ROMAN CIVIL LAW

Including

The Twelve Tables, The Institutes of Gaius,
The Rules of Ulpian and The Opinions of Paulus

ROMAN CIVIL LAW

Including

The Twelve Tables, The Institutes of Gaius,
The Rules of Ulpian and The Opinions of Paulus

Translated from the original Latin, edited, and compared
with all accessible systems of jurisprudence ancient and modern.

By S. P. SCOTT, A. M.

Author of **History of the Moorish Empire in Europe**,
Translator of **The Visigothic Code**

R. A. SITES BOOKS
Clearwater, Florida

This work originally appeared in the 17 volume work
THE CIVIL LAW
Translated by S. P. Scott
Copyright, 1932
by the Central Trust Company
Executor of the Estate Samuel P. Scott, Deceased
(Copyright expired without renewal)

ISBN-13: 978-1500237547

ISBN-10: 150023754X

Special Contents Of This Edition © 2014
By Roy Allen Sites

All rights to this edition reserved. No part of this book may be reproduced in any form or by any electronic or mechanical means, including information storage and retrieval systems, without the permission of the copyright holder, except by a reviewer who may quote brief passages in a review.

Disclaimer:
While every effort has been made to produce an edition of this book that is accurate and equivalent in content to the original printed edition, the editor is not legally responsible for any errors or omissions in the text. As with any information, use this edition with appropriate scholarly caution. If you discover errors in the text, please contact the editor at roysites@yahoo.com with details so corrections can be made.

TABLE OF CONTENTS

PREFACE, by S. P. Scott.. ix

THE LAWS OF THE TWELVE TABLES.. 1
    TABLE I. CONCERNING THE SUMMONS TO COURT 3
    TABLE II. CONCERNING JUDGMENTS AND THEFTS 4
    TABLE III. CONCERNING PROPERTY WHICH IS LENT....................................... 6
    TABLE IV. CONCERNING THE RIGHTS OF A FATHER, AND OF MARRIAGE.............. 7
    TABLE V. CONCERNING ESTATES AND GUARDIANSHIPS................................. 9
    TABLE VI. CONCERNING OWNERSHIP AND POSSESSION................................. 10
    TABLE VII. CONCERNING CRIMES... 11
    TABLE VIII. CONCERNING THE LAWS OF REAL PROPERTY............................... 11
    TABLE IX. CONCERNING PUBLIC LAW.. 12
    TABLE X. CONCERNING RELIGIOUS LAW.. 12
    TABLE XI. SUPPLEMENT TO THE FIVE PRECEDING ONES................................. 14
    TABLE XII. SUPPLEMENT TO THE FIVE PRECEDING ONES................................ 14

THE FOUR COMMENTARIES OF GAIUS ON THE INSTITUTES OF THE CIVIL LAW.. 15
    FIRST COMMENTARY... 17
        I. CONCERNING CIVIL AND NATURAL LAW... 17
        II. CONCERNING THE DIVISIONS OF THE LAW.. 19
        III. CONCERNING THE DIFFERENT CONDITIONS OF MEN.......................... 19
        IV. CONCERNING DEDITICII AND THE PROVISIONS OF THE LEX ÆLIA SENTIA........ 19
        V. CONCERNING ENEMIES WHO HAVE SURRENDERED AT DISCRETION............. 19
        VI. CONCERNING MANUMISSION, AND PROOF OF THE REASON FOR IT........... 20
        VII. CONCERNING THE CONSTITUTION OF THE COUNCIL............................ 20
        VIII: IN WHAT WAY LATINS MAY OBTAIN ROMAN CITIZENSHIP.................. 21
        IX: CONCERNING FIDUCIARY GUARDIANSHIP... 36
    SECOND COMMENTARY.. 40
        I: WHETHER OR NOT WARDS CAN ALIENATE PROPERTY.......................... 48
        II: CONCERNING MILITARY WILLS... 52
        III: CONCERNING SUBSTITUTIONS... 59
        IV: CONCERNING LEGACIES... 61
        V: ON THE FALCIDIAN LAW... 65
        VI: CONCERNING INOPERATIVE LEGACIES... 65
    THIRD COMMENTARY.. 71
    FOURTH COMMENTARY... 97

FRAGMENTS OF THE RULES OF DOMITIUS ULPIANUS........ 125
    TITLE I. CONCERNING FREEDMEN.. 127
    TITLE II. CONCERNING A SLAVE, OR SLAVES, WHO ARE TO BE FREE UNDER A CONDITION..... 129

TITLE III. CONCERNING LATINS..	130
TITLE IV. CONCERNING THOSE WHO ARE THEIR OWN MASTERS......................	130
TITLE V. CONCERNING THOSE WHO ARE UNDER CONTROL................................	130
TITLE VI. CONCERNING DOWRIES...	131
TITLE VII. CONCERNING THE LAW OF DONATIONS BETWEEN HUSBAND AND WIFE.........	132
TITLE VIII. CONCERNING ADOPTIONS...	133
TITLE IX. CONCERNING THOSE WHO ARE IN THE HANDS OF THEIR HUSBANDS........	133
TITLE X. IN WHAT WAY PERSONS UNDER THE CONTROL OR SUBJECT TO THE AUTHORITY OF OTHERS ARE RELEASED FROM THE EXERCISE OF THAT RIGHT..........	134
TITLE XI. CONCERNING GUARDIANSHIP...	134
TITLE XII. CONCERNING CURATORS...	136
TITLE XIII. CONCERNING A MAN WHO IS UNMARRIED, ONE WHO HAS NO CHILDREN, AND A FATHER WHO HAS BUT A SINGLE CHILD.............................	137
TITLE XIV. CONCERNING THE PENALTY OF THE LEX JULIA...............................	137
TITLE XV. CONCERNING TENTHS...	137
TITLE XVI. CONCERNING THE CAPACITY OF HUSBAND AND WIFE TO RECEIVE IN FULL WHAT MAY BE LEFT BY THE OTHER...	137
TITLE XVII. CONCERNING LAPSED LEGACIES...	138
TITLE XVIII. WHO ARE GOVERNED BY THE ANCIENT LAW IN THE CASE OF LAPSED LEGACIES..	138
TITLE XIX. CONCERNING OWNERS, AND THEIR ACQUISITION OF PROPERTY...........	139
TITLE XX. CONCERNING WILLS...	140
TITLE XXI. HOW AN HEIR SHOULD BE APPOINTED...	141
TITLE XXII. WHO CAN BE APPOINTED HEIRS..	141
TITLE XXIII. HOW WILLS ARE BROKEN..	144
TITLE XXIV. CONCERNING LEGACIES...	146
TITLE XXV. CONCERNING TRUSTS..	148
TITLE XXVI. CONCERNING HEIRS-AT-LAW...	149
TITLE XXVII. CONCERNING THE ESTATES AND PROPERTY OF FREEDMEN..............	150
TITLE XXVIII. CONCERNING THE GRANTING OF POSSESSION...............................	150
TITLE XXIX. CONCERNING THE ESTATES OF FREEDMEN......................................	151

THE OPINIONS OF JULIUS PAULUS ADDRESSED TO HIS SON...... 153

BOOK I..	155
TITLE I. PAGE CONCERNING AGREEMENTS AND CONTRACTS........................	155
TITLE II. CONCERNING ATTORNEYS AND AGENTS...	155
TITLE III. CONCERNING AGENTS...	156
TITLE IV. CONCERNING THE TRANSACTION OF BUSINESS.............................	156
TITLE V. CONCERNING CALUMNIATORS...	157
TITLE VI.a. CONCERNING FUGITIVE SLAVES..	157
TITLE VI.b. CONCERNING THE ACCUSATION OF DEFENDANTS.......................	157

TABLE OF CONTENTS

TITLE VII. CONCERNING COMPLETE RESTITUTION………………………………..	157
TITLE VIII. CONCERNING FRAUD……………………………………………………..	158
TITLE IX. CONCERNING MINORS UNDER THE AGE OF TWENTY-FIVE YEARS…………...	158
TITLE X. CONCERNING ONE WHO LOSES HIS CASE BY CLAIMING MORE THAN HE IS ENTITLED TO……………………………………………………….	159
TITLE XI. CONCERNING THE GIVING OF SECURITY……………………………….	159
TITLE XII. CONCERNING ALL CRIMINAL CASES………………………………..	159
TITLE XIII. CONCERNING JUDGMENT…………………………………………….	159
TITLE XIIIa. WHERE AN ESTATE, OR ANY OTHER PROPERTY IS CLAIMED………………	160
TITLE XIV. CONCERNING THE PUBLIC HIGHWAY………………………………….	160
TITLE XV. WHERE A QUADRUPED COMMITS DAMAGE……………………….	160
TITLE XVI. CONCERNING THE ESTABLISHMENT OF BOUNDARIES…………………..	160
TITLE XVII. CONCERNING SERVITUDES………………………………………..	161
TITLE XVIII. THE PARTITION OF ESTATES……………………………………...	161
TITLE XIX. IN WHAT WAY ACTIONS MAY BE DOUBLED BY THE DENIAL OF THE DEFENDANT……………………………………………………………...	161
TITLE XX. CONCERNING SURETIES AND SPONSORS…………………………..	161
TITLE XXI. CONCERNING SEPULCHRES AND MOURNING…………………………..	161
BOOK II……………………………………………………………………………..	162
TITLE I. CONCERNING PROPERTY LOANED, AND OATHS……………………………..	162
TITLE II. CONCERNING PRE-EXISTING PECUNIARY DEBTS…………………….	163
TITLE III. CONCERNING CONTRACTS……………………………………………..	163
TITLE IV. CONCERNING LOANS FOR USE AND DEPOSIT, AND ALSO PLEDGES AND TRUSTS………………………………………………………………..	163
TITLE V. CONCERNING PLEDGES………………………………………………….	163
TITLE VI. CONCERNING SHIPMASTERS…………………………………………….	164
TITLE VII. ON THE LEX RHODIA………………………………………………….	164
TITLE VIII. CONCERNING AGENTS……………………………………………….	165
TITLE IX. CONCERNING PROPERTY EMPLOYED FOR THE BENEFIT OF ANOTHER……….	165
TITLE X. CONCERNING THE MACEDONIAN DECREE OF THE SENATE………………..	165
TITLE XI. ON THE VELLEIAN DECREE OF THE SENATE………………………..	166
TITLE XII. CONCERNING DEPOSIT………………………………………………	166
TITLE XIII. CONCERNING THE LEX COMMISSORIA………………………………….	166
TITLE XIV. CONCERNING INTEREST…………………………………………….	167
TITLE XV. CONCERNING MANDATES……………………………………………..	167
TITLE XVI. ON PARTNERSHIP…………………………………………………….	167
TITLE XVII. CONCERNING PURCHASE AND SALE………………………………….	168
TITLE XVIII. CONCERNING LEASING AND HIRING……………………………….	169
TITLE XIX. CONCERNING MARRIAGE……………………………………………...	169
TITLE XX. CONCERNING CONCUBINES……………………………………………	169
TITLE XXI. CONCERNING WOMEN WHO FORM UNIONS WITH OTHERS' SLAVES, AND ON THE CLAUDIAN DECREE OF THE SENATE…………………………….	169

- TITLE XXI.a. CONCERNING DOWRIES.. 171
- TITLE XXII. CONCERNING AGREEMENTS ENTERED INTO BETWEEN HUSBAND AND WIFE.. 171
- TITLE XXIII. CONCERNING DONATIONS BETWEEN HUSBAND AND WIFE.............. 171
- TITLE XXIV. CONCERNING THE BIRTH OF CHILDREN.. 171
- TITLE XXV. IN WHAT WAY CHILDREN BECOME THEIR OWN MASTERS............... 172
- TITLE XXVI. CONCERNING ADULTERY.. 173
- TITLE XXVII. CONCERNING THE EXCUSES OF GUARDIANS................................. 174
- TITLE XXVIII. CONCERNING THE APPOINTMENT OF PERSONS OF SUPERIOR POWER...... 174
- TITLE XXIX. WHO CANNOT APPOINT PERSONS OF SUPERIOR AUTHORITY........... 174
- TITLE XXX. ON THE RESCRIPT OF THE DIVINE SEVERUS.................................... 174
- TITLE XXXI. CONCERNING THEFTS... 174
- TITLE XXXII. CONCERNING THE SERVICES OF FREEDMEN................................. 177

BOOK III... 177
- TITLE I. CONCERNING THE CARBONIAN EDICT... 177
- TITLE II. CONCERNING THE ESTATES OF FREEDMEN... 177
- TITLE III. CONCERNING THE FABIAN FORMULA.. 177
- TITLE IV.a. CONCERNING WILLS.. 177
- TITLE IV.b. CONCERNING THE APPOINTMENT OF HEIRS..................................... 179
- TITLE V. ON THE SILANIAN DECREE OF THE SENATE.. 179
- TITLE VI. CONCERNING LEGACIES.. 181
- TITLE VII. CONCERNING DONATIONS MORTIS CAUSA... 186
- TITLE VIII. ON THE LEX FALCIDIA.. 186

BOOK IV... 187
- TITLE I. CONCERNING TRUSTS.. 187
- TITLE II. CONCERNING THE TREBELLIAN DECREE OF THE SENATE................... 188
- TITLE III. CONCERNING THE PEGASIAN DECREE OF THE SENATE....................... 188
- TITLE IV. CONCERNING THE REJECTION OF AN ESTATE..................................... 188
- TITLE V. CONCERNING THE COMPLAINT THAT A WILL IS INOFFICIOUS................ 189
- TITLE VI. CONCERNING THE TAX OF THE TWENTIETH... 190
- TITLE VII. CONCERNING THE LEX CORNELIA.. 190
- TITLE VIII. CONCERNING THE SUCCESSION OF PERSONS DYING INTESTATE....... 191
- TITLE IX. ON THE TREBELLIAN DECREE OF THE SENATE................................... 192
- TITLE X. ON THE ORPHITIAN DECREE OF THE SENATE....................................... 193
- TITLE XI. CONCERNING DEGREES... 193
- TITLE XII. CONCERNING MANUMISSIONS... 194
- TITLE XIII. CONCERNING GRANTS OF FREEDOM UNDER A TRUST...................... 195
- TITLE XIV. ON THE LEX FUFIA CANINIA... 195

BOOK V.. 196
- TITLE I. CONCERNING CASES INVOLVING FREEDOM.. 196
- TITLE II. CONCERNING USUCAPTION.. 196

TABLE OF CONTENTS

TITLE III. CONCERNING ACTS COMMITTED BY A CROWD.	196
TITLE IV. CONCERNING INJURIES.	197
TITLE V. CONCERNING THE EFFECT OF DECISIONS AND THE TERMINATION OF ACTIONS AT LAW.	199
TITLE V.b. CONCERNING THE POSSESSION OF PROPERTY GRANTED BY THE AUTHORITY OF A JUDGE.	200
TITLE VI. CONCERNING INTERDICTS.	200
TITLE VII. CONCERNING VERBAL OBLIGATIONS.	201
TITLE VIII. CONCERNING NOVATIONS.	202
TITLE IX. CONCERNING STIPULATIONS.	202
TITLE X. CONCERNING AUTHORITY FOR MAKING CONTRACTS.	203
TITLE XI. CONCERNING DONATIONS.	203
TITLE XII. CONCERNING THE RIGHT OF THE TREASURY AND THE PEOPLE.	203
TITLE XIII. CONCERNING INFORMERS.	204
TITLE XIV. CONCERNING THE INFLICTION OF TORTURE.	204
TITLE XV. CONCERNING WITNESSES.	204
TITLE XVI. CONCERNING THE TORTURE OF SLAVES.	205
TITLE XVII. CONCERNING ACQUITTALS.	206
TITLE XVIII. CONCERNING CATTLE THIEVES.	206
TITLE XIX. CONCERNING SACRILEGE.	206
TITLE XX. CONCERNING INCENDIARIES.	206
TITLE XXI. CONCERNING SOOTHSAYERS AND ASTROLOGERS.	207
TITLE XXII. CONCERNING SEDITIOUS PERSONS.	207
TITLE XXIII. ON THE LEX CORNELIA HAVING REFERENCE TO ASSASSINS AND POISONERS.	208
TITLE XXIV. ON THE LEX POMPEIA RELATING TO PARRICIDES.	209
TITLE XXV. ON THE LEX CORNELIA HAVING REFERENCE TO WILLS.	209
TITLE XXVI. ON THE LEX JULIA RELATING TO PUBLIC AND PRIVATE VIOLENCE.	210
TITLE XXVII. ON THE LEX JULIA RELATING TO PECULATION.	211
TITLE XXVIII. ON THE LEX JULIA RELATING TO EXTORTION.	211
TITLE XXIX. ON THE LEX JULIA RELATING TO TREASON.	211
TITLE XXX. A. ON THE LEX JULIA RELATING TO CORRUPT INTRIGUING FOR OFFICE.	211
TITLE XXX. B. ON THE LEX FAVIA.	212
TITLE XXXI. CONCERNING MILITARY PUNISHMENTS.	212
TITLE XXXII. WHEN AN APPEAL CAN BE TAKEN.	212
TITLE XXXIII. CONCERNING THE SECURITIES AND THE PENALTIES OF APPEALS.	212
TITLE XXXIV. CONCERNING PROCEEDINGS SENT UP ON APPEAL.	213
TITLE XXXV. CONCERNING THE RETURN OF CASES WHICH HAVE BEEN APPEALED.	213
TITLE XXXVI. WHAT SHOULD BE OBSERVED AFTER AN APPEAL.	213
TITLE XXXVII. CONCERNING THE MERITS OF APPEALS.	213
APPENDIX.	215

THE CIVIL LAW

Translated and Edited by S. P. Scott

EDITOR'S PREFACE

THE original sources of Roman law, lost in the obscurity of bygone centuries, are unknown. All efforts to trace them have, in the absence of authentic records, or even of reliable tradition, proved fruitless and unprofitable. Any monuments of former legislation which may have existed during the regal domination, or subsequently under republican rule, undoubtedly perished at the time of the invasion by the Gauls, or in the domestic convulsions which, at frequent intervals, afflicted the ancient city. There is no doubt, however, that Roman jurisprudence, like that of every people in the early period of its history, was largely founded upon custom, partly indigenous, partly borrowed from other nations, and arranged, formulated, maintained, and perpetuated by sacerdotal influence. The first jurisconsults were invariably priests. So apparently indissoluble has always been the primitive connection between law and religion that, even in England, the office of Chancellor was, almost without exception, filled by ecclesiastics, until the second quarter of the seventeenth century. This universal and essential characteristic of legal establishment and knowledge indicates the difficulty experienced by ancient countries in the enforcement of the rules upon which their very existence depended, and which required the all-powerful aid of superstition to accomplish that purpose. The close union of the legal and sacerdotal systems is disclosed in the history of the Romans as in that of other races, by the custody of both religious and secular records and ordinances by the priesthood; by the semi-oracular decrees of the pontiffs; by the worship of ancestors, closely associated with the rule of succession; by the celebration of marriage, and the definition and observance of the rights and obligations resulting therefrom; by the constitution of the family, to whose head, invested with despotic authority, the designation "*Pius*," imparted the attributes of reverence, devotion, affection, and law.

The Roman Pontiff would naturally only preserve and admit to record such regulations as would, either directly or indirectly, have a tendency to increase or maintain the wealth, importance, and power of his order. His custody of the ordinances which governed all classes of the community, and which he had every opportunity and temptation to alter to suit his own purposes, together with the sacred character of his calling, gave him unbounded influence; an influence which continued to exist, despite the changes of government and religion, through all the centuries of Roman domination. The element of superstitious observance was conspicuous in every official ceremony, as well as in legal transactions and the multifarious occupations of private life. It was manifested alike in the selection and investiture of great dignitaries of state; in the solemn proceedings of popular assemblies; in the administration of civil and criminal justice; in the devotion of certain malefactors to the infernal gods; in the adoption of sanitary and sumptuary regulations; in the methods by which property of every description was acquired or lost. The earliest customs and legal enactments of the

Romans of which we have any knowledge whatever disclose unmistakably the religious source from which they derive their origin, and the sacerdotal spirit that dictated their provisions.

There were two distinct forms of worship observed at Rome, the *sacra publica* and the *sacra privata*. The first of these, as the term implies, referred to the religion of the State, and was celebrated at the public expense; the second involved the invocation of, and sacrifices to the tutelary gods of the *gens* (that is the race or clan), the household, or the individual. The *lares* or spirits of departed relatives, to whom this pious homage was addressed, were presumed to exercise a beneficent and protective influence upon their surviving descendants, and were the prototypes of the patron saints of the Roman Catholic calendar. The *jus sacrarum*, or right of ancestral worship, was, however, not indiscriminately enjoyed, but was the peculiar privilege of the patrician order. Members of the latter were *ingenui*, or freeborn — a term derived from *gens* — although the words *ingenuus* and *gentilis* were by no means synonymous, the latter being the more comprehensive of the two. To belong to the class of *gentiles*, freebirth, identity of name, the same worship, the fact that no ancestor had ever been subject to servile dependence or patronage, or the person in question had, at any time, suffered forfeiture of civil rights were indispensable requisites: "*Gentilis dicitur et ex eodem genere ortus, et is qui simile nomine appellatur.*" While the meaning and application of the term are at present uncertain, it is sufficiently established that the basis of the gentile tie was either actual or presumed consanguinity. It has been asserted that a common place of residence was also essential to the constitution of a *gens* in ancient times. Each *curia*, or division of a city corresponding to our ward, included ten *gentes* which were designated respectively by the family names of their members. The rights of the various *gentes* — the union of whose individual constituents, founded upon the blood-relationship to which was directly traceable their title to aristocratic superiority, formed the most important and powerful body of the State — were sedulously guarded and enforced by both the secular and religious authorities. In no part of the Roman polity is the intimate association of religion and law more conspicuous than in the institution of the *gens*, whose origin was patriarchal; and the privileges and responsibilities to which it gave rise were manifested in the administration of government, the control of the family, and the mutual relations existing between the members of the community and the ruling power. The establishment of the *sacra publica* was largely attributable to its influence, exerted in ages of which no record survives. It has even been suggested that the Roman Senate, in its inception, was organized as representative of the assembled *gentes*, an hypothesis supported by plausible inferences drawn from the statements of many classic writers.

Among the laws contained in the Code of Hammurabi, the Gentoo Code, and the Institutes of Menu, which have come down to us from antiquity, and antedate the foundation of the Eternal City by hundreds of centuries, are to be found many precepts and formulas identical in purport and expression with those scattered throughout the treatises of Roman jurisprudence. Their frequent occurrence suggests an origin that can hardly be accidental; and, considering the different conditions of race, religion, climate, society, and environment under which they were promulgated, would seem to indicate conclusively that their acknowledged usefulness and adaptability to the pursuits and exigencies of humanity have been transmitted to succeeding peoples through countless generations, rather than to assume that their presence in the volumes of the civil law is attributable to chance, or mere coincidence. The majority of these rules have reference to the legitimate union of the sexes, and the possession of means for the sustenance of offspring, thereby insuring the existence and survival of the race, subjects whose importance is conclusively emphasized by one of the most accomplished of English jurists, as follows: "Almost all the relative duties of human life will be found more immediately, or more remotely, to arise out of the two great institutions of property and marriage. They constitute, preserve, and improve society. Upon their gradual improvement depends the progressive civilization of mankind; on them rests the whole order of civil life." We are told by Horace, that the first efforts of law-givers to civilize men consisted in strengthening and regulating these institutions, and fencing them round with rigorous penal laws.

PREFACE

"*Oppida coeperunt munire, et ponere leges, Ne quis fur esset, neu latro, neu quis adulter.*"[1]

The force of custom cannot be ignored in the consideration of the sources of Roman jurisprudence.

The great mass of Roman law owed its establishment not to measures adopted by regularly qualified officials designated for that purpose, but to customs generally regarded as advantageous, and often confirmed by religious sanction which tacitly accepted as rules of public and private conduct, had in the course of centuries obtained the character and authority of legislative enactments. These were the *mores majorum*, so frequently mentioned by ancient jurisconsults and historians, and regarded by the people at large with far greater veneration, and as having a better claim to implicit obedience than the recent edicts of despotic sovereigns, or the inconsiderate and often suspicious acts of popular assemblies. The religious element which entered so largely into the composition and establishment of these time-honored customs was, as already stated, unquestionably the principal cause of their endurance and perpetuation. It has been most aptly remarked that the mental condition of primitive humanity, in considering the observances inculcated by a man's ancestors as public and private obligations, exactly corresponds with the feeling of reverence with which it contemplates the resistless and awe-inspiring manifestations of natural phenomena. The tenacity with which semibarbarians adhere to the long-continued practices of their ancestors is proverbial. The reunion of three different tribes — Romans, Sabines, and Luceres — formed the nucleus of that mighty state which in time bequeathed its enactments, its judicial organization, and its method of legal procedure, to subsequent ages. The customs of these tribes, while to some extent diverse, were undoubtedly in many respects similar, perhaps identical; as all three were subjected to practically the same environment, their amalgamation must have been effected without difficulty; and their incorporation into the polity of the growing commonwealth exerted no inconsiderable influence upon the destinies of the Kingdom, the Republic, and the Empire, as well as upon the innumerable tributary nations that acknowledged their supremacy.

Unwritten, or customary law, is said by Aulus Gellius to be that established by the implied consent and practice of illiterate men: "*Jus non scriptum tacito et illiterado hominum consensu et moribus expressum est.*" In connection with this, the opinion has been advanced that this definition does not preclude its original dependence upon a legislative act of some description, or upon some agreement, the circumstances and language of whose adoption or acceptance have long since vanished from the memory of man; a self-evident deduction, as any ordinance entitled to and requiring obedience, must necessarily have emanated from some generally recognized authoritative source.

With the disappearance of the actual participation of the Roman people in the affairs of government in consequence of the arbitrary measures of Constantine, which practically invested the emperor with all legislative power, the influence of custom in the formation of law permanently ceased to exist. The *vox populi* was suppressed; the duties of the Senate were restricted to registering the imperial edicts; the magistrate no longer enjoyed the latitude of interpretation possessed by his predecessors, who not infrequently exercised judicial functions in the formulation and promulgation of laws; and the sovereign, invested with divine attributes and despotic power, whose right it was both treason and sacrilege to dispute, became the acknowledged source of all legislation.

As a law could be established by custom, so it could be rendered inoperative by the adoption of one in opposition to it, or by being permitted to fall into desuetude. This rule, however, was not applicable to ordinary enactments or imperial decrees which, having been committed to writing and published, required a formal act to effect their repeal, which could not take place by implication. The doctrine prevalent at Rome that where the provisions of different statutes conflicted with one another the more recent one should be accepted: "*Jus posterius derogat priori,*" even without any special statement to that effect, is now of general

---

[1] Mackintosh, Miscellaneous Works, Vol. I, Page 368.

application everywhere.

In the interpretation of contracts classed as *bonæ fidei*, when any doubt existed as to the intention of the parties, the magistrate was required to decide in accordance with the custom applicable to such cases:

"*Ea enim quæ sunt moris et consuetudinis in bonæ fidei judiciis debent venire.*"

The Roman State was, in the first place, composed of two separate tribes or nationalities, the Ramnes, and the Quirites or Sabines, probably differing somewhat in habits, usages, government, and religion, whose contiguity led to their ultimate amalgamation, and whose traditions retained the memory of their dual origin even to the end of the Empire. Various institutions and observances of the two chief component elements of the Roman people have been mentioned as symbolical of the former separate existence of those tribes. The legend of the twins, as well as the empty throne, and the crown and sceptre said to have been placed beside his own by Romulus after the homicide of Remus, and referred to by Servius,[1] were indicative of this double origin. The head of Janus, which appears upon the earliest Roman coinage, is stated by Niebuhr[2] to be a reminiscence of a similar character. The extraordinary attachment which successive generations evince for a once well-established custom, no matter what may be its derivation, is again illustrated by the persistence of the twofold, supreme magisterial jurisdiction dating from the foundation of the City; suspended during the regal epoch; revived in the Consulate; represented by the municipal duumvirates; and which shorn of actual power, and subsisting merely as an honorary distinction, survived until the final period of imperial supremacy.

The original government of Rome was composed of the King, the Senate, and the *Comitia*, or popular assemblies. The monarch was the fountain of justice, and exercised the irresponsible power of a dictator. All legislative measures were instituted and framed by him, with the advice of the Senate, and the nominal approval of the people.

The *Leges Regiæ*, or laws of the regal period, by reason of the prevailing religious character of the fragments which have come down to us, have, with considerable probability, been ascribed to the College of Pontiffs. It has, indeed, been suggested that the primal form of government in Italy was purely sacerdotal, and that the King was merely an evolution of the priest; an hypothesis which, however plausible, derives no direct confirmation from either the authentic or legendary history of Rome. We are principally indebted to Dionysius for the meagre accounts of the *Leges Regiæ* that we possess, which are, for the most part, only allusions to their purport and effect; for none of these primitive laws have, even in the form of veritable extracts, been transmitted to posterity, although there is good reason to believe that some of their provisions were incorporated into the Twelve Tables. With the overthrow of the Kings all reference to the *Leges Regiæ* as a basis for judicial decisions ceased, as they could no longer be cited as of valid authority. A collection of these laws, called the "*Jus Civile Papirianum*," from Sextus Papirius, Pontifex Maximus, its compiler, was subsequently made; but it, like others which may have once existed, has disappeared.

Much uncertainty attaches to the sources from which the Twelve Tables were derived. While the greater portion of their contents may positively be said to have a Latin origin, still there remains much to be accounted for, and for whose existence neither history nor tradition offers a reliable or satisfactory explanation.

The generally indigenous character of this famous code is, however, apparent to everyone familiar with the worship, the customs, the prejudices, and the superstitions of the Roman people. Several hundred years had already elapsed since a vagrant tribe of freebooters were said to have fixed their residence upon the banks of the Tiber. Amalgamation with other semi-barbarians, somewhat superior in culture, increased their numbers and improved their manners, while communicating to them a certain amount of knowledge, even

---

[1] *De Æneide* 1, 276.
[2] History of Rome, I, 293.

though imperfect, of the arts of civilization. During those ages, a complex form of government had been evolved; rules for the administration of justice formulated; commercial relations with adjoining nations established; manufactures set in operation; and the various requisites for the maintenance of an ambitious and growing State provided. Such conditions were clearly incompatible with those prevailing at the period of the foundation of the city, and therefore certain laws, whatever their nature, must previously have been enacted for the efficient protection of the lives and property of the members of the community to insure its preservation.

To Greece has been wrongfully attributed much of the substance of the Twelve Tables, due to the fact that a commission was, after the expulsion of the kings by the Romans, despatched to that country with a view to the ascertainment and adoption of whatever might be found advantageous in Grecian jurisprudence, although the legislation of the Greeks was, notwithstanding their artistic and oratorical ascendency, notoriously crude and defective.

Judging from the writings of Cicero, a most respectable authority, who, while lavishing unbounded praise upon the philosophical wisdom which he asserted distinguished the Twelve Tables, entertained anything but a favorable opinion of Greek jurisprudence in general, much of their contents could not have been obtained from Greece.

It is, however, stated by him that some of Solon's laws were unquestionably inserted into the new code, one of them at least which related to the unseemly and vociferous mourning, and self-inflicted disfigurement of women at funerals — without any appreciable alteration: "*Quam legem eisdem prope urbis nostri decemviri in decimam tabulam coniecerunt; nam de tribus reciniis et pleraque illa Solonis sunt; de lamentis vero expressa verbis sunt. Mulieres gênas ne radunto nec lessum funeris ergo habento.*"[1]

It was not to the Greeks or their Italian colonies, but to their immediate neighbors, the Etruscans, that the Romans were principally indebted for their religion, their laws, and their rudiments of art which were largely the foundation of their future greatness. At a date, now unknown, but of remote antiquity, central and southern Italy had been occupied by foreign adventurers, most probably Lydians, who brought with them the customs, traditions, culture, and civilization of the Orient. At one time they possessed the greater part of the Italian peninsula, and their domination extended to the islands of Sardinia, Corsica, and Elba. Their country was divided into three great provinces, and the provinces into separate states or commonwealths, bound together in a confederacy for mutual protection, each of which had its separate capital, which exercised supreme jurisdiction over all the territory subject to its control; a system bearing a close analogy to those of Greece, and mediæval Italy, whose independent cities and principalities exerted such an important influence over their political destinies. This condition, and the peaceable character of the inhabitants, eventually subjected the latter to the authority of the truculent Romans, dominated from the very beginning by the spirit of war and conquest. In every walk in life; in every department of knowledge; in the ceremonies of religious worship; in the organization of government; in the manifestations and symbolism of art; in the formation of language; in the separation of classes and the rigid maintenance of caste; in military organization; in the existence of habits, usages, and amusements; are traceable the direct effect of intimate association with one of the most refined and polished nations of antiquity. The purple, the distinctive color reserved for the use of royalty, was borrowed from the Etruscans. So was the eagle, the object of superstitious reverence, borne at the head of the legion; the trumpet which sounded the charge; and the toga, the peculiar badge of Roman citizenship. The musical instruments, dances, and games, adopted and practised by the conqueror were mainly Etruscan. In ancient Etruria, as at Rome, Church and State were united in the ruler; a proud and powerful aristocracy was everywhere predominant; and the lower classes were divided into serfs and slaves, whose condition was far

---

[1] *De Legibus* II, 25, 68.

more pitiable than that of the later *coloni* and *servi*. The institutions and national traits of the Etruscans exhibited unmistakable indications of their Oriental origin, thus justifying the remark of Seneca: "*Tuscos Asia sibi vindicat.*" Nor was the influence of Etruria upon Rome confined to the mere adoption of the arts and conveniences of civilization; it extended even to the royal office. The elective character of the Roman kingdom permitted the accession of one of its citizens to the throne. Tarquinius Priscus was, on his mother's side, of Etruscan lineage.

A nation so prosperous and enlightened, which had attained to such superiority in the arts of peace as to rival the finished efforts of Grecian taste and genius, must necessarily have also had a well-established and efficient judiciary. Unfortunately none of its literary memorials have survived. We know, however, that they once existed; that writers in every branch of letters flourished; and that its institutions of learning were held in high repute by their neighbors; as it was the practice of the Roman youth to repair to the Etruscan academies for the completion of their education. In the presence of such conditions, the lack of a comprehensive body of laws and a judiciary competent to enforce them can hardly be imagined; even though the limitation of legislative functions to the sacerdotal order must often have been productive of serious embarrassment, both in the exertion of public authority, and in the adjustment of the relations of individuals with one another.

The downfall of the Monarchy, followed by the foundation of the Republic, which was inevitably attended by the rejection of many laws incompatible with the existence and administration of popular government, necessitated the formation of a new system of jurisprudence; for which purpose, however, no satisfactory materials and precedents were afforded by the customs, history, or traditions of Rome. Notwithstanding that the king had been chosen by the people, and was, in theory at least, responsible to them for any encroachment upon their rights, he ruled with despotic sway, and practically exercised unlimited power, not only in religious matters, but also in the framing and enactment of legislation. The conflict of the aristocracy and the rabble, always fierce, and now rendered even more bitter by the insolence of the latter intoxicated with their newly acquired influence, rendered a reorganization of the legislative and magisterial branches of the government imperative. In spite of the efforts of the patrician order, whose members saw in such a project an attempt to curtail their privileges and influence, a law was passed about the middle of the fifth century before Christ authorizing the appointment of a commission to completely revise the existing code, and introduce such new laws as might be deemed advisable. Although the patricians were unable to prevent the adoption of this measure, they seem to have had no difficulty in dictating the selection of those empowered to execute it; and, at their instance, three commissioners, presumably taken from the aristocratic class, were sent to Greece to study its legal and judicial systems, and by combining the information acquired with that already available at home, devise a new and more effective method for the administration of justice. Upon their return, the patricians who, although they had in the meantime lost most of their power, still managed to secure the appointment of ten extraordinary officials, the *Decemviri*, who were invested with full legislative and executive authority. From their labors emanated the first known body of Roman law, which, called the Twelve Tables from the fact that it was divided into twelve sections, was engraved upon plates of bronze and set up in the Forum, where everyone required to obey it might familiarize himself with its provisions. The Tables were originally ten in number, but two others were subsequently added.

Exhaustive and persistent efforts for the reconstruction of this venerable body of laws have repeatedly been made by scholars, no two of whose versions, however, coincide. In the prevailing lack of positive information or reliable data, all attempts to this end must of course be incomplete, and the results largely speculative. Still, despite their fragmentary character, enough has been ascertained from these researches to enable us to form an intelligent idea of the general scope of the laws of the Twelve Tables; the spirit which prompted their enactments; the principles they inculcated; the method of legal procedure which they prescribed; and the penalties inflicted upon those who ventured to violate them. As an index of popular manners, religious ceremonies and political conditions, they have, notwithstanding their mutilated condition,

PREFACE

proved invaluable to the historian.

The internal evidence of this compilation shows conclusively that the rules which it laid down, whatever might have been their origin, had long been established and obeyed by people accustomed to be subjected to the restraints essential to their intellectual and material development, and were not the mere haphazard and desultory efforts of a race like that of the Romans, which had not yet emerged from barbarism. But side by side with enlightened maxims of justice are to be seen doctrines embodying the most abject superstitions, and the imposition of penalties which well-informed, modern critics have pronounced incredible, on account of their atrocious and sanguinary character.

As in the case of the *Leges Regiæ*, from which as previously mentioned, many of their precepts undoubtedly were borrowed, the Twelve Tables disclose a sacerdotal influence which pervades them from beginning to end. The ritualistic element is everywhere prominent, revealing the primal sources of their derivation, and the union of the governing powers of Church and State. It is exceedingly improbable that any wholly original and untried regulations were incorporated into the Twelve Tables, although its compilers had authority to do this; nor is it likely that any important provision was adopted with which many Romans were not already more or less familiar, as no society, however backward, would be inclined to blindly accept laws whose operation had not hitherto been subjected to the decisive test of experience. Hence the collection may be considered as largely composed of legislative acts, and customs, which through immemorial observation had obtained legal force; in short, a concise summary of the rules of jurisprudence at that period existing at Rome, combined with many others taken from the codes of various nations, which the political sagacity of the compilers had deemed worthy of insertion into the one which they had been appointed to revise and amplify.

The most prominent characteristics of the Twelve Tables are their comprehensiveness and their conciseness. Every emergency which was likely to arise among the people for whose use they were established was fully provided for. The legal aspects and requirements of marriage and divorce; the reciprocal obligation of parent and child; the absolutely despotic paternal authority, peculiar to the Romans, deemed indispensable to the government of the family, and often exercised with merciless cruelty; the appointment and duties of guardians; the unrestricted right of testamentary disposition; the law of intestate succession; the sacred and inviolable nature of agreements formally executed; the sale and pledge of property; the transfer of ownership and possession; the qualifications of sureties; the duties of magistrates; the order of legal proceedings both in time and method; the rules governing the negotiation of loans and the payment of interest; the acquisition and loss of title by prescription; the fixing of responsibility in case of trespass; the organization and conduct of corporate bodies; the regulation of funerals and sepulture; and the penalties incurred by the commission of crimes, are enumerated and set forth with almost epigrammic terseness. This painstaking condensation of the legal principles and precepts applicable to the affairs of every-day life presents a remarkable contrast to the prolixity of many of Justinian's laws, absolutely irreconcilable with one another, and oppressed with a weight of high-sounding verbiage, whose interpretation increases the labors, contributes to the embarrassment, and evokes the anathemas of the student and the commentator.

The language in which the Twelve Tables were originally composed is harsh, unformed, and barbarous, bearing little resemblance to the elegant and polished idiom of subsequent times. Some of the words have long since become obsolete; the orthography of many of those that survive is radically altered; the numerous abbreviations contribute to their ambiguity; and it is said that even in the time of Cicero the most accomplished scholars and legal antiquaries differed as to their meaning and application, the ascertainment of which demanded the highest degree of expert knowledge.

Notwithstanding the obstacles which now confront the student in the restoration and construction of the phraseology and rules of this ancient compilation, its great value at the time when it was made cannot fail to be apparent to the most superficial observer, and its paragraphs, mangled, defective, and often unintelligible, as they are to-day, still afford us an instructive and suggestive picture of the primitive society for whose benefit they were framed, and represent the source of that vast and complex system of jurisprudence which, perfected by the accomplished lawyers of the Empire, now constitutes the foundation of modern legislative action and judicial procedure throughout the world.

History is silent as to the date when the Twelve Tables ceased to exist in their integrity, but their partial destruction and loss must, like those which attended the disappearance of other Roman monuments of law and literature, be ascribed to barbarian neglect and devastation.

The Twelve Tables were the epitome of the common law of Rome, which then renouncing its customary character, was thereafter to be considered as embraced in a number of statutes that had been solemnly accepted and sanctioned by a vote of the people. Prior to their adoption, the profession of advocate and jurisconsult had been exercised almost exclusively by the patricians, who composed the only class possessing a competent knowledge of jurisprudence, which practical monopoly they guarded as one of their most cherished privileges. All this, however, was changed when the inscriptions upon the bronze tablets posted in the Forum, enabled every citizen to become acquainted with the laws of his country and, in person, apply to the tribunals to redress his wrongs.

The provisions of the Twelve Tables required the defendant in an action to appear without delay; if he failed to do so, his adversary, having called the attention of bystanders to the fact, was authorized to arrest and bring him into court by force, of necessity. Personal service, however, could not be made upon a man outside the walls of his residence. Vehicles were despatched for those who, by reason of sickness or age, were unable to obey the summons. When security was demanded, only a person whose wealth was equal to that of him compelled to give it, was allowed to become surety; for a party litigant in indigent circumstances, anyone however poor, might act in that capacity. Compromise of all disputes was encouraged. The proverbial "law's delay" was not known to the ancient Romans. When the case came to trial, which had to take place in the morning, the parties themselves argued it, and the judge was compelled to render a decision before sunset of the same day. Continuances were always granted when either the magistrate, plaintiff, or defendant, was incapacitated from appearing on account of illness. Debtors were treated with great severity. After one had had judgment rendered against him, and did not discharge the obligation within thirty days, he could again be brought into court, the payment of the claim demanded, and, if it was not forthcoming, he could be loaded with chains, and imprisoned. When another term of sixty days had elapsed, he could be sold as a slave; or, where there were several creditors, his body might be divided among them.

A child born to a widow ten months after the death of her husband was legitimate. Unlimited authority for the disposition of their estates subject to the claims of creditors was conferred upon testators. When they did not appoint any heirs, and left no children, the nearest agnates were entitled to the succession; thus, while ignoring the right of primogeniture, the Twelve Tables always gave the preference to the direct descendants of males, to the prejudice of cognates. An estate could not legally be acquired by relatives in the ascending line. The next of kin were compelled to assume the guardianship of minors or spendthrifts, and as this trust was considered a public duty, only absolute incapacity for some reason or other, constituted a valid excuse. A sale was not held to have been concluded so as to pass the title to the property, even though delivery had actually taken place, unless the purchase-money had been paid, or security furnished. Undisputed enjoyment for one year in the case of personal, or for two years in that of real property, was sufficient to vest the ownership of the same in the possessor. Cohabitation uninterrupted by three nights of absence and continuing for one year, had the same effect as a legal marriage. When a man desired to divorce his wife, which he could do at his pleasure, he was required to state the reason for his act. While it is not expressly stated that the right was reciprocal, there is no doubt that this was the case, and that the wife enjoyed the same privilege. Divorce, however, is said to have been rare in the early ages of Rome, and a tradition of questionable authenticity asserts that it did not occur for five centuries after its foundation. If this were really the case, it cannot now be

PREFACE

determined how much the permanency of matrimonial unions was due to religious influence or public policy, or whether the *patria potestas* of the husband, who held his wife *in manum* as a daughter, was not largely responsible for it; as irreconcilable conjugal disagreements owing to the weakness of human nature, must have been as frequent at Rome as elsewhere, and there is no good reason to assume the contrary. Controversies with reference to boundary lines, were, as they often are at the present day, settled by the decision of three arbiters whose award was final. Similar proceedings were enjoined to prevent rainwater falling upon adjacent land from damaging the premises of the complainant. No privileges could be granted, or laws enacted to the injury of individuals, or in violation of the rights to which all persons were entitled. A judge, or arbiter who, having accepted a bribe, rendered an unjust decision in consequence, was punished with death. The expenses allowed, and ceremonies to be observed at funerals, were prescribed with extraordinary minuteness; indicative of the abuse and extravagance which, no doubt, had hitherto prevailed, rendering these solemn rites an occasion for vulgar display, and frequently imposing intolerable burdens upon the family of the deceased.

In the administration of criminal justice, great solicitude was manifested for the preservation of the rights of the Roman citizen, whose person was, under ordinary circumstances, considered inviolable. No *civis Romanus* could be deprived of life or liberty by any magistrate, unless with the consent of the people evidenced by vote of the largest popular assembly, the *Comitia Centuriata*. Capital punishment which, at first, was not inflicted at Rome, and was always regarded with marked disfavor by the masses, when prescribed by the Twelve Tables, had, almost always, some direct or indirect connection with an act of sacrilege, that subjected the culprit to the wrath of an offended deity. In this curious compendium of ancient laws, as in those of all nations during the establishment of their political and social organization, a distinction is made between offences committed against the government, and those of which an individual is the object. The latter, considered of a personal or private character, were to be expiated either by what might be deemed a pecuniary equivalent for the damage sustained; or, when this was not secure, by infliction of the same injury upon the accused by way of retaliation. The *Lex Talionis*, in all its harshness, is laid down in the Seventh Law of Table VII. The same principle appears elsewhere in the penalties prescribed for perjury and arson, since the false witness was not afterwards allowed to testify, and the incendiary was liable to death by fire. The next of kin was authorized to enforce the *Lex Talionis*, which, in default of payment of the customary compensation, was held to be the only means of redress available to the injured party. Hence it is apparent that the rules of criminal jurisprudence as applied by courts of the present day were not known to the early Roman legislators.

Judicial reparation for injury was obtained by means of *actiones ex delicto*, or penal actions, and whatever was recovered was considered to partake rather of the nature of a fine for an illegal act, than as an indemnity for the wrong sustained. Therefore, in this respect, they differed materially from our actions of tort; nor was liability for what his ancestor had done transmitted to the heir of the defendant; "*Nemo succedit in delicta*." The magistrate was accustomed to assess the damages, dependent upon the character of the offence, and this was afterwards limited to the sum of twenty-five *asses*, except where serious injury had resulted. In the case of certain misdemeanors or torts, double or quadruple the value of the property impaired or destroyed was collected. When rendering judgment, fully as much attention was paid to the degree of provocation which prompted the injury, as to the loss which it caused. Well defined ideas of the personal responsibility incurred by the publication of slanders and libels were entertained at the epoch of the adoption of the Twelve Tables, and he who defamed another by attacking his reputation for probity, or publicly insulted him, as well as the author of *pasquinades*, was scourged until he died. All breaches of trust, especially those affecting minors, were visited with severe penalties.

The great respect with which the Twelve Tables were always regarded by the most eminent authorities, as the exemplar of all law, and the embodiment of the juridical experience of centuries, was not diminished with the progress and development of Roman jurisprudence. Admirably adapted to the conditions of the society for whose regulation they were promulgated, it would be unfair to judge them by the standards of our superior civilization, or apply to them the moral and political principles of the present age.

Gaius, like Paulus and Ulpian, the contemporary of Papinian, most revered of Roman jurists, stands first in order of time among the great lawyers whose works have either created or interpreted the rules of ancient jurisprudence. He lived during the reign of Hadrian and the Antonines, during the middle and latter part of the second century. The place of his birth, the circumstances of his life, his residence, that branch of his profession to which he especially devoted his labors as a commentator or a practitioner, even his cognomen, are absolutely unknown. From the fact that his family name has not come down to us for he never was designated by it, it has been surmised that he was of foreign origin, probably a native of Asia. He must, however, have enjoyed the privileges of citizenship, as otherwise, the consideration in which his literary efforts were held would never have been accorded to the works of a barbarian. He was a most voluminous author, but all of his books have been lost, except his "Institutes," an elementary treatise, and the foundation upon which the entire more modern fabric of Roman jurisprudence was constructed. Critics differ as to its character and object, some being of the opinion that it constitutes a complete series of lectures; others maintaining that it is merely the outline of a course to be pursued and expanded by oral instruction.

Although many extracts from Gaius appear scattered through the laws of Justinian, none of his writings were known to be extant until the discovery of the Institutes of Niebuhr at Verona in 1816, on a palimpsest, which had been utilized by some more pious than enlightened copyist for the preservation of the Epistles of St. Jerome.

Most esteemed for legal learning and perspicuity of diction of all the Roman jurisconsults, with the sole exception of Papinian, was Domitius Ulpianus, a native of Phoenicia, who was first the teacher, and then the secretary and trusted adviser of the Emperor Alexander Severus, by whom he was raised to the highest and most responsible posts in the government of the Empire. The principal work by which he is now known is the "*Liber Singularis Regularum*," a collection of opinions, rules, and decisions, of which at present only an abridgment exists. In addition to his profound acquaintance with the law in all its aspects, historical, judicial, and executory, his conciseness of expression and lucidity of style are his most distinguishing qualities. His merits are frequently alluded to in the Pandects, to which, in quantity of matter as well as in valuable erudition, he contributed more than any other legal authority. Ulpian has incurred the condemnation of posterity, because of his attachment to the ancient faith, and his pronounced antagonism to Christianity, but his sagacious counsel and talents for administration were far more valuable to the Empire than the maintenance of any form of religion, however popular, ever could be. His integrity and moral principle are sufficiently disclosed by his refusal to accede to the demands of military tyranny, which was the cause of his murder by the Prætorian Guards. Historians and legal writers alike have paid deserved tribute to his genius; and the prosperity of the reign of Alexander Severus was largely attributed to the soundness of his advice, and the consummate skill with which he exercised the functions of the political and judicial employments with which he was invested: "*Quia Ulpiani consiliis rempublicam rexit.*"[1] Julius Paulus, who, to a thorough acquaintance with the law, added a taste for general literature and a talent for versification remarkable for his time, was another of that brilliant and accomplished body of lawyers who have, by their learning and abilities, immortalized the golden age of Roman jurisprudence. He, also, is only known to us through the survival of a single legal treatise, the "*Sententiæ*," in five books, addressed to his son; and a very small number of isolated fragments from his "*Institutiones*," which afford no adequate conception of the character or merits of the work from which they are derived. We are, however, to a certain extent, indemnified for this loss by the fact that the compilation of Justinian abounds in quotations from this author, the greater portion of the Digest alone being composed of extracts from the writings of Paulus and Ulpian.

---

[1] Lampridius, Alexander Severus, LXVI.

PREFACE

The reputation of Paulus for legal acumen and extraordinary professional attainments, like those of his two famous contemporaries, continued unimpaired until the final dissolution of the Empire. A part of his works was incorporated into one of the earliest codes whose publication signalized the advent of a new and improved order of juridical procedure eventually to be erected upon the ruins of the ancient one which, in common with all other institutions of culture and civilization, had been overwhelmed by the disastrous tide of barbarian conquest.

Not the least remarkable among the extraordinary circumstances attending the general revision and codification of the Roman law, was the origin of its author. We should naturally suppose that an undertaking of such magnitude and importance would only be projected and executed by a sovereign of gentle birth, finished education, literary taste, and profound legal knowledge. But this was far from being the case. Justinian, although educated at Constantinople by his uncle Justin — who, formerly a shepherd, had raised himself by his talents and courage to the highest civil and military offices — never displayed any unusual predilection for letters. Born in Dacia, the modern Bulgaria, his originally harsh and guttural name Uprauda, afterwards Latinized into the more elegant appellation by which he is generally known, suggests at once his plebeian antecedents and barbarian ancestry. While he, no doubt, enjoyed the highest advantages of instruction at that time to be obtained, and which were by no means contemptible, no evidence exists of his proficiency in any branch of science, or that he had improved the unusual opportunities placed at his disposal. His personal character was defiled by the practice of the most odious vices. He was cruel, tyrannical, treacherous, unprincipled, and corrupt. He obtained the passage of a law authorizing the nuptials of actresses with men of senatorial dignity, which had long been forbidden, in order to enable him to marry Theodora, a common prostitute, whose notorious licentiousness was the scandal of the capital, and whose shameless and incredible behavior at public banquets and upon the stage, had excited the wonder, and provoked the resentment of an age proverbially indulgent to the exercise of every kind of profligacy. It is certainly not to the possessor of such qualities that one is inclined to look for reform in legislation and morals, and the enforcement of regulations for the well-being of society. Yet from this unpromising source were derived both the preservation and arrangement of those principles of jurisprudence to whose excellence even the venerated expounders of the Common Law of England, irreconcilably and traditionally hostile to their full acceptance, have been compelled to yield reluctant tribute.

The *Responsa Prudentum*, or opinions of learned jurisconsults, given in answer to legal points submitted to them for determination, were an indirect and limited, but important source of Roman legislation. The custom of applying to persons distinguished by their legal acquirements for the solution of disputed questions, dated back to the days of the Republic. While the greatest respect was always entertained for these dicta, owing to the eminent ability of those who promulgated them, they were not invested with an official character until the reign of Augustus, and were long solely indebted for the credit which they acquired to the skill and knowledge exhibited in the treatment of the matters in controversy.

That sagacious monarch, quick to adopt and utilize any practice of former ages whose value had been confirmed by experience, provided it did not conflict with the objects of his own ambition; published a decree declaring such opinions to possess legal and official validity, when rendered by persons especially authorized by imperial appointment to give them, thus permanently establishing the *prudentes* and their *responsa* as a part of the juridical system of the Empire.

Their functions, however, were rather interpretative than creative, and were largely confined to the settlement of mooted points of law in particular cases; still, notwithstanding this restriction, the influence of their decisions as precedents was vast and decisive.

The assemblage and collation of the opinions of the most renowned of the ancient jurists, unquestionably preserved for posterity the most valuable results of their labors. Their works, of which more than two thousand were examined to obtain materials for the Digest, have nearly all perished. None of them remain in an unmutilated condition. A few are accessible through the medium of translations of doubtful authenticity. Some authors are known to us only by name, even the titles of their books have disappeared. It is true that the Edict of Justinian prohibiting the comparison of these authorities with their official abridgment — which was declared to be the immutable law of the land — or their citation before the tribunals, must have greatly contributed to their loss or destruction, as they would henceforth be of no legal value, and no sufficient incentive for their preservation would exist. Even an antiquary could have no use for an obsolete law-book, whose perusal was productive of no benefit either literary or financial, and whose study was practically forbidden by the government. Still, if, as has been popularly alleged, we are indebted to the discovery at Amalfi of a sole surviving copy of the laws of Justinian — a statement whose accuracy may, however, not improperly be challenged, since numerous volumes of the Digest and the Code must have been distributed throughout the Empire, and have been in the hands of every magistrate, as without access to them he would be incapacitated from dispersing justice, or rendering a valid decision — it may well be presumed that the rare and scattered treatises of the old commentators would have met with a similar fate, when the infinite number of copies issued by imperial authority for the guidance of the proconsuls, prætors, governors, and other officials charged with the administration of government, to say nothing of those obtained by lawyers and other individuals, did not avail to prevent their destruction.

The Institutes, the Digest, and the Code of Justinian were not originally written and promulgated in the order in which they now appear. The Code was issued first of all, and a second edition — which is the one we have, the other having been lost — was published after the completion of the Digest, in order to reconcile discrepancies existing between the two, and to provide for new laws which had been enacted since the first edition was ordered. The Institutes, which, being an elementary treatise intended for the use of students, would naturally be placed before the others, was composed after the Digest, but was published a few weeks before it, and became operative at the same time with the latter. The Institutes is, to all intents and purposes, a transcript of the work of Gaius, a few trifling alterations in the arrangement and discussion of the subjects involved having been introduced for the purpose of meeting the requirements exacted by subsequent legislation. The only material point in which it differs from the abridgment of Gaius, is that it includes a Title on crimes and their prosecution, a topic which is not touched upon by the latter author. The merits of the Institutes alone are sufficient to establish the reputation of the famous lawgiver.

The labors of the various jurists, twenty-seven in number, whose opinions, precepts, and arguments practically compose the Digest, embraced a period of seven centuries.

It has not escaped the notice of the commentator that the majority of those whose works were utilized lived in comparatively recent times, and that there are few citations which date back more than a century from the completion of the great undertaking of Justinian. The advantageous influence of that undertaking exerted, directly and indirectly, upon the general welfare of mankind; the inculcation and practice of morality; and the administration of justice, has been incalculable. Nor is the excellence, fame, and usefulness of the Digest confined to the enormous mass of legal information it contains, or the eminent character of the authorities placed under contribution by its compilers. Unlike the Code and the Novels, whose phraseology and style are more or less contaminated by barbarisms, the idiom in which it is written is of almost classic purity, and it has been said that if it alone of all Latin compositions survived, the entire language could be reconstructed by the study of its pages.

The Digest of Justinian remains, as it was at its completion, the most comprehensive, authoritative, and generally available source from which man, in his intercourse with his fellows, can ascertain those eternal principles of equity without the knowledge and application of which his happiness, and even his continued existence, would be impossible.

PREFACE

The Digest, with all its extraordinary merits, is, however, very far from being a perfect compendium of legal learning. This can scarcely be a matter of surprise, when the vast number of treatises to which it owed its origin, and the conflicting and often irreconcilable opinions of its authors are taken into consideration. Justinian, well aware of the discordant views on important points of law held by the prominent jurisconsults of his time, deemed it necessary to personally examine, and diligently scrutinize the work of his commissioners, as well as to prohibit, as previously mentioned, any criticism of, or commentary on, the product of their labors.

The arrangement of the Digest is defective, and lacks the method and convenience of reference which should characterize a work of this description. Notwithstanding the avowed intention of the Emperor that such imperfections would be avoided, it abounds in repetitions, contradictions, and irreconcilable statements — often occurring within a few pages of one another — which are the cause of infinite perplexity and annoyance. Despite its claim to condensation it is still far too diffuse, and, by means of intelligent revision, could be greatly abridged without detracting in any respect from its value, to the infinite advantage of those desirous of familiarizing themselves with its contents.

The Code consists of a series of imperial constitutions of the later emperors, none of them older than the reign of Hadrian. They are placed in chronological order, but the disposition of the topics is not judicious, nor well adapted to the purposes of either the student or the magistrate. The vast numbers of laws promulgated since the publication of the first edition, including fifty decisions rendered by Justinian in an attempt to reconcile the contradicting opinions of eminent legal authorities which are responsible for much of the obscurity and uncertainty attaching to certain parts of the Digest, imperatively demanded the issue of another edition of the Code, which would adequately provide for the changes introduced by the new legislation. It is well known that many fundamental changes in the constitutions were made by the commissioners, to whom was committed the revision of the original Code; full power having been conferred upon them — as in the case of the Digest — to do so, a privilege of which they did not hesitate freely to avail themselves. The text is frequently obscure, the style dry and involved, and the language indicative of the corrupt influence of a decadent age upon the literature of the Empire. The fact that the revised Code and the Digest were practically contemporaneous in completion and publication, and were drawn up under the same supervision, renders the inferiority of the former the more remarkable.

When he made his oft-repeated declaration that his decrees were unalterable, not susceptible of improvement, and destined to prevail for all time, Justinian failed to take into consideration that the law is a progressive science, and that, while its principles remain the same, their application must inevitably be modified, as occasion may demand, in order to adapt them to the ever-varying conditions and requirements of society. From the date of the conception of the Digest almost to the hour of his death, the Emperor was constantly employed in the revision and repeal of his own enactments. His last efforts to this end were embodied in the New Constitutions, or "Novels," as they are usually called, issued as explanatory of matters contained in the Code, which, in its turn, when any controverted point arose, took precedence of both the Institutes and Digest, as being the more recent authority: "*Leges posteriores priores contrarias abrogant.*"

Two editions of the Novels, one in Latin, of one hundred and thirty-four, the other in Greek, of one hundred and fifty-nine constitutions, have come down to us. The former is styled *Corpus Authenticum*, and is generally considered as possessing the highest authority.

The Novels were not published as a whole until after the death of Justinian. By far the greater portion have reference to the private interests of individuals, and to three of them we are indebted for the law of intestate succession which, substantially unaltered, has been adopted by all the civilized nations of the world.

The Constitutions of Leo are largely taken up with rules prescribing the selection and ordination of candidates for ecclesiastical offices; privileges granted to captives and slaves; regulations to be observed by fishermen in casting their nets; and provisions of minor importance concerning Jews, concubinage, marriage, wills, coinage, and sumptuary legislation.

The arrangement of the Titles of the entire Civil Law is more or less largely arbitrary, unmethodical, and without adequate classification. It is a singular fact that the confusion and uncertainty which must inevitably result from this was not anticipated and provided for by the commissioners of Justinian, whose labors would have been greatly lessened, and the convenience of future generations materially promoted by the reconciliation of conflicting opinions, the avoidance of repetition, and the disposition of the rules of law, together with the observations to which they gave rise, in regular and systematic order.

Law was usually divided by the Romans into three kinds, Natural Law, *Jus Naturale*; the Law of Nations, *Jus Gentium*; and the Civil Law, *Jus Civile*. With a view to the close analogy existing between the first two of these many learned authors included both in the term *Jus Gentium*, which, being considered as embracing that body of rules prompted by the innate sense of morality and justice which should govern intercourse between our neighbors and ourselves, and requiring no express enactment to establish its validity, was also known as the Law of Nature.

In the case of the Romans, who had conquered the world, the *Jus Gentium* was subject to a different interpretation than that generally accorded to it, as the peoples to whom it applied no longer enjoyed that independence which would enable them to assert their rights, and, if necessary, maintain them by force of arms; but being, for the most part, reduced to the condition of either tributaries or serfs, were necessarily obliged to comply with such regulations as the appointed magistrate, in the exercise of his discretion, might see fit to impose upon them, regardless of their former nationality or privileges.

The *Jus Civile*, analogous to the Common Law of England, was stated by the authors of the Digest to be based exclusively upon the verbal opinions of jurisconsults: "*Est proprium jus civile, quod sine scripto in solo prudentium interpretatione consistit.*"[1] The definition of Cicero is much more comprehensive, and included not only the Twelve Tables, but legislative enactments of every description, decrees of the Senate, judicial decisions, the precepts of learned jurists, imperial edicts, customs that from long usage had acquired legal force, and whatever was consistent with equity: "*Quod in legibus senatus consultis, rebus judicatis, jurisperitorum auctoritate, edictis magistratuum, more, equitate consistat.*" The *Jus Civile* was not a term exclusively applicable to the rules of action adopted by the Romans; it was understood to indicate those which any nation might prescribe for the ordinary regulation and obedience of its constituents.

Law was also either public or private; the first had reference to the mutual obligations of the State and those subject to its authority; the second concerned its relations of private individuals with one another. Public Law, therefore, dealt generally with the affairs of government, such as the maintenance and observance of the ceremonies of religion, which were usually political in their character, and the administration of criminal justice; private law with the enforcement of the rights upon which the acquisition and control of property principally depend; for example, those regulating contracts of every kind, the conveyance of land, testamentary disposition, and the settlement of the innumerable controversies, which, in the daily transaction of business, form so great a portion of the affairs of life.

The *Jus Civile*, which was only susceptible of a rigid interpretation, was also employed in contradistinction to the *Jus Honorarium*, or prætorian law, composed of magisterial edicts, in the formulation of which a large measure of discretion was conceded to the Prætor, who was authorized to mitigate the severity of existing statutes, and by reason of this extraordinary privilege, frequently exercised legislative as well as judicial functions. The *Jus Honorarium* in the course of centuries expanded to such dimensions as to be unavailable for reference, and an abridgment became necessary. This was effected during the reign of Hadrian by the existing Prætor, Salvius Julianus, to whose revision of the judicial acts of his predecessors was

---

[1] Digest, I, II, 13.

PREFACE

given the title of Perpetual Edict, which from that time was assigned a place as a part of the *lex scripta* of Roman jurisprudence.

Privilegia, as the etymology of the term implies, were exclusive laws having reference to certain persons or things. It was, however, generally used to indicate some unusual penalty. A *privilegium* was usually absolutely restricted to the individual who was the object of its provisions, and where it related to property, it also was applicable to the possessor or owner of the same. Legislation of this description was promulgated by the emperor, each rescript being circumscribed by the conditions of the particular case calling for its enactment; hence such laws could never be cited as precedents: "*Privilegia non sunt trahenda ad exemplum.*"

Roman jurisprudence, to a certain extent, sanctioned retroactive legislation. The pernicious effects of this doctrine are thus ably set forth by a distinguished authority: "A retrospective law is a phrase which abridges in two words every possible notion of oppression, wickedness, and wrong, and this was the Common Law of England, according to the unanimous opinion of the judges."

While such legislation is expressly and unqualifiedly prohibited by Article I, Section 9, of the Constitution of the United States, judicial interpretation has so greatly restricted the application of the provision relating to *ex post facto* laws, as to seriously impair its efficacy, and to suggest that, in the future, legal acumen may suggest a ground for entirely annulling it.

The three legislative bodies of the Roman government were the *Comitia Centuriata*, or general assembly of the people, the *Comitia Tributa*, or assembly of the tribes, and the Senate. The legislative acts passed by these were respectively designated *leges, plebiscita*, and *senatus-consulta*. The measure to be adopted by the *Comitia Centuriata* was drawn up by a magistrate of senatorial rank, presumably a consul, revised by some eminent jurist, and then submitted to the voters of the Centuries, among whom originally no distinction of rank existed, as far as their suffrages were concerned. In the *Comitia Tributa*, which at its inception was exclusively composed of plebeians, a tribune introduced the proposed *plebiscitum*, which, as the patricians had no voice in either its submission or passage — although it not infrequently curtailed their privileges, and menaced their influence — affords a striking instance of class legislation. While, during the existence of the Republic, full authority to pass laws was vested in the entire body of the people, still, it was customary to obtain the sanction of the Senate, which in the earliest ages was indispensable. The process was sometimes reversed, for in important questions of diplomacy, or matters seriously affecting the public welfare, the law was proposed in, and passed by the Senate, and afterwards confirmed by the popular vote.

The legislative powers of these different bodies varied greatly at different epochs of Roman history. At one time, no act of the *Comitia* was valid without senatorial confirmation; at another, the tribune could arbitrarily veto a *senatus-consultum* — a privilege subsequently exercised by the emperor as the successor of that official; and at first, under imperial rule, the Senate was presumed to enjoy full authority as the lawmaking power of which eventually scarcely the shadow remained, for the sovereign, absolute in this respect as in all others, communicated his will to the August but obsequious assemblage, and the populace by means of rescripts, edicts, mandates, and decrees.

Thus, at a period long antecedent to the reign of Justinian, the voice of the people, once dominant in the *Comitia* and the Senate, interdependent sources of legislation, had been silenced by the threatening and all-powerful influence of imperial authority. It is true that the shadow of its former greatness and dignity was still preserved in the deliberations of the Senate, but its acts were merely the expression of a prescribed and unimportant formality. After the third century, its approval was not deemed essential to render legislation valid; the sovereign rarely deigned to solicit the advice of the Conscript Fathers; and the decree which they were expected, and, in fact, ordered to confirm, already drawn up and ready for publication, was submitted to them by the Emperor in the form of the proposed law for their nominal consideration and actual passage. The functions of the *Comitia* were gradually assumed by the Senate, which, in turn, was compelled to relinquish its power to the sovereign, a power for centuries feared and respected throughout the world, and to whose exercise was largely attributable the glory and prestige attaching to the Roman name.

To no source, however, not even to the *Jus Civile* itself, is to be attributed a greater share in the formation and development of Roman jurisprudence than to the *Jus Prætorium*, or equity jurisdiction of the Prætor.

The Consuls succeeded the Kings as the highest judicial officers, whose duties, afterwards growing too onerous through the enormous increase of legal business due to the absorption of conquered territory, the extension of commerce, and the control of a turbulent and insolent populace, were eventually shared by inferior members of the magistracy, decemvirs, tribunes, and prætors, created from time to time as occasion demanded. Of these the prætors, during the latter part of the fourth and the middle of the third century before Christ, were recognized as judges with exclusive, original jurisdiction of legal questions, and general interpreters of the law.

Originally, there was but one of these magistrates, who was chosen with one of the Consuls by the *Comitia Centuriata*; afterwards, he was given a colleague, who heard and decided controversies arising between Roman citizens and foreigners. While they cast lots for the choice of jurisdiction, the former, styled *Prætor Urbanus*, was superior in rank to the latter, the *Prætor Peregrinus*.

Cicero informs us that the term "prætor" was originally a title of the Consuls, as military commanders, whose duties the magistrate subsequently designated by that name discharged in case of their absence or incapacity. After them, he was the most exalted dignitary of the state. He possessed the two extensive powers known as "*imperium*" and "*jurisdictio*," exercised together by no other Roman official except the Consuls. The former indicated his right to bring parties before his tribunal by summons, and to compel obedience to his decisions, or his edict; the latter had reference to his authority to render judgment and expound the law. While his principal functions were of a strictly judicial character, others were, from time to time, assigned to him, not the least important of which was the superintendence of the public games, with which the Urban Prætor was charged at a very early date. An office of such responsibility, and one which implied the possession of more than ordinary shrewdness, knowledge, discretion, and experience, was naturally only to be entrusted to a mature person of acknowledged capacity; hence the age requirement under the Republic was forty, under the Empire thirty years. The variety and complexity of the questions requiring examination by the courts, and which often demanded immediate consideration and settlement, necessitated an increase in the number of the functionaries of this branch of the Roman magistracy, and induced Sylla to order the appointment of eight Prætors, which figure Cæsar raised to sixteen. During the Empire, however, the original number was restored.

The Prætor first held his court in the Forum, and afterwards in the Basilica, not far away. Like all dignitaries of exalted rank, he was attired in a robe bordered with purple. His tribunal occupied the most honorable station in the former place of assemblage, and was semicircular in form, with a curule chair in the centre upon a slightly elevated platform, before which was erected a spear. This emblem of conquest and dominion, deemed the best evidence of the title to property, and set up in all courts, was the *quiris* of the Sabines, whence was derived the term *Quirites*, applied to Roman citizens in their civil capacity, as distinguished from the military. The inferior judicial officials were seated below the Prætor at his feet, and hence were designated *Judices Pedanei*; the lictors stood on either side. His exalted position did not require him always to render judgment in the tribunal; in *ex parte* matters he could decide and issue his order *de plano*; on the street, at his home, in the bath, or elsewhere; hence application for his sanction could be made to him at almost any time when no contested point was involved, as in the cases of the emancipation of children, or the manumission of slaves.

The Prætorian Tribunal was established for the purpose of affording relief in the administration of justice by determining questions which could not satisfactorily be disposed of under the ordinary rules of legal procedure; and which, if they remained unheard, or were decided strictly by law, would result in hardship and

PREFACE

pecuniary loss to the parties concerned. In this respect, as well as in others, it presents a striking analogy to our modern courts possessing equity jurisdiction, instituted to supply the deficiencies of laws of too general a character. It was, indeed, the prototype of the English Court of Chancery, created for the same ends, and largely governed by the same principles and precepts. As is well known to every lawyer, a judge sitting as chancellor can, in case of emergency, hear and decide numerous matters without the formality of going upon the bench, when personal liberty or the preservation of property requires immediate action.

Other analogies will readily suggest themselves; the Prætor was originally, before being charged with the duties of the Consuls during their absence, or when they were occupied in the convocation and presidency of the Senate, merely the legal adviser of these chief magistrates of the Republic. The latter, like the Kings, were the fountain of justice, and to the judicial officer appointed to relieve them of a portion of their arduous duties, a certain discretionary power, in matters where the law as set forth in the Twelve Tables and subsequent enactments appeared to be deficient, was delegated, in order to afford equitable relief which could not otherwise be obtained.

In like manner, in England, the royal prerogative of grace, subject to strict and well-defined limitations, was placed in the hands of the chancellor, representing the sovereign, who originally sat with his judges in the court of the King's Bench, to "temper justice with mercy," which the latter, bound by the requirements and traditions of their office, were not at liberty to do. As in the case of the Prætor at Rome, the chancellor was expected to follow the well-established Common Law of the realm, where this was possible, and its rigid enforcement did not result in a conclusion not justified by conscience, in compliance with the ancient maxim: *Æquitas sequitur legem*. Like his prototype, he did not always see fit to adhere to this rule, and, in fact, both sometimes either quietly evaded, or boldly violated it.

The decree of the Prætor for specific performance, or one issued under some pressing exigency, exactly corresponded to that of the English chancellor, and coincides with our writ of mandamus; the preventive remedy of the Roman interdict was the exemplar of the injunction. The Prætor, if application were made to him, could order *restitutio in integrum*, or complete restitution of the complainant to his former status, where a contract was tainted with fraud; the chancellor, under similar circumstances, is invested with the same authority. The jurisdiction of both was especially directed to the protection of minors; the enforcement of the responsibilities of guardians; the prevention of impositions upon the weak and helpless. Both could compel answers to be given, under penalty, where lists of interrogatories were submitted; each could assign to a deputy a cause to be heard, order evidence to be taken, and the facts ascertained, that a decree might subsequently be rendered, a functionary, who, in the Prætorian Tribunal, was styled a "*judex*" or "*arbiter*," in the Court of Chancery, a "master."

The equitable jurisdiction of the Prætor, and the restraints which it imposed upon the formal application of the principles prescribed by the Twelve Tables, accepted customs, and other sources of the Civil Law, were regarded with great disfavor by the ancient Roman jurists, who could not be reconciled to improvements in the dispensation of justice, however salutary they might be, which conflicted with their preconceived ideas of legal proceedings, sanctioned and consecrated as the embodiment of human wisdom by the approval of their predecessors, and the continuous observance of many generations.

The greatest prejudice was also manifested by the early common lawyers against the Court of Chancery and its decrees. They deplored the latitude granted the chancellor, which, at times, enabled him to exercise his discretion in contravening established rules, and openly defying the law. They foresaw untold evils in the abandonment of principles that for so long had guided the official conduct of the renowned jurisconsults of the English bar. Regardless of the fact that all law is, or should be, founded on equity, the maxim, *Lex aliquando sequitur æquitatem* — the converse of the more ancient one — was to them an abomination. Their position on this point found apt expression in the saying of Selden: "Equity is a roguish thing, and is in law what the Spirit is in Religion, what everyone pleases to make it." Even to this day, when courts of law and equity are almost everywhere practically consolidated, this feeling is by no means extinct among many members of the legal profession.

A considerable portion of the prejudice attaching to Roman law in England, has very properly been attributed to the machinations of the priesthood. "Perverted by the Canonists into an instrument of ecclesiastical ambition and rapacity, wielded in every part of Europe by the clergy, as a means of accomplishing their gigantic schemes of usurpation, it is not surprising that real patriots should oppose doctrines which were put forward ostentatiously by the most determined and implacable foes of English freedom."

There were other magistrates than the Prætor, such as tribunes, quæstors, censors, ædiles, triumvirs, and duumvirs, inferior in rank, and invested with more or less limited jurisdiction, some of whom could be classed under the modern appellation of commissioners. In the course of time the office of Prætor was curtailed of much of its importance by the transfer of many of its functions to the courts of the Urban and Prætorian Prefects.

As the duties of the Consuls frequently required them to be absent from Rome, the Prætor, under such circumstances, acted as their representative, and was invested with supreme executive as well as judicial authority. The difference between the two offices was, in fact, merely nominal. The Prætor, like the Consul, could exercise the right of military command, as well as discharge the functions of civil government. But his principal duties were those connected with his judicial power. His was the supreme tribunal for the administration of justice, whence legal principles emanated, and where laws were expounded, and often promulgated. In the Edict which he always published at the beginning of his term of office, he declared that he would afford relief to the severity imposed upon litigants by a strict construction of the civil law, either by employing what was lacking, or by correcting what was onerous, so far as might be advantageous to the public welfare: "*Adjuvandi vel supplendi vel corrigendi juris civilis propter publicam utilitatem.*" In the formulation of the rules for his official conduct during the year for which he was elected, he was, in this instance as elsewhere, guided largely by his own discretion. He could adopt the regulations established by his predecessor, change, or practically abrogate them, if he chose to do so. As a matter of fact, however, he generally confirmed at least a portion of them, adding such others as he considered either necessary or advisable. Thus he possessed a qualified legislative authority, whose effect upon the jurisprudence of Rome, both with respect to its formation and construction, and especially conspicuous in its beneficent influence, exceeded anything accomplished by the ordinary lawmaking powers. The independence of the Prætor was indeed so great, that, until less than a century before the Christian era, aside from custom, there was no legal way by which he could be compelled to observe the rules that he himself had prescribed, and which, when actuated by ambition or prejudice, he would naturally be tempted to disregard. The defect was eventually remedied by the enactment of the *Lex Cornelia de Edictis Perpetuiis*, which forbade him to violate the terms of his Edict.

The right to issue edicts was, by no means, the exclusive privilege of the Prætor, although his authority in this respect exceeded that of other judicial officers, for, as Gaius informs us, it was vested in all Roman magistrates: "*Jus autem edicendi habent magistratus populi Romani.*"[1]

In the alteration of the ancient law, and its adaptation to the new conditions of Roman society which had been evolved in the course of centuries, the influence of the Prætorian Tribunal was gradual, but none the less effective. The proverbial attachment of the people to established custom, or the practice of their ancestors, was such as to discourage any sudden or radical abolition of existing laws, even though obsolete, as many of the provisions of the Twelve Tables, together with others embodied in subsequent legislation, actually were. The

---

[1] Institutes, I, VI.

PREFACE

difficulty was increased by the incessant conflict between the patricians and the plebeians; the former unwilling to renounce any of their time-honored privileges, and the latter equally determined to secure for themselves a greater degree of freedom, and a decisive voice in the affairs of state. Great tact was therefore requisite, and, as the Prætor was always a patrician, he was necessarily often suspected as being constantly liable to temptation to unduly favor his own order. The fact that such important changes in jurisprudence were accomplished without serious disturbance at any time, speaks well not only for the talents with which the Prætorian magistracy was administered, but also indicates the laudable self-control of which the masses were susceptible, even when their most vital interests were involved.

The moral element was, of course, the most important consideration in the establishment of the equitable jurisdiction of the Prætor. He was expected, above all things, constantly to bear in mind the principles of justice, and to apply them without regard to the observance of the strict letter of the law — "*In summa æquitatem ante oculos habere debet judex.*" His innovations did not, however, go to the length of actually annulling a law which, either by special enactment, or through acknowledged custom, had been accepted as such; his authority rather consisted in a liberal interpretation and application of such rules as he had formulated as the basis of his decisions when he assumed the duties of his office, and which he was expected to adhere to, and, by means of them, modify and correct the inconveniences entailed by preexisting legislation. While he could not expressly abrogate a statute, he had the power to suspend its operation in matters which came before him for determination when this was required for the dispensation of equity, defined by Aristotle to be: "The correction of the law where it is defective by reason of the universality of its expression."

Notwithstanding the great latitude allowed him in rendering judgment, the Prætor was subject to certain restrictions; among others that of not being permitted to lay down rules or promulgate decisions either irreconcilable with the terms of his own Edict, or in absolute contravention of the civil law by which his official conduct was, in general, presumed to be regulated. The fact that the duties of this important office were almost uniformly discharged by men who were not lawyers, is one of the striking anomalies of Roman jurisprudence. Such technical legal knowledge as was necessary was supplied by the Assessors, otherwise known as *decemviri litibus judicandis*, ten in number, and taken equally from the senatorial and equestrian orders, who, although they were sometimes designated judges, acted only in an advisory capacity.

While the Prætor was empowered to hear and determine questions of both law and fact, the latter duty was generally performed by a *judex* or judge, a term which did not necessarily imply the possession of legal attainments. When the *judex* made his report, the Prætor rendered judgment in the case. When appointed for that purpose the *judex* could also interpret the law, but, under no circumstances, was he considered as the deputy of the Prætor, who only designated him to decide some special case, after which his authority was at an end. The parties litigant were expected to agree upon the selection of the judge, and when this had been done, the Prætor, on the motion of the plaintiff, appointed him. No matter how small the sum involved was, the appointment was not made without their consent.

Under the Roman practice there were three kinds of judges, who were designated respectively, *Judex*, *Arbiter*, and *Recuperatores*, the latter term never being used in the singular. The first of these had jurisdiction of actions *stricti juris*, or such as were instituted under the civil law to the rules of which he was obliged absolutely to adhere; the second heard cases *bonæ fidei*, that is those styled *arbitrariæ*, in which the sum to be recovered was undetermined, and the court was invested with full authority to fix it; the third, as previously stated, were jurymen appointed to assess damages in civil proceedings, when suit had not been brought to recover any certain article or specified sum of money, and in actions of tort; this, however, they only had a right to do when the value of the property in dispute was less than a thousand *asses*. Their number is not positively known, and, indeed, varied, ordinarily consisting of three or five, sometimes of many more. They first were appointed in cases where a foreigner was a party, but this rule was afterwards extended to include disputes existing between the Roman government and those of other states; their acts being, in such instances, invested with more or less of a diplomatic character.

While, properly speaking, there could only be a single *judex*, there might be several *arbitri*, as well as *recuperatores*. It was not essential that either of these should be Roman citizens, or that the *recuperatores* should be selected from the panel of *judices* posted up in the Forum, as bystanders could be called upon to serve, as in the case of modern talesmen. This fact, as well as the statement by Gaius that, in the case of the non-appearance of the defendant, judgment was at once rendered against him by the *recuperatores* for the penal sum mentioned in the bond: "*Ut qui non steterit, is protinus a recuperatoribus in summan uadimonii condemnatur;*"[1] would seem to indicate that they were principally considered available in instances where the rapid disposal of a controversy was deemed expedient. The functions of these officials were, to all intents and purposes, identical, the only difference between them was the number employed. This was the ordinary course of Roman civil procedure from the compilation of the Twelve Tables to the reign of Diocletian.

The Roman system of government invested all important dignitaries — Consuls, Proconsuls, Governors of Provinces, Prætorian Prefects, Quæstors, and Curule Ædiles — whom we would naturally class as exclusively executive officers, with judicial authority. Although after the institution of the Empire, the Consulate became a purely honorary office, eventually consolidated with that of the sovereign as supreme magistrate, the Consuls occasionally performed the duties of expounders of the law, so late as the fourth century, and to the last, the Prætor was considered a deputy, or supplementary Consul. To the arbitrary and uncertain character of the Consular decisions was chiefly to be attributed the great and beneficial change caused by the compilation of the Twelve Tables.

A love for grandiloquent titles, unknown to the ancient Romans, and an infallible symptom of national decadence, characterized the debased population of the Eastern Empire. The pompous and often absurd designations and attributes assumed by Justinian, and prefixed to the Digest, reveal the extent to which imperial vanity and exaggeration could go. The nobility, which included the magistrates, were divided into five grades or classes, *illustres, spectabiles, clarissimi, perfectissimi, egregii*, according to their rank and the official positions which they occupied.

Some confusion may naturally arise when the respective functions of the *Judices* under the Formulary System, and those of the later *Judices Pedanei* are considered. The duty of the former was simply to ascertain the facts at issue and report accordingly; the latter, however, being ordinarily trained and experienced jurists, and often acting as Assessors or advisers of the Prætor, were authorized to decide both the law and facts, and they, upon whose decisions he was almost wholly dependent for the information to enable him to render his decrees, had obviously far greater influence and power.

The imperial magistracy also included the *duumviri*, two in number as indicated by their name, municipal authorities of all cities except Rome and Constantinople, whose office was elective; and the *defensor civitatis*, appointed by the Prefect of the district as the representative of the poorer classes against the oppressive encroachments of powerful and unscrupulous persons. These functionaries, when acting in a judicial capacity, decided cases in which not more than three hundred *solidi*, about fifteen hundred dollars, were involved. The *duumviri* corresponded to the Consuls, from whom their office was derived, but did not possess the authority of the latter.

The original Romans were warriors pure and simple, whose emblem, the spear, was never lost sight of. It was the most important and significant token of their military, economic, and social life. When the commanding officer of an army wished to manifest his devotion to his soldiers he stood upon a spear while making the prescribed declaration to that effect. Conquered enemies were marched under it to denote their

---

[1] Gaius, Institutes, IV, 185.

subjection. The shaft of such a weapon was bestowed as a reward of military merit. A spear, the symbol of legal authority and possession, was erected at all auctions of both public and private property, as well as when the Censor sold the right to collect taxes to farmers of the revenue. A spear-head, which had transfixed a gladiator in the ampitheatre, was employed instead of a comb, to part the hair of a prospective bride. As the emblem of property and quiritarian right, representative of the principle of force upon which the Roman polity depended for its existence and continuance, its appearance perpetually called to mind the valor and constancy which enabled those who wielded it to vanquish their enemies, and had prompted them to include among their possessions even their children, who were practically slaves, and their wives, who themselves had originally been obtained by violence. It is therefore only natural that what was regarded as the symbol of all power should eventually occupy a prominent place in the judicial tribunals.

Much of the severity manifested in early Roman legislation, both as regards its formulation and its enforcement, is attributable to the ruling impulse of the nation, the worship of force. Despite the nominal supremacy of Jupiter, Mars and Hercules were in fact the dominant spirits of its Pantheon. The arts of peace, which bring in their train the virtues of sympathy and benevolence, and the amenities of social intercourse, were always subordinated to the battle, the triumph, and the lust of universal empire. In the words of a famous writer: "*Les hommes extrêmement heureux et les hommes extrêmement malheureux sont également portés à la dureté; témoin les moines et les conquérants. Il n'y a que la médiocrité et le mélange de la bonne et de la mauvaise fortune qui donnent de la douceur et de la pitié.*"[1]

The civil and military history of a nation is thus reflected in its laws. The two are inseparably connected, and each is the necessary complement to the other. The circumstances attending the origin and growth of a people must be ascertained in order to grasp intelligently the motives which prompted its legislation; the character of its ordinances must be thoroughly understood to enable the chronicler to effectively depict and explain the consequences of the acts of the lawmaking power. Hence it has been most pertinently observed that a jurist should be acquainted with history, and an historian versed in jurisprudence: "*Tout historien devrait être jurisconsulte, tout jurisconsulte devrait être historien.*"[2] No more faithful or suggestive picture of the rise, development, and destruction of a race can be obtained, than by the philosophical study of the laws by which it was governed, as well as of the political considerations that caused their enactment, and to no state is this remark more applicable than to Rome.

Roman jurisprudence was exclusively devised for, and applicable to those enjoying Roman citizenship. He only, was a citizen in whom were vested the rights of *connubium* and *commercium*; that is, one who could marry, and enter into a valid contract, an essential requisite for the prosecution of any kind of business. The enjoyment of the *jus civitatis* implied not only the exercise of many privileges, but the assumption of responsibilities which could not be evaded. The *civis* was registered in the census, and was subject to taxation; he could be enrolled in the army, which was closed to slaves, freedmen, and foreigners; he could take part in the proceedings of the various popular assemblies, and was eligible to the highest official dignities; his person was sacred, in early times it was unlawful to put him to death, and in subsequent ages, even though by conviction for crime he forfeited his citizenship, he was permitted to avoid the penalty by going into voluntary exile; it was his duty to be present on important occasions, at sacrifices and the celebration of other religious ceremonies, and at the public games; he participated in all civil benefits. Liberty was his birthright, and despotic control of his household his peculiar privilege; upon him alone was conferred testamentary capacity and the power to take under a will, or succeed to an estate; upon him were imposed the charges of guardianship, responsibility for whose assumption and exercise could not be renounced, and whose faithful performance was insured by the most exacting safeguards. The highest grade of citizenship was that to which

---

[1] Montesquieu, Works, *De l'Esprit des Lois*, page 231.

[2] Ortolan, Histoire de la Legislation Romaine, I, XVII.

the *jus suffragii et honorum*, the right to vote in the *Comitia*, and to administer the office of magistrate, attached. The possession of political rights, which we are accustomed to associate exclusively with the term, was not, however, absolutely necessary, as many *ingenui* were not entitled to it; but the enjoyment of civil privileges was indispensable to enable a man to contract a marriage recognized as legal, or engage in transactions which necessitated the acquisition and alienation of property, including the succession to intestates.

Residence at Rome was attended with greater prestige and the enjoyment of superior advantages than were accorded to dwellers in municipal towns.

The original division of the people was into two classes, the *Cives*, and the *Peregrini*. To these were subsequently added that of the *Latini*, who could buy and sell merchandise, but to whom matrimonial connection with the *Cives* was denied. *Peregrini*, or strangers, were not necessarily aliens, but any persons who could claim no rights either private or political; even plebeians were placed in this category. They had, at first, no standing in the tribunals, and, being to all intents and purposes outlaws, could not obtain legal redress unless they enjoyed the patronage of some influential citizen. It was mainly for their benefit that the office of *Prætor Peregrinus* was created. The severity of these rules was, from time to time, relaxed; with the institution of the Empire the honorable appellation of *civis* was deprived of much of its meaning and importance; the privilege was bestowed by the Emperors indiscriminately at mere solicitation; and, as the climax of this violation of ancient usage and tradition, Caracalla, by an edict, constituted every freeman in his dominions a Roman citizen.

The *Jus Civitatis* and the *Jus Quiritium* were not synonymous, the latter, from which the *Jus Civitatis* obtained nearly all that rendered it desirable or advantageous, namely, the private rights which its enjoyment conferred, being embraced in it.

The *lex originis*, or municipal law of man's birthplace, always took precedence of the rules affecting his Roman citizenship, in case any conflict arose between the two. The *munera publica*, or civil obligations, which the former entailed, could not be declined or avoided by him whom, by the accident of nativity, fortune had rendered liable to their performance. Among these requirements were the holding of certain offices and the gratuitous discharge of public duties, which frequently demanded great personal sacrifices, involving loss of time, and a considerable expenditure of money.

The extraordinary power wielded by municipalities over their citizens, and which had been so long and despotically exercised, vanished with the overthrow of the Western Empire by the barbarians.

Attention has been called to the remarkable fact that the Roman is the only system of jurisprudence mentioned in history which was established and developed under a Republican form of government; as well as to its difference from others in that its authority was not, for many centuries, exerted for the propagation of any special form of superstition. Religious toleration was a cardinal principle of the Roman polity. The statue of every divinity, the ritual of every sect, found a place in the Roman Pantheon and its services; admission was even given to the altar of the "Unknown God." In common with other Italian towns, Rome possessed a tutelary deity whose name, known only to the initiated, was secret, and was impiety to utter; a custom which may have been derived from the Hebrews, who observed it with reference to one of the synonyms or attributes of Jehovah. And yet this government, in common with those of all primitive races which depend at first upon credulity and fear for the enforcement of their decrees, was absolutely controlled by sacerdotal power. The Roman cult was, as previously stated, always political, and the College of Pontiffs was far from being an association of a purely sacred character. The primary functions of the *Pontifex Maximus* and the augur were civil, not religious. The priests not only framed and promulgated laws, but were the custodians of the official records in which they were preserved; saw to their execution; and guarded most jealously, as their special prerogative, the knowledge of the formalities requisite for their enforcement. This association of secular and

PREFACE

religious authority was reflected in a not less marked degree in the Roman households, or *familiæ*, of which the State was but an aggregation, and where the head was the celebrant of the *sacra privata*, as well as the ruler in mundane affairs of those subject to his arbitrary, domestic jurisdiction. The inevitable result of this confusion of religious precept and temporal law was that every violation of the established ordinances was held to be more or less of a sacrilegious character, and a sin, invoking upon the head of the offender not only the anathemas of the priesthood, but the general execration of all pious citizens, and rendering him and his family outlaws, a condition which was found to be so effective in the maintenance of papal authority, that it was frequently created in mediæval times by the imposition of an interdict upon recalcitrant or offending communities.

The duty of the presiding magistrate was primarily, but not exclusively, the construction and application of the law; and his ruling was termed *jus*. The facts were passed upon, and reported by, the *judex*, or *recuperatores*, who, appointed by the Prætor, with the consent of the parties, had little or nothing to do with the legal aspects of the case, but heard the evidence, and made a report, which was styled *judicium*. The *litis contestatio*, or joinder of issue, was held to take solace at the time when the claims of both parties were submitted to the Prætor for examination. If a compromise could not be effected, the judge was selected from a list of persons whose names were enrolled upon the Prætor's *album judicium*, their eligibility being dependent upon pecuniary qualifications prescribed by law. The appointee was usually a senator, but this was not indispensable.

This separation of matters of law and fact naturally suggests the impanelling and functions of the English jury. The number, and the effect of the votes of both do not coincide, but this is of little consequence when their original selection, duties, and proceedings are considered. The source from whence our jury system is taken has long been a subject of controversy. The weight of authority seems to point to the Frankish inquest as its prototype. The Franks, however, were an offshot of a Teutonic tribe domiciled on the Rhine; and the *Schöffen*, or *facti judices* of the Germans, decided questions of fact in the same manner as the *Recuperatores*; and, like the original English jurymen, based their verdict largely upon matters within their own knowledge. Hence the jury was called *testes*, and what would now be a ground for exclusion, was, in the beginning, an indispensable requisite. The *Compurgatores*, whose number varied from five to twelve, were also of German origin, and a judicial body, the eligibility of whose members and whose decisions were founded upon personal acquaintance with the matters at issue. It may also be remarked here that the primary meaning of the term *arbiter* was, also, "a witness." This general similarity would seem to be more than a mere coincidence, and, bearing in mind the boundless influence of the Roman Empire upon the barbarous, as well as the civilized nations with which it was brought in contact, or which, at some time, were subject to its domination, in the absence of positive evidence, it is not unreasonable to infer that the origin of the modern jury may be attributed to the judicial polity of that imperial race whose genius has left such enduring traces upon others of our legal institutions.

No nation can construct for itself a rational and efficient system of criminal jurisprudence, until it abandons the primitive conception that a violation of the rights of man, founded upon, and confirmed by ancient custom, or forbidden by express enactment, is an offense against the deity. The persistence of this idea among the Romans even after the second edition of Justinian's Code, had a conspicuous effect upon their penal laws, which were far less complete and judicious than their wise and admirable scheme of civil legislation.

This was also the case in England during the age preceding the Norman conquest when reparation for what were considered private wrongs, was made either according to a regular schedule of penalties, or by the application of the *Lex Talionis*. The punitive character of the legislation of uncivilized nations bears no resemblance to what we designate criminal law. Its object is not the same. Its application is private and personal, and has no connection with the supreme authority of the State. None of the technicalities which abound in modern judicial systems exist to render its interpretation ambiguous, its enforcement difficult. Its precepts are rather advisory than mandatory, the expression of customs long and unhesitatingly observed, until all classes came to regard them as rules which must not be disobeyed.

The postulate that no Roman citizen could, according to the ancient law, legally suffer the penalty of death, was evaded by the ingenuous expedient of reducing him to servitude prior to his execution by declaring him to be *servus pœnæ*, the slave of punishment. Conviction of a serious crime also involved the forfeiture of citizenship, a condition equivalent to outlawry.

At the era when the Twelve Tables were the supreme law of the land, only four actions, strictly speaking, were recognized in legal procedure. The equitable jurisdiction of the Prætor not being, as yet, established, all suits were perpetual, that is the right to bring them was not barred by prescription, no matter how long a period had elapsed since its accrual. When, however, honorary or prætorian actions found their way into Roman jurisprudence, they were subject to limitation of time, and were only available during the year in which the Prætor held office; hence they were designated *temporales*, or temporary. An *actio directa* was one instituted for the recovery of property, or to compel the observance of a contract by the defendant, who, in case he had sustained any damage, or had been subjected to expense by reason of the transaction, had a right to bring the *actio contraria*, or counter-action, for the purpose of indemnification. Actions were either real, personal, or mixed. A real action (*in rem*), was one in which the right to proceed arose from the property or subject itself; a personal action (*in personam*) was based on the breach of an obligation contracted by another, and for which he and his heirs and successors were liable. A mixed action, to a certain extent, possessed the character of both the others. *Actiones stricti juris* were those in which the court was obliged to adhere to the law as laid down by the authorities, and had no latitude of interpretation whatever, as contrasted with *actiones bonæ fidei*, in which the discretionary power of the magistrate in rendering a decision consonant with the principles of equity could be properly exercised. Hence it appears that real and personal actions at civil law differ from those of common law practice, as, under the latter, suit could only be brought for the specific recovery of lands, or rights arising therefrom, and hence was applicable to real property alone; a limitation not recognized by Roman jurists. *Actiones in personam*, arising either from contracts or torts, closely resemble the personal actions of English jurisprudence. The difference between actions *in rem* and those *in personam* was entirely dependent upon the character of the rights which those two forms of legal procedure were respectively designed to protect. The Roman *actio in rem*, which lay where the title to any kind of property whatever was involved, was obviously much more extended in its application than the corresponding action of the common law, which was restricted to the recovery of land, or some interest in it, claimed under a free tenure as an indispensable condition of its availability. Despite those distinctions, which are more apparent than real, a general analogy exists between the two methods, and no reasonable doubt can exist that, in this as in so many other instances, the English is indebted to the Roman law for formulas whose origin is of such high antiquity that it cannot definitely be established.

The term *in rem* indicates its general application, so far as the property or right involved is concerned; the liability of the defendant either as claimant, possessor, or as responsible for damage, not being considered material, but of secondary importance. Hence an action of this kind being unlimited so far as persons were concerned, and directly relating to what it was designated to recover, could be brought against the party in possession. The principal distinction between real and personal actions stated concisely, was that the former were based upon ownership, or what was called by the Romans *jus in re*; the latter was available when anyone was entitled to something arising from a contract or obligation, a right designated *jus ad rem*; or, in the words of Bacon: "the one is an estate, which is *jus in re*, the other a demand, which is *jus ad rem*."[1] All prætorian actions, no matter what their nature, whether personal or real, could be heard and decided by an *arbiter*, who,

---

[1] Bacon, Works, Reading on the Statutes of Uses, Vol. IV, Page 161.

PREFACE

invested with somewhat greater authority than the *judex*, was defined as follows: "*Arbiter est qui totius rei arbitrium habet et potestatem.*"

Fleta adopts the Roman division of actions verbatim, without allusion to its derivation: "*Placitarum alius personale, aliud reale, aliud mixtum.*"[1]

Under the practice of the later period of the Empire, actions of every description were no longer perpetual, but the right to bring them was barred after the lapse of thirty years. As a rule, a criminal accusation could not be filed where twenty years from the date of the offence had expired. During the reign of Justinian, the difference between proceedings *in jure* and *in judicio* was abolished, and all points of law and fact were heard and determined by one magistrate, who was also invested with the authority necessary to carry his decrees into execution; that is, the *imperium mixtum* in civil actions, and the *imperium merum* in those involving punishment for crime.

The Roman Empire, from the reign of Constantine, was, for both administrative and judicial purposes, divided into four Prætorian Prefectures, which were in turn, subdivided into twelve dioceses, or districts, each governed by a deputy. The tribunals of those officials constituted supreme courts of appeal from the decisions of judges of inferior jurisdiction. Governors of provinces came next in the exercise of magisterial authority, and after them, the *duumviri* or municipal authorities, the *judices pedanei*, and the popular defenders, or *defensores civitatum*. The Prætorian Prefects of the two great capitals were the successors of the Urban Prætor. To the Emperor and his Council were occasionally referred questions which the exalted rank or powerful influence of the parties interested enabled them to remove from the consideration of the ordinary tribunals.

The jurisdiction of the Urban Prefect extended a hundred miles from Rome in every direction. To it the Latins were not subject, but enjoyed the privilege of being governed by their own laws. They were also, under certain circumstances, entitled to the freedom of the capital, and permitted to take part in important religious ceremonies. Their right of citizenship was restricted, but it could be claimed when they had either occupied the position of magistrate, or had left an heir. Italians, outside of Latium, were even less favored than those who enjoyed *Latinitas*. Justinian was the first to abolish the distinction existing between Italy and the remaining provinces, so far as the application of the civil law was concerned.

Under the improved system of practice introduced by this Emperor, the plaintiff first filed a *libellus conventionis*, or notice of suit, a concise statement of the cause of action, asking the magistrate to notify the defendant, and compel his appearance. Security was required from the plaintiff, or he was obliged to swear that he would have the action heard in sixty days, or reimburse the defendant double the amount of the expenses he had incurred, as well as prosecute the case to final judgment, and, if defeated, pay all costs. If the court found upon examination that the claim was not good in law, he dismissed the case, a proceeding resembling the sustaining of a demurrer, except that it effectually disposed of the suit. If, on the other hand, he considered the complaint to be well founded, he issued a summons to the defendant, who filed his answer, or *libellus contradictionis*, and was at the same time compelled to furnish security for damages and costs.

A plea to the jurisdiction could then be entered, and if it was found against the defendant, the oath of calumny was taken, and the case proceeded in due course. Institution of legal proceedings by *libellus* was almost identical with what was known as *cognitio extraordinaria*, with which all magistrates were now invested, and the only system authorized by Justinian. The effect of *litis contestatio* was that the parties litigant bound themselves under what was practically a stipulation to acquiesce in the decision of the judge, to whom the matter in controversy was referred; and, in early times, indicated the beginning of the proceedings *in judicio*; afterwards, however, when the magistrate determined questions of both law and fact, it dated from

---

[1] Commentarius Juris Anglicani, I, 1.

the day when the preparations for trial had been completed. The ancient law of Rome required each party to file the pleadings and conduct his own case. This was subsequently changed by permitting the appointment of a procurator, or agent, who was a mere attorney-in-fact, and, standing in the place of his constituent, became individually responsible for the result. Under the old common law of England, the same rule prevailed, and no one could empower another to appear for him without having first obtained permission of the court to do so. When a magistrate, through ignorance or design, rendered an illegal decision, he was held strictly accountable for any loss or expense resulting from his want of knowledge, or duplicity. If guilty of fraud, he incurred liability for the entire amount involved in litigation. The law of England and America is more indulgent, and an erroneous ruling by the judge cannot ordinarily be made the subject of judicial inquiry, either civil or criminal, as his acts are presumed to have been dictated by motives worthy of the honor and dignity of his exalted office.

The profound influence of Roman law upon that of England although never expressly admitted by the ancient jurists who appropriated many of its doctrines and precepts without alteration, cannot consistently be denied. Their treatises, constituting the very foundation of English jurisprudence, contain innumerable technical expressions and forms of procedure taken bodily, beyond all question, from the compilation of Justinian. Among these is the reference to the verbal contract familiar to the Romans as *stipulatio*, unknown to the common law, and from which the Action of Covenant is said to have been derived. The Roman element is remarkably conspicuous in the work of Fleta.

The Conquest of England by the Normans, and the resultant introduction of the canon law by ecclesiastics, the only class of persons at all conversant with letters in that age, had more to do with the study of the *Jus Civile*, and the adoption of its principles, than any other cause. Again, many of the chief dignitaries of the Church were either foreigners, special emissaries of the Holy See, or priests educated in Italy, and thoroughly imbued with the doctrines of the Civil Law and the Roman polity, upon which the entire fabric of their religion and the rules by which it was governed were based. The vast and irresponsible papal authority, almost faultless in the details of its organization and the adroitness with which its mandates are executed, is the direct heritage of the imperial system of Rome, and Italian influence is especially noticeable in the survival of these ancient forms in the practice of the Ecclesiastical Courts and those of the two Universities. The greater portion of the Common Law, however, dates back to the Saxon occupation, and the Teutonic love of liberty, inherited from remote antiquity, caused the British mind to revolt at the idea of such subjection to despotic will, as the Roman system, which practically concentrated all legislative, executive, and judicial functions in a single individual, enjoined as compulsory; notwithstanding the dictum of Glanvil, "The pleasure of the king is law, and has the force of law;" "*Hoc ipsum Lex fit quod Principi placet & Legis habet vigorem.*"[1] It was not until the fourteenth century, that the Civil Law, which for the period of nearly three hundred years had, chiefly through the agency of ecclesiastics appealing to the most powerful instincts and prejudices of humanity, been largely instrumental in the formation and development of English jurisprudence, began no longer to arouse the interest of jurists who had hitherto devoted themselves to its study. The immediate cause of this was not only the hatred entertained by the English for the exercise of arbitrary power by secular rulers, but the well-founded apprehension of papal supremacy, exemplified in many instances by the arrogant usurpation of civil authority by foreign prelates, acting under the direction of the See of Rome. The effects produced upon the laws of England by this influence, notwithstanding its unpopularity, never were effaced. In the law of contracts, especially that portion of it requiring a consideration to establish the validity of an agreement and render it legally enforceable; in the rules governing intestate succession; in the forms and titles of legislation; in the pleadings, examination of witnesses, and general order of judicial procedure; in the close resemblance of the interdict and injunction which suggests identity of origin; in the adoption, and constant use

---

[1] Glanvil, Tractatus de Legibus & Consuetudinibus Angliæ, Prologus, 3.

PREFACE

of maxims borrowed without alteration and without credit from the Institutes and the Digest; in the easement, corresponding to the servitude, of which it is the derivative and counterpart, and the means by which the right may be exercised, maintained, and lost; in the doctrine of natural accessions; in the authority of the chief law officer of the Crown to file informations, which was one of the duties of the Imperial Procurator representing the Emperor; in the innumerable other analogies existing between the Roman and English systems of jurisprudence, which, though often indefinite, are none the less convincing when the principles of the Civil and the Common law are subjected to comparison and contrast.

Numerous orders prohibiting the study and application of the rules of the civil law were issued at different epochs by the English authorities. Stephen, influenced as much by personal resentment against the Pope for his interference in the affairs of his kingdom as by the representations of his legal advisors, forbade the books of Roman law to be read. Henry III did not allow them to be taught in London, but confined the restriction to the capital. During the reign of Richard II, the recalcitrant nobles promulgated a resolution solemnly adopted, stating that: "The realm of England had never been until this hour, nor, by consent of our Lord the King and the Lords of Parliament, shall it ever be ruled or governed by the civil law." So great was the prejudice entertained by the English lawyers against Roman jurisprudence, that whenever a copy of the compilation of Justinian came into their hands, they immediately destroyed it. Despite these menacing prohibitions, and the bulls of several popes interdicting it, the study of the civil law was still pursued with avidity, especially by churchmen. Very properly regarded as the fundamental basis of the canon law, it was deemed essential for the magistrates, who were almost invariably priests, to be thoroughly familiar with both systems; versed "*in utroque jure canonico scilicet et civili.*"

Ecclesiastical influence succeeded in establishing and preserving for centuries the Roman forms of procedure in the various tribunals, presided over by members of the clergy, not the least important of which was the Court of Chancery.

It was stated by Selden that the reign of Edward I should be accepted as marking the epoch from which the constructive legislation of England — which country had hitherto been almost exclusively dependent upon other nations for its laws — dated its origin, and the formulation of a juridical system peculiarly its own began. The labors of Glanvil and Bracton, with their wholesale appropriation of the maxims and practice of the great Roman jurists, had already been accomplished. The former of these two authors who may with propriety be designated the Fathers of English jurisprudence, however, borrowed far less from Roman sources than his more learned and illustrious successor, of whom it was said: "There is scarcely a principle of law incorporated in the treatise of Bracton, that has survived to our times, which may not be traced to the Roman law, Bracton's direct references evidently do not comprise the whole of what he adopted immediately from the "*Corpus Juris.*" It has been estimated that at least one third of his work is taken from it. Not only Bracton, but other ancient legal writers, among whom, is Plowden, refer to many of the axioms and rules, which, constituting part of its common law, they quote as having originated in England, when in fact, they have been copied from the Digest, a misrepresentation hardly attributable to ignorance.

The arrangement and titles of some of the topics discussed by Bracton, Fleta, and Blackstone exactly coincide with those adopted by the commissioners of Justinian; and the phraseology employed by the first two, is, in numerous instances, identical with that of the Roman jurisconsults, whose observations appear substantially as transcripts in the treatises of these English commentators.

As there can be no doubt that the laws of Italy were administered in the British Isles during the Roman occupation, it is strange that their influence seems absolutely to have disappeared with the cessation of imperial supremacy. The impression, if any, left by those laws upon the jurisprudence of England, at that time seems to have been negligible, and their re-introduction in another form, under the auspices of the clergy, was, as above stated, one of the most important incidents of the Norman Conquest. Scarcely a vestige of the prior existence of the laws of Rome appears in the legal history of the preceding seven centuries.

The first Anglo-Saxon Code with its Teutonic legislation, which formed one of the original sources of the Common Law of England, was not promulgated until about the beginning of the seventh century. The Salic law, dating back to the fifth century, and consisting principally of a schedule of fines to be imposed by way of compensation for personal physical injuries, while to some extent instrumental in the formation of English jurisprudence, is of much less importance than the laws introduced by the Saxons. In these primitive compilations, as in the Twelve Tables, if the fine was not forthcoming, the relatives of the deceased were at liberty to exercise the right of blood-revenge. The *Lex Talionis* was not, however, so specifically set forth in those codes, as it was in the ancient Roman one. The influence of custom, long perpetuated and supreme among nations whose political organization was based upon clan, tribe, or family, is clearly discernible in these venerable collections. But, after all, to no source does the common law lie under such obligations for its doctrines and practice as to the rules and maxims of Rome. When compared with them the other legislation from which that law is derived applies inequitable, barbarous, and imperfect. The bitter hostility of the old English lawyers has never succeeded in even temporarily impairing the value of the *Corpus Juris Civilis*, upon the application of whose imperishable principles the administration of justice in the British Empire, as well as among all other civilized peoples as fully depends to-day as it did upon the Bosphorus and the Tiber in the age of Justinian.

Certain tribunals of special jurisdiction, that is such as have now, or formerly did have cognizance of matters relating to the Church and military and naval affairs, as well as those exercising control over members of the two Universities, were authorized to employ a course of procedure almost identical with that of the civil law. This privilege, originally obtained through the insistence of ecclesiastics, was based either upon the assent of the Crown, statutory enactment, or royal charter subsequently confirmed by Act of Parliament. The Ecclesiastical Courts, in which until 1857, were heard cases involving marriage, divorce, the probate of wills, and the testamentary distribution of estates, traced their origin to the period preceding the Norman invasion, when no distinction existed between secular and religious tribunals, so far as the questions which came before them for determination was concerned. The clergy, however, always favorable to the civil law, and jealous of the interference of laymen in matters in which the interests of the Church were concerned, and, in general, far better versed in jurisprudence than any other part of the population, not even excepting the common lawyers themselves, subsequently effected a separation of the two systems, asserting the superiority of the canon law over all others, including that of Justinian, notwithstanding it was so largely indebted to the latter.

This assumption of superiority was carried to such lengths that it was even acknowledged by English writers that the king had no jurisdiction over an ecclesiastic until after he had been degraded, and that, no matter of what crime he was guilty, his deprivation of sacerdotal functions was a sufficient expiation for it, and no other punishment could be imposed. Bracton, in the discussion of this subject, considers degradation as equivalent to the highest degree of forfeiture of civil rights under the Roman law: "*Satis enim sufficit ei pro pœna degradatio, quæ est magna capitis diminutio.*"

The civil law has long since ceased to be cited as authority in the judicial tribunals of England. With the exception of Louisiana, its force has never been officially recognized in any part of the United States. Despite these facts, its silent and unacknowledged influence in the determination of abstruse questions, in the application of legal principles, and in the administration of justice in both countries, is none the less powerful and significant. Generally speaking, the origin of this influence is, as above stated, traceable to the acceptance of the precepts of Roman jurisprudence by the old English commentators; to the power of the clergy, long paramount in secular as well as ecclesiastical affairs; and to the procedure and decisions of Courts of Equity, the heirs and beneficiaries of Prætorian jurisdiction. No treatises of ancient or modern times will bear comparison with the laws of Justinian as set forth in the Digest. Of unknown antiquity and origin they represent the very sum and substance of the rules by which civilized society is now, and always has been

PREFACE

governed and preserved. There is probably no branch of Roman jurisprudence which has exerted such a marked influence upon that of Europe as the law of contracts. The leading principle of the civil law with reference to obligations, a term which has a broader signification in England and America than it had at Rome, was that a mere agreement, or *nudum pactum*, being void for want of *causa*, or consideration, could not be enforced: "*Ex nudo pacto non oritur actio*." While this rule was substantially the same under both systems, it was not held by the Romans to be invariably applicable; as when a *stipulatio* was formally concluded it was valid whether there was any consideration or not. In England, all oral agreements without consideration are absolutely void, there must always be a *quid pro quo*. The canon law, having in view the moral obligation or motive of a promise, declares such contracts to be valid.

A marked distinction was recognized between the words *contractus* and *pactum*, the first, meaning a formal agreement under which suit could be brought; the second, an informal one which originally was not actionable. The Romans considered all contracting parties as principals, and did not admit the doctrine of contractual agency, except in the case of sons under paternal control and slaves, who, being legally incapable of acquiring property except for those upon whom they were dependent, were deemed to have obtained it for them, consensual and innominate contracts, based respectively upon common consent and concluded without further ceremony, or becoming operative following the performance of an agreement by one of the parties, and so designated because there was no specific action to compel their enforcement, are unknown to the law of England.

The *nexum*, or obligation contracted *per ses et librum*, or bronze and balance, like *mancipium*, which it resembled, was the oldest species of formal agreement known to the Romans, and involved the surrender of a man's liberty in consideration of a loan, in case he failed to discharge the debt when it became due. It, in fact, implied provisional servitude, and was often inexorably enforced, the person of the debtor being hypothecated, and he remaining in a servile condition until, by means of his services, the claim of the creditor had been fully satisfied. The latter had a right to imprison him, if he wished to do so. The *mutuum*, or loan for consumption, to be repaid in kind was afterwards substituted for the *nexum*.

Another division was that of *stricti juris* and *bonæ fidei*. The former embraced everything that an obligation rendered operative through the use of a prescribed formula; the latter referred to all agreements not included in that category. Under a contract *stricti juris* no interest could be collected; but under one *bonæ fidei* this might be done in case of default in payment. The stipulation, the principal elements of which were a verbal promise and its acceptance accomplished by specific interrogation and reply, was the formal engagement generally in use among the Romans. When it had once been concluded, it was not susceptible of alteration, which was not the case with the innominate contract, whose distinctive feature was the fact that either party might, under certain circumstances, withdraw without incurring liability. The stipulation, being *stricti juris* and hence admitting of no modification, was the only one of this kind which survived the sweeping changes effected by Justinian in Roman jurisprudence. While contracts *stricti juris* were required to be absolutely and literally fulfilled in accordance with their terms, this rule did not apply to such as were designated *bonæ fidei*, in which class were included sales, leases, and bailments of every description, admitting of the performance of any additional acts which, being customary and implied, might be deemed necessary to render the agreement fully effective. Proof of fraud did not, of itself, rescind a contract *stricti juris*, but only opened the way to a complete restitution of former conditions, but as soon as it became evident that a contract *bonæ fidei* was of a fraudulent character it immediately became of no force or effect.

The stipulation was ordinarily employed for the purpose of giving security for indebtedness contracted at the same time by the person who had negotiated a loan. Such an engagement was binding in the case of an obligation coming under the law of nature or nations, and which otherwise would not legally be capable of enforcement. When a contract dependent upon a condition was entered into, and it became evident that the condition could not be carried out, it was void *ab initio*, just as if no agreement had ever been made; and if it failed of performance it could not be renewed: "*Conditio semel defecta non resumitur.*"

Under the old Roman law, a woman was absolutely forbidden to become a surety, and she could not afterwards bind herself, even under a stipulation, unless this was done in behalf of the guardian of her children, or when she was proved to have deliberately been guilty of fraud. She could also render herself liable by the commission of an act which would redound to her injury, provided its disadvantageous character was apparent to every one, and she herself was aware of it. These restrictions were the result of the general legal incapacity attaching to her sex.

The position of a woman under the Roman system was one of absolute dependence during life. When the *patria potestas* was terminated by death, she at once became subject to either legal or testamentary guardianship. A male child could be released from tutelage at puberty; a female never was entitled to absolute freedom. If she married, she occupied the place of a daughter of her husband with all its incident restraints and disabilities. Thus, as remarked by Livy: "To every act, even of a private character, performed by a woman, our ancestors required the sanction of a guardian."

The barbarian nations that overwhelmed the Roman Empire had formed no conception of any rules by which agreements solemnly concluded bind the parties concerned, a condition which presupposes a certain advance in the arts of civilization, and a knowledge of the requirements of commercial intercourse to which they had not yet attained, and with which they, of course, were unfamiliar. This ignorance of one of the fundamental principles of ordinary business seems to have been shared by all Teutonic peoples, as the Anglo-Saxons, whose laws made so deep an impression upon English jurisprudence, had hardly a rudimentary conception of the obligatory nature of a contract.

An important class of engagements recognized by Roman legislation were certain rights established by operation of law under what were known as quasi-contracts. Among them were the *negotiorum gestio*, or voluntary agency, by which a man who undertook the management of another's affairs without authority, was thereby held to the exercise of the strictest diligence; the responsibility of a guardian for the proper discharge of the duties of his trust — and, on the other hand, his own right of action against the ward for money expended, or security furnished for his benefit; the obligation of the heir to satisfy all claims against the estate, and especially legacies and trusts, even though he may not have been benefited by the will; the power to recover anything paid or delivered under the impression that it was due, when in fact it was not; the liability of one joint-owner to another for necessary expense incurred on account of the common property, or for the recovery of his share of the profits when they had been enjoyed by either one to the exclusion of the other; and the rule laid down by the *Lex Rhodia de jactu*, which required compensation for merchandise thrown overboard at sea to lighten the ship, for the benefit of all, to be made by those whose goods had not been sacrificed; these are all examples of obligations arising by implication, *quasi ex contractu*, when no formal or express agreement was entered into by either party, the law prescribing that liability should attach to one or the other of them according to the circumstances of each particular case.

The earliest form of matrimony among the Romans was that of marriage by purchase, or *coemptio*, which was reciprocal, as the name implies. By means of it the wife was said to come under the control of her husband, "*convenire in manum mariti*," and was legally regarded in the same light as his daughter. Hence, if the husband did not make a will and died without issue, she succeeded to his entire estate; and if there were children she was entitled to share on equal terms with them in the distribution of the same. In ancient times, as at the present day, marital unions were invested with a certain religious character, being fully as much designed for the preservation of the public *sacra*, and private sacerdotal rites of the Roman *familia*, or household, as for the perpetuation of the race. For this reason, and incidentally to maintain the social and political ascendency of the patrician order, it was essential to the validity of a marriage that both the parties should be members of the same *gens*. The fact that plebeians originally were not allowed to participate in the

PREFACE

celebration of the public religious ceremonies, is stated by Latin writers to have been the cause of the prohibition of marriage between the higher and lower classes of the Roman commonwealth.

Coemptio, in the general sense, was a method of transference of the title to property by quiritarian right. As applicable to marriage, it denoted a form of adoption by means of which the *patria potestas*, or paternal control of the father over his daughter, was conveyed to her husband. She was said to be the *mancipium* of the latter, a term to a certain extent synonymous with "slave," and indicating that her husband's power over her might be relinquished in the same manner as that by which he had acquired it. *Mancipatio*, referred to by Gaius as a fictitious sale, "*imaginaria quædam venditio*," and devised for the purpose of establishing the status of the person who was the subject of it, was originally solely employed when either adoption or emancipation were to be effected. The reciprocity of the transaction did not imply an interchange of money or other property by which the purchase was concluded, but that, by means of the imaginary sale to the husband, certain rights and obligations were contracted on both sides by means of which the *unitas personæ*, or the unification of the two participants into a single legal personality, was accomplished, a principle long recognized to the fullest extent in England and the United States. The sale of wives in market overt, known as Smithfield marriages, and in former times frequently resorted to by the lower classes, is undoubtedly a survival of the ancient *coemptio*, and a reminiscence of the Roman domination in Britain, of which few other traces remain.

From *coemptio* is to be deduced the origin of *dos*, dower or dowry, a term used by Roman jurists in the opposite sense to that in which it is understood by us, and actually meaning the marriage gift by the wife, intended as compensation for the burdens assumed by the husband: "*Ibi dos esse debet, ubi onera matrimonii sunt.*"[1] This was symbolized by the delivery of an *as*, the coin in common use, by the bride, upon her entrance into her husband's house.

Notwithstanding that it is styled by Justinian, "*Divini et humani juris communicatio*," marriage among the Romans was, with the exception of the religious ceremony known as *confarreatio*, never anything but a civil contract, and, like many other similar obligations, was dissoluble by the common consent of the parties interested.

With the progress of time, the absolute rights of the husband over his wife and her property were materially curtailed; his control of her possessions was limited to the dowry; the *unitas personæ* was, to all intents and purposes, abolished; and to each party was conceded a distinct legal existence. The increased privileges of the wife ultimately enabled her to demand the exercise of ordinary diligence in the management of her dowry, and to have recourse to the tribunals to prevent its waste; to hold and dispose of her *parapherna* without consulting her husband, and sue to recover it, in case of necessity; as well as to dispose of her estate by will without any restriction.

As the dowry was constituted for the purpose of providing for the expenses incurred by marriage, it naturally ceased to exist, and became returnable to the woman when the marriage was dissolved, whether by death, captivity, slavery, or divorce. The provision of a *dos* obtained from some source was always presumed, it being in fact the consideration of the matrimonial contract. This principle of compensation has been retained in the jurisprudence of Continental Europe, and is not unknown in practice in this country. As no bond could be executed, or other security furnished to insure the return of the dowry, the plan was devised of making a marriage settlement of equal value, designated *donatio propter nuptias*, for the benefit of the wife, which operated as a set-off in case the dowry was retained by the husband. In England, a settlement of this description, or jointure, when made before marriage, is a bar to the collection of the dowry, as being an equivalent for it. The Roman woman had, by virtue of a tacit hypothecation, a prior lien on her dos, as against all creditors. This was not the case, however, in early times, when the husband was substantially the owner of

---

[1] Digest, XXIII, III, 56, 1.

his wife, and the right to everything she possessed was vested in him. Gradually, either by custom, or by express acts of legislation, he was deprived of this right, and from being the absolute owner, he became a mere tenant or usufructuary, without the power of alienation, even with his wife's consent, when the dowry consisted of real property; and when it was composed of chattels, while he was at liberty to dispose of them, he was required to replace them with similar articles of the same nature, equal in number and value. On account of the favor conceded to liberty, a husband was permitted to manumit dotal slaves in his possession, while he was living, or under the terms of his will. He could not, however, by so doing, defraud his wife, who was entitled to an action against him or his heir to recover what the slaves actually were worth, regardless of the price which he had obtained for them.

The Romans, having in view the interests of children already born, regarded second marriages with disfavor; and for this reason encouraged the institution of concubinage. This relation was not attended with the opprobrium which at present attaches to it, and was legalized and regulated by statutory enactment, as an union which differed mainly from marriage in the fact that the father did not acquire paternal control over the issue resulting therefrom, as he did over his legitimate offspring, nor could they succeed to him as heirs. The children of the quasi matrimonial connection were acknowledged by their father, and could exact maintenance from him, if he refused it. The general rights of the parties in marriage and concubinage were almost identical.

The disabilities of married women, as exemplified in the jurisprudence of both England and Scotland, have very properly been attributed to the influence of the Canon Law. The Romans, especially in the later days of the Empire, were much more indulgent in this respect than the churchmen, whose intolerance and jealousy of power induced them to restrict to the utmost the freedom of the marriage relation, and especially with reference to wives, over whom, by means of their spiritual ministrations, they exercised almost absolute control.

Modern jurisprudence, not only in Continental Europe, but also in England and America, is indebted to the Civil Law for the greater portion of the rules regulating the constitution of dower, and the rights and duties of matrimony; and wherever these have undergone alteration in the interest of the clergy it has almost invariably been for the worse.

The institution of marriage, as the basis of the Roman *familia*, whose existence was held to be eternal, was also regarded merely as a means for the creation and continuance of the *patria potestas*, or paternal authority, from which was derived some of the most prized and exclusive privileges of Roman citizenship. This arbitrary power has no parallel anywhere in the irresponsible and despotic authority which the Roman father could legally exert over his offspring and the other members of his household. The person in whom it was vested was declared by law to be him, "*Qui in domo dominium habet*";[1] and it was of such antiquity that the Romans themselves were ignorant of its source. It has been suggested that it may have been a consequence of the office of celebrant of the ceremonies of private family worship, as well as a participant in the public *sacra*, rights enjoyed by every Roman citizen; and hence had a semi-religious origin. Only extinguished with the fall of the Empire, it is a significant indication of the general acknowledgment of the unrestricted control of a parent over the destinies of his children, that the *paterfamilias* is not mentioned by the *Lex Pompeia de Paricidiis*, enacted for the punishment of persons guilty of the murder of those closely related to them by the bond of consanguinity.

Subject to paternal ownership, children in the early days of Rome were treated with no more consideration than domestic animals. It was entirely optional with the father whether his offspring should be spared and brought up, or abandoned and suffered to die of starvation. Even during the palmy days of the Empire, infanticide was frequently practised to avoid expense. Under the reign of Constantine it was made

---

[1] Digest, L, XVI, 195.

PREFACE

legal for parents to sell their children as soon as they were born, when they were too poor to support them; and this inhuman and unnatural privilege was freely exercised for many subsequent centuries. A child, like a slave or an ox, could be surrendered by its father by way of reparation for any damage it had caused; thus enabling him to evade responsibility on the ground that it attached to whatever had committed the act: "*Noxa caput sequitur.*"

Under the Roman law, which differed in this respect from that of England, a child was obliged to provide for the necessities of its parents if the latter were in indigent circumstances, the duties of the relation being reciprocal.

Patria potestas was lost by death, forfeiture of civil rights, adoption, and emancipation, but neither marriage nor the attainment of majority, had any effect, so far as the release of paternal authority was concerned.

Whenever it became necessary to protect the rights of a child, its birth was considered to date from the hour of its conception. An infant under the Roman law was one less than seven years old; a minor, a male under fourteen, and a female under twelve, indicative of the age of puberty; an adult a youth who had reached that age. The issue of parents, one of whom was an alien, were not entitled to citizenship. The term natural, when applied to children, did not, as with us, denote an illegitimate origin, but meant such as had been begotten, as distinguished from those who were adopted. Legitimation of bastards by subsequent marriage was limited to the progeny of concubines; a rule utterly at variance with the Common Law of England, by which the stigma of illegitimacy always attached to children born out of wedlock.

The Roman law of descent and testamentary distribution was mainly borrowed from Greece, but in time underwent such radical changes that its original feature can now with difficulty be recognized. The appointment of an heir, who in many respects corresponded to an executor, was indispensable to the validity of the will. Before the adoption of the Laws of the Twelve Tables, wills were always oral, and could only be made in the presence of the *Comitia Calata*, or popular assembly, which was regularly convoked semi-annually principally for this purpose, and this, in every instance, practically amounted to the enactment of a special statute authorizing the bequests by the testator. This of course, it has been conjectured, was considered necessary on the ground that when anyone died his estate reverted to the community at large and this right had to be publicly renounced by his representatives to enable the testator to dispose of his property.

Testamentary capacity did not merely refer to a man's legal competency to make a will, but whether he was qualified to take under it, or even act as a witness to the same; and it was essential that such competency should not only exist at the time when the will was executed, but that it should also continue until the hour of his death.

The doctrine of *unitas personæ* was applicable to the testator and the *suus hæres*, or direct and proper heir of the deceased; hence the estate was not held to be in reality transmitted, but simply to remain under the control of one who already was a legal possessor of it; and all existing rights, privileges, duties, and liabilities, were either enjoyed by, or charged upon the survivor. Until the appearance of the heir, the estate was the legal representative of the deceased. The law of primogeniture was unknown to the Romans, who, also, from the era of the Twelve Tables, made no distinction with regard to sex in the matter of inheritance. At Civil Law, the heir succeeded to the entire estate, in which respect he differed from the heir at Common Law, who, by right of consanguinity, succeeded only to the real property. Sons and daughters, alike, succeeded *per capita*, while grandchildren the issue of a son succeeded *per stirpes*; in England they succeed *per capita*. Under the Civil Law, the rule of descent to ascertain the next of kin required the calculation to be made up through the ascending, and then down through the collateral line; in which respect it differed from the Canon Law, according to which the count was only made down, and in divergence from the direct line. In England, the degrees determining the next of kin in the distribution of chattels are ascertained in compliance with the rule of the civil law; the canon law however, is followed when the question of the descent of real property arises.

The right of representation in the collateral line was not admitted, but the next in degree took precedence, and the succession was never *per stirpes*. From the Twelve Tables to the reign of Justinian, the claim of cognates, or heirs in the female line, were not recognized when settling the right of inheritance in case of intestacy; for the reason that if this had been done, the estate would have passed into some other *gens*, a condition contrary to all the maxims and traditions of the Roman polity. This doctrine was carried to such an extent that when a woman entered another family, whatever she possessed was at once transferred to her next of kin. Property of any description could not ascend, as a child under paternal control was incapable of ownership, and whatever he might have belonged to his father. A similar rule existed at common law so far as land was concerned, as it could not pass to ascendants.

Justinian changed the ancient practice by which if a son was neither appointed heir nor specifically disinherited, the will was void, by extending this regulation to all legitimate children, without exception.

Previous to the adoption of the Laws of the Twelve Tables, no rule of testamentary disposition had been either devised or formulated at Rome. Where a man had not already actually transferred his estate to some one, it passed to those legally entitled to it, who were styled *hæredes legitimi*, or heirs-at-law. The Twelve Tables conferred upon the owner of property unrestricted authority to dispose of it at his pleasure, regardless of the moral claims which might with justice be urged by his descendants. The harshness of this custom was subsequently modified on the ground of paternal duty, and the estate at once remained entirely in the hands of the heir, who, prior to that time, had through the legal fiction of the *unitas personæ*, been regarded as invested with a quasi joint-ownership of the same.

The rules of intestate succession as laid down in the Institutes and Digest, were materially altered in the Novels, which now constitute the basis of all jurisprudence on the subject. Under the original provisions of the Civil Law, in determining the distribution of estates in case of intestacy, the *sui heredes* took precedence; and, in default of them the agnates, or persons related solely through males, succeeded; and after these came the members of the *gens*. Various decrees of the Senate, and the equitable ruling of the Prætor, from time to time modified the severe restrictions imposed by the Twelve Tables, in this as in many other instances; and grandchildren, mothers, and sisters, in addition to the others above mentioned, were allowed to share in the distribution. The reforms instituted by Justinian in the Seventy-fourth, Eighty-ninth, and One hundred and eighteenth Novels, disposed of the *sui heredes*; abolished all distinction between agnates and cognates; and admitted to the succession ascendants and certain relatives in the collateral line, who had hitherto been absolutely excluded. Among the latter were brothers and sisters of the half blood and their issue. All descendants, without reference to sex, came first in the order of succession; and, in the case of the failure of blood relatives, either the husband or wife became the legal heir. Where no wife or children survived, a concubine and her offspring could claim one sixth of the parent's property. An adopted child could inherit the estate of its adoptive father. Anyone who was both an agnate and a cognate derived his title as heir from cognation. The cardinal principle of the right of intestate succession, established by Justinian, was founded upon consanguinity.

Under the *Lex Julia et Papia*, when no one appeared to claim the inheritance, it escheated to the Public Treasury; except under certain circumstances when the comrades-in-arms of a deceased soldier, the municipality, the *curia*, or a corporation to which the decedent belonged, could demand it to the exclusion of the State.

A radical difference exists under the civil and the canon law, in the calculation of degrees of descent in the collateral line. The former counts the number from the ancestor on both sides; the latter only on one. Hence, by the civil law, brothers are related in the second and by the canon law in the first degree. The rule of the canon law has been adopted in England, while that of the civil law generally prevails in the United States.

PREFACE

Under the more recent legislation of Justinian, no one was qualified to inherit who was not a member of the orthodox Christian communion. This provision, undoubtedly to be ascribed to the sinister influence of ecclesiastics, was largely instrumental in extending the authority of the Church to all matters connected with the inheritance and distribution of estates in England; and, contributing greatly to the power and wealth of the clergy, ultimately manifested itself in the gross abuses arising from the claim of papal supremacy.

The genius of the Roman, as disclosed by his attainments in arts, arms, and literature, was eminently practical. The inconclusive subtleties of philosophy, the sophistry and speculative dissertations of the various Grecian schools, exerted no important influence on the intellectual or political life of the stern and utilitarian masters of the world. In the formulation and application of legal principles, their inclinations and their administrative ability were eminently favorable to the development and exercise of their talents in this direction. To the enlightened wisdom and example of the renowned Roman lawyers are to be credited the maxims and doctrines which find expression in the proceedings of every judicial tribunal of to-day. The rules of the civil law, as laid down and promulgated by Justinian, more than any other factor, have contributed to the establishment of modern civilization, to the maintenance of good government and public order, and to the preservation of the vital interests of society; well meriting as its own the encomium so aptly bestowed upon jurisprudence in general, when it was designated as: "The pride of the human intellect, which, with all its defects, redundancies, and errors, is the collected reason of ages, combining the principles of original justice with the infinite variety of human concerns."

The jurisprudence of all nations, with the exception of ancient Egypt and Phœnicia, of which no legal memorials are extant, and of modern Greece — with whose idiom the translator is not sufficiently familiar — which however, corresponds with that of the other countries of Continental Europe, has been made the subject of examination in these volumes. Reference to the various Codes of Spanish America, whose provisions are almost identical with those of France and Spain, has, for this reason, also been omitted.

The comparison of the various judicial systems as set forth in the notes to this work have been made, not so much to show their present resemblances or discrepancies, as to bring to the attention of the reader their original derivation from the civil law and the obligations they owe to the most voluminous and comprehensive body of legislation which has ever been compiled.

In making the translation, which it has taken eight years to complete, attention has been paid rather to the accurate rendering of the letter and spirit of the text, whenever this was possible, than to the strict rules of grammar.

The substance of the citations in French, Spanish, Portuguese, Italian, German, Dutch, Danish, Swedish, and Latin, has almost invariably been given in English, for the benefit of persons not conversant with those languages; the excerpts in the antiquated legal jargon employed by Britton, Staunforde, Littleton, and Plowden, which every well-informed lawyer is presumed to understand, have, for the most part, been left for the decipherment of the reader.

February 11, 1922.

S. P. SCOTT: ROMAN CIVIL LAW

THIS TRANSLATION HAS BEEN MADE FROM:

(The following lists of references pertains to S. P. Scott's complete 17 volume edition of The Civil Law. The list has been included in its entirety here for the benefit of readers interested in pursuing a more in-depth study of the history of law from the primary sources.—RAS-ED.)

Leges XII Tabvlorvm, Svis Qvotqvot Reperiri Potvervnt Fragmentis Restitvtæ, A Ioh, Nicolao Fvnccio, 4to. Rintelii, MDCCXLIV.

Gaii, Institutionum Ivris Civilis, Commentarii Quattvor, 12mo. Lipsiæ, MDCCCLXXXVI.

Ivlii Pavlii, Sententiarum ad Filium, Libri Quinque, 12mo. Lipsiæ, MDCCCLXXXVI.

Domitii Vlpiani, Fragmenta, 12mo. Lipsiæ, MDCCCLXXXVI.

Fontes Iuris Romani Antejustiniani, 12mo. Florentiæ, MCMVIII.

Corpus Juris Civilis Pandectis ad Florentinum archetypum expressis, Institutionum, Codice et Novellis, cum notis integris repetitæ quintum prælectionis. Dionysii Gothofredi JC. 2 vols. Fo. Amstelodami, MDCLXIII.

Corpus Juris Civilis, Recognoverunt Adnotationibusque Criticis Instructum, Ediderunt D. Albertus et D. Mauritius, Fratres Kriegelii. D. Aemilius Hermann. D. Eduardus Osenbruggen, 3 vols. 8vo. Lipsiæ, 1872.

Pandectæ Justinianeæ in Novum Ordinem Digestæ (Pothier), 20 vols. 8vo. Paris, 1823.

IT HAS BEEN COMPARED WITH THE FOLLOWING AUTHORITIES:

Corpus Ivris Canonici, Notis Illvstratvm Gregorii XIII Ivssy Editvm, 2 vols. 4to. Lygdvni, MDCLXI.

The Code of Hammurabi (Harper), 8vo. Chicago, 1904.

Babylonian and Assyrian Laws, Contracts and Letters (Johns), 8vo. New York, 1904.

Avesta, The Religious Books of the Parsees, from Professor Spiegel's Translation of the Original MSS. (Bleeck), 8vo. London, 1864.

A Code of Gentoo Laws, or Ordinations of the Pundist, 4to. London, 1776.

Mishnah, A Digest of the Basic Principles of the Early Jewish Jurisprudence (Goldin), 8vo. New York, 1913.

Old Testament, 12mo. Oxford, 1897.

Lex Salica, The Ten Texts with the Glosses (Hessels), 4to. London, 1880.

Forum Judicum (por la Real Academia Española), Fo. Madrid, 1815.

The Koran (Sale), 8vo. New York, 1867.

The Quran (Palmer), 2 vols. 8vo. Oxford, 1880.

The Hedaya or Guide; A Commentary on the Mussulman Laws (Hamilton), 8vo. London, 1870.

Hughes, A Dictionary of Islam, 8vo. London, 1885.

Syed Ameer Ali, Mohammedan Law, Compiled from Authorities in the

Original Arabic, 2 vols. 8vo. Calcutta, 1892. Baillie, The Moohummudan Law of Sale, 8vo. London.

Macnaghten, Principles and Precedents of Mohammedan Law, 8vo. Calcutta.

Eschbach, Le Droit Musulman, 8vo. Paris, 1860. The Medjellé or Ottoman Civil Law (Grigsby), 8vo. London, 1895. Potter, The Antiquities of Greece, 2 vols. 8vo. Edinburgh, 1808.

Gilbert, The Constitutional Antiquities of Sparta and Athens, 8vo. London, 1895.

St. Louis, Etablissements, 4 vols. 8vo. 1888.

PREFACE

Domat (translated by Strahan), The Civil Law in its Natural Order, together with the Publick Law, 2 vols. Fo. London, MDCCXIII.
Nouveau Coutumier General de France et des Provinces, 4 vols. Fo. Paris, 1724.

Capitularia Regum Francorum, 2 vols. Folio. Parisiis, MDCCLXXX.

La Coutume de Normandie, 4to. Paris, 1707.

El Fuero Viejo de Castilla, Fo. Madrid, MDCCLXXI.

Las Siete Partidas del Muy Noble Rey Don Alfonso et Sabio, Glosadas por EL. LIC. Gregorio Lopez. 4 vols. 4to. Madrid, 1844.

Ancient Laws and Institutes of England. Fo. London, 1840.

Wingate, An Exact Abridgment of all the Statutes in Force and Use from the beginning of Magna Charta, 12mo. London, 1700.

Glanvilla, De Legibus & Consuetudinibus Regni Angliæ, 16mo. London, MDCLXXIII.

Bracton, De Legibus & Consuetudinibus Angliæ, Libri Quinque, Fo. Londini, 1569.

Fleta, seu Commentarius Juris Anglicani. Londini, 1685.

Britton, De Legibus Anglicanis, 16mo. London, 1640.

Plowden, Les Commentaries Ou Reports, Fo. London, 1613.

Littleton, Tenures, 16mo. London, 1671.

Coke, Institutes of the Laws of England, 5 vols. 8vo. London, 1797.

Bacon, Works, 10 vols. 8vo. London, 1824.

D'Anvers, A General Abridgment of the Common Law, 3 vols. Fo. London, 1705.

Spelman, English Works, Fo. London, MDXXVII.

Staunforde, Les Plees del Coron. London, 1583.

Selden, An Historical and Political Discourse of the Laws and Government of England (Edit. Bacon), Fo. London, 1739.

Hale, The History of the Pleas of the Crown, 2 vols. 8vo. London, 1778.

Probert, The Ancient Laws of Cambria, 8vo. London, 1823.

Broom, Commentaries on the Common Law. London, 1888.

Blackstone, Commentaries of the Laws of England, 2 vols. 8vo. Philadelphia, 1875.

Stephen, New Commentaries of the Laws of England, 4 vols. 8vo. London, 1908.

Stephen, A Digest of the Criminal Law. London.

Stephen, A Digest of the Law of Evidence, 12mo. London, 1899.

Pollock and Maitland, The History of English Law before the time of Edward I, 2 vols. 8vo. Cambridge, 1899.

Crabb, A History of English Law, 8vo. London, 1829.

Holdsworth, A History of English Law, 3 vols. 8vo. London, 1903.

Stephen, A History of the Criminal Law in England, 3 vols. 8 vo. London, 1883.

Pike, A History of Crime in England, 2 vols. 8vo. London, 1873.

Montesquieu, De l'Esprit des Lois, 8vo. Paris, 1835.

Erskine, Principles of the Laws of Scotland, 8vo. Edinburgh, Fifteenth Edition.

More, Lectures on the Law of Scotland, 2 vols. 8vo. Edinburgh.

Dickson, A Treatise on the Law of Evidence in Scotland, 2 vols. 8vo. Edinburgh.

Stair, The Institutions of the Law of Scotland, Fo. Edinburgh, 1693.

Paterson, A Compendium of English and Scotch Law, 8vo. Edinburgh.

Mackenzie, The Laws and Customes of Scotland in Matters Criminal, 4to. Edinburgh, 1678.

Burnett, A Treatise on Various Branches of the Criminal Law of Scotland, 4to. Edinburgh.

The Fundamental Law of the Penal Code of China (Staunton), 4to. London, 1810.

The Code of Japan (Gubbins), 2 vols. 8vo. Tokio, 1897.

New Criminal Code of Japan (Becker), 8vo. Yokohama, 1903.

Japanese Code of Criminal Procedure, 8vo. Yokohama.

Code Civil (de France), 12mo. Paris, 1911.

Code Pénal, 12mo. Paris, 1911.

Code de Procédure Civile, 12mo. Paris, 1915.

Code de Commerce et Sociétés, 12mo. Paris, 1912.

Código Civil (de España), 12mo. Valencia, 1910.

El Código Penal (Garcia), 2 vols. 8vo. Madrid, 1908.

Código de Commercio, 12mo. Valencia, 1910.

Blanco-Constans, Estudios Elementales de Derecho Mercantil, 2 vols. 8vo. Madrid, 1911.

Herrero-Martinez, Ley de Enjuiciamiento Criminal Reformada, 8vo.

Valladolid. Code Civil (de Belgique), 12mo. Bruxelles, 1911.

Code des Lois Pénales Belges, 12mo. Bruxelles, 1909.

Codice Civile del Regno d'Italia, 12mo. Firenze (Eighth edition).

Codice Penale, 12 mo. Firenze (Seventh edition).

Codice di Commercio, 12mo. Torino, 1910.

Bürgerliches Gesetzbuch (Germany), 12mo. Berlin, 1920.

Strafgetzbuch für das Deutsche Reich, 12mo. Berlin.

Zivilprozetzordnung mit Gerichtsverfassungsgesetz und Einfuhrungsgesetzen, 12mo. Berlin, 1909.

Bürgerliches Gesetzbuch (Austria), 12mo. Wien, 1900.

Allgemeines Strafgesetz, 12mo. Wien, 1904.

Burgerlijk Wetboek (Holland), 12mo. Zwolle (Eighth edition).

Wetboek van Strafrecht, 12mo. Zwolle (Sixth edition).

Almindelig Borgerlig Straffelov (Denmark), 8vo. Kobenhavn, 1909.

Sveriges Rikes Lag (Sweden), 8vo. Stockholm (Thirty-fifth edition).

Schweizerisches Zivilgesetzbuch, 8vo. Bern, 1912.

Kovalevsky, Modern Customs and Ancient Laws of Russia, 8vo. London, 1891.

Code Pénal Russe (Eberlin), 8vo. Paris, 1906. Hunter, Roman Law, 8vo. London, 1876.

Justice, A General Treatise on the Dominion and Laws of the Sea, 4to. London, 1705.

Smith, A Compendium of Mercantile Law, 8vo. London (Ninth edition).

PREFACE

Barrell, An Outline of Anglo-Saxon Law, 8vo. New York, 1885.

Mackintosh, Miscellaneous Works, A Discourse on the Law of Nature and Nations, 3 vols. 8vo. London, 1846.

Maine, Early Law and Custom, 8vo. London, 1890.

Pufendorf, De Jure Naturæ et Gentium, 4to. Amstelædami.

Vattel, The Law of Nations (Chitty), 8vo.

Lorimer, The Institutes of the Law of Nations, 2 vols., 8vo. Edinburgh, 1883.

Baker, First Steps in International Law, 8vo. London, 1899.

Pollock, The Law of Torts, 8vo. London (Fifth edition).

Bodington, An Outline of the French Law of Evidence, 8vo. London, 1904.

Archbold, A Complete and Practical Treatise on Criminal Procedure, Pleading and Evidence, 2 vols. 8vo. New York (Seventh edition).

Wilson's Practice of the Supreme Court of Judicature, 8vo. London, (Seventh edition).

Kent, Commentaries on American Law, 4 vols., 8vo. Boston (Eleventh edition).

Parsons, The Law of Contracts, 3 vols., 8vo. Boston (Fifth edition).

Washburn, A Treatise on the American Law of Real Property, 3 vols., 8vo. Boston (Third edition).

Starkie, A Practical Treatise on the Law of Evidence, 3 vols., 8vo. Philadelphia (Third edition).

Greenleaf, A Treatise on the Law of Evidence, 3 vols., 8vo. Boston (Twelfth edition).

Story, Commentaries on the Law of Partnership, 8vo. Boston.

Hilliard, The Law of Torts, 2 vols., 8vo. Boston (Third edition).

Hilliard, The Law of Sales of Personal Property, 8vo. Boston (Third edition).

Story, A Treatise on the Law of Sales of Personal Property, 8vo. Boston.

Byles, A Treatise of the Law of Bills of Exchange, Promissory Notes, Bank Notes and Checks, 8vo. Philadelphia (Fifth edition).

Wharton, A Treatise on Criminal Law, 3 vols., 8vo. San Francisco, 1912.

Wheeler, A Practical Treatise on the Law of Slavery, 8vo. New York, 1837.

Goodell, The American Slave Code, 12mo. New York, 1853.

Stroud, A Sketch of the Laws relating to Slavery, 12 mo. Philadelphia, 1856.

The Code of 1650, Being a Compilation of the Earliest Laws and Orders of the General Court of Connecticut, 12mo. Hartford, 1836.

Civil Code of the State of Louisiana, 4 vols., 8vo. New Orleans, 1838.

Barnes' Federal Code, 8vo. Charleston, W. Va., 1919.

THE TWELVE TABLES

THE LAWS OF THE TWELVE TABLES

TABLE I

CONCERNING THE SUMMONS TO COURT

Law I. When anyone summons another before the tribunal of a judge, the latter must, without hesitation, immediately appear.[1]

Law II. If, after having been summoned, he does not appear, or refuses to come before the tribunal of the judge, let the party who summoned him call upon any citizens who are present to bear witness.[2] Then let him seize his reluctant adversary; so that he may be brought into court, as a captive, by apparent force.

Law III. When anyone who has been summoned to court is guilty of evasion, or attempts to flee, let him be arrested by the plaintiff.

Law IV. If bodily infirmity or advanced age should prevent the party summoned to court from appearing, let him who summoned him furnish him with an animal, as a means of transport. If he is unwilling to accept it, the plaintiff cannot legally be compelled to provide the defendant with a vehicle constructed of boards, or a covered litter.[3]

Law V. If he who is summoned has either a sponsor or a defender, let him be dismissed, and his representative can take his place in court.[4]

---

[1] Under the Roman method of procedure, until the thorough organization of the judicial system by the emperors, service of summons was always made by the plaintiff in the action. This was even sometimes done after the custom of regularly appointing court officials for that purpose had been established. — ed.

[2] Notification of the bystanders was made to show that the arrest of the defendant was to compel his appearance before the tribunal, a proceeding authorized by law; and not to insult him, or forcibly restrain him of his liberty, which might form the ground of prosecution for an illegal act. — ed.

[3] Litters were originally used exclusively by women and sick persons during the early ages of Greece and Rome. They, afterwards, in the time of the Empire, became a favorite mode of conveyance with the Romans, and especially with the wealthy nobles, who vied with one another in the profuse and costly decoration of their luxurious *lecticæ*, upholstered in silk, embellished with ebony, ivory, and lazulite, and glittering with precious stones and gold. The *sella*, one form of the litter, was almost identical with the sedan chair of the eighteenth century. The vehicle referred to in the text was probably a public one, like our cabs and carriages for hire. — ed.

[4] From this it will be seen that the office of defensor, or "defender," of the party sued was one of the most ancient recognized by Roman jurisprudence. Its duties were often undertaken without solicitation, through motives of friendship or compassion, or the

Law VI. The defender, or the surety of a wealthy man, must himself be rich; but anyone who desires to do so can come to the assistance of a person who is poor, and occupy his place.

Law VII. When litigants wish to settle their dispute among themselves, even while they are on their way to appear before the Prætor, they shall have the right to make peace; and whatever agreement they enter into, it shall be considered just, and shall be confirmed.

Law VIII. If the plaintiff and defendant do not settle their dispute, as above mentioned, let them state their cases either in the *Comitium* or the Forum, by making a brief statement in the presence of the judge, between the rising of the sun and noon; and, both of them being present, let them speak so that each party may hear.

Law IX. In the afternoon, let the judge grant the right to bring the action, and render his decision in the presence of the plaintiff and the defendant.

Law X. The setting of the sun shall be the extreme limit of time within which a judge must render his decision.

TABLE II

CONCERNING JUDGMENTS AND THEFTS

Law I. When issue has been joined in the presence of the judge, sureties and their substitutes for appearance at the trial must be furnished on both sides. The parties shall appear in person, unless prevented by disease of a serious character; or where vows which they have taken must be discharged to the Gods; or where the proceedings are interrupted through their absence on business for the State; or where a day has been appointed by them to meet an alien.

Law II. If any of the above mentioned occurrences takes place, that is, if one of the parties is seriously ill, or a vow has to be performed, or one of them is absent on business for the State, or a day has been appointed for an interview with an alien, so that the judge, the arbiter, or the defendant is prevented from being present, and the furnishing of security is postponed on this account, the hearing of the case shall be deferred.

Law III. Where anyone is deprived of the evidence of a witness let him call him with a loud voice in front of his house, on three market-days.

Law IV. Where anyone commits a theft by night, and having been caught in the act is killed, he is legally killed.[1]

---

influence of family ties; and, as the defendant's representative, he occupied the legal position of the former, including the unqualified assumption of all his liabilities arising from, or dependent upon the matter in litigation. — ed.

[1] While the ordinary presumption certainly arises that no one can encounter a desperate malefactor in his house at night without incurring risk of serious injury; still, the Roman jurists, in enacting this provision, evidently had in view the prevention of homicide except when absolutely necessary, even under circumstances which might justify almost any violent act in the defence of life and property. Other lawgivers, generally speaking, did not recognize such nice distinctions.

The rule, somewhat modified, has been adopted by the majority of subsequent judicial systems as being thoroughly consonant with the principles of justice. It was incorporated, with but slight alteration, into the Visigothic Code, and Las *Siete Partidas*. "Fur nocturnus captus in furto, dum res furtivas secum portare conatur, si fuerit occisus, mors eius nullo modo vindicetur." (Forum Judicum, VII, II, 16.) "Otro tal decimos quo seria, si algun one /allasse algun ladron de noche en su casa, e lo quisiesse prender para darlo a la justicia del lugar, si el ladron se amparasse con armas. Ca entonce, si lo matare, non cæ por esso en pena." (Las Siete Partidas, VII, VIII, 3.) As stated above, to render the modicide justifiable, the Visigoths required that the thief should be in possession of the stolen

THE LAWS OF THE TWELVE TABLES

Law V. If anyone commits a theft during the day, and is caught in the act, he shall be scourged, and given up as a slave to the person against whom the theft was committed. If he who perpetrated the theft is a slave, he shall be beaten with rods and hurled from the Tarpeian Rock.[1] If he is under the age of puberty, the Prætor shall decide whether he shall be scourged, and surrendered by way of reparation for the injury.

Law VI. When any persons commit a theft during the day and in the light, whether they be freemen or

---

property; and the Castilian law provided that he should be armed and resist arrest while in the house of the owner. Under the law of Athens, a thief taken *flagrante delicto*, at night, could be killed with impunity. (Potter, Antiquities of Greece, I, 24, 126.)

With the Jews, homicide was not punishable when the culprit was killed under circumstances essential to constitute the crime known to us as burglary. "If a thief be found breaking up, and he be smitten that he die. no blood shall be shed for him; but if the sun be risen upon him, there shall blood be shed for him; for he should have made full restitution." (Exodus XXII, 2.)

With the Anglo-Saxons, a thief caught in the act, at any time, either by day or by night, could be slain with impunity. "He who slays a thief must declare on oath that he slew him offending." (Ancient Laws and Institutes of England; Laws of King Ine, 16.)

This principle does not appear to have been accepted in the earliest age of the Common Law. Glanvil does not mention it. Bracton, however, refers to it as being sound, and applicable by day or by night, without regard to place, if the homicide, at the time, could not avoid serious personal injury. "*Qui latronem occiderit, non tenetur, nocturnum vel diurnum, si aliter periculum evadere non possit.*" (Bracton, *De Legibus et Covsuetudinibus Angliæ*, III, 155, 36.)

Fleta says: "*Quicunqiie enim furem nocturnum interfecerit, non teneatur, & qui invasorem domus suæ, se ipsum & hospitium suum saltem illa hora defendendo interfecerit, juste interficit.*" (Fleta, *Commentarius Juris Anglicanæ*, I, XXIII, 14.) This applied not only to a burglar, but to anyone found in the "curtilage," or enclosure containing the residence, at any hour between nine P. M. and six A. M.; and under these conditions, homicide was authorized either in self-defense, or when it occurred in an attempt to arrest the intruder, or was committed in order to prevent his escape. The necessity for the homicide must be absolute in order to render it justifiable. "*Si necessitas evitabilis fuerit, absque occasione, reus est homicidii, qui si fuerit inevitabilis, ad pœnam homicidii non tenebitur, eo quod felonice non occidit.*" *(Ibid.* I, 23.) It is held by Coke that the act of killing must be in self-defence, and be preceded by violent aggression on the part of the thief. "If a thiefe offer to rob or murder B, either abroad or in his house, and thereupon assault him, and B, defend himself without any giving back, and in his defence killeth the thiefe; this is no felony." (Coke, Institutes of the Laws of England, Vol. IV, Ch. 8.)

This doctrine is explicitly set forth in Stat. 24, Hen. VIII, Chap. 5. "If any person do attempt to break any mansion-house in the night time, and shall happen to be slain by any person or persons, etc. (tho a lodger or servant) they shall upon their trial be acquitted and discharged." The above mentioned Statute, as is held by a high authority, may be construed to apply to an illegal act of this kind committed during the day with felonious intent "It seems it extends not to a braking the house in the day-time, unless it be such a braking, as imports with it, apparent robbery, or an intention or attempt thereof." (Hale, The History of the Pleas of the Crown, I, XL, Page 488.)

This was also the rule in Scotland, "It is lawful to kill a Thief, who in the night offers to break our Houses, or steal our Goods, even though he defend not himself, because we know not but he designs against our Life; and Murder may be easily committed upon us in the night, but it is not lawful to kill a Thief who steals in the day time, except he resist us when we offer to take him, and present him to Justice." (Mackenzie, The Laws and Customes of Scotland in Matters Criminal, I, XI, III.) The general rule, while well established, was formerly, to a certain extent, so far as its application is concerned, largely dependent upon the circumstances of each particular case. No distinction was made between an invasion of the house and an attack upon the person, provided the alarm experienced by the homicide was considered to be so well founded as to justify his act. In some respects great latitude was allowed the injured party. "The same right of defending our property, may also justify our killing a thief, or predonious invader, in the act of running away with our goods, if he cannot otherwise be taken, or the goods secured." (Burnett, A Treatise on the Criminal Law of Scotland, I, page 57.)

The laws of France and Italy excuse the homicide of an intruder who commits burglary or theft with violence. (*Code Pénal de France*, III, II, Arts. 322, 329.) (*Codice Penale*, II, III, Art. 376.)

In the United States, killing is only justifiable where the crime could not otherwise have been prevented, and where force is employed. When an attempt is made to commit a secret felony, without violence, the right does not exist. It is different, however, where the precincts of a man's home are invaded in the daytime, or at night. "An attack on a house or its inmates may be resisted by taking life. This may be when burglars threaten an entrance, or when there is apparent ground to believe that a felonious assault is to be made on any of the inmates of the house, or when an attempt is made violently to enter the house in defiance of the owner's rights."

"But this right is only one of prevention. It cannot be extended so as to excuse the killing of persons not actually breaking into or violently threatening a house." (Wharton, A Treatise on Criminal Law, Secs. 629, 630, 634, 635.) — ed.

[1] This mode of punishment was considered especially ignominious by the Romans, and was usually inflicted upon traitors. "The rock Tarpeian, Fittest goal for treason's race, The promontory whence the traitor's leap Cured all ambition." — ed.

slaves, of full age or minors, and attempt to defend themselves with weapons, or with any kind of implements; and the party against whom the violence is committed raises the cry of thief, and calls upon other persons, if any are present, to come to his assistance; and this is done, and the thieves are killed by him in the defence of his person and property, it is legal, and no liability attaches to the homicide.

Law VII. If a theft be detected by means of a dish and a girdle, it is the same as manifest theft, and shall be punished as such.[1]

Law VIII. When anyone accuses and convicts another of theft which is not manifest, and no stolen property is found, judgment shall be rendered to compel the thief to pay double the value of what was stolen.

Law IX. Where anyone secretly cuts down trees belonging to another, he shall pay twenty-five *asses* for each tree cut down.

Law X. Where anyone, in order to favor a thief, makes a compromise for the loss sustained, he cannot afterwards prosecute him for theft.

Law XI. Stolen property shall always be his to whom it formerly belonged; nor can the lawful owner ever be deprived of it by long possession, without regard to its duration; nor can it ever be acquired by another, no matter in what way this may take place.[2]

TABLE III

CONCERNING PROPERTY WHICH IS LENT

Law I. When anyone, with fraudulent intent, appropriates property deposited with him for safe keeping, he shall be condemned to pay double its value.

Law II. When anyone collects interest on money loaned at a higher rate per annum than that of the *unciæ*, he shall pay quadruple the amount by way of penalty.[3]

---

[1] Various explanations have been suggested for the elucidation of this obscure passage. It has been supposed by some that a dish, perforated with two holes for the eyes, was carried by the thief to hide his face and conceal his identity; the girdle being intended for the removal of the booty. Others have advanced the theory that religious impostors, masquerading as members of the priesthood, passed the dish for the collection of money for alleged sacrificial purposes, and appropriated the amounts obtained to their own use. A few have maintained that the dish was employed to hold a piece of bread which had been subjected to certain magic ceremonies, and, for this reason compelled the thief to confess as soon as he had eaten it, a species of ordeal, as it were. The most plausible interpretation of the *furtum per lancem et licium refertum* is, however, that when the officer appointed for that purpose entered a house to seek for property which had been stolen, he was required to be naked, except for a girdle, and to hold a dish before his face, as a concession to the modesty of any woman he might encounter. The owner of the property was also entitled to make search under the same conditions. Nakedness was regarded as necessary in order to avoid anything being carried into the house which might afford ground for a false accusation. — ed.

[2] This doctrine as set forth in the maxim "*Spoliatus debet, ante omnia, restitui*," is recognized by the courts of all civilized, and most semi-barbarous nations. — ed.

[3] The rate of interest authorized by law at Rome was, despite statutory regulations, often a matter of avarice on one side and necessity on the other. Money lenders were accustomed to wring from distressed borrowers the last *sesterce* which heartless rapacity and extortion could exact. The rate was usually dependent upon agreement, and while the collection of compound interest was illegal, a bond for the increase of what was in arrears was sometimes required, which amounted to the same thing.

As shown by the text, the Twelve Tables forbade anything in excess of the *unciarum fœmus*, or interest on the twelve "ounces" into which the *as*, the integral amount representing capital for one year, as well as an estate when its assets were estimated for distribution, were divided. The term, however, is ambiguous, and has been interpreted in several ways. The best authorities hold that ten per cent is the rate referred to. — ed.

Law III. An alien cannot acquire the property of another by usucaption; but a Roman citizen, who is the lawful owner of the property, shall always have the right to demand it from him.

Law IV. Where anyone, having acknowledged a debt, has a judgment rendered against him requiring payment, thirty days shall be given to him in which to pay the money and satisfy the judgment.

Law V. After the term of thirty days granted by the law to debtors who have had judgment rendered against them has expired, and in the meantime, they have not satisfied the judgment, their creditors shall be permitted to forcibly seize them and bring them again into court.

Law VI. When a defendant, after thirty days have elapsed, is brought into court a second time by the plaintiff, and does not satisfy the judgment; or, in the meantime, another party, or his surety does not pay it out of his own money, the creditor, or the plaintiff, after the debtor has been delivered up to him, can take the latter with him and bind him or place him in fetters; provided his chains are not of more than fifteen pounds weight; he can, however, place him in others which are lighter, if he desires to do so.

Law VII. If, after a debtor has been delivered up to his creditor, or has been placed in chains, he desires to obtain food and has the means, he shall be permitted to support himself out of his own property. But if he has nothing on which to live, his creditor, who holds him in chains, shall give him a pound of grain every day, or he can give him more than a pound, if he wishes to do so.

Law VIII. In the meantime, the party who has been delivered up to his creditor can make terms with him. If he does not, he shall be kept in chains for sixty days; and for three consecutive market-days he shall be brought before the Prætor in the place of assembly in the Forum, and the amount of the judgment against him shall be publicly proclaimed.

Law IX. After he has been kept in chains for sixty days, and the sum for which he is liable has been three times publicly proclaimed in the Forum, he shall be condemned to be reduced to slavery by him to whom he was delivered up; or, if the latter prefers, he can be sold beyond the Tiber.

Law X. Where a party is delivered up to several persons, on account of a debt, after he has been exposed in the Forum on three market days, they shall be permitted to divide their debtor into different parts, if they desire to do so; and if anyone of them should, by the division, obtain more or less than he is entitled to, he shall not be responsible.[1]

TABLE IV

CONCERNING THE RIGHTS OF A FATHER, AND OF MARRIAGE

Law I. A father shall have the right of life and death over his son born in lawful marriage, and shall also have the power to render him independent, after he has been sold three times.[2]

---

[1] While a strict construction of the provisions of this law has been rejected by some jurists, there can be little doubt that its abhorrent features, far worse than those of the famous claim of Shylock, were susceptible of literal interpretation, and that the partition of the body of the unfortunate debtor was entirely dependent upon the inclination of his creditors to whom he had been adjudged. The statement of Aulus Gellius relative to a fact evidently well known to his countrymen, would seem to be conclusive upon this point. "*Nam, si plures forent, quibus reus esset judicatur, secare si vellent, atque partiri corpus addicti sibi hominis permiserunt.*" (Aul. Gell. *Nodes Atticæ*. I. XX. 1.) Fabius, alluding to the same law, says that public sentiment was opposed to its enforcement. "*Quam legem mos publicus repudiavit.*" In view of the eminent authority of these Roman writers, and the clear meaning of the text, the opinion entertained by some respectable commentators, that the word "*secare*," "to divide," merely has reference to the apportionment of the debtor's property, is hardly tenable, as it must have been already taken in execution and divided, before his person was delivered up to gratify the resentment of his disappointed creditors. — ed.

[2] This privilege, the *patria potestas*, enjoyed by Roman fathers, was a relic of the patriarchal authority originally asserted by a man over his household, including the members of his immediate family, his slaves, and other dependents. Derived from ancient custom, it

Law II. If a father sells his son three times, the latter shall be free from paternal authority.

Law III. A father shall immediately put to death a son recently born, who is a monster, or has a form different from that of members of the human race.

Law IV. When a woman brings forth a son within the next ten months after the death of her husband, he shall be born in lawful marriage, and shall be the legal heir of his estate.[1]

---

continued to exist for centuries after Rome had attained an exalted rank in the scale of civilization, and other practices of barbarous origin and primitive character had long been abandoned. It is said by Justinian (Code VI, 26) to have been an institution peculiar to the Romans; for while other nations possessed authority over their children unlimited by any legislative provision, few of their regulations bore even a distant resemblance to those which confirmed the Roman father in the exercise of his unquestioned and arbitrary power, the *jus vitæ et necis*. This power in early times was unbounded, and usually endured through life.

A marked peculiarity of this relation was what was known as the *unitas personæ*, under which a father and his son subject to his control were, by means of a legal fiction, held to be but a single person in law. Hence, when the father died, the son at once succeeded him; for the reason that, during his father's lifetime he had been a joint owner of the undivided estate. Despite the *unitas personæ*, the child was strictly not a person but a thing, one of the *res mancipi*, which by quiritarian right could be sold by the owner. The father was authorized to make any disposition of his offspring that he chose; he could scourge, maim, imprison, torture, or execute them at his pleasure. Nor was this right infrequently or sparingly exercised; the Roman annals are full of instances where sons were inhumanly treated and put to death by their fathers.

The acquisition of the *patria potestas* was dependent upon the status of the parent at the time of the birth of the child; he must be free, or *sui juris*, to be entitled to exercise paternal control, for if he were subject to the authority of another ascendant, his child would also come under the power of the latter.

Under ordinary circumstances, a son could acquire no property for himself, all he obtained belonged to his father. Exceptions were subsequently made in the cases of private, independent ownership of what was received by him while preparing for, or engaged in military service, or as a member of the priesthood; and finally of all acquisitions derived from maternal or other inheritances, or which were the remuneration of his individual labor or skill. This species of property designated *peculium castrense*, and *quasi peculium castrense*, was the subject of numerous Imperial enactments, which, in the course of time, afforded substantial relief to children oppressed by this legalized tyranny; as the censors, in the time of the Republic, had frequently exerted their authority for the same purpose.

Patria potestas was a necessary incident of lawful wedlock, which indeed was indispensable; and the authority thereby obtained was imposed on all the descendants through the son, but did not affect the offspring of a daughter who was subject to the *paterfamilias* of the family into which she had married. In addition to birth, paternal power could be acquired by means of the public acknowledgment of legitimacy, by adoption, and by matrimony.

As a natural result of placing children in the same category with slaves and domestic animals, liable to sale, barter, and the most cruel abuse, there was a time at which a child could be given up to the injured party by way of reparation for some unlawful act, or *noxa*, which it had committed; a practice condemned by Justinian in unmeasured terms.

It was not until about 370, during the reign of Valentinian and Valens, that measures were taken to place restrictions upon the irresponsible power of the head of the household; an example which was followed by many succeeding emperors. The sentiment expressed by Hadrian in condemning to exile a father who had killed his son, discloses the change of public opinion with which the excessive exercise of paternal authority was, even in that day, regarded. "*Patria potestas in pietate debet, non in atrocitate, consistere.*"

This right, in a greatly modified form, and relating principally to the obligations of obedience and support, is explicitly recognized by the jurisprudence of Continental Europe. — ed.

[1] At Common Law, the time prescribed was forty weeks. "*Et si ele eyt un enfant dedens t's XL semaines adõques soit cel enfant receu el heritage.*" (Britton, Chap. 66, p. 166.) The countries whose jurisprudence is directly derived from that of Rome, as well as Japan, follow the rule of the text, and fix the limit at three hundred days. (*Code Civil de France*, Art. 315. *Código Civil de España*, Art. 108. *Codice Civile de Italia*, Art. 160. *Codigo Civil Portugues*, Art. 101. *Civil Code of Japan*. Art. 820.) According to Moslem law, the presumption of legitimacy may be established at any time from six lunar months — adopted as the shortest period of gestation — to two years. (*Syed Ameer Ali*, Mohammedan Law, Vol. II. II, 2, p. 191.) As is well known, the Civil Law maxim, "*Pater est quem nuptiæ demonstrant*," is not accepted by the Common Law, which requires the birth to precede the marriage in every instance. The law of Scotland coincides with that of Rome on both the above-mentioned points. (More, Lectures on the Laws of Scotland, Vol. I, Chap. I. Sec. II.) — ed.

THE LAWS OF THE TWELVE TABLES

TABLE V

CONCERNING ESTATES AND GUARDIANSHIPS

Law I. No matter in what way the head of a household may dispose of his estate, and appoint heirs to the same, or guardians; it shall have the force and effect of law.[1]

Law II. Where a father dies intestate, without leaving any proper heir, his nearest agnate, or, if there is none, the next of kin among his family, shall be his heir.

Law III. When a freedman dies intestate, and does not leave any proper heir, but his patron, or the children of the latter survive him; the inheritance of the estate of the freedman shall be adjudged to the next of kin of the patron.

Law IV. When a creditor or a debtor dies, his heirs can only sue, or be sued, in proportion to their shares in the estate; and any claims, or remaining property, shall be divided among them in the same proportion.

Law V. Where co-heirs desire to obtain their shares of the property of an estate, which has not yet been divided, it shall be divided. In order that this may be properly done and no loss be sustained by the litigants, the Prætor shall appoint three arbiters, who can give to each one that to which he is entitled in accordance with law and equity.

Law VI. When the head of a family dies intestate, and leaves a proper heir who has not reached the age of puberty, his nearest agnate shall obtain the guardianship.[2]

---

[1] This law, which placed the distribution of his estate absolutely in the hands of the testator, without regard to the natural claims of consanguinity, was strictly observed for centuries. The abuse to which the privilege was liable became in time so flagrant that various measures were introduced to correct it. If the legacies bequeathed were large enough to include all, or so much of the assets as to render the remainder undesirable or burdensome, the estate was forthwith rejected by the heir. This act invalidated the will, and the heir-at-law took possession, the legacies being, of course, no longer of any effect. To obviate the confusion and injustice resulting from this proceeding, the Tribunal of the Centumviri devised the *querela inofficiosi testamenti*, or complaint of inofficious testament; by means of which the will was declared void on account of the mental incapacity of the testator, which was considered to be established *prima facie* by the existence of the clause of disinheritance. The *Lex Furia Testamentaria* limited the amount of a bequest to the insignificant sum of one thousand asses, which the ingenuity of testators evaded by simply increasing the number of legacies.

The *Lex Voconia*, passed A. U. C. 594, prohibited any legatee from accepting a bequest which exceeded in value the amount obtained by the heir. Women were also discriminated against by this law, presumably to prevent the affection of the testator from being indulged in their favor at the expense of members of his family; as well as to avoid the excessive accumulation of property in the hands of persons generally considered as ill-qualified to make a proper use of it.

The *Lex Voconia* having proved ineffective, the *Lex Falcidia*, by which the previous enactments on this subject were repealed, was introduced one hundred and twenty years later. It provided that the heir, should, under ordinary circumstances, be entitled to one-fourth of the estate after all claims had been paid; and that no legacy should exceed three-fourths of the amount of the same. In case this rule was violated, the heir was authorized to diminish the bequests *pro rata*, until the sum to which he was entitled was made up. This apportionment, known as the "*Quarta Falcidia*," or "*Falcidian Fourth*," has, without substantial change, under the name of "*legitime*," been incorporated into much of the jurisprudence of Europe. It is in force in Louisiana, where it exists in favor of all direct descendants, and of ascendants in the first degree. "Donations *inter vivos* or *mortis causa* cannot exceed two thirds of the property of the disposer, if he leaves at his decease a legitimate child; one half, if he leaves two children, and one third, if he leaves three or a greater number." (Civil Code of Louisiana, Arts. 1480, 1481.) With the exception of the above-mentioned State, no similar restraints are, in this country, imposed upon the testamentary disposition of property, which is, of course, always subject to the dower of the widow. The same rule prevails in England. — ed.

[2] This was done under the presumption that the person most closely connected with the minor by the ties of consanguinity, and being next in the order of succession and hence directly interested in the preservation of the estate, would be most likely to properly discharge the duties of the trust. The English doctrine, which coincides with that adopted by the Greeks at the instance of Solon, is

Law VII. When no guardian has been appointed for an insane person, or a spendthrift, his nearest agnates, or if there are none, his other relatives, must take charge of his property.

TABLE VI
CONCERNING OWNERSHIP AND POSSESSION

Law I. When anyone contracts a legal obligation with reference to his property, or sells it, by making a verbal statement or agreement concerning the same, this shall have the force and effect of law. If the party should afterwards deny his statements, and legal proceedings are instituted, he shall, by way of penalty, pay double the value of the property in question.

Law II. Where a slave is ordered to be free by a will, upon his compliance with a certain condition, and he complies with the condition; or if, after having paid his price to the purchaser, he claims his liberty, he shall be free.

Law III. Where property has been sold, even though it may have been delivered, it shall by no means be acquired by the purchaser until the price has been paid, or a surety or a pledge has been given, and the vendor satisfied in this manner.

Law IV. Immovable property shall be acquired by usucaption after the lapse of two years; other property after the lapse of one year.

Law V. Where a woman, who has not been united to a man in marriage, lives with him for an entire year without the usucaption of her being interrupted for three nights, she shall pass into his power as his legal wife.[1]

Law VI. Where parties have a dispute with reference to property before the tribunal of the Prætor, both of them shall be permitted to state their claims in the presence of witnesses.

Law VII. Where anyone demands freedom for another against the claim of servitude, the Prætor shall render judgment in favor of liberty.

Law VIII. No material forming part of either a building or a vineyard shall be removed therefrom. Any one who, without the knowledge or consent of the owner, attaches a beam or anything else to his house or vineyard, shall be condemned to pay double its value.

Law IX. Timbers which have been dressed and prepared for building purposes, but which have not yet been attached to a building or a vineyard can legally be recovered by the owner, if they are stolen from him.

Law X. If a husband desires to divorce his wife, and dissolve his marriage, he must give a reason for doing so.

---

directly the opposite. It excludes from guardianship those who could, under any circumstances, become heirs, and therefore evinced a preference for cognates. The temptation to foul play to which the next of kin to the minor was supposed to be liable, is stated by the early English jurists in very energetic language. "*Nunquam enim custodia alicujus de jure alicui remanet, de quo habeatur suspicio quod possit vel velit aliquod jus in ipsa, hereditate clamare.*" (Glanvil VII, II.) Coke compares a guardian of this description to a ravening wolf: "*quasi agnem committere lupo ad devorandum,*" are the terms in which he characterizes such an appointment. (Coke Inst. I. 88.) — ed.

[1] This indicates the existence of woman as a mere chattel to be acquired by uninterrupted possession and use for a year, like any other species of personal property. It has been stated, with much probability, that this kind of matrimonial union was the most common and popular one in the early days of Rome. Our Common Law marriage authorized by some States, and which requires the public acknowledgment of the woman as a wife, bears a considerable analogy, in certain respects, to the cohabitation, *matrimonii causa*, of the text. — ed.

THE LAWS OF THE TWELVE TABLES

TABLE VII

CONCERNING CRIMES

Law I. If a quadruped causes injury to anyone, let the owner tender him the estimated amount of the damage; and if he is unwilling to accept it, the owner shall, by way of reparation, surrender the animal that caused the injury.[1]

Law II. If you cause any unlawful damage . . . .[2] accidentally and unintentionally, you must make good the loss, either by tendering what has caused it, or by payment.

Law III. Anyone who, by means of incantations and magic arts, prevents grain or crops of any kind belonging to another from growing, shall be sacrificed to Ceres.[3]

Law XVII. When a patron defrauds his client, he shall be dedicated to the infernal gods.

TABLE VIII

CONCERNING THE LAWS OF REAL PROPERTY

Law I. A space of two feet and a half must be left between neighboring buildings.[4]

Law II. Societies and associations which have the right to assemble, can make, promulgate, and confirm for themselves such contracts and rules as they may desire; provided nothing is done by them contrary to public enactments, or which does not violate the common law.

Law III. The space of five feet shall be left between adjoining fields, by means of which the owners can visit their property, or drive and plow around it. No one shall ever have the right to acquire this space by usucaption.

Law IV. If any persons are in possession of adjoining fields, and a dispute arises with reference to the boundaries of the same, the Prætor shall appoint three arbiters, who shall take cognizance of the case, and, after the boundaries have been established, he shall assign to each party that to which he is entitled.

Law V. When a tree overhangs the land of a neighbor, so as to cause injury by its branches and its shade, it shall be cut off fifteen feet from the ground.

Law VI. When the fruit of a tree falls upon the premises of a neighbor, the owner of the tree shall have a right to gather and remove it.

Law VII. When rain falls upon the land of one person in such a quantity as to cause water to rise and injure

---

[1] This was the origin of the proceedings growing out of *noxa*, an injurious or unlawful act committed by an animal, a slave, or a child under paternal control, for which the owner, master, or parent was held responsible. Whatever caused the damage was held to be primarily liable, under the rule, "*omnes noxales actiones caput sequntur*"; hence the injured party had a right to seize the offending animal or slave, and hold it as security until his claim was satisfied; which has an exact parallel in the case of a stray found upon the premises of another, and detained or impounded under the English or American law. At first, in neither instance, could the author of the damage be sold, or the injury be otherwise redressed; this defect was, however, subsequently remedied by the passage at Rome of the *Lex Aquilia*, which granted an action directly against the owner; and by the enactment of the Statutes 5 & 6 Wm. IV. which permitted a sale of the animal in question, after certain legal formalities had been complied with. The American law is similar. — ed.

[2] Original manuscript illegible.

[3] The intimate association of religion with law in the early life of Rome is disclosed by the frequent appearance of the formula "*sacer esto.*"

[4] This was done in order to render access to the owner's property more convenient, to prevent conflagrations, and to facilitate the extinguishing of fire. — ed.

the property of another, the Prætor shall appoint three arbiters for the purpose of confining the water, and providing against damage to the other party.

Law VIII. Where a road runs in a straight line, it shall be eight feet, and where it curves, it shall be sixteen feet in width.

Law IX. When a man's land lies adjacent to the highway, he can enclose it in any way that he chooses; but if he neglects to do so, any other person can drive an animal over the land wherever he pleases.

TABLE IX

CONCERNING PUBLIC LAW

Law I. No privileges, or statutes, shall be enacted in favor of private persons, to the injury of others contrary to the law common to all citizens, and which individuals, no matter of what rank, have a right to make use of.

Law II. The same rights shall be conferred upon, and the same laws shall be considered to have been enacted for all the people residing in and beyond Latium, that have been enacted for good and steadfast Roman citizens.

Law III. When a judge, or an arbiter appointed to hear a case, accepts money, or other gifts, for the purpose of influencing his decision, he shall suffer the penalty of death.

Law IV. No decision with reference to the life or liberty of a Roman citizen shall be rendered except by the vote of the Greater *Comitia*.

Law V. Public accusers in capital cases shall be appointed by the people.[1]

Law VI. If anyone should cause nocturnal assemblies in the City, he shall be put to death.

Law VII. If anyone should stir up war against his country, or delivers a Roman citizen into the hands of the enemy, he shall be punished with death.

TABLE X

CONCERNING RELIGIOUS LAW

Law I. An oath shall have the greatest force and effect, for the purpose of compelling good faith.

Law II. Where a family adopts private religious rites every member of it can, afterwards, always make use of them.[2]

---

[1] "*Quæstores Paricidii*." These officials discharged the triple functions of detectives, State attorneys, and executioners. They were two in number, and are supposed by some authorities to have been identical with the urban quæstors of subsequent times, which conjecture, however, has no positive evidence to support it. They were originally appointed by the King, and, under the Republic, by the consuls. It was their duty to investigate and prosecute capital crimes, such as arson, murder, witchcraft, and the destruction of growing crops, all of which in ancient times were punishable with death. They summoned the *Comitia*, or Assembly of the People, for the trial of an offender, and executed the sentence after it had been pronounced. — ed.

[2] The Romans, like all primitive peoples, originally worshipped their ancestors, of whom one, styled the *lars familiaris*, was always selected as the tutelary diety. The various ceremonies attending this worship were of a private character, and hence were entirely

THE LAWS OF THE TWELVE TABLES

Law III. No burial or cremation of a corpse shall take place in a city.[1]

Law IV. No greater expenses or mourning than is proper shall be permitted in funeral ceremonies.

Law V. No one shall, hereafter, exceed the limit established by these laws for the celebration of funeral rites.

Law VI. Wood employed for the purpose of constructing a funeral pyre shall not be hewn, but shall be rough and unpolished.

Law VII. When a corpse is prepared for burial at home, not more than three women with their heads covered with mourning veils shall be permitted to perform this service. The body may be enveloped in purple robes, and when borne outside, ten flute players, at the most, shall accompany the funeral procession.

Law VIII. Women shall not during a funeral lacerate their faces, or tear their cheeks with their nails; nor shall they utter loud cries bewailing the dead.

Law IX. No bones shall be taken from the body of a person who is dead, or from his ashes after cremation, in order that funeral ceremonies may again be held elsewhere. When, however, anyone dies in a foreign country, or is killed in war, a part of his remains may be transferred to the burial place of his ancestors.

Law X. The body of no dead slave shall be anointed; nor shall any drinking take place at his funeral, nor a banquet of any kind be instituted in his honor.

Law XI. No wine flavored with myrrh, or any other precious beverage, shall be poured upon a corpse while it is burning; nor shall the funeral pile be sprinkled with wine.

Law XII. Large wreaths[2] shall not be borne at a funeral; nor shall perfumes be burned on the altars.

Law XIII. Anyone who has rendered himself deserving of a wreath, as the reward of bravery in war, or through his having been the victor in public contests or games, whether he has obtained it through his own exertions or by means of others in his own name, and by his own money, through his horses, or his slaves, shall have a right to have the said wreath placed upon his dead body, or upon that of any of his ascendants, as long as the corpse is at his home, as well as when it is borne away; so that, during his obsequies, he may enjoy the honor which in his lifetime he acquired by his bravery or his good fortune.

Law XIV. Only one funeral of an individual can take place; and it shall not be permitted to prepare several biers.

Law XV. Gold, no matter in what form it may be present, shall, by all means, be removed from the corpse at the time of the funeral; but if anyone's teeth should be fastened with gold, it shall be lawful either to burn, or to bury it with the body.

Law XVI. No one, without the knowledge or consent of the owner, shall erect a funeral pyre, or a tomb, nearer than sixty feet to the building of another.

---

distinct from those performed in the temples and at the public altars. Religion being so closely interwoven with State affairs in the Roman polity, its mode of celebration was, in every instance, rigidly prescribed by law. — ed.

[1] It was the custom at Rome, prior to the enactment of the Laws of the Twelve Tables, for the deceased relatives of the family to be buried in their own homes, which gave rise to the worship of the *Lares*, above referred to. The inconvenience and unsanitary results growing out of this practice no doubt contributed largely to its abrogation. — ed.

[2] "*Longæ Coronæ*." This term, while obscure, would seem to refer to garlands of excessive size, exhibited by way of pomp and ostentation at the celebration of funeral rites. The greater part of the legislation of this Table was evidently framed for the correction of the inordinate display of wealth and luxury already becoming prevalent at the burial of the dead. — ed.

Law XVII. No one can acquire by usucaption either the vestibule or approach to a tomb, or the tomb itself.

Law XVIII. No assembly of the people shall take place during the obsequies of any man distinguished in the State.

TABLE XI
SUPPLEMENT TO THE FIVE PRECEDING ONES

Law I. Affairs of great importance shall not be transacted without the vote of the people, with whom rests the power to appoint magistrates, to condemn citizens, and to enact laws. Laws subsequently passed always take preference over former ones.

Law II. Those who belong to the Senatorial Order and are styled Fathers, shall not contract marriage with plebeians.

TABLE XII
SUPPLEMENT TO THE FIVE PRECEDING ONES

Law I. No one shall render sacred any property with reference to which there is a controversy in court, where issue has already been joined; and if anyone does render such property sacred, he shall pay double its value as a penalty.

Law II. If the claim of anyone in whose favor judgment was rendered after the property had been illegally seized, or after possession of the same had been delivered, is found to be false, the Prætor shall appoint three arbiters, by whose award double the amount of the profits shall be restored by him in whose favor the judgment was rendered.

Law III. If a slave, with the knowledge of his master, should commit a theft, or cause damage to anyone, his master shall be given up to the other party by way of reparation for the theft, injury, or damage committed by the slave.

END OF THE LAWS OF THE TWELVE TABLES.

THE FOUR COMMENTARIES
OF GAIUS ON THE
INSTITUTES OF THE CIVIL LAW

THE FOUR COMMENTARIES OF GAIUS ON THE INSTITUTES OF THE CIVIL LAW

FIRST COMMENTARY

I. CONCERNING CIVIL AND NATURAL LAW.

(1) All peoples who are ruled by laws and customs partly make use of their own laws, and partly have recourse to those which are common to all men; for what every people establishes as law for itself is peculiar to itself, and is called the Civil Law, as being that peculiar to the State; and what natural reason establishes among all men and is observed by all peoples alike, is called the Law of Nations, as being the law which all nations employ. Therefore the Roman people partly make use of their own law, and partly avail themselves of that common to all men, which matters we shall explain separately in their proper place.[1]

---

[1] With the Romans the *Jus Gentium* and the *Jus Naturale* were practically synonymous. The greater number of ancient authorities made two divisions of jurisprudence, the Law of Nations and the Civil Law; some added another, the *Jus Privatum*, or *Familiæ*, that is to say, private law.

The precepts of morality, as in most human enactments, form the basis of this most comprehensive system of jurisprudence which all civilized peoples are presumed to acknowledge.

By what we designate the Law of Nature, the Roman jurists understood the rules by which all living beings were governed: "*Quod natura omnia animalia docuit.*" The Law of Nations was known to them as *Jus Feciale*.

No lawyer of ancient or modern times has given such a lucid, comprehensive, and eloquent description of the Law of Nature as Cicero. In glowing language, eminently worthy of the distinguished scholar and jurist, he sets forth its constant and universal blessings; a law which summons all to the performance of their duties, and deters the hesitating from the commission of fraud; from whose observance even those highest in authority are not exempt; whose application is universal; whose precepts are eternal and immutable; which cannot be disregarded or abrogated with impunity; of which God is the originator, the interpreter, the proposer; and he who refuses to obey it flees from himself, and rejects the claims of humanity, by this very act rendering himself liable to the severest penalties, even if he be able to escape others which have been prescribed.

"*Est quidem vera lex recta ratio, naturæ congruens, diffusa in omnes, constans, sempiterna; quæ vocet ad officium iubendo, vetando a fraude deterreat, quæ tamen neque probos frustra iubet aut vetat, neque improbos iubendo aut vetando movet. Huic legi neque obrogari fas est, neque derogari ex hac aliquid licet, neque tota abrogari potest. Nec vero aut per senatum aut per populum solvi hac*

(2) The Civil Law of the Roman people consists of statutes, plebiscites, Decrees of the Senate, Constitutions of the Emperors, the Edicts of those who have the right to promulgate them, and the opinions of jurists.

(3) A statute is what the people order and establish. A plebiscite is what the commonalty order and establish. Moreover, the commonalty is distinguished from the people by the fact that the entire body of citizens including the patricians, is designated by the appellation, "the people"; but the other citizens, exclusive of the patricians, are indicated by the term commonalty; for which reason the patricians formerly declared that they were not bound by plebiscites, as they were enacted without their sanction; but subsequently the *Lex Hortensia* was passed, by which it was provided that plebiscites should bind the entire people; and hence, in this way, they were placed on the same footing as laws.

(4) A Decree of the Senate is what the Senate orders and establishes, and therefore it obtains the force of law, although this formerly was disputed.

(5) An Imperial Constitution is what the Emperor establishes by a decree, an edict, or a letter, and there was never any doubt that it had the force of a law, as the Emperor himself derives his authority from a statute.

(6) The magistrates of the Roman people have the power of promulgating edicts, but the highest authority attaches to the edicts of the two prætors, the urban and the foreign, whose jurisdiction is vested in the governors of the provinces; as well as to the edicts of the curule Ædiles, whose jurisdiction the quæstors administer in the provinces of the Roman people, for quæstors are not appointed in the provinces of the Emperor and, therefore, the latter edict is not published in these provinces.

(7) The answers of jurists are the decisions and opinions of those who are authorized to define the law. If the opinions of all of them concur, what they agree upon obtains the force of law; if, however, they disagree, the judge has a right to follow whichever opinion he may wish, and this is set forth in a rescript of the Divine Hadrian.[1]

---

lege possumus: neque est quærendus explanator aut interpres eius alius. Nec erit alia lex Romæ, alia Athenis, alia nunc, alia posthac; sed et omnes gentes et omni tempore una lex et sempiterna, et immutabilis continebit; unusque erit communis quasi magister et imperator omnium Deus, ille legis huius inventor, disceptator, lator: cui qui non parebit ipse se fugiet et naturam hominis aspernabitur, atque hoc ipse luet maximas pœnas, etiamsi cætera, supplicia, quæ putantur, effugerit." (De Repub. lib. III, cap. 22.)

The importance of considering man as an individual, distinct from his association with his fellows in communities, is emphasized by Montesquieu in determining the principles of the Law of Nature.

"*Avant toutes ces lois sont celles de la nature, ainsi nommées parce qu'elles dérivent uniquement de la constitution de notre être. Pour les connaître bien, il faut considérer un homme evant l'établissement des sociétés. Les lois de la nature seront celles qu'il recevroit dans un état pareil.*"

"*Il songeroit à la conservation de son être, avant de chercher l'origine de son être." (De l'Esprit des Lois, I, II, Page 191.)*

The Law of Nations he concisely states to be based upon the bestowal of the greatest benefits in peace and the infliction of the least injury in war consistent with the public interests involved.

"*Le droit des gens est naturellement fondé sur ce principe, que les diverses nations doivent se faire dans la paix le plus de bien, et dans la guerre le moins de mal qu'il est possible, sans nuire à leurs véritables intérêts." (Ibid I, II, 191.)*

No ancient classic work on the Law of Nations has survived, if, indeed, one ever was written. The formulation and perfection of its rules as a science were worthily accomplished by the genius, learning, philosophical discernment, and industry of Grotius, Pufendorf, and Vattel. — ed.

[1] The *Responsa Prudentum* were at first only the opinions of eminent lawyers imparted to anyone who consulted them. Subsequently, by decrees of Augustus and other sovereigns, they were invested with legal validity, and obtained all the force of regularly enacted statutes. They were directly addressed to the judge, or, having been reduced to writing, were submitted to the court in the presence of witnesses who had seen them drawn up. The *Responsa* formed one of the most important sources from whence was derived the maxims and principles of the Civil Law, and indeed, of all modern jurisprudence. The Digest is largely composed of them. From the

II. CONCERNING THE DIVISIONS OF THE LAW.

(8) All the law which we make use of has reference either to persons, to things, or to actions. Let us first consider persons.

III. CONCERNING THE DIFFERENT CONDITIONS OF MEN.

(9) The principal division of the law of persons is the following, namely, that all men are either free or slaves.

(10) Again, men who are free are either freeborn or freedmen.

(11) Freeborn are those who are free by birth, freedmen are those who have been manumitted from legal slavery.

(12) Moreover, there are three classes of freedmen, namely, Roman citizens, Latins, and *dediticii*. Let us consider each of these separately, and, in the first place, *dediticii*.

IV. CONCERNING DEDITICII AND THE PROVISIONS OF THE LEX ÆLIA SENTIA.

(13) It is provided by the *Lex Ælia Sentia* that slaves who have been placed in chains by their masters, or have been branded, or have been subjected to torture for some offence and convicted, or have been delivered up to fight with others or with wild beasts, or to contend with gladiators, or have been thrown into prison and have afterwards been manumitted by the same, or by another master, shall become free, and belong to the same class as that of enemies who have surrendered at discretion.

V. CONCERNING ENEMIES WHO HAVE SURRENDERED AT DISCRETION.

(14) Those enemies are called *dediticii* who, having formerly taken up arms and fought against the Roman people afterwards have been conquered and have surrendered at discretion.

(15) From this it is evident that slaves who have been guilty of criminal acts of this kind, no matter in what way, or at what age they may have been manumitted, and even though their masters had complete authority over them, can never become either Roman citizens or Latins, but must always be classed among enemies who have surrendered at discretion.

(16) If, however, a slave has not been guilty of such criminality, we declare that by manumission he sometimes becomes a Roman citizen, and sometimes a Latin.

(17) Where the following three requisites are combined in the person of a slave, that is to say where he is over thirty years of age, where his master is invested with full civil rights, and he is set free by proper and lawful manumission through the intervention of the prætor, by enrollment on the register of the census, or

---

fragments it contains we can form some idea of the vast knowledge and attainments possessed by these old Roman lawyers, whose works have perished, and whose names would hardly be known, were it not for the compilation of Justinian. As legal dicta they are, as a rule, models of perspicacity and conciseness. Their language is terse, comprehensive, elegant. The ingenuity with which their conclusions are formed is admirable. The dominating sentiments which pervade them are a love of truth and a reverence for justice, qualities, it is scarcely necessary to add, which do not always characterize modern legislation.

These opinions, originally intended to mitigate the severity of the Civil Law, whose basis was the harsh and inflexible collection of the Twelve Tables, by enabling the magistrate to modify his decisions, and evade the cruel legislation of a barbarous age, laid the foundation of equity jurisprudence. After the *Responsa* had, by Imperial sanction and general acceptance, acquired full legal effect, they were designated *sententiæ receptæ*. — ed.

by will, he becomes a Roman citizen; if, however, one of these requisites should be lacking, he will become a Latin.

VI. CONCERNING MANUMISSION, AND PROOF OF THE REASON FOR IT.

(18) The requisite of the age of the slave was introduced by the *Lex Ælia Sentia*, for this law did not permit slaves under the age of thirty years, who had been manumitted, to become Roman citizens unless they were set free by the wand of the prætor, after proof of good reason for the manumission had been established in the presence of the Council.

(19) A good reason for manumission exists where, for instance, anyone offers for manumission before the Council a natural son or daughter, or brother or sister, or foster-child or teacher, or a slave with the intention of appointing him a steward, or a female slave on account of prospective marriage.

VII. CONCERNING THE CONSTITUTION OF THE COUNCIL.

(20) The Council in the City of Rome consists of five senators and five Roman knights of the age of puberty. In the provinces it consists of twenty magistrates who are Roman citizens, and who are convoked on the last day of the term. At Rome, however, manumissions take place in the presence of the Council upon certain days. Slaves who are more than thirty years of age can be manumitted at any time, and the ceremony can be performed even while walking in the streets, as for instance, when the prætor or the proconsul is on his way to the bath or the theatre.

(21) A slave, who was under the age of thirty years when manumitted, can become a Roman citizen if he was granted his freedom and appointed heir by the will of his master who died insolvent. . . .[1]

(22) Slaves manumitted in certain ways are called *Latini Juniani; Latini* for the reason that they are classed with Latin colonists, *Juniani* because they received their freedom under the terms of the *Lex Junia*, as before it was passed they were considered slaves.

(23) The *Lex Junia* does not, however, permit them either to make a will, or to take under the will of another, or to be appointed testamentary guardians.

(24) What we have said with reference to their being unable to take under a will must be understood to mean that they cannot take anything directly as heirs, or legatees, but, on the other hand, they have a right to take under the terms of a trust.

(25) Those, however, who belong to the class of *dediticii* can, under no circumstances, take under a will, any more than a foreigner; nor can they, in accordance with a majority of the decisions, themselves make a will.

(26) Hence, only the lowest degree of freedom is possessed by those who belong to the class of *dediticii* nor is any way afforded them of obtaining Roman citizenship either by a law, by a Decree of the Senate, or by an Imperial Constitution.

(27) Moreover, they are forbidden to dwell in the City of Rome or within the hundredth mile-stone of the Capitol; and if they should disobey, they and their property are ordered to be publicly sold under the condition that they shall remain slaves beyond the hundredth milestone of the City of Rome, and that they shall never be manumitted; and if they should be manumitted, they are ordered to become the slaves of the Roman people; and these things are included in the *Lex Ælia Sentia*.

---

[1] Original manuscript illegible.

VIII. IN WHAT WAY LATINS MAY OBTAIN ROMAN CITIZENSHIP.

(28) Latins obtain Roman citizenship in many ways.

(29) For, by the *Lex Ælia Sentia*, where slaves under the age of thirty years are manumitted and become Latins, if they marry either women who are Roman citizens or Latin colonists, or those who belong to the same condition as themselves, and prove this by the testimony of not less than seven Roman citizens who have arrived at the age of puberty; and they have sons, and the latter are a year old, authority is granted them by this law to appear before the prætor — or, in the provinces before the governor — and prove that they have married wives in accordance with the terms of the *Lex Ælia Sentia*, and have sons by them who are a year old; and if the magistrate before whom this proof is adduced should declare it to be true, then the Latin and his wife, provided she and her son are of the same condition, are ordered to become Roman citizens.

(30) I added the clause, "If the son is of the same condition", for the reason that if the wife of the Latin aforesaid is a Roman citizen, her son is a Roman citizen by birth under the terms of the recent Decree of the Senate promulgated by the Divine Hadrian.

(31) This right of acquiring Roman citizenship, though at first only conferred upon those who had been manumitted under thirty years of age and had become Latins by the *Lex Ælia Sentia*, was afterwards, by a Decree of the Senate issued under the consulship of Pegasus and Pusio, granted to all Latins, even though they were more than thirty years of age at the time when they were manumitted.

(32) However, even if the Latin should die before he was able to prove that his son was a year old, the mother of the latter can prove his condition, and hence both she and her son (if she is a Latin) will become Roman citizens. If the mother should not be able to prove this, the son himself can do so when he reaches the age of puberty. If the son himself is a Roman citizen, for the reason that he is born of a mother who is a Roman citizen, he must still prove his condition in order to become the heir of his father.

(32a) What we have stated with reference to a son being a year old we also understood to apply to a daughter of the same age.

(32b) Moreover, by the *Lex Visellia*, persons become Roman citizens, where by manumission they have become Latins, when either under or over thirty years of age, if they have served for six years in the guards at Rome. A Decree of the Senate is said to have been subsequently enacted by which Roman citizenship was bestowed on Latins if they had served for three years in the army.

(32c) Likewise, by an Edict of the Divine Claudius, Latins obtain the rights of Roman citizens if they build a ship with a capacity not less than ten thousand measures of grain, and the said ship, or one substituted for it, should transport grain to Rome for the term of six years.

(33) Moreover, it was established in an Edict published by Nero that if a Latin who had property worth two hundred thousand sesterces, or more, should build a house in the City of Rome on which he expended not less than half his estate, he should obtain the right of Roman citizenship.

(34) Finally, the Divine Trajan decreed that if a Latin should exercise the calling of a miller in the City of Rome for the term of three years, and should grind each day not less than a hundred measures of grain, he could acquire Roman citizenship.

(35) Slaves who become Latins either because they are under thirty years of age when manumitted, or, being over that age, have been informally manumitted, may become Roman citizens by being again manumitted either by the wand of the prætor, or by inscription on the register of the census, or by will; and

in either of these cases they become the freedmen of the party who manumitted them a second time. Therefore, if a slave forms part of your property by bonitarian right and belongs to me by quiritarian right, he can be made a Latin solely by you, and he can be manumitted a second time by me but not by you, and in this way he will become my freedman; and if he obtains the right of citizenship in other ways he still will be my freedman. The possession of his estate at the time of his death is however granted to you, no matter in what way he may have obtained Roman citizenship. But, if he is manumitted by one who has in him both bonitarian and quiritarian rights he can be manumitted by the said party, and become both a Latin and a Roman citizen.

(36) Every one who desires to manumit a slave is not permitted to do so.

(37) For he who manumits a slave for the purpose of defrauding his creditors or his patron, commits an act which is void, for the reason that the *Lex Ælia Sentia* prevents the grant of freedom.

(38) Likewise, by the same law a minor owner under the age of twenty years is not permitted to manumit a slave, except by the intervention of the prætor, after proper cause has been shown for the manumission in the presence of the Council.

(39) The following are proper causes for manumission, for instance, where anyone manumits his father, his mother, his teacher, or his foster-brother. Moreover, the reasons which we have designated above with reference to a slave under thirty years of age may be adduced also in the case of which we speak; and likewise, on the other hand, the same reasons which we stated with reference to an owner under the age of twenty years may be advanced where the slave is less than thirty years old.

(40) Therefore, as a certain restriction on the manumission of slaves is imposed upon owners under the age of twenty years by the *Lex Ælia Sentia*, the result is that anyone who has completed his fourteenth year, although he can make a will, appoint an heir to his estate, and bequeath legacies, still, if he is under the age of twenty years, he cannot grant freedom to his slave.

(41) And even though an owner under the age of twenty years may desire to constitute a slave a Latin, he must, nevertheless, prove before the Council, that he has a good reason for doing so, and afterwards manumit the said slave in the presence of friends.

(42) Moreover, by the *Lex Fufia Caninia* a certain limit is established with reference to the manumission of slaves by a will.

(43) Hence, he who has more than two slaves and not more than ten, is permitted to manumit as many as half of that number. He, however, who has more than ten and not more than thirty slaves, is permitted to manumit a third of that number; and he who has more than thirty slaves and not more than a hundred, is granted authority to manumit one fourth of his slaves. Finally, he who has more than one hundred and not more than five hundred, is not permitted to manumit more than a fifth; and, no matter how many slaves a man may have, he is not permitted to manumit more than this, as the law prescribes that no one shall have the right to manumit more than a hundred. Still, where anyone has only one or two slaves, his case does not come under this law, and therefore he has free power of manumission.

(44) Nor does this law have any reference whatever to persons who manumit in any way except by will, and therefore those who do so either in the tribunal of the Prætor, or by enrollment on the registers of the census, or in the presence of friends, are permitted to liberate their entire bodies of slaves; provided however, that no other reason prevents their receiving their freedom.

(45) What we have stated with reference to the number of slaves which can be manumitted by will should be understood to mean that where a man has a right to liberate the half, the third, the fourth, or the fifth part

of his entire body of slaves, he shall in no case be restricted to a smaller number than he would have been permitted to manumit had the estimate been made according to the next preceding scale. This provision is in accordance with reason, for it certainly would be absurd for any one to be permitted to liberate five out of his ten slaves, because he is granted authority to manumit half of that number; while another, having twelve slaves, would not be permitted to manumit more than four; and anyone who has more than ten and not more than thirty, under the same rule should be permitted also to manumit five, the same number which he who has ten is allowed to liberate.

(46) If freedom should be granted by a testator in his will to a greater number of slaves than is above mentioned, and the names are written in a circle so that no order of manumission can be ascertained, none of the said slaves shall become free; because the *Lex Fufia Caninia*, as well as other special Decrees of the Senate, have declared all testamentary provisions devised for the purpose of evading the law to be void.

(47) In conclusion, it should be noted that, as it is provided by the *Lex Ælia Sentia* that slaves who have been manumitted for the purpose of defrauding a patron, or creditors, do not become free; for the Senate, at the suggestion of the Divine Hadrian, decreed that this rule should also apply to foreigners, while the other provisions of the same law do not apply to them.

(48) There is another division with reference to the law of persons, for some persons are their own masters, and some are subject to the authority of others.

(49) Again, of those persons who are subject to the authority of another, some are in his power, others are in his hand, and others are considered his property.

(50) Let us now consider those that are subject to the authority of another, for, when we ascertain who they are, we shall then understand what persons are their own masters.

(51) In the first place, let us examine those who are in the power of another.

(52) Slaves are in the power of their masters, and this power is acknowledged by the Law of Nations, for we know that among all nations alike the master has the power of life and death over his slaves, and whatever property is acquired by a slave is acquired by his master.

(53) At the present time, however, neither Roman citizens nor any other persons who are under the empire of the Roman people are permitted to employ excessive or causeless severity against their slaves; for by a constitution of the Most Holy Emperor Antoninus anyone who kills his slave, without good reason, is not less liable than one who kills the slave of another; and the excessive harshness of masters is restrained by another constitution of the same Emperor; for he, having been consulted by certain governors of provinces with reference to slaves who flee for refuge to the temples of the Gods or the statues of the Emperor,[1] ordered that if the cruelty of masters appeared to be intolerable, they should be compelled to sell their slaves; and in both cases he acted justly, for we should not make a bad use of our rights, in accordance with which principle the administration of their own property is forbidden to spendthrifts.

(54) But, as among Roman citizens, a double ownership may exist (for a slave is understood to be subject to bonitarian or quiritarian right or to belong to both these classes) so we merely say that a slave is in the power of his owner if he forms part of his property by bonitarian right, even if at the same time he may not

---

[1] The right of asylum, derived by Rome from Greece, did not attach to all temples, or Imperial statues, but only to such as long continued custom had invested with that privilege, of which debtors, slaves, and violators of the law constantly availed themselves. The clergy, after the introduction of Christianity, being well aware of the financial and political advantages which would accrue to them by the perpetuation of this practice, encouraged and confirmed it, until the abuse of the right of sanctuary, through the immunity enjoyed by notorious criminals, became one of the worst scandals of mediæval times. — ed.

belong to him by quiritarian right; for anyone who has the bare quiritarian right in a slave is not understood to have him in his power.

(55) In like manner, our children whom we have begotten in lawful marriage are under our control. This right is peculiar to Roman citizens, for there are hardly any other men who have such authority over their children as we have, and this the Divine Hadrian stated in the Edict which he published with reference to persons who petitioned for Roman citizenship for themselves and for their children, for he said: "It does not escape my knowledge that the Galatians hold that children are in the power of their parents."

(56) Roman citizens are understood to have contracted marriage according to the Civil Law and to have the children begotten by them in their power if they marry Roman citizens, or even Latins or foreigners whom they have the right to marry; for the result of legal marriage is that the children follow the condition of the father and not only are Roman citizens by birth, but also become subject to paternal authority.

(57) Therefore, certain veterans are usually granted permission by the Imperial Constitutions to contract civil marriage with those Latin or foreign women whom they first marry after their discharge, and the children born of such unions become Roman citizens by birth, and are subject to the authority of their fathers.

(57a) Marriage, however, cannot take place with persons of servile condition.

(58) Nor are we permitted to marry any free woman, as we should refrain from contracting matrimony with certain ones of this class.

(59) For marriage cannot be contracted between persons who sustain to one another the relation of ascendants and descendants, nor can legal matrimony exist between them; for instance, between father and daughter, mother and son, or grandfather and granddaughter; and if such persons form unions they are said to have contracted nefarious and incestuous marriages. To such an extent does this rule apply that, although the relationship of parents and children may have been established by adoption, they cannot contract matrimony with one another, and even if the adoption has been dissolved, the same rule of law will continue to apply; so that I could not take as a wife a woman who sustains to me the relationship of daughter or granddaughter by adoption, even if I have emancipated her.

(60) This rule also applies to persons related in the collateral degree, but not to the same extent.

(61) Marriage is indeed prohibited between brother and sister, whether they are born of the same father or mother or merely of one of these parents in common; but although legal marriage cannot take place between me and my sister by adoption as long as the adoption continues to exist, still if the adoption is dissolved by emancipation I can marry her, and if I should be emancipated, no impediment to the marriage will exist.

(62) It is lawful for a man to marry the daughter of his brother, and this first became customary when the Divine Claudius married Agrippina, his brother's daughter, but it is not lawful for anyone to marry his sister's daughter, and this rule is stated in the Imperial Constitutions. It is likewise illegal for a man to take as his wife his paternal or maternal aunt.

(63) Moreover, I cannot marry my former mother-in-law or daughter-in-law, or my step-daughter or step-mother. We make use of the word "former," because if the marriage by which affinity of this kind was established is still in existence, there is another reason why I cannot marry her, for a woman cannot marry two men, nor can a man have two wives.

(64) Therefore, if anyone should contract a nefarious and incestuous marriage he is considered to have

neither a wife nor children, hence the issue of such a union are considered to have a mother but no father, and for this reason are not subject to paternal authority, but resemble children whom the mother has conceived through promiscuous intercourse; and they, in like manner, are understood to have no father, as he also is uncertain; therefore they are ordinarily called illegitimate children, either from the Greek word meaning conceived indiscriminately, or because they are children without any father.

(65) It sometimes happens that children when born are not under the control of their fathers but are afterwards subjected to their authority.

(66) For instance, under the *Lex Ælia Sentia*, if a Latin, after having married, should have a son who is a Latin by a Latin mother, or who is a Roman citizen by a Roman mother, he will not have him under his control; but if he should afterwards obtain the right of Roman citizenship by the evidence required by law, his son will, at the same time, be brought under his power.

(67) Likewise, if a Roman citizen should marry a Latin or a foreign woman through ignorance, believing that she was a Roman citizen, and should have a son, the latter will not be under his control because he will not be a Roman citizen, but either a Latin or a foreigner; that is to say, he will belong to the same condition as his mother, as no child follows the condition of its father unless the right to legal marriage existed between its parents; but by a Decree of the Senate it is permitted to prove the cause of error, and in this way the wife and the son will both obtain Roman citizenship, and the son will, from that time, begin to be under the control of his father. The same rule applies where a Roman citizen marries a woman belonging to the class of the *dediticii*, except that the wife does not become a Roman citizen.

(68) Moreover, if a female Roman citizen should, through mistake, marry a foreigner under the impression that he was a Roman citizen, she will be permitted to prove the cause of error, and in this way both her son and her husband will obtain Roman citizenship, and, at the same time, the son will begin to be subject to the authority of the father. The same rule also applies if the woman marries a foreigner as a Latin under the terms of the *Lex Ælia Sentia*, as provision for a case of this kind is specially made by the Decree of the Senate. Again, the same rule applies to a certain extent if she should marry a man belonging to the class of the *dediticii*, as being either a Roman citizen or a Latin under the provisions of the *Lex Ælia Sentia*, except that her husband belonging to the class of the *dediticii* remains in the same condition, and therefore his son, although he becomes a Roman citizen, is not subjected to the authority of his father.

(69) Likewise, if a Latin woman should marry a foreigner believing him to be a Latin in accordance with the *Lex Ælia Sentia*, on the birth of a son she can, under the Decree of the Senate, prove the cause of her error, and then all the parties will become Roman citizens, and the son will pass under the control of his father.

(70) The same rule has been established where a Latin man marries a woman who is a foreigner under the impression that she is either a Latin or a Roman citizen, with a view to taking advantage of the *Lex Ælia Sentia*.

(71) Moreover, a Roman citizen who thinks that he is a Latin, and for this reason marries a Latin woman, will be permitted to prove the cause of his error in case of the birth of a son, just as if he had married his wife under the provisions of the *Lex Ælia Sentia*. Likewise, those who being Roman citizens think that they are foreigners and marry foreign women, are permitted by the Decree of the Senate, on the birth of a son, to prove the cause of their error; and this having been done, the wife becomes a Roman citizen, and the son not only obtains to Roman citizenship but also is brought under the authority of his father.

(72) Whatever we have said with reference to a son is also understood to apply to a daughter.

(73) And, so far as proving the cause of the error is concerned, as nothing with reference to this was provided by the Decree of the Senate, it makes no difference how old the son or daughter may be unless he or she should be a Latin; because it was also declared by the *Lex Ælia Sentia* that in this case if the son or daughter is less than a year old the cause cannot be proved. It has not escaped my observation that it was stated in a rescript of the Divine Hadrian, with reference to the proof of the cause of the error, that the child must be a year old, but the right did not seem to be of general application, as the Emperor issued the rescript under peculiar circumstances.

(74) If a foreigner, believing himself to be a Roman citizen, married a woman who is a Roman citizen, the question arises whether he could prove the cause of error under the Decree of the Senate. He could not do so, however, as this privilege is not granted by the Decree of the Senate to a foreigner, even though he, being mistaken, should have married a Roman citizen, unless this right was especially conferred upon him. But, when a foreigner married a woman who is a Roman citizen, and after a son was born, he obtained Roman citizenship in some other way, then when the question arose whether he could prove the cause of error, the Emperor Antoninus stated in a rescript that he could do so, just as if he had remained a foreigner; from which we gather that even a foreigner can prove the cause of error.

(75) From what we have said, it is apparent that where either a Roman citizen marries a foreign woman or a foreigner marries a woman who is a Roman citizen, the child born of the union is a foreigner. If, however, a marriage of this kind should have been contracted through mistake, the defect can be remedied in the manner which we explained above. But if no error took place, and the parties, aware of their condition, contracted marriage, the defect of an union of this kind can, under no circumstances, be remedied.

(76) We, however, are speaking of persons who have not the right to contract legal marriage; for, otherwise, if a Roman citizen should marry a foreign woman with whom civil marriage can be contracted as is stated above, a legal marriage takes place, and a son born to the parties is a Roman citizen, and will become subject to the authority of his father.

(77) Likewise, if a female Roman citizen should marry a foreigner who is entitled to contract a legal marriage, and a son is born, he will be an alien, and the lawful son of his father, just as if he had begotten him with a foreign woman. At the present time, however, by a Decree of the Senate enacted at the instance of the Divine Hadrian, even if the right of civil marriage did not exist between a woman who is a Roman citizen and a foreigner, the child born of the union is the lawful son of his father.

(78) What we have stated, however, with reference to a female Roman citizen marrying a foreigner, and their issue being an alien, is derived from the *Lex Minicia*, by which it is provided that where a child is born of an unequal marriage it follows the condition of the parent of inferior rank. On the other hand, it is provided by the same law that if a Roman citizen should marry a foreign woman with whom the right of legal marriage did not exist, the child born of this union will be a foreigner. The *Lex Minicia* was not especially necessary in a case of this kind, for, without this law, the child would have followed the condition of its mother, as this is the rule by the Law of Nations, among those between whom the right of civil marriage does not exist. This provision of the law which directs that the issue of a Roman citizen and a foreign woman shall be a foreigner seems to be superfluous, for even without this law this would be the case under the Law of Nations.

(79) Moreover, to such an extent does this rule apply that the issue of the marriage between a Roman citizen and a Latin woman follows the condition of its mother, for in the *Lex Minicia* not only are alien nations and peoples designated as "foreigners," but also those who are called Latins; and it also refers to other Latins who had their own peoples and states, and were included under the head of foreigners.

(80) On the other hand, by the same rule, the son of a Latin father and a mother who was a Roman citizen, whether the marriage was contracted under the provisions of the *Lex Ælia Sentia* or not, is born a Roman citizen. There were some authorities, however, who held that where a marriage was contracted under the *Lex Ælia Sentia* the child was born a Latin; for the reason that in this instance the right of legal marriage was conferred upon the parties by the *Lex Ælia Sentia et Junia*, and legal marriage always has the effect of giving the child the same condition as its father; for, if the marriage were otherwise contracted, the child, by the Law of Nations, would follow the condition of its mother, and for this reason would be a Roman citizen. We, however, make use of the rule established by the Decree of the Senate at the instance of the Divine Hadrian, by which it is declared that, under all circumstances, the child of a Latin man and a woman who is a Roman citizen is born a Roman citizen.

(81) In conformity with these provisions, the said Decree of the Senate, enacted at the instance of the Divine Hadrian, also prescribes that the issue of a Latin man and a foreign woman, as well as that of a foreign man and a Latin woman, follows the condition of the mother.

(82) The result of this is that the child of a female slave and a freeman is, by the Law of Nations, born a slave; and, on the other hand, the child of a free woman and a male slave is free by birth.

(83) We should note, however, whether any law or enactment having the force of law, in any case changes the rule of the Law of Nations.

(84) For example, under the Claudian Decree of the Senate, a woman who is a Roman citizen and has sexual intercourse with a slave belonging to another with the consent of his master will, in accordance with the agreement, remain free herself while she gives birth to a slave; for the contract entered into between her and the owner of the slave is declared to be valid by the Decree of the Senate. Afterwards, however, the Divine Hadrian, influenced by the injustice and impropriety of the law, restored the rule of the Law of Nations, so that as the woman herself remains free, her child is also born free.

(85) Likewise, by another law, children born of a female slave and a freeman could be born free; for it is provided by the said law that if anyone should have sexual intercourse with a female slave belonging to another and whom he believed to be free, and any male children should be born, they will be free; but any female children would be the property of him to whom their mother, the female slave, belonged. In this case, however, the Divine Vespasian, influenced by the impropriety of the law, restored the rule of the Law of Nations, so that, in every instance, even if female children should be born, they will become the slaves of the person who owned their mother.

(86) Another section of the same law remains in force, namely, that any children born to a free woman and a slave who is the property of another, and whom she knew to be a slave, are born slaves; hence among those who are not subject to this law, the child follows the condition of its mother[1] by the Law of Nations, and on this account is free.

(87) In those cases, however, where the child follows the condition of the mother and not that of the father, it is perfectly clear that it is not subject to the authority of his father, even though the latter may be a Roman citizen; and therefore we stated above that in certain instances where a marriage which was not lawful was contracted through a mistake, the Senate could intervene and remedy the defect of the marriage, and in this way generally bring it about that the son should be subjected to the authority of his father.

(88) If a female slave should conceive by a Roman citizen and afterwards, having been manumitted, should

---

[1] This rule, as expressed in the maxim: "*Partus sequitur ventrem*," has always been recognized. It not only applied to slaves, but also to illegitimate children, with reference to whom it is everywhere in force to-day. — ed.

become a Roman citizen and a child should be born, although the latter would be a Roman citizen like its father, it would still not be under the control of the latter, for the reason that it was not conceived in lawful marriage, and because an union of this kind is not declared to be legal by any decree of the Senate.

(89) The decision which was made that if a female slave should conceive by a Roman citizen and then, after having been manumitted, her child should be born free, is in accordance with natural law, for children who are illegitimately conceived assume their status at the time when they are born, and therefore, if they are born of a free woman, they will be free, nor does it make any difference by whom their mother conceived them while she was a female slave; but those who are lawfully conceived assume their status at the time of conception.

(90) Therefore, where a female citizen at Rome, who is pregnant at the time, is interdicted from fire and water,[1] and for this reason having become a foreigner, gives birth to a child; many authorities make a distinction, and are of the opinion that, as she conceived in lawful marriage, her child is born a Roman citizen, but if she conceived as the result of promiscuous intercourse, her child will be an alien.

(91) Likewise, where a woman who is a Roman citizen while pregnant, becomes a slave under the Claudian Decree of the Senate, for the reason that she had intercourse with a slave belonging to another, against the consent and protest of his master, many authorities make a distinction and hold that as the child was conceived in lawful marriage, it will be born a Roman citizen, but if it was conceived as the result of promiscuous intercourse, it will be born the slave of the person to whom his mother belongs.

(92) Again, if an alien woman should conceive as the result of promiscuous intercourse, and afterwards become a Roman citizen and bring forth a child, the latter will be a Roman citizen. If, however, she should conceive by an alien whom she married in accordance with foreign laws and customs, she will, under the terms of the Decree of the Senate enacted at the instance of the Divine Hadrian, be held to give birth to a Roman citizen, provided Roman citizenship has also been conferred upon the father.

(93) Where an alien has acquired Roman citizenship for himself and his children, the latter do not pass under the control of their father unless the Emperor should expressly cause them to do so; and this he only does when, after the case has been examined, he thinks that this would be advantageous to the children. He, moreover, makes a more diligent and minute investigation with reference to children who are under the age of puberty and absent; and this rule is set forth in an Edict of the Divine Hadrian.

(94) Likewise, where anyone with his wife, during her pregnancy, is presented with Roman citizenship, although the child, as we have mentioned above, is born a Roman citizen, he still does not pass under the control of his father; and this is stated in a rescript of the Divine Hadrian. For this reason if he knows that his wife is pregnant, and he petitions the Emperor for citizenship for himself and his wife, he should, at the same time, ask that his child shall be subjected to his authority.

(95) The rule is otherwise in the case of those who, together with their children, attain to Roman citizenship

---

[1] Prohibition of the use of water and fire was a death penalty introduced by Sylla in the *Lex Cornelia*. The person upon whom it was imposed being by its terms excluded from the enjoyment of the absolute necessaries of life, was certain to perish miserably if the sentence had been literally executed, which it never was, in reality. It operated, however, as a forfeiture of civil rights, and was avoided by voluntary exile. Certain limits were prescribed within which the privileges of citizenship could not be exercised; and if the guilty party remained, he became a social outcast with whom all ordinary intercourse was prohibited, and whose acts were void in law. Those who were convicted of capital crimes either took refuge in foreign countries, or changed their residence beyond the radius prescribed by the sentence, trusting to good fortune or the efforts of their friends to have it annulled, and their disabilities removed by legislation, which was usually effected in the *Comitia Centuriata* where the trial had taken place. Many distinguished Romans were subjected to the interdiction from fire and water, among them Cicero, who was, in this way, banished four hundred miles from Rome. — ed.

by the right of being Latins, for their children pass under their control.

(96) This right has been granted to certain foreign States, either by the Roman people, or by the Senate, or by the Emperor. The right of Latinity is either greater or less. Greater Latinity is that of those who are elected decurions or administer any honorable office or magistracy, and by this means obtain Roman citizenship. The lesser right of Latinity is where only those who administer the office of magistrate or any other honorable employment attain to Roman citizenship; and this difference is referred to in many Imperial rescripts.

(97) Not only as we have stated are natural children in our power, but also those whom we adopt.

(98) Adoption takes place in two ways; either by the authority of the people, or by the command of the magistrate, as for instance, of the Prætor.

(99) We adopt, by the authority of the people, those who are their own masters, which kind of adoption is called arrogation, for the reason that he who adopts is asked, that is to say, interrogated, whether he desires to have the person whom he intends to adopt as his lawful son; and he who is adopted is asked whether he is willing to have this done; and the assembled people are asked whether they direct this to take place. By the command of the magistrate we adopt those who are under the control of their parents, whether they are in the first degree of descendants, as a son or a daughter, or whether they belong to an inferior degree, as a grandson or a granddaughter, a great-grandson or a great-granddaughter.

(100) Adoption by the people can only take place at Rome; and the other usually takes place in the provinces before the governors of the same.

(101) The better opinion is that women cannot be adopted by the voice of the people; but women may be adopted in the tribunal of the Prætor at Rome, or in the provinces in the tribunal of the proconsul or the lieutenant.

(102) The adoption of a child under the age of puberty by the vote of the people was at one time forbidden, and at another permitted; but at present, by the Epistle of the Emperor Antoninus addressed to the pontiffs, it is allowed under certain conditions, if there seems to be good cause for the adoption. We can, however, adopt persons of any age in the tribunal of the Prætor at Rome, or in the provinces in that of the proconsul, or the lieutenant.

(103) It is a rule common to both kinds of adoption that persons who are incapable of begetting children, such as eunuchs, can adopt.

(104) Women, however, cannot in any way adopt other persons, for the reason that they cannot exercise authority even over their natural children.

(105) Likewise, if anyone adopts another, either by the vote of the people, or by the consent of the Prætor or the governor of a province, he can give the son whom he has adopted in adoption to another.

(106) It is a question, however, with reference to both forms of adoption, whether a person can adopt another who is older than himself.

(107) It is peculiar to that kind of adoption which takes place by the vote of the people, that if he who gives himself to be arrogated has children under his control, he will not only himself be subject to the authority of the arrogator, but his children will also be under the control of the latter, as grandchildren.

(108) Now let us consider those persons who are in our hand, which right is also peculiar to Roman citizens.

(109) Both males and females are under the authority of another, but females alone are placed in the hands.

(110) Formerly this ceremony was performed in three different ways, namely, by use, by confarreation, and by coemption.

(111) A woman came into the hand of her husband by use when she had lived with him continuously for a year after marriage; for the reason that she was obtained by usucaption, as it were, through possession for the term of a year, and passed into the family of her husband where she occupied the position of a daughter. Hence it is provided by the Law of the Twelve Tables that if a woman was unwilling to be placed in the hand of her husband in this way, she should every year absent herself for three nights, and in this manner interrupt the use during the said year; but all of this law has been partly repealed by legal enactments, and partly abolished by disuse.

(112) Women are placed in the hand of their husbands by confarreation, through a kind of sacrifice made to Jupiter Farreus, in which a cake is employed, from whence the ceremony obtains its name; and in addition to this, for the purpose of performing the ceremony, many other things are done and take place, accompanied with certain solemn words, in the presence of ten witnesses. This law is still in force in our time, for the principal flamens, that is to say, those of Jupiter, Mars, and Quirinus, as well as the chief of the sacred rites, are exclusively selected from persons born of marriages celebrated by confarreation. Nor can these persons themselves serve as priests without marriage by confarreation.

(113) In marriage by coemption, women become subject to their husbands by mancipation, that is to say by a kind of fictitious sale; for the man purchases the woman who comes into his hand in the presence of not less than five witnesses, who must be Roman citizens over the age of puberty, and also of a balance-holder.

(114) By this act of sale a woman can not only make a coemption to her husband but also to a stranger, that is to say, the sale takes place either on account of marriage or by way of trust; for a woman who disposes of herself in this way to her husband for the purpose of occupying the place of his daughter is said to have done so on account of matrimony; but where she does this for some other purpose, either to a husband or to a stranger, as for instance in order to avoid a guardianship, she is said to have made a coemption by way of trust.

(115) The method by which this is done is as follows: If a woman wishes to get rid of her present guardians and obtain another in their stead, she makes this disposal of herself with their consent; and then the other party to the sale sells her again to him to whom she wishes to be her guardian, and he manumits her by the ceremony of the wand of the Prætor, and by this means becomes her guardian, and is designated a fiduciary guardian, as will hereafter appear.

(115a) Formerly a fiduciary coemption took place for the purpose of acquiring power to make a will, for women, with some exceptions, did not then have testamentary capacity unless they had made fictitious sales of this kind, and after having been resold, were manumitted; but the Senate, at the suggestion of the Divine Hadrian, abolished this necessity of making a fictitious sale.

(115b) Even if the woman makes a fiduciary sale of herself to her husband, she nevertheless occupies the place of his daughter; for if a wife comes into the hand of her husband for any reason whatsoever, it has been decided that she enjoys the rights of a daughter.

(116) It remains for us to explain what persons are subject to mancipation.

(117) All children of either the male or female sex who are under the control of their father can be mancipated by him in the same way as that in which slaves can be mancipated.

(118) The same rule of law applies to those persons who are in the hand of others, and they can be mancipated in the same way by those to whom they have been sold, just as children may be mancipated by their father; and while she who is married to the purchaser may only occupy the place of his daughter; still, though she may not be married to him, nor occupy the place of his daughter, she can still be mancipated by him.

(118a) Generally speaking, mancipation takes place either by parents or by those who obtain possession by coemption, when the parents and the so-called purchasers desire to release the persons from their authority, as will appear more clearly hereafter.

(119) Mancipation, as we have mentioned above, is a kind of fictitious sale, and the law governing it is peculiar to Roman citizens. The ceremony is as follows: After not less than five witnesses (who must be Roman citizens above the age of puberty) have been called together, as well as another person of the same condition who holds a brazen balance in his hand and is styled the "balance holder," the so-called purchaser, holding a piece of bronze in his hands, says: "I declare that this man belongs to me by my right as a Roman citizen, and let him be purchased by me with this piece of bronze, and bronze balance." Then he strikes the scales with the piece of bronze, and gives it to the so-called vendor as purchase money.

(120) In this manner both slaves and free persons are mancipated, as well as such animals as are subject to sale, among which are included oxen, horses, mules, and asses, as well as urban and rustic estates; for instance, Italian lands are usually disposed of in the same manner.

(121) The sale of land differs from the mancipation of other things, in that both slaves and free persons, as well as animals subject to mancipation cannot be disposed of in this way unless they are present; as it is necessary for him who acquires the object by mancipation to be able to grasp it with his hands, and the ceremony is designated mancipation because the property is seized with the hands. Lands, however, are usually mancipated at a distance.

(122) A piece of brass and a balance are employed for the reason that in former times only brazen money was in circulation, and this consisted of asses, double asses, half asses, and quarter asses; nor was any gold or silver coin in circulation, as we learn by the Law of the Twelve Tables. The value of the purchasing power of these coins was not estimated by their number, but by their weight; hence an as consisted of a pound of bronze, a double as of two pounds (whence it derived its name, which is still retained), while the half-asses and quarter-asses were estimated by their respective parts of a pound. Therefore, in former times, those who paid out money to anyone did not count it but weighed it, and the slaves who were permitted to disburse money were called "weighers."

(123) If anyone should ask what is the difference between coemption and mancipation, the reply is that the first ceremony does not reduce the party to a servile condition; but persons of either sex mancipated by parents or others are reduced to the condition of slaves, to such an extent that they cannot take either an estate or a legacy under the will of the party by whom they have been mancipated, unless they have been ordered to be free by the terms of the same will; just as the law is with reference to the persons of slaves. The reason for this distinction is clear, as the words used by parents and so-called purchasers are the same as those employed in the mancipation of slaves, but in the coemption of women this is not the case.

(124) Let us now consider in what ways those who are subject to the authority of another are released from it.

(125) And, in the first place, let us examine those who are under the power of others.

(126) We can understand from what has been stated above with reference to the manumission of slaves, how they are freed from the power of their masters.

(127) Children who are under the authority of their father become their own masters at his death. The following distinction, however, must be made, namely: When a father dies, his sons and his daughters always become independent; but when a grandfather dies, his grandsons and granddaughters do not, under all circumstances, become independent, but only where, after the death of their grandfather, they do not again pass under the control of their father. Therefore, if at the time of the death of their grandfather their father was living and was under the control of his father, they pass under the control of their father after the death of their grandfather; but if, at the time of the death of their grandfather, their father was either dead or had been released from the control of his father, then the grandchildren, for the reason that they cannot pass under his control, will become their own masters.

(128) As a person who, on account of the commission of some crime, has been interdicted from water and fire under the *Lex Cornelia*, loses his Roman citizenship, and for this reason is excluded from the number of Roman citizens, his children cease to be under his control, just as if he were dead; for reason does not permit that a person of the condition of an alien should have a Roman citizen subject to this authority. In like manner, if anyone who is in the power of his father is interdicted from water and fire, he ceases to be under his control, as it is not reasonable that a man of the condition of an alien should be under the parental authority of a Roman citizen.

(129) Even if the father should be taken captive by the enemy and thereby become the enemy's slave, nevertheless, his authority over his children remains in abeyance under the law of *postliminium*, by which those who were captured by the enemy and return, recover all their former rights; and, therefore, if he should return, he will have his children in his power. If, however, he should die while in captivity, his children will become their own masters; but it may be doubted whether this took place at the time when the father died in the hands of the enemy, or at the time when he was captured. Likewise, if the son himself, or a grandson, should be taken captive by the enemy, we say that the authority of the father remains in abeyance on account of the law of *postliminium*.

(130) Moreover, male children are released from paternal authority if they are installed priests of Jupiter; and females, if they are chosen Vestal Virgins.

(131) In former times also, when the Roman people were accustomed to establish colonies in Latin territory, sons, who, by the order of their father, placed their names upon the roll of the Latin colony, ceased to be under the control of their father, because they became citizens of another State.

(132) Again, children cease to be under parental authority by means of mancipation. A son, however, by three mancipations, and other children either of the male or female sex by a single mancipation, are released from parental authority; for the Law of the Twelve Tables only mentions three mancipations with reference to a son, as follows: "If a father sells his son three times, let him be free from the control of his father." This ceremony takes place in the following manner. The father sells his son to a third party, and the latter manumits him by the wand of the prætor, and by doing so, he is restored to the control of his father; and the latter then sells him a second time, either to the same person or to another (but it is customary to sell him to the same person); and he again manumits him in the same way, and by this act the son is again placed in the power of his father; and the father then sells him a third time, either to the same person or to another (it is customary, however, for him to be sold to the same person), and by virtue of this sale he ceases to be under the control of his father, even though he has not yet been manumitted, but still remains in the condition of one who has been sold.

(133) It should, however, be noted that one who has a son, and by him a grandson under his control, has full power to release his son from his control, and still to retain authority over his grandson; or, on the other hand, he has the right to manumit his grandson, or to render both parties their own masters. We understand

that this rule also applies to great-grandsons.

(134) Again, parents also lose their authority over their children by giving them in adoption. Where a son is given in adoption, three sales are required, and two intervening manumissions must take place, as is customary when the father releases a son from his authority, in order that he may become his own master. Then, the son is either resold to the father and he who adopts him claims him as his son before the prætor; and, if his natural father does not claim him, he is given by the prætor to the party who claims him by adoption; or, if he is not sold again to his father, he who adopts him claims him from him to whom he was sold for the third time. It is, however, more convenient for him to be resold to his natural father. In the case of other offspring of either sex, one sale is sufficient, whether a resale is made to the natural father or not. The same ceremony ordinarily takes place in the provinces, in the presence of the governor.

(135) When a grandson is conceived after the first or second sale of a son, although he may not be born until after the third sale of his father, he, nevertheless, remains under the control of his grandfather, and may be emancipated, or given in adoption by him. A grandson, however, who is begotten after the third sale of a son, is not born under the control of his grandfather; but Labeo holds that he is born under the control of him to whom his father was sold. We, however, make use of the following rule, that as long as its father is in mancipation the right of the child remains in suspense; and if the father should be manumitted, the child will pass under his authority; but if he should die before the ceremony of mancipation has been completed, the child will become its own master.

(135a) We understand that the same rule applies to the case of a grandson who has been mancipated once, as it does to that of a son who has been mancipated three times, for, as we stated above, what three sales accomplished with reference to a son, one accomplishes in the case of a grandson.

(136) A woman placed in the hand of her husband by confarreation is not, for this reason, at present, released from paternal authority unless the ceremony of coemption has been performed; for it is provided by the *Lex Asinia Antistia* enacted during the Consulate of Cornelius Maximus and Tubero, with reference to priestesses of Jupiter being in the hand of their husbands as far as relates to the sacred rites; but in all other respects they are considered as not being under such restraint. Where, however, women are placed in the hand of their husbands by coemption, they are released from parental control; and it makes no difference whether they are placed in the hand of their husbands, or in that of strangers; although those alone are considered to occupy the place of daughters who are placed in the hand of their husbands.

(137) Women placed in the hand of their husbands by coemption cease to be subject to this authority in the same way as daughters under the control of their father; that is to say, either by the death of him in whose power they are, or because he has been interdicted from water and fire.

(137a) They also cease to be in the hand of their husbands by remancipation; and if emancipated after a single sale they become their own mistresses. A woman who has concluded a coemption with a stranger by way of trust, can compel him to sell her again to anyone whom she may select; but one who has been sold to her husband, in whose hand she is, cannot compel him to do so, any more than a daughter can compel her father, even though she may be an adopted daughter. A woman, however, can, by serving notice of repudiation, force her husband to release her, just as if she had never been married.

(138) As persons who have been sold in this way are considered to occupy the position of slaves, if they should be manumitted either by the prætor, or by enrollment in the census, or by will, they become their own masters.

(139) In this instance, however, the *Lex Ælia Sentia* does not apply. Therefore, we do not require the party who manumits, or the one who is manumitted, to be of any particular age; and no attention is paid to

whether the party granting the manumission has either a patron or a creditor; and not even the number prescribed by the *Lex Fufia Caninia* is considered with reference to persons of this description.

(140) But even if the party having possession of the one who is sold should be unwilling, the latter can obtain his freedom by being enrolled on the register of the census; except in the case of one whom his father has mancipated under the condition that he should be again sold to him; for, in this instance, the father is considered to have reserved, to a certain extent, his own power for himself which he received by mancipation. And, indeed, he is not said to have received his freedom by enrollment on the register of the census, against the consent of the party who holds him in mancipation, if his father gave him up as the result of a noxal action; for instance, where his father has been condemned on account of a theft committed by his son and has surrendered him by mancipation to the plaintiff, for then the plaintiff holds him instead of the payment of a sum of money.

(141) In conclusion, we observe that no insulting act should be committed by us against persons whom we hold in mancipation; otherwise, we shall be liable to a suit for injury committed. And, indeed, men should not be retained for any length of time in this condition, but, for the most part, as a matter of form, and only for an instant, unless the parties are mancipated on account of a noxal action.

(142) Let us now pass to another division. For persons who are neither subject to paternal authority, nor are in the hand, nor are held in mancipation by another, may still be under guardianship or curatorship, or may be free from either of these restrictions. Let us first consider those who may be under guardianship and curatorship; for then we shall understand who the other persons are who are subject to neither of these restraints.

(143) And, first, let us examine those who are under guardianship.

(144) Parents are permitted to appoint testamentary guardians for their children who are subject to their authority, who are under the age of puberty, and of the male sex; and for those of the female sex, no matter what their age may be, and even if they are married; for the ancients required women, even if they were of full age, to remain under guardianship on account of the levity of their disposition.

(145) Therefore, if anyone appoints a guardian for his son and daughter by will, and both should arrive at the age of puberty, the son will cease to have a guardian, but the daughter will nevertheless remain subject to guardianship; for it is only under the *Lex Julia et Papia* that women are released from guardianship by the birth of children. Those whom we speak of do not include Vestal Virgins, whom the ancients desired to be free on account of the honor of the priesthood; hence this was provided by the Law of the Twelve Tables.

(146) We can, however, only appoint testamentary guardians for grandsons and granddaughters, if after our death they do not again pass under the control of their father. Therefore, if my son was under my control at the time of my death, my grandsons by him cannot have a guardian appointed by my will, although they were under my control at the time; for the reason that by my death they were placed under the control of their father.

(147) As in many other instances posthumous children are considered as already born, in this case also it has been decided that testamentary guardians can be appointed for posthumous children, as well as for those previously born; provided, however, that if born during our lifetime, they would have been subject to our authority. We can also appoint them our heirs, but it is not permitted to appoint posthumous strangers heirs.

(148) A testamentary guardian can be appointed for a wife who is in the hand of the testator; just as if she

were a daughter; and, likewise, one may be appointed for a daughter-in-law who is in the hand of a son, just as if she were a granddaughter.

(149) A guardian can most properly be appointed in the following manner, namely: "I appoint Lucius Titius guardian of my children." If, however, the appointment was made as follows: "Let Lucius Titius be the guardian of my children and my wife," it is understood to be legally made.

(150) The choice of a guardian may be left to a wife who is in the hand of the testator, that is to say, he can permit her to select any guardian whom she may choose, as follows: "I give to Titia, my wife, the selection of her guardian." In this instance, the wife is permitted to appoint a guardian either for the administration of all the property, or only of one or two things.

(151) Moreover, the choice may be granted either absolutely or with restrictions.

(152) It is ordinarily granted absolutely in the way that we have mentioned above. Where it is granted with restrictions, the following form is usually employed: "I grant to Titia, my wife, only one choice of a guardian"; or: "I only grant her the right to make two selections."

(153) These privileges of selection are very different, for she who has an unlimited right of choice, can choose a guardian twice or three times, or oftener; but she who has a limited right of choice cannot make more than one if only one is granted; and if only two are granted she has no right to make more than two selections.

(154) Guardians who are especially appointed by will are called "dative"; and those to whom the selection of a guardian is left are called "optative."

(155) By the Law of the Twelve Tables the nearest agnates become the guardians of children for whom no guardian was appointed by will, and they are styled legal guardians.

(156) Agnates are blood relatives through the male sex, for instance, through the father; as a brother having the same father, the son of a brother, or a grandson by him, and also a paternal uncle and his son and grandson. Those who are related through the female sex are not agnates, but cognates, according to natural law. Therefore, agnation does not exist between a maternal uncle and a son or a sister, but cognation does. In like manner, the son of my maternal aunt, or the sister of my mother, is not my agnate, but my cognate; and, on the other hand, I am related to him by the same rule, because children follow the family of their father, and not that of their mother.

(157) Formerly, however, according to the Law of the Twelve Tables, females had agnates as legal guardians, but afterwards the *Lex Claudia*, which abolished the guardianship of agnates, so far as females were concerned, was enacted, and therefore a male child under the age of puberty has his brother, who is above the age of puberty, or his paternal uncle, as his guardian; but a female child cannot have a guardian of this kind.

(158) The right of agnation is extinguished by the loss of civil rights, but the right of cognation is not affected by it, for the reason that a civil law can abrogate civil rights, but cannot extinguish natural rights.

(159) The loss of civil rights is a change of former condition, and this takes place in three ways; it is either greatest, or less, which some call intermediate, or least.

(160) The greatest loss of civil rights occurs when anyone forfeits at the same time both his citizenship and his freedom, which happens to those who are not inscribed on the register of the census, and are in consequence ordered to be sold; which rule has for some time been abolished by disuse. Under the terms of the *Lex Ælia Sentia, dediticii* are liable to the same penalty for violation of its provisions if they have

established their domicile in the City of Rome. It also takes place where, under the Claudian Decree of the Senate, free women become the slaves of the owners of other slaves with whom they have cohabited against the consent and protest of their masters.

(161) Less, or intermediate, loss of civil rights occurs when citizenship is forfeited but freedom is retained, which happens when anyone is interdicted from fire and water.

(162) The least loss of civil rights results when both citizenship and freedom are retained, but a man's domestic condition is altered; which happens to those who are adopted, as well as to women subject to coemption, and also in the case of those who are given in mancipation and are afterwards manumitted; so that as often as anyone is mancipated, or remancipated, or manumitted, he suffers a loss of civil rights.

(163) The right of agnation is extinguished not only by the two greater losses of civil rights but also by the least; and therefore if a father should emancipate one of two children, neither can be the guardian of the other by the right of agnation after his death.

(164) When agnates have a right to guardianship, all of them are not entitled to that right at once, but only those in the nearest degree.

(165) By the same law of the Twelve Tables, the guardianship of freedwomen and freedmen under the age of puberty belongs to their patrons and the children of the latter. This kind of guardianship is also styled legal, not because special provision is made for it by this law, but for the reason that this has been accepted by interpretation just as if it had been expressly stated in the words of the statute; for as the law directed that the estates of freedmen and freedwomen who died intestate should belong to their patrons and the children of the latter, the ancient authorities held that the law intended that they should be entitled to their guardianship because it ordered that agnates whom it called to the succession should also be guardians.

IX. CONCERNING FIDUCIARY GUARDIANSHIP.

(166) As in the case of patrons, another kind of guardianship which is also designated legal, has been established. For, if anyone should give in mancipation to another, under the condition that he would remancipate him to himself, either a son or a grandson by that son, who is under the age of puberty, or a daughter or a granddaughter by a son, and their descendants, whether they have arrived at the age of puberty or not; and he should manumit them after they have been remancipated, he will become their legal guardian.

(166a) There are other kinds of guardianship which are styled fiduciary, that is to say, such as we are entitled to for the reason that a free person has been mancipated by us, or by a relative, or by a party to coemption and afterwards has been manumitted.

(167) The guardianship of Latins of both sexes who are under the age of puberty does not invariably belong to those who manumit them, but to those to whom they belonged by quiritarian right before their manumission. Therefore, if a female slave who belonged to you by quiritarian right, but who was mine by bonitarian right, should be manumitted by me alone without your taking part in the ceremony, she would become a Latin, and her property will belong to me; but you will have the right to her guardianship, as provision for this is made by the *Lex Junia*. Hence, if the said slave should be made a Latin by one who had both the bonitarian and quiritarian rights, her property as well as her guardianship will belong to him.

(168) Agnates, patrons, and those who manumit free persons are permitted to transfer the guardianship of a female ward to another in court; it is not, however, permitted to transfer the guardianship of male wards, for the reason that this is not considered onerous, as it terminates at the age of puberty.

(169) He to whom a guardian is thus transferred is designated a cessionary guardian.

(170) If he dies, or loses his civil rights, the guardianship reverts to the party who transferred it; and if the latter should be either dead or have forfeited his civil rights, the guardianship will leave the cessionary guardian and pass to the one next in degree to the party who transferred it.

(171) So far as agnates are concerned, however, cessionary guardianship does not at present exist, as guardianship of female wards by agnates was abolished by the *Lex Claudia*.[1]

(172) Certain authorities hold that fiduciary guardians also have no right to transfer their guardianship, as they themselves have voluntarily assumed the burdens of the same; but, although this has been decided, still in the case of a parent who have given either a daughter, granddaughter, or a great-granddaughter in mancipation to another under the condition that she shall be again mancipated to him, and, this having been done, he manumits her, the same rule should not apply; as he is considered a legal guardian, and the same privilege should be granted to him as to a patron.

(173) Moreover, by a Decree of the Senate, women are permitted to demand another guardian to take the place of one who is absent; and this having been granted, the first guardian ceases to hold his office, nor does it make any difference how far he may be from home.

(174) An exception, however, is made in the case of an absent patron, as a freedwoman is not permitted in this instance to demand another guardian.

(175) Again, in the same class with the patron we have a parent who has obtained legal guardianship from the fact that he has manumitted his daughter, granddaughter, or great-granddaughter, who has previously been remancipated by himself. His sons, however, are only considered to occupy the places of fiduciary guardians, but those of a patron obtain the same guardianship which their father possessed.

(176) Sometimes, however, it is permitted to demand a guardian to take the place of an absent patron; as for instance, where an estate is to be entered upon.

(177) The Senate decreed that the same rule should apply to the son of a patron who was himself a ward.

(178) For by the *Lex Julia*, enacted for the purpose of regulating marriages, a female who is under the legal guardianship of a ward is permitted to demand a guardian from the Prætor of the City for the purpose of constituting her dowry.

(179) For the son of a patron, even if he is under the age of puberty, becomes the guardian of a freedwoman, although he cannot perform any legal act, as he is not permitted to do anything without the authority of his guardian.

(180) Likewise, if any female is subject to the legal guardianship of a person who is insane, or dumb, she is permitted by the Decree of the Senate to demand a guardian for the purpose of constituting her dowry.

(181) In these instances, it is clear that the patron or the patron's son is unquestionably entitled to the guardianship.

(182) Moreover, the Senate decreed that, if the guardian of a male or female ward was suspected of maladministration, and was removed from the guardianship; or if he should be excused for some good reason, and another guardian be appointed in his stead; after this has been done, the former guardian shall

---

[1] Prior to the enactment of the *Lex Claudia*, the *res mancipi* of a woman under the tutelary control of agnates, were not subject to usucaption, unless the transfer had previously been sanctioned by her guardian. — ed.

lose the guardianship.

(183) All of these provisions are observed both at Rome and in the provinces, but at Rome application for the appointment of a guardian should be made to the Prætor, and in the provinces to the governor.

(184) Formerly, when the ancient mode of procedure was in use, a guardian was appointed for another reason, namely, where a suit was about to be brought between the guardian and the woman, or the ward; since because the guardian could not grant authority in his own case, another guardian was appointed by whom the legal proceedings were instituted; and he was called a prætorian guardian, because he was appointed by the Urban Prætor. Some authorities, however, think that, after the ancient mode of procedure was abolished, this method of appointing a guardian became obsolete, but it is held by others that it is still the practice where an action is to be brought.

(185) If there should be no lawful guardian for a person, one is appointed for him under the *Lex Atilia*, in the City of Rome by the Urban Prætor and a majority of the tribunes of the people, who is styled an "Atilian guardian"; and in the provinces he is appointed by the governor under the *Lex Julia et Titia*.

(186) Hence if a guardian is appointed of anyone by will under a condition, or from a certain day, a guardian can be appointed while the condition is pending, or before the time arrives. Likewise, if a guardian should be appointed absolutely, a guardian can be demanded under these laws, so long as no heir appears, and he will cease to hold his office as guardian when the one appointed by will acquires the right to act.

(187) When a guardian is captured by the enemy, a substitute should be demanded under these laws, and he will cease to be guardian if the one who was taken captive should return, for, on his return, he will recover the guardianship by the law of *postliminium*.[1]

---

[1] The *jus postliminii* of the Civil Law, was the privilege enjoyed by prisoners of war of being, upon their return, restored to all the rights which they possessed previous to their captivity. By the effect of this legal fiction they were considered never to have been absent at all. "*Postliminium fingit eum qui captus est, in civitate semper fuisse.*" The rule was also applicable to real, but not to personal property, unless the latter was speedily retaken, and hence became readily susceptible of identification.

Under the Law of *Postliminium*, freemen were said to "return"; slaves to be "received"; and property to be "recovered". The *animus revertendi* was absolutely essential for the enjoyment of the rights which it conferred; if a prisoner of war was surrendered against his will, he was not entitled to them. Deserters were also excluded from participation in these advantages.

As long as a father was in captivity, the exercise of paternal control remained in abeyance, dating from the moment of capture, but the right again vested at the time of release. Marriage was voidable at the option of the parties interested; hence its suspension might be indefinitely prolonged. As a captive was temporarily *civiliter mortuus*, he could perform no legal act; but if he died while in the hands of the enemy his decease was presumed to have occurred in his own country, at the instant when he lost his liberty.

The general principles of the *jus postliminii* as laid down by the Romans, are recognized by all writers on international law. "*Per bellum capti, ubi manus hostium quocunqua modo evaserint, neque illis fide data sint obstricti, atque ad suos redierint, non modo pristinum statum, sed & omnia sua bona ac jura recuperent. Quod autem res attinet, quamdiu bellum durât, si hostibus iterum sint ereptæ sive per nos ipsos, sive per nostros cives aut milites, eas ad antiquos dominos redire par est, non immobiles tantum, sed & mobiles, modo liquido a nobis possint dignosci.*" (Pufendorf, *De Jure Naturæ et Gentium*, VIII, VI, 25.)

"It is therefore with reason that movables or booty are excepted from the right of *postliminium*, unless retaken from the enemy immediately after his capture of them; in which case, the proprietor neither finds a difficulty in recognising his effects, nor is presumed to have relinquished them." (Vattel, *The Law of Nations*, III, XIV, Page 393.)

"The right of postliminy is founded upon the duty of every State to protect the persons and property of its citizens against the operations of the enemy. When, therefore, a subject who has fallen into the hands of the enemy is rescued by his State, he is restored to his former rights and condition under his State. So, of the property of a subject recaptured from the enemy by his State; it is no more the property of the State than it was before it fell into the hands of the enemy; it must, therefore, be restored to its former owner. But if, by the well-established rules of public law, the title to the captured property has become vested in the enemy captor, the former owner cannot claim its restoration from the recaptor, because his original title has been extinguished." (Baker, First Steps in

(188) From this it is apparent how many different kinds of guardianships there are, and if we consider into how many classes they may be divided a long discussion will be required, for the ancient authorities entertained many doubts on this subject, and as we have examined it very carefully, both in the interpretation of the Edict and in the books which we have written on Quintus Mucius, it will be sufficient to state that certain jurists, for instance, Quintus Mucius, say that there are five classes, and others, like Servius Sulpicius, say that there are three; and still others, as Labeo, say that there are two; and others again, hold that there are as many kinds of guardianship as there are forms of the same.

(189) The law of all states declares that persons who have not reached puberty shall be under guardianship, because it is consonant with natural reason that one who is not of full age should be controlled by the guardianship of another. Indeed, there is scarcely any state in which parents are not permitted to appoint testamentary guardians for their children; although, as we have stated above, only Roman citizens are considered to have their children subject to paternal authority.

(190) There does not seem to be any good reason, however, why women of full age should be under guardianship, for the common opinion that because of their levity of disposition they are easily deceived, and it is only just that they should be subject to the authority of guardians, seems to be rather apparent than real; for women of full age transact their own affairs, but in certain cases, as a mere form, the guardian interposes his authority, and he is often compelled to give it by the Prætor, though he may be unwilling to do so.

(191) Therefore, a woman has no right of action under the guardianship against her guardian, but where guardians transact the business of their male and female wards, they must render an account of their guardianship in court, after their wards arrive at the age of puberty.

(192) The legal guardianship of patrons and parents are indeed understood to have a certain effect, for the reason that they cannot be forced to give their consent to the making of a will, to the alienation of property subject to mancipation, or to the assumption of obligations; unless there should be some urgent reason for the alienation of such property, or for undertaking the obligations aforesaid. These provisions have been made for their own benefit, in order that where the estates of persons who have died intestate belong to them, they can neither be excluded from them by will, nor have the estate come into their hands diminished in value on account of debts which have been incurred, or through the alienation of the most valuable part of the property.

(193) Women are not held in guardianship among foreigners as they are with us; still, they are generally, as it were, in a state of tutelage; as, for example, the law of the Bythinians directs that if a woman enters into a contract it must be authorized either by her husband or by a son who has reached the age of puberty.

(194) Moreover, a freeborn woman is released from guardianship if she is the mother of three children, and a freedwoman if she is the mother of four, and is under the legal guardianship of her patron. Those who have other kinds of guardians, as, for instance, Atilian[1] or Fiduciary, are released from guardianship by having three children.

(195) A freedwoman may, however, have a guardian appointed in several other ways; for example, where she has been manumitted by a woman, for then she must demand a guardian under the *Lex Atilia*, or in the

---

International Law, XXXV, Pages 364, 365.) — ed.

[1] The *tutor Atilianus* was appointed by the Prætor and the tribunes, under the *Lex Atilia*, when no guardian existed. This became necessary when there was a will, and the heir had not accepted the estate; or the designated guardian was incapacitated; or the testament from which he derived his authority was defective. — ed.

provinces under the *Lex Julia et Titia*, for she cannot be under the guardianship of a patroness.

(195a) Again, if she has been manumitted by a male and should enter into coemption with his consent, and then should be remancipated and manumitted, she ceases to have her patron as her guardian, and begins to have as a guardian the party by whom she was manumitted, who is designated a fiduciary guardian.

(195b) Likewise, if her patron, or his son, gives himself in adoption, a freedwoman should demand a guardian for herself either under the *Lex Atilia,* or the *Lex Julia et Titia.*

(195c) Likewise, under the same laws, a freedwoman should demand a guardian, where her patron dies and leaves no child of the male sex in the family.

(196) Again, when males reach the age of puberty they are released from guardianship. Sabinus and Cassius and our other preceptors hold that a person has arrived at the age of puberty who manifests this by the condition of his body, that is to say, if he is capable of procreation; but in the case of those who cannot show this condition, as for instance, eunuchs, their age should be considered to be that at which persons ordinarily reach puberty. Authorities belonging to another school, however, think that the age of puberty should be estimated by years; that is to say, they hold that a person has arrived at the age of puberty who has completed his thirteenth year. . . .[1]

(197) After having been released from guardianship, the affairs of a minor are administered by a curator until he reaches the age when he is qualified to transact his own business; and this rule is observed among foreign nations, as we have stated above.

(198) In cases of this kind, in the provinces, curators are usually appointed by the governor.

(199) In order to prevent the property of wards and persons who are under the charge of curators from being wasted or diminished in value by their guardians and curators, it is the duty of the Prætor to compel guardians and curators to furnish security for this purpose.

(200) This, however, is not always the case, for guardians appointed by will are not compelled to furnish security, because their fidelity and diligence have been approved by the testator himself; and curators who have not obtained their office by law, but who are appointed either by a consul, a Prætor, or the governor of a province, are, for the most part, not required to furnish security, for the reason that they have been chosen on account of their being considered sufficiently trustworthy.

SECOND COMMENTARY

(1) In the former Commentary we explained the law of persons; now let us consider the law of things, which either form part of our property or do not form part of it.

(2) The principal division of things is under two heads, namely, those that are subject to divine right, and those that are subject to human right.

(3) Things which are subject to divine right are such as are sacred and religious.

---

[1] Original manuscript illegible.

(4) Sacred things are those which are consecrated to the gods above; religious things are those which are dedicated to the spirits of the departed.

(5) That only is considered sacred which has been consecrated by the authority of the Roman people; that is to say, by a law or a Decree of the Senate enacted for that purpose.

(6) We, however, render things religious by our own will, when we bury a body in our own ground, provided we have a right to conduct the funeral of the deceased.

(7) Moreover, it has been held by the greater number of authorities that, in the provinces, ground does not become religious, as the ownership of the same belongs to the Roman people or to the Emperor, and we are only considered to have the possession or the usufruct of the same, and though it may not actually be religious, it is regarded as such. Likewise, in the provinces, while property which has not been consecrated by the authority of the Roman people is, properly speaking, not sacred, it is still considered as such.

(8) Holy places are those which are, to a certain extent, subject to divine right, as for instance, the walls and gates of a city.

(9) Again, things which are subject to divine right are not included among the possessions of any individual; that is to say, things which are subject to human right are, for the most part, included in the property of someone, they may, however, belong to no one; for an estate before any heir appears is without an owner, as a rule.

(10) Things subject to human right are either public or private.

(11) Things which are public are considered to be the property of no individual, for they are held to belong to the people at large; things which are private are the property of individuals.

(12) Moreover, some things are corporeal and others are incorporeal.

(13) Corporeal things are those that can be touched, as, for instance, land, a slave, clothing, gold, silver, and innumerable other objects.

(14) Incorporeal things are such as are not tangible, and are those consisting merely of rights, as, for instance, inheritances, usufructs, and obligations, no matter in what way the latter may have been contracted. For while corporeal things are included in an estate, and the crops gathered from land are corporeal, and what is due to us under the terms of some obligation is, for the most part, of a corporeal character, for example, land, slaves, money; still, the right of succession, the right of use and enjoyment, and the right of obligation, are incorporeal. To the same class belong rights attaching to urban and rustic estates, which are also called servitudes. Among these are the right to raise a building higher and obstruct the lights of a neighbor; the right to prevent a building from being raised, so that the lights of a neighbor may not be obstructed; the right to the use of streams, and to have rainwater fall upon the premises of another. . . . [1]

(14a) Things are either susceptible, or not susceptible of mancipation by sale.[2] Those susceptible of sale by

---

[1] Original manuscript illegible.

[2] The early Roman law divided property of every description into two classes, *res mancipi* and *res nec mancipi*. Ownership of the first could only be transferred by compliance with certain prescribed legal formalities, either involving a fictitious sale in the presence of witnesses and a balance-holder, or a public surrender of the property in court. The legal capacity to acquire *res mancipi* was vested only in those enjoying the privileges of Roman citizenship, who were said to obtain their title *ex jure quiritium*, by quiritarian right. Where neither of these formal methods of transfer was employed, the ownership did not pass until sufficient time had elapsed to establish title by prescription, and in the meantime, the property was considered to be *in bonis*, or merely in possession of the holder

mancipation are lands and houses in Italy, slaves, domestic animals and rustic servitudes; but servitudes attached to urban estates are not thus subject to sale.

(15) Likewise, estates subject to taxation and tribute are not subject to sale. According to what we have stated, cattle, horses, mules, and asses are held by some authorities to be susceptible of sale as soon as they are born; but Nerva, Proculus, and other jurists of a different school think that such animals are not subject to sale unless they have been tamed; and if this cannot be done on account of their extreme wildness, then they are considered to be salable when they reach the age at which others of the same kind are usually tamed.

(16) In like manner, wild beasts, as for instance, bears, lions, and those animals which can almost be classed as wild beasts, for example, elephants and camels, are not subject to sale; and therefore it makes no difference whether these animals have been broken to harness or to carry burdens, for they were not even known at the time when some things were decided to be saleable and others were not.

(17) Again, almost all things which are incorporeal are not subject to sale, with the exception of servitudes attached to rustic estates; for it is established that these can be sold, although they are included in the number of incorporeal things.

(18) A great difference exists between things which are saleable by mancipation and things which are not.

(19) Things which are not saleable by mancipation become the property of others absolutely by mere delivery; if they are corporeal and on this account are capable of being delivered.

(20) Therefore, if I deliver to you a garment, or some gold or silver, either by way of sale or donation, or for any other reason, the property immediately becomes yours, provided I am the owner of the same.

(21) To the same class belong lands in the provinces, some of which we designate as taxable, and others as tributary. Those are taxable which are situated in the provinces and are understood to be the property of the Roman people; those are tributary which are situated in the provinces and are considered the property of the Emperor.

(22) On the other hand, things susceptible of sale are such as are transferred to another by mancipation, from whence they are styled mancipable, and this has the same validity as a transfer in court.

(23) We explained mancipation and the manner in which it takes place in the preceding Commentary.

(24) A transfer of property in court takes place as follows: He to whom the property is to be conveyed appears before a magistrate of the Roman people, for example, the Prætor, and holding the property in his hands, says: "I declare that this slave belongs to me by quiritarian right." Then, after he makes this claim, the Prætor interrogates the other party to the transfer as to whether he makes a counter-claim, and if he does not do so, or remains silent, he adjudges the property to the party who claimed it. This is called an act of legal procedure, and it can even take place in a province before the governor of the same.

(25) For the most part, however, indeed almost always, we make use of sales by mancipation; for while we ourselves can transact our business in the presence of our friends, there is no reason or necessity for us to do so with greater difficulty before the Prætor, or the Governor of the province.

---

by bonitarian right. *Res nec mancipi*, which included everything not coming under the first head, and not belonging to the State, as set forth in the text, were transferable by mere delivery. The distinction between *res mancipi* and *res nec mancipi* which, for many years previously, had practically been ignored in business transactions, was abolished by Justinian. — ed.

(26) If the property susceptible of alienation is neither sold nor transferred in court . . . .[1]

(26a) In the provinces, however, no private property in land exists, nor is there any free citizenship.

(27) Moreover, in this place we should note that where the property is merely attached to the soil of Italy, it is not attached to the soil of a province; for the term "attached" only applies where the property is mancipable, and land in a province is not saleable by mancipation. . . .[1]

(28) It is clear that incorporeal property is not susceptible of delivery.

(29) The rights of urban estates can only be transferred in court; those attached to rustic estates can also be sold.

(30) Usufruct is only susceptible of transfer in court, for the owner of property can transfer the usufruct of the same to another so that the latter may have the usufruct, and he himself retain the bare ownership. The usufructuary, by transferring his right to the owner of the property in court, causes himself to be divested of it, and the usufruct to be merged in the ownership. Where, however, the right is transferred by him to another in court, it is, nevertheless, retained by the usufructuary, for such a transfer is held to be void.

(31) These proceedings only relate to lands in Italy, for only such lands can be transferred by mancipation, or surrendered in court. On the other hand, with reference to lands situated in the provinces, if anyone desires to create either the usufruct of the same, or the rights of way on foot, on horseback, and for vehicles; or of conducting water, or of raising houses to a greater height, or of preventing this from being done to avoid obstructing the lights of a neighbor, and other servitudes of this description, he can do so by means of agreements and stipulations, for the reason that the lands themselves are not susceptible of either mancipation or surrender in court.

(32) However, as an usufruct can be created in slaves and other animals, we must understand that the usufruct in them can also be created, even in the provinces, by a surrender of this right in court.

(33) But when we said that a usufruct could only be created by a surrender in court, this was not a rash statement, although it may be established by mancipation in such a way that in disposing of the property the usufruct of the same be reserved; for the usufruct itself is not sold but is reserved in the disposal of the property; and the result is that the usufruct is vested in one person and the ownership of the property in another.

(34) Estates also are only susceptible of alienation by a surrender in court.

(35) For if the party to whom an estate belongs as heir-at-law surrenders the same in court before it is entered upon, that is before any heir appears; the person to whom the surrender is made becomes the heir, just as if he himself had been called by law to the inheritance; but if he should surrender it after having incurred the obligation imposed by acceptance, he will, nevertheless, remain the heir, and for this reason will be responsible to the creditors. The debts will also be extinguished, and in this way the debtors of the estate will be benefited; and the corporeal property of the said estate will pass to him to whom the estate was surrendered, just as if separate portions of the same had been surrendered to him.

(36) A testamentary heir, by the surrender of an estate in court to another before it has been accepted, performs an act which is void; but if he should surrender it after he has entered upon it, what we recently stated with reference to one to whom the estate legally belongs by law as the heir of a person dying intestate will apply, if he surrenders the estate in court after assuming the obligations entailed by the

---

[1] Original manuscript illegible.

acceptance of the same.

(37) The same opinion is held by the authorities of a different school with reference to necessary heirs, namely, that it appears to make no difference whether a party becomes an heir by entering on an estate, or whether he becomes heir-at-law without his own consent; which will be explained in its proper place. Our preceptors, however, hold that the act of a necessary heir is void when he surrenders the estate in court.

(38) Obligations, no matter how they may have been contracted, cannot be transferred in either of these ways; for if anything is due from someone to me, and I wish to transfer the claim to you, I cannot do this in any of the ways by which corporeal property is transferred to a third party; but it will be necessary for you to stipulate with the debtor under my direction, with the result that he will be released by me and becomes liable to you, which is called the novation of an obligation.

(39) Without this novation, you cannot sue in your own name, but you must bring your action in my name, as my agent or attorney.[1]

(40) In the next place, we should note that only one ownership exists for aliens, for any one of them is considered either to be the owner, or not the owner, of property. The Roman people, in former times, made use of this rule, for every one was either the owner under quiritarian right, or he was understood to have no ownership whatever; but subsequently, they established a division of ownership, so that one person could own property by quiritarian right and another could hold it by bonitarian right.

(41) But if I neither sell an article to you nor surrender it in court, but only deliver it to you, the said article becomes yours by bonitarian right, but still remains mine by quiritarian right, until you, through possession, acquire it by usucaption; for as soon as usucaption is completed, the article becomes absolutely yours, that is, the bonitarian and quiritarian rights vest in you, just as if it had been sold or surrendered in court.

(42) Usucaption of movable property, however, is completed within a year, that of lands and houses within two years; and this was provided by the Law of the Twelve Tables.

(43) Again, we are entitled to usucaption of property of this kind where it has been delivered to us by a party who is not its owner; and this rule applies whether the property is subject to sale or not, provided we received it in good faith, and believed that he who delivered it was the owner.

(44) This regulation seems to have been adopted to prevent the ownership of property from being uncertain for a long period of time, as the term of one or two years should be sufficient to enable the owner to inquire after his property, which time is granted to the possessor to acquire it by usucaption.

---

[1] Among the Romans, the origin of legal representation in court is directly traceable to the close relations existing between patron and client. The former, invariably of patrician rank, was, at all times, obliged to protect the interests of his illiterate and inexperienced dependents; and especially was this the case when they became involved in litigation. This duty was not only a point of honor with the patron, but its observance was enforced by the infliction of severe penalties, and its violation incurred public reproach and infamy. A patron was never permitted to accept any compensation for his services, no matter how important or valuable they were. His influence, however, in time declined, and as the study of the law developed, and men chose it as a profession, all classes of the people sought the advice and assistance of jurisconsults of acknowledged learning and ability, whose attainments had kept pace with the progress and technical requirements of legal procedure. Still, no fees were actually charged, but custom demanded that one styled an *honorarium*, should always be offered, the amount of this was subsequently fixed by law, and the provision of the *Lex Cincia*, prohibiting any remuneration for legal services — "*Ne quis ob causam orandam mercede aut donis emeretur*" — *was* abrogated. After the patron came the *procurator*, who was only an agent, or the attorney-in-fact of his constituent, and generally possessed of little or no legal knowledge. The *cognitor*, who was the original attorney-at-law, and the advocate, were those who usually tried and argued cases before the Roman tribunals. The *procurator* absolutely took the place of his principal, and became personally responsible if an adverse decision was rendered; but the *cognitor* merely appeared for his client, just as a modern lawyer does. — ed.

(45) Sometimes, however, a party who possesses property in the utmost good faith still cannot acquire the same by usucaption; for instance, where he has possession of an article which has been stolen or obtained by violence, for the Law of the Twelve Tables forbids stolen property to be acquired by usucaption, and the *Lex Julia et Plautia* makes the same provision with reference to property obtained by force.

(46) Likewise, lands situated in the provinces are not susceptible of usucaption.

(47) Again, in former times, property susceptible of mancipation which belonged to a woman under the guardianship of agnates could not be acquired by usucaption, unless it had been delivered by herself with the authority of her guardian; and this rule was established by the Law of the Twelve Tables.

(48) It is also clear that men who are free, as well as sacred and religious property, cannot be acquired by usucaption.

(49) The common saying that the usucaption of property which has been stolen or obtained by force is prohibited by law, does not mean that the thief himself, or the party who obtains possession by violence, cannot acquire it by usucaption (for he is not entitled to usucaption for another reason, namely, because he is a possessor in bad faith), but that no one else, even though he purchased the property in good faith, has the right to acquire it by usucaption.

(50) Wherefore, with reference to movable property, a possessor in good faith does not readily acquire it by usucaption, because a person who sells the property of another and delivers it, commits a theft; and the same thing happens if the property is delivered for any other reason. Sometimes, however, this is not the case, for if an heir believes that property which has been loaned, hired, or deposited with the deceased, belonged to the estate, and he should sell or give it away, he is not guilty of theft; and also if one to whom the usufruct of a female slave belongs, believing that her child was his, should sell or give it away, he does not commit a theft, for theft cannot be committed without the intention of stealing. This may also happen in other ways, as where anyone transfers property belonging to another to a third party, without the defect of theft, and enables it to be acquired by usucaption by the possessor of the same.

(51) Anyone can obtain possession of land belonging to another without the exertion of violence, if it either becomes vacant through the neglect of the owner, or because he died without leaving any heir, or was absent for a long time; and if he should transfer the said land to another who received it in good faith, the possessor can acquire it by usucaption. And although the party who obtained the land when vacant may be aware that it belongs to another, still, this does not in any way prejudice the right of usucaption of the possessor in good faith, as the opinion of those who held that land could be the subject of theft is no longer accepted.

(52) Again, on the other hand, it happens that anyone who knows that the property which he possesses belongs to another can acquire it by usucaption; as, for instance where someone has possession of property belonging to an estate of which the heir who is not yet born has not obtained possession; for he is permitted to acquire it in this manner, provided the said property is of a nature which admits of usucaption, and this kind of possession and usucaption is styled that of a person representing an heir.

(53) Usucaption of this kind is so readily granted that real property may be acquired by usucaption within the space of a single year.

(54) The reason why, in this instance, land can be acquired by usucaption in a single year, is because that, in former times, through the possession of property belonging to an estate the estate itself was considered to be acquired by usucaption, that is to say, in a year; for, though the Law of the Twelve Tables establishes the term of two years for the usucaption of land and one year for that of other property, an estate "was

considered to be included in the latter, as it is neither part of the soil nor corporeal; and although it was afterwards held that estates themselves were not capable of usucaption, still the right to usucaption with reference to all property belonging to an estate, even land, remained in force.

(55) The reason why such thoroughly dishonorable possession and usucaption was allowed was because the ancient authorities desired that estates should be entered upon more quickly, and that there should be persons to perform the sacred ceremonies to which, in those times, the greatest importance was attached; and also that the creditors might have someone from whom they might collect their claims.

(56) This species of possession and usucaption is called lucrative, for the party knows that he is profiting by the property of another.

(57) At the present time, however, it is not lucrative, for a Decree of the Senate, enacted at the instance of the Divine Hadrian, provided that usucaptions of this kind could be revoked; and therefore an heir can recover the property by bringing an action for the estate against him who acquired it by usucaption, just as if the usucaption had never taken place.

(58) Where there is a necessary heir, usucaption of this kind cannot take place under the law.

(59) A person can knowingly acquire the property of another by usucaption under other circumstances; for if anyone makes a fiduciary sale of the property of another or surrenders it in court to a third party, and the owner himself should obtain possession of the same, he can acquire it by usucaption, even in the case of land, after the expiration of a year. This species of usucaption is called a recovery by use, because property which we owned at a former time we recover in this way by usucaption.

(60) Fiduciary ownership, however, is contracted either where the creditor holds the property by way of pledge, or through a friend with whom our property is placed for safe-keeping; and, when the trust is contracted with a friend, recovery by use can, under all circumstances, take place; but where this is done with a creditor, the money must, by all means be paid, and when it has not yet been paid, the property can only be recovered in this way provided the debtor has not hired it from the creditor, or have obtained possession of it during pleasure; as in this instance lucrative usucaption will take place.

(61) Moreover, if the people should sell property pledged to satisfy a claim, and the owner should become possessed of it, recovery by use is permitted; but in this case land will be recovered after the lapse of two years. This is what is commonly called recovery of possession after public sale, for he who buys it from the people is called a purchaser of mortgaged land.

(62) It sometimes happens that an owner has not the power to alienate his property, and that one who is not the owner can do so.[1]

(63) For, by the *Lex Julia*, a husband was forbidden to alienate dotal land against the consent of his wife, although the land may have become his own either by sale to him as dowry, or by surrender in court, or by usucaption. It is doubtful whether this rule is applicable only to lands in Italy, or also to those in the provinces.

(64) On the other hand, an agnate who is the curator of an insane person can, by the Law of the Twelve Tables, alienate the property of the latter; and an agent can also, as well as a creditor, alienate that of his principal, if authorized to do so under an agreement, although the property does not belong to him. This

---

[1] In the text, Sections 62, 63 and 64, follow immediately after Section 79. As there does not appear to be any reason for this and it evidently is an error, I have placed them in their regular order. — ed.

may perhaps be considered to be done for the reason that the pledge is understood to be alienated with the consent of the debtor, who previously agreed that the creditor might be permitted to sell the pledge, if the money was not paid.

(65) Therefore, from what we have stated, it appears that certain property can be alienated by Natural Law; as, for instance, that which is transferred by mere delivery, and that other property can be alienated by the Civil Law, as through sale, surrender in court, and usucaption, for these rights are peculiar to Roman citizens.

(66) Property which becomes ours by delivery can be acquired by us not only by natural law but also by occupancy, and hence we become the owners of the same because it previously belonged to no one else; and in this class are included all animals which are taken on land, or in the water, or in the air.

(67) Therefore, if we should take captive any wild animal, bird, or fish, it is understood to be ours only as long as it is in our custody; for when it escapes from our control and recovers its natural liberty, it again becomes the property of the first occupant, because it ceases to be ours. It is considered to recover its natural liberty when it escapes from our vision, or, although it may be in our sight, its pursuit is difficult.

(68) In the case of those animals, however, which are accustomed to go away and return, as for instance pigeons, and bees, and also deer which are accustomed to go into the forests and return, we have adopted the rule which has come down to us from former times, namely, that if these animals should not have the intention to return, they also cease to be ours and become the property of the first occupant; and they are considered to have ceased to have the intention to return when they abandon their habit of returning.

(69) Property taken from the enemy also becomes ours by Natural Law.

(70) Land acquired by us through alluvion also becomes ours under the same law. This is held to take place when a river, by degrees, makes additions of soil to our land in such a way that we cannot estimate the amount added at any one moment of time; and this is what is commonly stated to be an addition made by alluvion, which is added so gradually as to escape our sight.[1]

(71) Therefore, if the river should carry away a part of your land and bring it to mine, that part will still continue to be yours.

(72) But, if an island rises in the middle of a river, it is the common property of those who possess land on both sides of the stream; but if it is not in the middle of the river, it will belong to those who have land on the nearest bank of the stream.

(73) Moreover, any building erected on our land by another, even though the latter may have erected it in his own name, is ours by Natural Law, for the reason that the surface is part of the soil.

(74) This rule applies with still greater force to trees planted on our soil by another, provided, however, they have taken root in the earth.

(75) The same rule also applies to grain which has been sowed by another upon our land.

---

[1] These rules regulating the acquisition and loss of the qualified ownership in animals *feræ natural*, as well as those relating to alluvial deposits, were adopted bodily from Roman jurisprudence by the early writers on the Common Law, and are in. force to-day. "*Omnia animalia que in terra & in mari & in cælo & in aëre nascuntur vbicunq (ubicunque); capiantur, et cu capta fuerint incipiunt esse mea; quia mea custodia cœrcetur. & eadem ratione si euaserint custodiam meam & in naturalem libertatem se receperint, desinunt esse mea & rursus fiunt occupantis. Est autem alluvio latens incrementum & alluvione adjici dicitur quod ita paulatim adjicitur, quod intelligere non possis quo momento teporis adjicitur.*" Bracton, *De Leg. et Consuet. Ang.* II, I, 9. — ed.

(76) But if we bring an action against him to recover the land or the building, and we refuse to pay him the expenses he has incurred in constructing the building or in sowing the crop, we can be barred by an exception on the ground of fraud, that is to say, if he was a possessor in good faith.

(77) It is settled by the same rule that whatever anyone has written on my paper or parchment, even in letters of gold, is mine, because the letters are merely accessory to the paper or parchment; but if I should bring an action to recover the books or parchments, and do not reimburse the party for the expense incurred in writing, I can be barred by an exception on the ground of fraud.

(78) If, however, anyone paints anything on a tablet belonging to me, as for instance, a portrait, the contrary rule is adopted, for it is said that the tablet is accessory to the painting; but a good reason for this difference hardly exists. According to this rule it is certain that if you bring an action for the portrait as yours, while I am in possession of the same, and you do not pay me the value of the tablet, you can be barred by an exception on the ground of fraud. But, if, you are in possession, the result will be that I should be granted an equitable action against you, in which instance unless I pay the expenses of the painting, you can bar me by an exception on the ground of fraud, just as if you were a possessor in good faith. It is clear that if either you, or anyone else should steal the tablet, I will be entitled to an action of theft.

(79) Where the nature of the article is changed recourse to natural law is also required. Hence, if you make wine, oil, or grain, out of my grapes, olives, or heads of wheat, the question arises whether the said wine, oil, or grain is mine or yours. Likewise, if you manufacture a vase out of my gold or silver, or build a ship, a chest, or a bench with my lumber, or you make a garment out of my wool, or mead out of my wine and honey; or a plaster or eye-wash out of drugs belonging to me, the question arises whether what you have made out of my property is yours or mine. Certain authorities hold that the material or substance should be taken into consideration, that is to say, that the article manufactured should be deemed to be the property of him to whom the material belongs, and this opinion was adopted by Sabinus and Cassius. Others, however, hold that the article belongs to him who manufactured it, and this doctrine was approved by authorities of the opposite school, who also agreed that the owner of the material and substance was entitled to an action of theft against the party who had appropriated the property; and also that a personal action would not lie against him because property which has been destroyed cannot be recovered; but, notwithstanding this, personal actions can be brought against thieves and certain other possessors.

I. WHETHER OR NOT WARDS CAN ALIENATE PROPERTY.

(80) We must next call attention to the fact that neither a woman nor a ward can alienate property by mancipation without the authority of their guardians, but a woman can alienate property not subject to mancipation without such authority, which a ward cannot do.

(81) Hence, if a woman lends money to anyone without the authority of her guardian, for the reason that she transfers it to him, and as money is not subject to sale, the borrower contracts an obligation.

(82) If, however, a ward should do this, as he does not transfer the money to the borrower, the latter does not contract an obligation; and therefore the ward can recover his money, provided it is in existence; that is to say he can claim it as his under quiritarian right, but a woman can only recover the money by an action for debt. Hence the question arises whether the ward who lent the money can, in any action whatever recover it from the person who borrowed it if it has been expended, as recovery must be had for a party in possession.

(83) On the other hand, all property, whether subject to sale or not, can be transferred to women and to wards without the authority of their guardians; and this is granted them because their condition is improved

by the transaction.

(84) Hence if a debtor pays any money to a ward, he transfers the ownership of the same to him, but he himself is not released from liability, for the reason that a ward cannot release a debtor from an obligation without the authority of his guardian, as he is not permitted to alienate any property without his guardian's consent; still, if he receives any benefit from the money, and continues to demand payment of the debt, he can be barred by an exception on the ground of fraud.

(85) A woman, however, may be legally paid without the authority of her guardian; and he who makes payment is released from liability, because, as we have previously stated, women can, even without the authority of their guardians, alienate property not mancipable. Although this rule only applies where she actually received the money, still if she did not receive it, but merely says that she has, and wishes to discharge her debtor by giving him a formal release without the authority of her guardian, she cannot do so.

(86) Again, we acquire property not only by ourselves but through those whom we have under our control, in our hand, or in *mancipium*. We can also acquire it through slaves in whom we have the usufruct, as well as through freemen, and slaves belonging to others whom we have possessed in good faith. Let us now carefully examine these different cases.

(87) Anything which our children, who are under our control, as well as anything which our slaves acquire by sale, delivery, or stipulation, or in any other manner whatsoever, is acquired for us; for he who is subject to our authority can have nothing of his own. Hence if such a person should be appointed an heir he cannot enter on the estate without our order, and if he should do so under our direction the estate will be acquired for us, just as if we ourselves had been appointed heirs; and in accordance with this rule a legacy is acquired by such parties for us in the same manner.

(88) We should, however, note that where a slave belongs to one person by bonitarian right, to another by quiritarian right, in every instance whatever is acquired by him belongs to the party in whom the bonitarian right is vested.

(89) Not only is the ownership of property acquired for us by those whom we have under our control, but possession is also; for if they obtain possession of property we are considered to have possession of the same, hence property can even be acquired through them by usucaption.

(90) Ownership is indeed acquired for us, in every instance, through those persons whom we have in our hand or in *mancipium*, just as it is by those who are under our control; but whether possession is also acquired is a question, for the reason that we do not have possession of the said persons.

(91) Moreover, it has been decided with reference to slaves in whom we only have an usufruct that anything which they acquire by the employment of our own property, or by their labor, is acquired for our benefit; but what they acquire by any other means belongs to the owner of the property. Therefore, if a slave of this kind is appointed an heir, or a legacy should be left to him, it would not be acquired for my benefit, but for that of the owner of the property.

(92) The same rule applies to anyone who is possessed by us in good faith, whether he is free or the slave of another; for what has been decided with reference to an usufructuary also holds good with reference to a *bona fide* possessor; and hence any property which is acquired in any other way than the two above mentioned will belong to the party himself, if he is free, or to the owner, if he is a slave.

(93) But after a *bona fide* possessor has obtained a slave by usucaption,[1] for the reason that he becomes his

---

[1] Usucaption was originally only applicable to corporeal property, but was afterwards extended by custom so as to include incorporeal

owner in this way, anything which the slave may acquire will be for his benefit. An usufructuary, however, cannot acquire a slave by usucaption; first, because he does not have possession, but only the right of use and enjoyment; and second, because he knows that the slave belongs to another.

(94) It is a matter of doubt whether we can hold possession of property and acquire it by usucaption through a slave in whom we have the usufruct, because we are not in possession of the slave. There is no question, however, that we can both hold possession of property and acquire it by usucaption, through a slave of whom we have possession in good faith. But in both these cases we have reference to the distinction which we explained above; that is to say, where the slave acquires anything by means of our property, or by his own labor, it is acquired for our benefit.

(95) From this it is apparent that under no circumstances can property be acquired for our benefit through freemen who are not subject to our authority, and of whom we do not have possession in good faith, nor by slaves belonging to others in whom we neither have the usufruct, nor of whom we have legal possession. This is what is meant by the common saying that property cannot be acquired for us through a stranger; and the only question relating to possession is whether it can be acquired for our benefit through a person who is free.

(96) In conclusion, it should be remembered that nothing can be surrendered in court by persons who are under the control, or in the hand or mancipation of another, as nothing can belong to persons of this description; and the result is that they cannot claim anything as their own in court.

(97) Up to this point it is sufficient to have stated how separate property can be acquired by us; for we shall hereafter, and in a more suitable place discuss the law of legacies, by which also we acquire individual property. Now let us see in what ways property can be acquired by us in the aggregate.

(98) If we become the heirs of any person, or demand prætorian possession of an estate, or purchase the inheritance of anyone, or adopt anyone, or receive a wife in our hand; the entire property of any of said persons passes to us.

---

hereditaments. It differed from prescription in that good faith was absolutely essential to its operation; and was invented as a penalty to be inflicted upon the actual owner for permitting his right to remain unexercised or unclaimed through gross and inexcusable negligence. Anyone who lost his property in this way was considered to have transferred it: "*Videtur alienare qui patitur usucapi.*"

Usucaption, as such, was recognized by the Common Law, and the doctrine of the Twelve Tables, that it only applied to corporeal objects, was accepted in all its rigidity. "*Incorporealia verò possideri non poterunt, nec usucapi, nec sine corpore tradi, quia per se traditionem non patirentur. Quasi possidere tamen non poterunt per patientiam & per usum.*" (Fleta, III, XV, 1.)

According to Bracton, no certain time for the title to vest was established by law, but this was left entirely to the discretion of the Court.

"*Rerum dominia transferuntur per usucaptionem s. p. longam, continuam et pacificam possessionem, ex diuturno tempore et sine traditione; sed quam longa esse debeat non definitur a jure, sed ex Iustitiariorum discretione.*" (Bracton *De Leg. et Consuet, Ang.* II, 22.)

Prescription, at Common Law, was based on the enjoyment of a right from time immemorial, and did not apply to land. It is now regulated by statute, and in England depends upon uninterrupted use for twenty years, where an easement is concerned. The ownership of immovable property is acquired in France by continuous possession for ten years, if the true owner resides within the jurisdiction of the Court of Appeal; and for twenty, if he does not. (Cod. *Civ.* Art. 2265); in Spain, for the same periods, when the parties are present, or absent, (*Cod. Civ.* Art. 1957); in Portugal, for five years where possession, and for ten years where the title of acquisition, is registered; in both cases from the date of registry. (Cod. *Civ.* Art. 526); in Italy, for ten years where all legal requirements have been complied with. (Cod. *Civ.* Art. 2137); in Japan, for from ten to twenty years, where the party in interest has had undisturbed possession with the intention of owning the property. (Civ. Cod. of Japan, Arts. 162, 163.) By the Civil Code of Louisiana ten or twenty years are required to obtain a good title to immovable property by prescription, dependent upon whether the owner resides in or out of the State; and three years when title to chattels is involved. In former times, the right of ownership to slaves was lost by uninterrupted possession for half the time necessary for the acquisition of real-estate. Good faith was indispensable in the abovementioned cases, and was always presumed. (Civil Code of Louisiana, Arts. 3437, 3439, 3440, 3442, 3447.) — ed.

(99) And, first, let us discuss inheritances, the condition of which is twofold; for an inheritance either comes to us by will, or on account of intestacy.

(100) And first we shall examine what comes to us by will.

(101) Originally there were two kinds of wills; for parties either made a will at the *Comitia Calata*, which were assembled twice a year for that purpose; or in the face of the enemy, that is to say when the testator took up arms for the purpose of making war; for the term has reference to an army ready and armed for service. Hence, persons made one kind of a will in time of peace and tranquillity, and another when about to go into battle.

(102) Afterwards, a third kind of will was introduced, which was executed by bronze and balance. Where a man who had not made a will at the *Comitia Calata* or in the face of the enemy was apprehensive of sudden death, he usually transferred his estate by sale to a friend, and requested him to distribute it to whomever he desired to have it after his death. This kind of testamentary disposition is styled a will by bronze and balance, because it is effected by the ceremony of mancipation.

(103) The two kinds of wills above mentioned have, however, fallen into disuse; and only the one effected by bronze and balance has been retained, but it is now changed from what it was in ancient times. For formerly the purchaser of the estate, that is to say the party who received it by a sale from the testator, occupied the place of the heir, and for this reason the testator directed him with reference to what he desired to be given to anyone after his death. Now, however, another person is appointed heir under the will who is charged with the distribution of legacies, and differs from the one who, as a matter of form and in imitation of the ancient law, represents the purchaser of the estate.

(104) This transaction takes place as follows: The party who executes the will having, as in the case of other sales, called together five Roman citizens of the age of puberty as witnesses, and a balance holder, and having reduced his will to writing, sells his estate as a matter of form to a certain person, and the said purchaser makes use of the following words: "Let your family and money pass into my charge and custody, and, in order that you may make your will properly in accordance with the public law, let them be purchased by me with this bronze" (or as some authorities add) "with this brazen balance." Then he strikes the balance with the piece of bronze, and delivers the latter to the testator as purchase money. Next the testator, holding the will in his hands, says, "I do give and bequeath, and declare that I do so, everything written in these tablets and this wax, and do you, Roman citizens bear witness to my act." This ceremony is called nuncupation, for this term means to declare publicly; and indeed what the testator specially stated in writing in his will is considered to have been declared and confirmed by this general affirmation.

(105) Anyone who is under the control of, or belongs to the family of the purchaser or to that of the testator himself, should not be one of the witnesses; because, in imitation of the ancient law, the entire transaction which takes place for the purpose of establishing the will is considered to be carried on between the purchaser of the estate and the testator; and in former times, as we stated above, anyone who purchased the estate of the testator occupied the position of an heir, and therefore the testimony of persons belonging to the family taken in a proceeding of this kind was rejected.

(106) Wherefore, if the purchaser of the estate is under the control of his father, neither his father, nor anyone in the power of the latter, for instance his brother, can be a witness. If, however, a son under parental control, after his discharge from the army, should make a will disposing of his *castrense peculium*, neither his father, nor anyone who is subject to the authority of the latter, can be a witness.

(107) We understand that the same rules which have been established with reference to witnesses, also apply to the balance-holder, for he is included in the number of witnesses.

(108) Not only can he who is under the control of the heir or legatee, or who is also under the control of the same person as the heir or the legatee be a witness and a balance-holder, but the heir, or the legatee himself, has a right to act in this capacity. Still, so far as the heir is concerned, as well as with reference to him who is in his power, and the party under whose control he himself is, we should not, by any means, make use of this right.

II. CONCERNING MILITARY WILLS.

(109) The rigid observation of these rules in the making of wills is not required of soldiers, by the Imperial Constitutions on account of their extreme want of legal knowledge. For, even if they should not summon the lawful number of witnesses, or sell the property, or declare the will to be theirs, they nevertheless have the right of testamentary disposition.

(110) Moreover, they are permitted to appoint even aliens and Latins as their heirs or legatees; while under other circumstances aliens are forbidden by the Civil Law from receiving estates and legacies, and Latins are forbidden to do so by the *Lex Junia*.

(111) Unmarried persons who are prohibited by the *Lex Julia* from receiving estates or legacies, and likewise bereaved persons, that is to say those who have no children and upon whom the *Lex Papia* forbids to take more than half an estate or legacy, are not disqualified from taking all of it under a military will.

(112) A Decree of the Senate was enacted at the instance of the Divine Hadrian, by which women were permitted to make a will even without the ceremony of coemption; provided, however, they were not under twelve years of age; and if they were not released from guardianship, they were required to execute their wills with the consent of their guardians.

(113) Females therefore appear to be in a better position than males, but a male under the age of fourteen cannot make a will, even with the authority of his guardian; but a female obtains the right of testamentary disposition with the consent of her guardian, after she has reached her twelfth year.

(114) Hence, if we wish to know whether or not a will is valid, we must ascertain in the first place whether the party who executed it had testamentary capacity, and next, if he had it, we must learn whether he made the will in accordance with the requirements of the Civil Law; with the exception of soldiers, who, as we have stated, are, on account of their want of legal knowledge, permitted to make a will in any way that they may desire, and in any way that they can.

(115) In order that a will may be valid under the Civil Law, it is not sufficient that the rule which we have laid down above with reference to the sale of an estate, the qualification of witnesses, and the declaration of the testator should be observed.

(116) But, above all things, it should be ascertained whether the appointment of the heir was made in regular form; for, where the appointment was made otherwise, it makes no difference whether the estate of the testator was sold, the witnesses assembled, and the declaration published in a proper manner, as we stated above.

(117) The regular appointment of an heir is as follows: "Let Titius be my heir." The following form at present seems to be approved, namely: "I order that Titius be my heir." This one, however, "I desire Titius to be my heir" is not recognized as correct; and the following expressions, "I appoint Titius my heir," and "I make Titius my heir," are not admitted as valid by the greater number of authorities.

(118) Moreover, it should be observed that if a woman, who is under guardianship, makes a will, she must do so with the consent of her guardian; otherwise her will is void by the Civil Law.

(119) The prætor, however, promises the heirs mentioned in the will to place them in possession of the estate in accordance with the provisions of the same, if the will is attested by the seals of seven witnesses, and if there is no one to whom the estate will belong as heir-at-law under the rule of intestacy; as, for example, a brother by the same father, or a paternal uncle, or the son of a brother, the heirs mentioned, in the will can retain the estate; "for the same rule of law applies as in the case where a will is not valid for some other reason, for instance because the estate was not sold, or the testator did not utter the words required for the declaration.

(120) But let us consider, even if there should be a brother or a paternal uncle, whether the heirs mentioned in the will should be preferred to them; for it is stated in a rescript of the Emperor Antoninus that parties who have obtained prætorian possession of an estate in accordance with the terms of a will not properly executed, can, by means of an exception based on fraud defend themselves against parties claiming the estate on the ground of intestacy.

(121) It is certain that this rule applies to the wills of males as well as to those of females which were not properly executed, as, for example, where they did not make use of the mere formality of selling the estate, or of speaking the words required for the declaration; and we shall see whether this constitution also applies to the wills of women which have been executed without the authority of their guardians.

(122) We are not speaking, however, of those women who are under the legal guardianship of their parents or patrons, but of those who have guardians of another kind that are compelled, even if unwilling, to grant their consent; otherwise it is evident that a parent or a patron cannot be removed by a will made without his sanction.

(123) Again, anyone who has a son under his control must take care either to appoint him as his heir or to disinherit him by name; otherwise, if he passes him over in silence this renders his will void. To such an extent is this true, that our preceptors hold that even if the son should die during the lifetime of his father, no one can be an heir under the will, for the reason that the appointment was not valid in the beginning. Authorities of the other school, however, are of the opinion that although the son, if he is living at the time of his father's death, becomes his father's heir on the ground of intestacy, without being barred by the mention of the heirs in the will; still, if he should die before his father, they hold that the said heirs can enter on the estate under the will, without the son being any longer an impediment; for the reason that they think that the will was not valid from the beginning, on account of the son having been passed over.

(124) If, however, the testator should pass over others of her children, the testament is valid, but the persons who have been passed over will have a right, with the heirs mentioned therein, to equal shares of the estate, if they are proper heirs; and to half of it if they are strangers. For example, if anyone should appoint his three sons his heirs, but should pass over his daughter, the daughter will become a co-heir to a fourth part of the estate; and for this reason will obtain the same share that she would have been entitled to if her father had died intestate; but if he should appoint foreign heirs, and pass over his daughter, the latter will be entitled to half of his estate. What we have mentioned with reference to a daughter we understand to apply to a grandson and to all the children of a son, of both sexes.

(125) What course then should be pursued? Although according to what we have stated the heirs mentioned in the will are only deprived of half the estate by the children of the testator, still, as the prætor promises to give the latter possession contrary to the provisions of the will, and according to this rule, foreign heirs are excluded from the entire estate, and merely become heirs without obtaining any of the property,

(126) We formerly made use of this law as no difference between females and males existed; but the Emperor Antoninus recently stated in a rescript that women who were proper heirs could not obtain more

by acquiring prætorian possession of an estate than they would by the right of accrual. This rule should also be observed in the case of daughters who have been emancipated; that is, they will obtain the same amount through prætorian possession of the property as they would have obtained by the right of accrual, if they had remained under the control of their father.

(127) A son, however, must be expressly disinherited by his father, otherwise he is not considered to have been disinherited. A son is held to be expressly disinherited when the following expressions are used, "Let my son Titius be disinherited"; or "Let my son be disinherited"; without mentioning his name.

(128) Other children of both sexes may be properly disinherited, among others, by the use of the following words: "Let all those remaining be disinherited"; which words are usually added after the appointment of the heirs. This, however, is only prescribed by the Civil Law.

(129) For the prætor requires all descendants of the male sex that is to say sons, grandsons, and great-grandsons, to be disinherited by name; but he considers it sufficient if descendants of the female sex, that is to say, daughters, granddaughters, and great-granddaughters, are either disinherited by name, or among others.

(130) Posthumous children must be either appointed heirs, or disinherited.

(131) In this respect the condition of all is the same, so that if a posthumous son, or any other child of either sex is passed over, the will is indeed valid; but after the birth of the posthumous child it will be broken, and for this reason will be absolutely void. Therefore, if a woman who is expected to give birth to a posthumous child should have an abortion, there will be nothing to prevent the heirs mentioned in the will from entering on the estate.

(132) Persons of the female sex are either expressly, or generally disinherited, but if they are disinherited with others, something must be bequeathed to them in order that they may not appear to have been passed over through forgetfulness. It has been decided, however, that persons of the male sex cannot legally be disinherited unless this is done expressly, for instance as follows: "Let any son who may be born to me be disinherited" . . . .[1]

(133) In the same category with posthumous children are placed those who, by succeeding as proper heirs, become such to their relatives, just as posthumous children are by birth. For example, if I have a son, and by him a grandson, or a granddaughter in his power, because the son precedes by a degree, he alone enjoys the rights of a proper heir; although the grandson and granddaughter by him are both under the same authority. If, however, my son should die during my lifetime, or should, for any reason whatsoever, be released from my control, the grandson and granddaughter will succeed to his place, and in this way acquire the rights of proper heirs just as if they were posthumous children.

(134) Therefore, to avoid my will being broken in this way, just as I must appoint either my son my heir, or expressly disinherit him, otherwise my will will not be valid; so it is necessary for me to appoint my grandson or granddaughter my heir, or disinherit them; lest, if my son should die during my lifetime, my said grandson or granddaughter, by succeeding to his place, may break my will in the same way as if they had been posthumous children. This is provided by the *Lex Junia Vellæa*, in which the method of disinheritance is prescribed, that is to say, posthumous children of the male sex shall be expressly disinherited, and those of the female sex shall be disinherited expressly, or generally with others; provided, however, that something is bequeathed to those who are disinherited with others.

---

[1] Original manuscript illegible.

(135) It is not necessary for children emancipated by the Civil Law to either be appointed heirs, or disinherited, for the reason that they are not proper heirs. The prætor, however, orders all children of both sexes to be disinherited if they are not appointed heirs; if they are of the male sex they must be expressly mentioned, and if of the female sex they must either be expressly mentioned, or disinherited among others; and if they are neither appointed heirs nor disinherited the prætor, as we have stated above, promises to grant them possession of the estate in opposition to the terms of the will.

(135a) Children who have been granted Roman citizenship along with their father, are not subject to his authority, if at the time citizenship was granted or afterwards, the father did not petition to retain them under his control — and the rule is the same if he did petition but did not succeed — for children who are placed under the control of their father by the Emperor differ in no respect from those who are subject to his authority from their birth.

(136) Again, adopted children, as long as they remain in this condition, occupy the place of natural children; but when they have been emancipated by their adoptive father, they are not included among his children, either by the Civil Law, or by the Edict of the Prætor.

(137) On the other hand, for this reason it happens that as long as they remain in the adoptive family, they are considered as strangers so far as their natural father is concerned; but if they should be emancipated by their adoptive father, they will then be in the same condition as they would have been had they been emancipated by their natural father.

(138) If anyone, after having made a will, should either adopt a son, who is his own master, in an assembly of the people, or one who is under the control of his parent through the intervention of the Prætor, his testament will undoubtedly be broken, just as it would have been by the subsequent birth of a proper heir.

(139) The same rule applies where, after having made a will, a wife comes into the hand of the testator, or he marries a woman who is in his hand; for in this way she takes the place of a daughter, and becomes a proper heir.

(140) It makes no difference whether either of the parties adopted was appointed an heir by the will, for, so far as their disinheritance is concerned, the question would seem to be superfluous; as, at the time the will was made, they were not included in the number of proper heirs.

(141) Likewise, a son who has been manumitted after the first or second sale, breaks a will previously executed; for the reason that he is restored to the authority of his father, and it makes no difference whether he was appointed an heir, or disinherited by the said will.

(142) The same rule formerly applied to one for whose benefit proof of error is permitted by the Decree of the Senate, for the reason that he was born of an alien, or of a Latin woman who was married with the understanding that she was a Roman citizen; for, whether he was appointed heir, or disinherited by his father, or whether, during the lifetime of the latter, the error was proved, or this was done after his death; the will was absolutely broken, as by the birth of a posthumous child.

(143) Now, however, by a late Decree of the Senate enacted at the instance of the Divine Hadrian, if the error is proved during the lifetime of the father, the will is in every instance broken, as in former times; but where it is proved after the death of the father, if the son was passed over in silence, the will is broken. But if he was mentioned in it as the heir, or disinherited, the will is not broken, in order that carefully executed wills may not be rescinded at a time when they cannot be renewed.

(144) A former will is revoked by one subsequently executed; nor does it make any difference whether an heir ever appears or not, for it only is considered whether he might take under it if he did appear. Therefore,

if the heir appointed by the last will, which was legally executed, is unwilling to take under the same; or if he should die during the lifetime of the testator, or after the death of the latter, and before he had entered upon the estate; or if he should be excluded for not having accepted the estate within the prescribed time, or on account of the condition under which he was appointed not having been complied with; or by the *Lex Julia* on account of celibacy; in all these cases the testator dies intestate; for the first will having been revoked by the subsequent one is not valid, and the last will also has no effect, as there is no heir under it.

(145) Wills legally executed may become void in another way, as for instance, when he who executed the will loses his civil rights, and how this may happen was stated in the First Commentary.

(146) Moreover, in a case of this kind we say that a will may become inoperative; for although wills which are revoked, and those which in the beginning are not legally executed are alike invalid, and those which have been properly executed become invalid on account of loss of civil rights, they, nevertheless, may be said to be rescinded; still, for the reason that it is more convenient for the different cases to be designated by different names, some of these wills are said not to have been legally executed, and others which have been legally executed are either broken or become void.

(147) However, wills which in the beginning were not legally executed, or if they were legally executed afterwards became void, or were revoked, are still not absolutely inoperative; for if they have been sealed with the signets of seven witnesses, the appointed heir can demand possession of the estate in accordance with the provisions of the will, provided the deceased testator was a Roman citizen and his own master at the time of his death; but if the will became inoperative, for example, because the testator lost his citizenship or his freedom, or gave himself in adoption, and he dies under the control of his adoptive father, he cannot demand possession of the estate in accordance with the provisions of the will.

(148) Therefore, those who obtain prætorian possession of an estate in accordance with the provisions of a will which was not properly executed in the first place, or which if it was properly executed, was subsequently broken, or became void; provided they can establish their right to the estate can obtain actual possession of the same. If, however, they can be deprived of the estate by some one having a better claim they will be entitled only to nominal possession.

(149) For, if anyone has been appointed heir under the Civil Law by either a former or a subsequent will; or is the heir-at-law to an intestate estate, he can deprive the nominal possessor of the same; but, if no one else is an heir under the Civil Law, the possessor can retain the estate, nor will cognates, who have no legal title, have any right to deprive him of it.

(149a) Sometimes, however, as we have mentioned above, heirs who were appointed by will are preferred to heirs-at-law; for instance if the will was not legally executed either because the estate was not sold, or because the testator did not utter the formula of declaration; for if the agnates of the deceased should claim the estate they can be barred on the ground of fraud in accordance with the Constitution of the Divine Antoninus.

(150) Prætorian possessors of an estate are not excluded under the provisions of the *Lex Julia*, by which estates which have no heirs are ordered to escheat to the government, if the deceased left no successor of any kind.

(151) A will legally executed may be rendered void by the expression of a contrary intention, but it is evident that it cannot be rendered inoperative by such an intention alone; because after the testator was unwilling that it should stand, and even if he went so far as to cut the cord with which it was tied, it will, nevertheless, continue to be valid under the Civil Law. Moreover, if he should erase or burn the will, what he wrote will still be valid, although the proof of it may be difficult. What then should be done? If anyone

demands prætorian possession of an estate on the ground of intestacy, and he who is appointed by the will claims it, the latter may, in this instance, be excluded by an exception on the ground of fraud, provided it is proved to have been the intention of the testator that the estate should go to those entitled to the same as heirs-at-law; and this rule is set forth in a rescript of the Emperor Antoninus.

(152) Again, heirs are either designated necessary, or necessary and proper, or foreign heirs.

(153) A necessary heir is a slave appointed with the grant of his freedom; and he is so called because at the death of the testator, whether he is willing or unwilling, he at once becomes free and his heir.

(154) For this reason anyone who suspects that he is insolvent, usually appoints his slave his heir with the grant of his freedom as a substitute in the second or any inferior degree; so that, if his creditors are not satisfied in full, the property of his estate may be sold rather as belonging to the heir than to the testator himself, and the disgrace which results from the sale of the property of an insolvent estate may attach rather to the heir than to the testator; although as was held by Sabinus, according to Fufidius, that he ought not to suffer ignominy because the sale of the property of the estate was not caused by his fault but through the requirements of the law. We, however, adopt a different view.

(155) As a recompense for this inconvenience, the benefit is conferred upon the slave of acquiring for himself everything which 'he obtains after the death of his patron, whether it was reserved for him before or after the sale of the property; and although only a part of the claim may have been paid by the proceeds of the sale, his subsequently acquired property cannot again be sold on account of the debts of the estate, unless he should have acquired something on account of his being the heir, for example, the estate of a Latin freedman, and thereby have become more wealthy; while if the property of other persons when sold only pays a portion of the indebtedness, and they afterwards acquire any other property, the latter may be sold time and again.

(156) Proper and necessary heirs are, for instance, a son or a daughter, a grandson or a granddaughter by a son, and their descendants, provided they were under the control of the testator at the time of his death. In order, however, that a grandson or a granddaughter may become a proper heir, it is not sufficient for him or her to have been under the control of their grandfather at the time of his death, but it is necessary that their father should, during the lifetime of his father, have ceased to be a proper heir, either on account of death, or because of having been released from parental control in any other way whatsoever, for then the grandson or granddaughter will succeed to the place of his or her father.

(157) They are called proper heirs because they are family heirs, and even during the lifetime of their parent are to a certain extent considered to be joint owners of the estate, and therefore where anyone dies intestate, the first right to the succession belongs to his children. They are called necessary heirs for the reason that, under all circumstances, whether they are willing or unwilling, they become heirs in case of intestacy, as well as under the will.

(158) The prætor, however, permits them to relinquish the succession, in order that the estate of their father may be sold for the payment of debts.

(159) The same rule applies to the case of a wife who is in the hand of her husband, because she occupies the place of a daughter; as well as to a daughter-in-law who is in the hand of a son of the testator; for the reason that she occupies the place of a granddaughter.

(160) Moreover, the prætor gives the same power to reject an estate to one *in mancipium*, who has been appointed heir with the grant of freedom, although he is merely a necessary heir, and not a proper one, as is the case with a slave.

(161) Others who are not subject to the control of the testator are designated foreign heirs. Therefore, children who are not under our control when appointed heirs by us, are considered as strangers, for which reason children who are appointed heirs by their mother are also included in this class because women cannot have children subject to their authority. In like manner, slaves who are appointed heirs with the grant of their freedom, and are afterwards manumitted by their owner, are included in the same class.

(162) Moreover, power is granted to foreign heirs to deliberate whether they will, or will not, accept an estate.

(163) If, however, one who has the power to reject an estate should interfere with the property of the same, or one who is permitted to deliberate as to whether he will enter on an estate or not, should accept it, he has no power to reject it afterwards, unless he is a minor under twenty-five years of age; for the prætor comes to the relief of persons of this age when they rashly accept an estate which is injurious to them; as in all other cases where they are deceived. I remember that the Divine Hadrian even excused a person over the age of twenty-five years, where, after he had entered on an estate, a great debt was discovered, which at the time of the acceptance of the estate was not known to exist.

(164) Time to make up their minds, that is to say, a certain term for deliberation, is usually granted to foreign heirs in order that they may enter upon an estate within the prescribed period, and if they do not do so, they are barred from accepting it. Hence this is called "*cretio*," for the reason that the word "*cernere*" means, in one sense, to decide and to determine.[1]

(165) Therefore, after the following clause: "Titius, be my heir," we should add: "and within a hundred days after you learn of your appointment, and are able to do so, you must state whether you accept or not; and if you do not do so, you shall be disinherited."

(166) And if an heir appointed in this manner desires to accept, he should do so within the prescribed time, that is to say he should utter the following words: "As Publius Mævius appointed me his heir by his will, I decide to accept the estate"; but if he should not make such a declaration, after the time has elapsed he shall be excluded; nor will it be of any benefit to him to act as the heir, that is to say, for him to make use of the property of the estate just as if he were the heir.

(167) But if an heir should be appointed without giving him time for deliberation, or be called to the succession as heir-at-law on the ground of intestacy, he can, either by deliberating or as acting as the heir, or by the mere intention of accepting the estate, become the heir, and he will be free to accept at any time, when he may desire to do so; but the Prætor, on the demand of the creditors of the estate, usually fixes a time within which if the party may enter on it if he wishes; and if he does not, the creditors may be permitted to sell the property of the deceased.

(168) But, just as one who has been appointed heir with time for deliberation does not actually become the heir unless he formally accepts the estate, so he will not be excluded unless he fails to make the declaration to that effect within the prescribed time; and, therefore, although before the time has expired he may have decided not to accept the estate, still, by having changed his mind and declared that he will accept, before the time for deliberation has elapsed, he can become the heir.

---

[1] By the Roman law, the beneficiary under a will was not permitted to accept or reject the estate until the death of the testator; before which event, of course, title to it could not vest. The *cretio* was adopted for the purpose of enabling creditors to present and collect their claims within a reasonable time. If the declaration of acceptance was not made within the period specified, the heir forfeited all his rights under the will. So long as the inheritance was not accepted, it was held, by a legal fiction, to personally represent the deceased, "*Personam defuncti sustinet*," who was presumed still to have possession. — ed.

(169) But just as he who was appointed heir without time for deliberation, or who was called to the succession as heir-at-law on the ground of intestacy, becomes heir by the mere expression of his will; so, by a contrary statement he is immediately excluded from the inheritance,

(170) Moreover, every period granted for deliberation has a prescribed limit, and in such cases a reasonable time is considered to be a hundred days. Still, by the Civil Law, a longer or a shorter period can be granted, though the Prætor sometimes shortens a longer one.

(171) Although the time for deliberation is limited to certain days, still, one kind of limitation is designated common and the other certain; common, being that which we have described above, that is, where the following words: "When he has learned of it, and is able," are added; certain, is that in which other words are written instead of those above mentioned.

(172) A great difference exists between these two grants of time, for in the common one no days are computed except those during which the party knows that he has been appointed heir, and is able to decide; but where a certain time has been granted, notwithstanding the party may not know that he has been appointed heir, the days are reckoned continuously; and, likewise, if for any reason he is prevented from stating his decision, or, further, if he has been appointed heir under some condition, the time will still continue to be reckoned, and hence it is better and more convenient to make use of the common method.

(173) This certain period of computation is called continuous for the reason that the days are reckoned without cessation; but, still, on account of the harshness of this method, the other is ordinarily employed, and hence is styled common.

III. CONCERNING SUBSTITUTIONS.

(174) Sometimes, we appoint two or more degrees of heirs in the following manner: "Lucius Titius, be my heir, and make your declaration within the next hundred days after you know of your appointment, and are able to do so; and if you should not announce your decision in this manner, you shall be disinherited. Then you, Mævius, be my heir, and announce your decision within a hundred days, etc." And afterwards we can make as many substitutions as we desire.

(175) We are permitted to substitute one or several persons in the place of one; and, on the other hand, to substitute one or several in the place of several.

(176) Therefore, where the heir is appointed in the first degree he becomes such by acceptance and the substitute is excluded; if he does not declare his acceptance, he will be excluded, even if he acts as heir, and the substitute will succeed in his stead; and if there are several degrees in succession, the same thing takes place under this rule in every instance.

(177) Where, however, the time for acceptance is fixed without mentioning disinheritance, that is to say as follows: "If you do not announce your acceptance of the estate, then let Publius Mævius be my heir," a different rule will apply; for if the party first appointed — even though he does not announce his acceptance — acts as heir, the substitute is only admitted to share in the estate, and both parties become heirs to equal portions of the same; and if he neither announces his acceptance, nor acts as heir, he will then be excluded from the entire estate, and the substitute will succeed to the whole of it.

(178) It was held by Sabinus that a substitute is not admitted as long as the heir first in degree has the right to announce his decision, even though he should have acted as heir, and in that way have become the heir; but that when the time prescribed for making a decision has expired, the substitute could be admitted, instead of the party who had been acting as heir. It was held by others, however, that even while the term

prescribed for making the decision was pending the heir, by the exertion of authority as such, would admit the substitute to share in the estate, and that the former could not again revert to his right to decide.

(179) As we have stated above, we can not only appoint a substitute for our children under the age of puberty, who are subject to our authority, that is, if we have another heir and they should fail to inherit; but also even if they should become our heirs and die before reaching the age of puberty, another may be their heir; as for example, "Let my son Titius be my heir; and if my son does not become my heir, or if he should do so and die before he becomes his own guardian, then let Seius be my heir."

(180) In this instance, if the son does not become the heir, the substitute will be the heir to the father; but if the son should become the heir and die before reaching puberty, the substitute will become the heir to the son himself. On this account there are, as it were, two wills, one that of the father, the other that of the son, just as if the son himself had appointed an heir; or, in fact, there is one will disposing of two estates.

(181) However, in order that the minor may not be subjected to the risk of treachery after the death of his parent, it is the usual practice to make the substitution publicly, that is to say, in the same part of the will in which we appoint the minor our heir; for as ordinary substitution only calls a substitute to the succession if the minor should not become the heir, which takes place where he dies while his parent is still living; in which instance we cannot suspect the substitute of being guilty of foul play, as during the lifetime of the testator everything which is contained in the will is unknown. A substitution like the one above mentioned by which, even if the minor should become an heir but should die before attaining the age of puberty, we call the substitute to the succession, is one which we write separately on tablets subsequently executed, and seal up by our own cord and wax after having provided in the first tablets that those written afterwards shall not be opened before he reaches the age of puberty. It is much safer, however, for both kinds of substitution to be sealed up in different tablets subsequently executed, for if this should be done, or separate substitutions be made, as we have stated, it can be understood from the first that the same substitution is made in the second.

(182) Not only where children under the age of puberty are appointed heirs, can we make a substitution for them, so that, if they should die before attaining puberty, the person whom we designated shall be our heir, but this will even be the case if they are disinherited; therefore, in this instance, if anything should be acquired by the minor from the estates of relatives either by inheritance, legacies, or donations, it will all belong to the substitute.

(183) What we have stated with reference to the substitution for children under the age of puberty, whether they have been appointed heirs or disinherited, we understand also to apply to posthumous children.

(184) We cannot, however, appoint a substitute for a stranger who is appointed an heir in such a way that if the stranger should become the heir and die within a certain time, another shall be his heir; but we are only permitted to bind him by means of a trust to transfer our estate, either wholly or in part, and what this rule is we shall explain in its proper place.

(185) Freemen as well as slaves, whether they belong to us or to others, may be appointed heirs.

(186) A slave belonging to us must, however, be appointed heir and declared to be free at the same time, that is to say, in the following manner: "Let Stichus, my slave, be free and my heir," or "Let him be my heir and be free."

(187) For if he is appointed heir without the grant of his freedom, even if he should subsequently be manumitted by his owner, he cannot be the heir, because his appointment, in the first place, is not valid, and therefore although he may have been alienated, he cannot declare his acceptance of the estate, even by

the order of his new master.

(188) When a slave is appointed with the grant of his freedom, and remains in the same condition he becomes free by the terms of the will, and hence is a necessary heir. If, however, he should be manumitted by the testator himself, he can use his own discretion as to entering on the estate. If he is alienated, he should enter on the estate by the order of his new master, for which reason the latter becomes the heir through him, as he himself cannot be either the heir, or free.

(189) When a slave belonging to another is appointed heir and he remains in the same condition, he should enter on the estate by the order of his master. If, however, he has been alienated by him, either during the lifetime of the testator, or after the death of the latter, before he makes up his mind whether he will accept the estate or not, he must act by the order of his new master; but if he has been manumitted, he can use his own judgment as to the acceptance of the estate.

(190) If, however, a slave belonging to another is appointed heir with the period usually allowed for acceptance, it is understood only to date from the time when the slave himself knew that he had been appointed heir, and no obstacle existed to prevent him from notifying his master, in order that he might accept the estate by his order.

(191) Let us next consider legacies, a part of the law which does not seem to have any reference to the subject under consideration, for we are discussing these legal titles by which rights are acquired by us in the aggregate; but we have, at all events, to discuss wills and testamentary heirs, and it is not without reason that this legal subject should, in the next place be examined.

IV. CONCERNING LEGACIES.

(192) There are four kinds of legacies, for we either make bequests by asserting a claim, by condemnation, by permission, or by way of preference.

(193) We bequeath legacies by way of claim as follows: "I give and bequeath my slave Stichus to Lucius Titius"; or if only one of the expressions, "I give" or "I bequeath" be employed, the legacy is properly bequeathed by way of claim, and the prevailing opinion is that if the bequest was made in the following language: "Let him take," or "Let him have for himself," or "Let him seize"; the legacy will also be bequeathed as a claim.

(194) .A legacy bequeathed in this manner is so called because after the estate has been entered upon, the property immediately vests in the legatee by quiritarian right; and if the legatee claims the property from the heir, or from anyone else who has it in his possession, he should bring an action to recover it, that is to say, claim that the property is his by quiritarian right.

(195) Jurists differ only upon one point, namely, Sabinus, Cassius, and our other preceptors hold that what has been bequeathed in this manner becomes the property of the legatee as soon as the estate has been accepted, even if he is ignorant that the legacy was left to him; but that after he does know it, and has rejected it, the legacy will no longer be valid. Nerva, Proculus, and the authorities of the other school, however, do not think that the bequest becomes the property of the legatee if he should refuse to accept it. But at present, in accordance with the terms of a Constitution of the Divine Pius Antoninus, the opinion of Proculus seems to be the one which has been adopted; for when a Latin was bequeathed to a colony in this manner, the Emperor said: "Let the decurions deliberate whether they wish him to be their property, just as if he had been bequeathed to an individual."

(196) Only those things can be legally bequeathed, subject to be claimed, which belonged to the testator

himself by quiritarian right. It has been decided however, that those, which are estimated by weight, number, or measure are required to only belong to the testator by quiritarian right at the time of his death; as for instance, wine, oil, grain, and coin. It has also been held that other property must have belonged to the testator by quiritarian right at both times; that is to say, when he made the will, and when he died, otherwise the legacy will be void.

(197) This, however, is the rule only under the Civil Law. Subsequently a Decree of the Senate was enacted at the instance of the Emperor Nero, by which it was provided that if a testator bequeathed anything which had never belonged to him, the legacy would be valid just as if it had been left in the most approved manner, "the most approved manner" meaning where it is left by condemnation, in which way property belonging to another can be bequeathed, as will appear hereafter.

(198) If anyone should bequeath property belonging to him, and, after having made his will, should alienate it. the greater number of authorities hold that the legacy is not only void under the Civil Law, but that it does not become valid by the Decree of the Senate. This opinion was promulgated for the reason that even if anyone should bequeath his property by condemnation, and afterwards should alienate it, many authorities think that although, by strict law, the legacy is still due, if the legatee demands it, he can be barred by an exception on the ground of fraud as claiming something contrary to the intention of the deceased.

(199) It has been established that if the same property is bequeathed by way of claim to two or more persons, whether jointly or severally, and all of them demand the legacy, each of them is only entitled to a certain portion of the same; and if any share is rejected it will vest in the co-legatee. A legacy bequeathed jointly as follows: "I do give and bequeath my slave Stichus to Titius and Seius"; severally, as follows: "I do give and bequeath my slave Stichus to Titius," "I do give and bequeath the same slave to Seius."

(200) Where a legacy is bequeathed as a claim, conditionally, the question arises to whom does it belong while the condition is pending? Our preceptors hold that it belongs to the heirs, as in the case of a slave to be conditionally free, that is to say, a slave who has been ordered to be free by a will under a certain condition, and who, it is established, in the meantime belongs to the heir. The authorities of the other school however, think, that the property does not belong to anyone in the meantime; and they assert that this rule applies even more forcibly in the case where a legacy has been bequeathed absolutely, before the legatee has accepted it.

(201) We bequeath a legacy by condemnation, as follows: "Let my heir be condemned to give my slave Stichus"; or if it is only written, "Let him give my slave Stichus"; this is a legacy by condemnation.

(202) By this same form of a bequest property belonging to another can also be bequeathed, so that the heir will be obliged to purchase either the article referred to and deliver it, or pay its estimated value.

(203) Any property which is not yet in existence may be bequeathed by condemnation provided it comes into existence hereafter; as for instance, any crops which may be produced on such-and-such land, or any child which may be born from such-and-such a female slave.

(204) Any bequest made in this way, after an estate has been entered on, even though it has been made unconditionally, unlike a bequest left to be claimed, is not immediately acquired by the legatee, but still belongs to the heir, and therefore the legatee must bring an action to recover it, that is to say, he must allege that the heir is required to transfer it to him; and then if the property is subject to mancipation, the heir should either transfer it to him in this way, or surrender it in court, and give him possession. If, however, it is not subject to mancipation, it will be sufficient if he merely delivers it, for if he should only deliver but not sell anything susceptible of mancipation, the legatee will obtain complete ownership only by

usucaption; and as we have mentioned in another place, usucaption of movable property is acquired after a year's possession, and real property after possession for the term of two years.

(205) Another distinction exists between a bequest by claim and one by condemnation; for where property is left to two or more persons by condemnation, and this is done jointly, each is entitled to a certain share, as in the case where a legacy is bequeathed by claim; but if the bequest is made severally the entire amount is due to each legatee, and the result is that the heir must deliver the article itself to one and pay its value to another. In a joint bequest, a share which has lapsed does not belong to the co-legatee, but remains a part of the estate.

(206) What we have stated with reference to the lapsed share of a legacy bequeathed by condemnation remaining as a part of the estate, and where it is left as a claim, accruing to the co-legatee, we should observe was established by the Civil Law before the enactment of the *Lex Papia*; but after the *Lex Papia* a lapsed share of the legacy is considered to have no owner, and belongs to those who are mentioned in the will as having children.

(207) And although heirs who have children have the best right to a legacy which is considered to have no owner, and heirs who have no children have the next best right to the same; still, it is stated by the *Lex Papia* itself that a co-legatee who has children shall be preferred to heirs, even though they also may have them.

(208) It is held by the greater number of authorities with reference to the rights conferred upon joint legatees by the *Lex Papia*, that it makes no difference whether the legacy is bequeathed by claim or by condemnation.

(209) We make a bequest by permission as follows: "Let my heir be condemned to permit Lucius Titius to take and to have my slave as his own."

(210) This kind of a legacy has a broader application than one bequeathed by claim, but a narrower one than a bequest by condemnation, for in this way a testator can legally bequeath not only his own property, as well as that of his heirs; while by claim he can only bequeath his own property, and by condemnation he can bequeath any property belonging to any stranger whomsoever.

(211) If the property bequeathed belonged either to the testator himself or to his heirs at the time of his death, it is clear that the legacy is valid, even if at the time of making the will the property belonged to neither of them.

(212) If, after the death of the testator, the property vests in the heir, the question arises whether the legacy is valid; and most authorities hold that it is not. What then is the law? Although anyone can bequeath property which never belonged to the testator, and never after his death belonged to his heir, by the Decree of the Senate promulgated during the reign of Nero, all bequests are considered as having been left by condemnation.

(213) Just as property left by condemnation does not immediately belong to the legatee as soon as the estate has been entered upon, but remains the property of the heir until he transfers it to the legatee, either by delivery, sale, or surrender in court; so, in the form of bequest by permission the same rule applies; and therefore a personal action is also brought in the name of a legatee of this kind to recover or enforce, "Whatever the heir is required by the will to give or to perform."

(214) Nevertheless, some authorities are of the opinion that an heir is not bound by this kind of a legacy, either to sell the property, surrender it in court, or deliver it; but that it will be sufficient for him to permit the legatee to take the property, because the testator did not order him to do anything else than to grant him

permission, that is to say, to allow the legatee to have it for himself.

(215) A more important distinction arises with reference to a legacy of this description, where the same property is left separately to two or more persons; for some authorities hold that each one is entitled to the whole, as where a bequest is left by claim; and others think that the condition of the first occupant is the better one, because in this kind of a legacy the heir is condemned to permit the legatee to have the property, and the consequence is, that if he allows the first one to take it, and he does so, he will be secure against anyone who afterwards demands the legacy from him; for the reason that he neither has the property so as to permit it to be taken by the second claimant, nor was he guilty of fraud in order to avoid having possession of the same.

(216) We bequeath property by a preferred legacy as follows: "Let Lucius Titius have my slave Stichus as a preferred legacy."

(217) Our preceptors, however, hold that property cannot be bequeathed in this way to anyone except to a person who has been appointed heir to a certain share of an estate, for to take as a preferred legatee is to receive something more than what he is entitled to as heir; and he only can do so who has been appointed heir to a certain part of the estate, and is entitled to it as a preferred legacy over and above his share of the said estate.

(218) Therefore, if a legacy of this kind is bequeathed to a stranger, it will be void, and to such an extent is this true that Sabinus was of the opinion that the defect could not even be remedied by the Decree of the Senate of Nero; for he says that by this decree only those faults are corrected which render a bequest invalid under the Civil Law, and not such as have reference to the person of the legatee. It was, however, held by Julian and Sextus that, even in this instance, the legacy was rendered valid by the Decree of the Senate, for it might happen, in a case of this kind, that by the words employed a legacy would be void at civil law; and hence it is clear that a proper bequest could be made to the same person by other words, for example, by claim, by condemnation, or by permission, for then the legacy is not valid on account of the defect in the person of the legatee, as when it is bequeathed to one to whom it can, under no circumstances, be left, as for instance, to an alien who cannot receive anything by a will; in which case it is evident that the Decree of the Senate does not apply.

(219) Likewise, our preceptors are of the opinion that a bequest made in this manner can be recovered by the party to whom it was bequeathed, in no other way than by the action for partition of the estate, that is to say, for the purpose of dividing the same; for it is part of the duty of the judge to decide with reference to the bequest of a preferred legacy.

(220) From this we understand that, according to the opinion of our preceptors, nothing can be left as a preferred legacy except what belongs to the testator; for no other property than that forming part of an estate can become the subject of this action. Hence, if a testator should, in this manner, bequeath property which is not his own, the bequest will be void by the Civil Law, but will be rendered valid by the Decree of the Senate. In one instance, however, they admit that property belonging to another may be left as a preferred legacy, as, for instance, where anyone bequeaths property which he has transferred to his creditors by a fiduciary sale; for they hold that it is the duty of the judge to compel the co-heirs to release the property from liability by payment of the debt, so that he to whom it has been bequeathed may be able to obtain it as a preferred legacy.

(221) Authorities of the other school are of the opinion that a preferred legacy may be bequeathed even to a stranger, just as if it were written in the will as follows: "Let Titius take my slave Stichus," and that the addition "as a preferred legacy" is superfluous; and therefore that the legacy would appear to be left by

claim; and this opinion is said to be confirmed by a Constitution of the Divine Hadrian.

(222) Therefore, in accordance with this opinion, if the property belonged to the deceased by quiritarian right, it can be recovered by the legatee, whether he be an heir or a stranger; but if it only belonged to the testator by bonitarian right, the legacy will be valid under the Decree of the Senate even if left to a stranger, and must be delivered by the heir under an order of court in an action for partition of the estate. If, however, it did not belong to the testator by any title, it would be valid under the Decree of the Senate, whether it was left to the heir or to a stranger.

(223) Where the same property is left, either jointly or severally, to two or more legatees, each will be entitled to only proportionate shares, whether they are heirs, in accordance with the opinion of our preceptors, or whether they are strangers, in accordance with that of authorities belonging to the other school.[1]

V. ON THE FALCIDIAN LAW.

(224) Formerly, anyone was permitted to exhaust his entire estate by legacies and the enfranchisement of slaves, thus leaving nothing to his heir but an empty name; and the Law of the Twelve Tables, by which it is provided that a person may dispose of his property absolutely by will, seems to permit this to be done in the following words: "In whatever way a man may bequeath his property it shall have legal effect"; and for this reason, those who were appointed heirs rejected the inheritance and therefore the majority of persons died intestate.

(225) Hence the *Lex Fufia* was enacted, by the terms of which (except in the case of certain persons) it was not permitted to accept more than a thousand asses either as a legacy or as a donation in anticipation of death. This law, however, did not accomplish what was intended; for example, anyone who had an estate of five thousand asses, could leave to five men a thousand asses each, and, by doing so, exhaust the entire estate.

(226) In consequence of this, the *Lex Voconia* was subsequently passed, by which it was provided that no one could, as a legatee, *mortis causa*, take more than the heirs received. It is clear that by this law the heirs appeared to receive a part of the estate, but it still contained almost the same defect, for the testator could, in distributing his estate among many legatees, manage to leave so little to the heir that it would be of no advantage to him, for the sake of the profit, to assume the burdens of the entire estate.

(227) Then the *Lex Falcidia* was enacted, by which it was provided that no more than three-fourths of an estate could be bequeathed; and therefore it was necessary for the heir to have a fourth part of the same, and this is the law at the present time.

(228) The *Lex Fufia Caninia* also repressed inordinate license in the bestowal of grants of freedom to slaves, as we have stated in the First Commentary.

VI. CONCERNING INOPERATIVE LEGACIES.

(229) A bequest made before the appointment of an heir is void, for the reason that wills derive their force and effect from the appointment of an heir, and on this account the appointment of the heir is considered to be the beginning and foundation of the entire will.

(230) A grant of freedom cannot be made before the appointment of an heir, for the same reason.

---

[1] [1] The ancient forms of legacies described above were greatly modified by Nero and his successors, and were entirely abolished by Justinian, who decreed that no distinction, in this respect, should exist between bequests of every description. — ed.

(231) Our preceptors do not think that a guardian can be appointed under such circumstances, but Labeo and Proculus hold that a guardian can be appointed, because by such an appointment nothing is taken from the estate.

(232) A bequest made after the death of an heir is void, that is to say, if it is made as follows: "After my heir dies, I do give and bequeath," or "Let my heir give"; the following provision, however, is legal: "When my heir dies"; because it is not made after the death of the heir, but will become operative at the last instant of his life. Again, a bequest cannot be made as follows: "On the day before my heir dies," as this is not considered to be founded on any good reason.

(233) We understand that these rules also apply to the enfranchisement of slaves.

(234) Whether a guardian can be appointed after the death of an heir may perhaps give rise to the same doubt which arose with reference to his appointment before the institution of the heir.

(235) Legacies bequeathed by way of penalty are void. A legacy is considered to have been bequeathed by way of penalty, where it is left for the purpose of compelling the heir either to perform some act, or to refrain from doing so; as, for instance, where the bequest is made: "If my heir gives his daughter in marriage to Titius let him pay ten thousand sesterces to Seius"; or as follows: "If you do not give your daughter in marriage to Titius, you shall pay him ten thousand sesterces"; and again, for example, where the testator orders that if his heir did not build him a monument within the term of two years he should pay ten thousand sesterces to Titius, this bequest being by way of penalty; and finally, in accordance with this definition, we can suggest many similar cases of this kind.

(236) Freedom cannot be granted by way of penal bequest, although a question has arisen on this point.

(237) We cannot, however, raise any dispute with reference to the appointment of a guardian, because by such an appointment an heir cannot be compelled either to perform some act, or to refrain from performing it; and therefore, if a guardian is appointed by way of penalty, the appointment will appear rather to have been made under a condition, than by way of penalty.

(238) A legacy left to an uncertain person is void. An uncertain person is considered to be one of whom the testator has only an indistinct idea in his mind; as for example, where a bequest is made in the following terms: "Let my heir pay ten thousand sesterces to the first person who comes to my funeral." The same rule of law applies if he makes a bequest in general terms to all, as: "Whoever comes to my funeral"; or where the bequest is left as follows: "Let my heir pay ten thousand sesterces to whoever gives his daughter in marriage to my son." It also applies where the bequest is in the following terms: "Whoever shall be the first consuls nominated after the execution of my will," for all these bequests are deemed to have been made to uncertain persons; and, finally, many other instances of this kind might be adduced. The bequest of a legacy is legal where the designation of the class to which the person belongs is described with certainty, but the individual to whom it is left is uncertain; as, for instance: "Let my heir pay ten thousand sesterces to that one of my relatives now living who comes first to my funeral."

(239) A testamentary grant of freedom, however, cannot be made to an uncertain person, because the *Lex Fufia Caninia* directs that slaves be enfranchised by name.

(240) A certain person must also be appointed a guardian.

(241) A legacy bequeathed to a posthumous stranger is void. A posthumous stranger is one, who, after his birth, will not be included among the proper heirs of the testator; and therefore a grandson born to an emancipated son is a posthumous stranger to his grandfather, and likewise the unborn child of a woman who is not considered a wife at Civil Law, is a posthumous stranger to his father.

(242) A posthumous stranger cannot even be appointed an heir, for he is an uncertain person.

(243) What we stated above properly has reference to legacies, although it was not unreasonably held by certain authorities that the appointment of an heir by way of penalty could not be made; as it makes no difference whether the heir is ordered to pay the legacy in case he should either perform or not perform some act, or whether a co-heir is appointed with him; for he is just as much compelled by the addition of a co-heir as by the payment of a legacy either to do, or not to do something contrary to his intention.

(244) It is a question whether we can legally bequeath a legacy to one who is in the power of him whom we have appointed the heir. Servius thinks that the legacy can be legally bequeathed, but that it will lapse if the legatee continues to be under control when the time arrives for the legacy to vest; and therefore, whether the bequest is absolute, and the party ceases to be under the control of the heir during the lifetime of the testator, or whether it is left under a condition, and this takes place before the condition is complied with; the legacy will be due. Sabinus and Cassius think that a legacy can be legally bequeathed under a condition, but not absolutely; for, although the legatee may cease to be subject to the authority of the heir during the lifetime of the testator, still, the legacy must be understood to be void; because it would be considered as of no effect if the testator should die immediately after making his will, but that it would be valid if he should live longer would be absurd. The authorities of the other school, however, are of the opinion that a legacy left under a condition is inoperative, for the reason that we cannot be indebted any more conditionally than absolutely to those whom we have under our control.

(245) On the other hand, it is settled that if anyone under your control is appointed an heir, he can be charged with the payment of a legacy to you, but if you should become an heir through him the legacy will be extinguished, because you cannot owe yourself a legacy. If, however, your son should be emancipated, or your slave manumitted or transferred to another party, and he himself should become the heir, or make the other party his heir, the legacy will be due.

(246) Let us now pass to the consideration of trusts.

(247) And first let us examine trusts connected with estates.

(248) In the first place, it should be ascertained that the heir has been duly appointed according to law, and that he has been entrusted to transfer the estate to another; as otherwise, a will is void by which no one has legally been appointed an heir.

(249) The proper forms of words creating a trust, and employed are: "I beg, I ask, I wish, I entrust"; and these are just as binding when used separately as when they are united in a single phrase.

(250) Therefore, when we have written: "Let Lucius Titius be my heir," we can add: "I ask you, Lucius Titius, and I beg you, that as soon as you can enter on my estate you deliver and transfer it to Gaius Seius"; and we can also ask him to transfer a part of the same. It is likewise permitted to leave the trust under a condition, or absolutely, or after a certain day.

(251) After the estate has been transferred, he who transferred it will, nevertheless, continue to be the heir; and he who received the estate sometimes occupies the position of an heir, and sometimes that of a legatee.

(252) Formerly, however, he did not occupy the position of either heir or legatee, but rather that of a purchaser; for in those days it was customary for the party to whom the estate was transferred to give a coin as an evidence of the purchase of the same; and the stipulations usually entered into between the vendor and the purchaser of an estate were accustomed to take place between the heir and the party to whom the estate was conveyed, that is to say, as follows: The heir stipulated with the party to whom the estate was transferred that he would be indemnified for anything which he might be compelled to pay on account of

the estate, or might otherwise pay in good faith; and if anyone were to bring an action against him on account of the estate, that it would be properly defended; and, on the other hand, the party who received the estate stipulated that if anything should come into the hands of the heir which belonged to the estate it should be delivered to him, and also that he should be permitted, either as the agent or attorney of the heir, to bring any actions which the latter was entitled to bring in his own name.

(253) In subsequent times, however, during the Consulate of Trebellius Maximus and Annseus Seneca, a decree of the Senate was enacted, by which it was provided that where an estate was transferred under a trust, the actions to which the heir was entitled, and also those which could be brought against him under the Civil Law, should be granted for and against the beneficiary of the trust. Under this Decree of the Senate, the judicial securities formerly in use were abandoned, and the Prætor was accustomed to grant equitable actions both in favor of, and against the party who received the estate as heir, and these are set forth in the Edict.

(254) But again, for the reason that the appointed heirs when requested to transfer either all the estate, or nearly all of it, refused to accept it on account of the little or no advantage received, and hence the trusts were extinguished, it was afterwards decreed by the Senate during the Consulate of Pegasus and Pusio, that the heir who was requested to transfer an estate should be permitted to retain a fourth part of the same, just as he is permitted to do under the *Lex Falcidia*, in the case of legacies; and the same permission was granted where separate things were left under the terms of a trust. By the provisions of this Decree of the Senate, the heir himself sustains all the burdens of the estate, and he who receives the remainder of the estate as the beneficiary of the trust, occupies the position of a partial legatee; that is to say, of one to whom a portion of the property has been left; which species of legacy is called partition, because the legatee divides the estate with the heir. Hence, the result is that the stipulations usually entered into by the heir and the partial legatee also take place between the person who receives the estate as the beneficiary of the trust, and the heir; that is to say, that the profit and loss arising from the estate shall be divided among them *pro rata*.

(255) Therefore, if the appointed heir is asked to transfer no more than three-fourths of the estate, it will then be transferred under the Trebellian Decree of the Senate, and rights of action will be granted *pro rata* on both sides against the heir under the Civil Law, and against the beneficiary of the trust under the Decree of the Senate; for, although the heir continues to be such even with reference to that part of the estate which he has transferred, and actions for the entire indebtedness of the estate can be brought against him; still, he cannot be made liable for anything more, nor can actions be granted against him for any further claims beyond the amount of interest which he has in the estate.

(256) If anyone is requested to transfer more than three-fourths of the estate, or all of it, there is ground for the application of the Pegasian Decree of the Senate.

(257) When, however, the heir has once entered upon the estate, provided he does so voluntarily — whether he retains a fourth of the same, or refuses to do so — he will be liable to the entire indebtedness of the estate; but if he retains a fourth, stipulations should be entered into between the partial legatee and the heir with reference to their respective shares; but if he transfers the entire estate, a stipulation should be entered into just as if the estate had been purchased and sold.

(258) But where the appointed heir refuses to enter on an estate for the reason that he says that he suspects it of being insolvent, it is provided by the Pegasian Decree of the Senate that, on the request of the party to whom he is asked to transfer it he may be compelled to accept and convey it, by order of the Prætor, and actions shall be granted both for and against him who received the estate as beneficiary of the trust, just as under the Trebellian Decree of the Senate. In this instance, no stipulations are required, because at the same

time security is given to the party who transferred the estate, and rights of action with reference to the estate are transferred for and against the party who obtained it as beneficiary.

(259) It makes no difference, however, whether anyone who is appointed heir to the entire estate is asked to transfer all, or a portion of the same; or whether he who was appointed heir to a share is asked to transfer the entire share, or only a portion of it, for, in this instance also, the rule of the Pegasian Decree of the Senate is understood to apply to the fourth part of the share.

(260) Anyone can also leave single articles under a trust, as for instance, a tract of land, a slave, a garment, silver plate, money; and he may either charge the heir himself, or a legatee to deliver it, although a legatee cannot be charged with a legacy.

(261) Likewise, not only the property of the testator can be left under the terms of a trust, but also that of an heir, a legatee, or any other person whomsoever. Hence, a legatee may not only be charged to deliver the legacy bequeathed to him to another, but he may also be charged with the delivery of anything else belonging either to himself or to another; only it must be observed that no one can be asked to deliver to others more than he himself received under the will, for any bequest in excess of this would be void.

(262) Moreover, when property belonging to another is left under the terms of a trust, it is necessary for the party who is asked to deliver it either to purchase and transfer the said property, or to pay its value; just as in the case where property belonging to another is bequeathed by condemnation. Still, there are some authorities who hold that if the owner refuses to sell property left under the terms of a trust, the trust will be extinguished; though the rule is different where a legacy is bequeathed by condemnation.

(263) Freedom can also be conferred upon a slave under the terms of a trust, and either the heir or the legatee may be charged to manumit him.

(264) Nor does it make any difference whether the testator makes the request with reference to one of his own slaves, or to one belonging to the heir himself, or to the legatee, or even to a stranger.

(265) Therefore, a slave belonging to another must be purchased and manumitted; but if his owner is unwilling to sell him, the grant of freedom is extinguished; because in this instance no computation of value can be made.

(266) When a slave is manumitted under the terms of a trust, he does not become the freedman of the testator, even though he may have been his slave, but of the person who manumitted him.

(267) Where a slave is ordered to be free by a direct provision of a will, for instance, as follows: "Let my slave Stichus be free," or "I order my slave Stichus to be free," he becomes the freedman of the testator himself. No other slave can obtain his freedom by a direct provision of the will but one who belonged to the testator by quiritarian right at both times, that is to say, the time when he executed the will, and when he died.

(268) A great difference exists between bequests made under the terms of a trust and those left directly.

(269) Hence a bequest may be left under a trust, to be discharged by the heir of the heir, while a bequest of this kind made in any other way in the beginning of a will is inoperative.

(270) Likewise, a person about to die intestate can charge his heir to deliver his estate to a third party under the terms of a trust, but on the other hand, he cannot charge him with the payment of a legacy.

(270a) Moreover, a legacy left by a codicil is not valid unless it has been confirmed by the testator, that is, unless the testator provided in his will that whatever he might insert in a codicil would be ratified; a trust, however, may be left without any confirmation of a codicil.

(271) Again, a legatee cannot be charged with a legacy, but the beneficiary of a trust can himself be charged with the execution of a trust in favor of another.

(272) Likewise, freedom cannot be left directly to a slave belonging to another, but this can be done under the terms of a trust.

(273) No one can be appointed an heir or disinherited by a codicil, even though it may have been confirmed by the will; but the testamentary heir may be asked by a codicil to transfer the estate either wholly or in part, to another, although the codicil may not have been confirmed by the will.

(274) Moreover, a woman appointed an heir by anyone who is registered in the census as possessing a hundred thousand sesterces, cannot take under the *Lex Voconia*; but she can still receive an estate left to her under a trust.

(275) Latins who are forbidden by the *Lex Junia* to receive estates or legacies directly under a will, can do so under the terms of a trust.

(276) Moreover, while the slave of a testator under the age of thirty years is prohibited by a decree of the Senate from being appointed an heir, and declared free; still, it is held by many authorities that we can direct him to become free when he reaches the age of thirty years, and that then the estate may be transferred to him.

(277) In like manner, although we cannot, after the death of a person who was our heir, appoint another in his stead, still, we can request him to transfer the entire estate, or a portion of the same, to another party when he dies; and for the reason that a trust may be created to take effect after the death of an heir, we may bring about the same result by inserting in the will: "When my heir Titius is dead, I desire my estate to belong to Publius Mævius"; and, whichever method is employed, Titius will leave his heir bound to transfer the estate under the terms of the trust.

(278) Moreover, we can sue for legacies under the Formulary System, but we enforce the performance of trusts, at Rome, either before the Consul or the Prætor, who is especially charged by the law with this duty; in the provinces, however, it is done by the Governor.

(279) Again, legal questions arising from trusts are decided in the City of Rome at all times, but those having reference to legacies only during the regular sessions of the tribunals.

(280) The interest and profits of property left in trust are payable, provided the party charged with the trust is in default, but the interest of legacies is not payable; and this is stated in a rescript of the Divine Hadrian. I am aware, however, that it was held by Julianus that, where a legacy was left under the form of permission, the same rule applies as in the case of trusts, and this opinion is the one accepted at the present time.

(281) Legacies bequeathed in the Greek language are not valid; trusts bequeathed in this way are valid.

(282) Moreover, where an heir disputes a legacy left by way of condemnation, an action can be brought against him for double the amount of the claim; but he can only be sued for simple damages where he acts as trustee.

(283) Likewise, where anyone, through mistake, pays more than was due under the terms of a trust, he can recover the excess; but where, in the case of a legacy by condemnation, payment is made for more than was due, through mistake, the excess cannot be recovered. The same rule of law applies where nothing at all

was due, and through some mistake or other, payment has been made.

(284) There were formerly other differences which at present no longer exist.

(285) For instance, aliens could take as beneficiaries of a trust, and which was, generally speaking, the original cause of trusts, but this was subsequently prohibited, and now a Decree of the Senate, enacted at the instance of the Divine Hadrian, provides that trusts left for the benefit of aliens shall be claimed by the Treasury.

(286) Persons who are unmarried are, by the *Lex Julia*, relating to wills, prohibited from receiving estates and legacies, and formerly were considered capable of being the beneficiaries of a trust.

(286a) Likewise, persons who have no children, and who for this reason under the terms of the *Lex Papia* lose half of their estates and legacies, were formerly considered capable of receiving the full benefit of trusts. Afterwards, however, they were forbidden by the Pegasian Decree of the Senate to enjoy the benefit of trusts, just as in the case of legacies and estates; and the property passed to those named in the will who have children, and, if none of them have any, to the people; as in the law with reference to legacies and estates which, for this or a similar reason, are deemed to have no owners.

(287) Again, in former times, property could be left under the terms of a trust to an uncertain person, or to a posthumous stranger, although he could neither be appointed an heir nor a legatee; but, by a Decree of the Senate, enacted at the instance of the Divine Hadrian, the same rule which applied to legacies and estates was adopted with reference to trusts.

(288) Likewise, there is no doubt that property cannot be left under a trust by way of penalty.

(289) Although in many branches of the law a much broader application to trusts exists than in the case of direct bequests, in other respects they are equally valid; still, a guardian cannot be appointed by will unless this is done directly, for instance, as follows: "Let Titius be the guardian of my child"; or "I appoint Titius guardian of my children"; but he cannot be appointed under a trust.

THIRD COMMENTARY

(1) By the Law of the Twelve Tables, the estates of persons dying intestate belong to their proper heirs.

(2) Children who were under the control of the deceased at the time of his death are held to be proper heirs, as for instance, a son or a daughter; a grandson or a granddaughter by a son; a great-grandson or a great-granddaughter by a grandson; nor does it make any difference whether these children are natural or adopted. Provided, however, that a grandson or a granddaughter, and a great-grandson or a great-granddaughter, are to be classed as proper heirs only when the party in the preceding degree has ceased to be under the control of his parent, either by the death of the latter, or for some other reason, for instance, emancipation; for if the son was in the power of the deceased at the time of his death, the grandson by that son cannot be a proper heir; and we understand that the same rule applies to all other descendants.

(3) A wife who is in the hand of her husband is a proper heir because she occupies the position of his daughter; as well as a daughter-in-law who is in the hand of his son, for she occupies the place of a granddaughter; she will, however, only be a proper heir if the son in whose hand she is was not under the control of the father at the time of his death. We also say that the same rule applies to her who is in the hand of a grandson on account of marriage, for the reason that she occupies the place of granddaughter.

(4) Posthumous children also, who if born during the lifetime of their parent would have been under his control, are proper heirs.

(5) The same rule of law is applicable to those in whose cases proof of error has been established after the death of the father under the provisions of the *Lex Ælia Sentia*, or the Decree of the Senate; for, if the error had been proved during the lifetime of the father, they would have been under his control.

(6) We understand that the same rule also applies to a son who, having been mancipated once or twice, is manumitted after the death of his father.

(7) Therefore, when a son or a daughter, and grandchildren of both sexes by another son, are equally called to the succession, the one who is nearest in degree does not exclude the one who is more remote; for it seems to be just that grandchildren should succeed to the place and share of their father. Under the same rule, if there is a grandson or a granddaughter by a son, and great-grandchildren by a grandson, they are all called at once to the succession.

(8) And, as it was decided that grandchildren and great-grandchildren of both sexes should succeed to the place of their father, it seems to be proper that the estate should be divided not *per capita* but *per stirpes;* so that the son should have half of the estate, and that two or more grandchildren by another son the remaining half; and if there should be one or two children by one son, and three or four by the other, half of the estate should belong to the two grandchildren by the son, and the other half to the three or four grandchildren by the other.

(9) If there is no proper heir, then the estate by the same Law of the Twelve Tables belongs to the agnates.

(10) Those are called agnates who are connected by lawful relationship. Lawful relationship is that which unites persons through the male sex. Therefore, brothers by the same father are agnates to those who are of the same blood, and it is not even required that they should have the same mother. Hence a paternal uncle is the agnate of the son of a brother, and *vice versa*. The sons of brothers are included in the same category, that is to say, those who are descended from two brothers and are usually called cousins, according to which rule also we can compute several degrees of agnates.

(11) The Law of the Twelve Tables does not grant an estate to all agnates at once, but only to those who are the nearest in degree at the time when it is certain that the deceased died intestate.

(12) Succession does not exist under this right of descent; therefore, if the agnates nearest in degree should fail to accept the estate, or should die before entering on it, the agnates next in degree will not legally be entitled to it.

(13) Moreover, we require that agnates should be the next in degree, not at the time of death, but when it became certain that the party died intestate, because if anyone should die after having made a will, it seemed to be better to accept the agnate next in degree, when it is certain that no one will be an heir under the will.

(14) With reference to women, however, it has been decided that one rule applies to the taking of estates left by them, and another to the taking of the estates of others by them. For the estates of women pass to us by the right of agnation, just as do those of males; but our estates do not belong to females who are beyond the degree of sisters by the same father. Therefore, the sister of a brother by the same father is his heir-at-law, but a father's sister and a brother's daughter cannot be the heir-at-law of one who occupies the place of a sister. A mother, or a stepmother, who passes into the hand of a father by marriage, is entitled to the same rights as a daughter.

(15) If the deceased leaves a brother and the son of another brother, as was previously stated, the brother is to be preferred, for the reason that he is nearest in degree; but another interpretation of the law is made in the case of proper heirs.

(16) If, however, no brother should survive the deceased, but there are children of more than one brother, the estate will belong to all of them; but the question arose if they were unequal in number, and one of the brothers left one or two, and the other three or four children, whether the estate shall be divided *per stirpes*, as is the rule among proper heirs, or *per capita*. It has, however, been long since decided that the estate shall be divided *per capita*; and therefore the estate shall be divided into as many portions as there are persons on both sides, so that each individual may have an equal share of the same.

(17) If there is no agnate, the same Law of the Twelve Tables calls *gentiles* to the inheritance. Who *gentiles* are we explained in the First Commentary, and as we called attention to the fact that the entire law relating to *gentiles* had fallen into disuse, it would be superfluous in this place to discuss the point with any degree of minuteness.

(18) The rules prescribed by the Law of the Twelve Tables with reference to the succession of intestate estates end here, and it is easy to understand how strict they were.

(19) For as soon as children were emancipated, they had no right to the estate of their parents under this law, as they had ceased to be proper heirs.

(20) The same rule applies to children who are not under the control of their father, for the reason that they, together with their father, had received Roman citizenship, and had not again been brought under his authority by the Emperor.

(21) Likewise, agnates who have suffered a loss of civil rights are, under this law, not admitted to the estate, for the reason that title by agnation is extinguished by the forfeiture of civil rights.

(22) Again, if the agnate next in degree should not enter on the estate, the one nearest to him is not legally admitted to the succession.

(23) Female agnates who are beyond the degree of sisters by the same father, have no right to succession under this law.

(24) In like manner, cognates who trace their relationship through persons of the female sex are not admitted; and, to such an extent does this rule apply, that even a mother and a son or daughter have no right reciprocally to an estate, unless by the mother having been placed in the hand of the husband by marriage, the rights of consanguinity should thereby have been established between them.

(25) But these unjust provisions of the law are now corrected by the Edict of the Prætor.

(26) For he calls to the succession all children whose legal title is defective, just as if they had been under the control of their father at the time of his death, whether they are alone, or there are also proper heirs; that is to say, they also come in with children who are under the control of their father.

(27) He does not, however, call agnates who have suffered a loss of civil rights and are not in the second degree after proper heirs; that is, he does not call them in the same degree in which they would be called by the law if they had not forfeited their civil rights, but in the third degree of proximity; for, although by forfeiture of civil rights they have lost their legal title, they certainly retain their rights of cognation. Hence, if there is anyone else who has an unimpaired right of agnation, he will be preferred, even though he may be in a more remote degree.

(28) The same rule applies, as some authorities hold, to the agnate who, if the next of kin should fail to accept the estate, would, nevertheless, be entitled to it by law. There are others, however, who hold that he should be called by the Prætor in the same order by which an estate is given to agnates under the law.

(29) It is certain that female agnates, who are beyond the degree of sisters, are called in the third degree; that is to say, where there is no proper heir, nor any other agnate.

(30) Those are also called in the same degree who are related through persons of the female sex.

(31) Also, children belonging to an adoptive family are called to the succession of their natural parents in this same order.

(32) Moreover, those whom the Prætor calls to a succession do not indeed become heirs by law, for the Prætor has no power to make heirs, and they become such only by some law, or some enactment which resembles a law; for example, by a Decree of the Senate, or an Imperial Constitution. When, however, the Prætor grants them possession of an estate they are placed in the position of heirs.

(33) In granting possession of an estate, the Prætor also takes cognizance of several other degrees, and he does this in order that no one may die without leaving a successor. We purposely do not treat of this matter in these Commentaries, as we have discussed this entire right in other Commentaries specially devoted to the subject.

(33a) It will be sufficient only to note the fact that, as we have already stated in the distribution of estates by law, cognation alone, as established by the Twelve Tables, would be of no advantage in taking an estate; and, therefore, unless a mother, in obtaining the estate of her children, has acquired the rights of consanguinity by being in the hand of her husband through marriage, she will have no right whatever under the law.

(34) Sometimes, however, the Prætor promises possession of an estate neither for the purpose of correcting or opposing the ancient law, but for the sake of confirming it; as he also grants possession of an estate in accordance with the provisions of the will to those persons who have been appointed heirs under a properly executed testament. He also calls the proper heirs and agnates to the possession of an estate *ab intestato*. In this instance, the only benefit derived from his act is that he who, in this way, demands prætorian possession of the estate, can avail himself of the interdict which begins with the words: "Whatever portion of the property"; and the advantage of this interdict we shall explain in its proper place. On the other hand, if prætorian possession of the estate is not granted, it will belong to the said parties by the Civil Law.

(35) Moreover, possession of an estate is often granted to persons in such a way that they will not be able to obtain it, and possession of this kind is said to be inoperative.

(36) For example, if an heir is appointed by a properly executed will, and declares his acceptance of the estate, but refuses to demand prætorian possession of the same in accordance with the provisions of the will, being content with the fact that he is the heir under the Civil Law; still, those who, if a will had not been made, would have been entitled to the estate of the party who died intestate, can demand possession of the property, but the grant will be inoperative, as the testamentary heir can evict the estate.

(37) The same rule applies where a person having died intestate, his proper heir refuses to demand prætorian possession, being content with his title of heir-at-law, for an agnate will have a right to obtain possession of the estate; but the grant will be inoperative because the estate can be evicted by the proper heir. In like manner, if the estate should belong to an agnate by the Civil Law, and he should enter upon the same, but should fail to demand prætorian possession, a cognate in the nearest degree can demand it; but his possession of the estate will be inoperative for the same reason.

(38) There are other similar cases, some of which we have discussed in the preceding Commentaries.

(39) Let us now consider the estates of freedmen.

(40) Formerly, a freedman was permitted to pass over his patron in his will, with impunity, for the Law of the Twelve Tables only called a patron to the estate of his freedman, when the latter died intestate without leaving any heirs. Hence, if the freedman died intestate but left a proper heir, the patron was not entitled to any of his estate, but if he left a proper heir who was one of his natural children, no complaint could be made on this account. If, however, the proper heir was an adopted son or daughter, or a wife who was in his hand, it was evidently unjust that the patron should have no right to the estate.

(41) For this reason, this injustice of the law was afterwards corrected by the Edict of the Prætor, for if a freedman made a will, he is ordered to do so in such a way as to leave half of his estate to his patron; and if he left him either nothing, or less than half, the possession of half the estate is granted to the patron in opposition to the provisions of the will. If, however, the freedman died intestate, leaving as his heir an adopted son, or a wife who was in his own hand, or a daughter-in-law who was in the hand of his son; possession of half the estate is also granted to the patron as against these proper heirs. The fact that he has natural children will, however, permit the freedman to exclude his patron from the succession, not only with reference to the children whom he has under his control at the time of his death, but also those that have been emancipated, or given in adoption; provided any of them have been appointed to shares of the estate under the will, or if, having been passed over, they have, under the Edict, demanded prætorian possession contrary to the provisions of the will; for if they have been disinherited they do not, by any means, exclude the patron.

(42) Subsequently, by the *Lex Papia*, the rights of patrons were increased, so far as the wealthier freedmen were concerned; for it is provided by this law that where a freedman left an estate of a hundred thousand sesterces, or more, and had less than three children, an equal share of his estate was due to the patron, whether he made a will or died intestate. Therefore, if a freedman should leave but one son or daughter, his patron will be entitled to half his estate, just as if he had died without leaving either a son or a daughter; and if he should leave two sons or two daughters, a third part of his estate will be due to the patron; but if he left three children, the patron will be excluded from the succession.

(43) By the ancient law, patrons suffered no injury so far as the estate of freedwomen were concerned; for, as the latter were under the legal guardianship of their patron, they could not make a will without the consent of their patron; and, therefore, if he agreed to the execution of the will, he would either be appointed the heir, or if he was not, it was his own fault; for, if he did not consent to the will being made and the freedwoman should die intestate, he would obtain her property, because a woman cannot have proper heirs; and formerly no other heir could exclude a patron from the estate of his freedwoman.

(44) Afterwards, however, by the *Lex Papia*, the birth of four children released the freedwoman from the guardianship of her patron; and, for this reason, she was permitted to make a will without the consent of her guardian; and the law provided that a share equal to that of each of the children whom the freedwoman had at the time of her death, should be due to her patron. Therefore, if a freedwoman left four children and no more, a fifth part of her estate — if she died before they did — belonged to her patron, and if any of her children died before her, the share of the patron would be proportionally greater; and if all of them died, her entire estate would pass to him at her death.

(45) What we have stated with reference to a patron we understand to apply as well to his son, and also to his grandson by a son, as well as to a great-grandson born to the grandson by a son.

(46) The daughter of a patron, a granddaughter by a son, and a great-granddaughter by a grandson, were

entitled to the same rights as the patron, under the Law of the Twelve Tables. Children of the male sex, however, are only called by the Edict to the succession, but the daughter of a patron can demand the possession of half the property of the estate of a freedman contrary to the provisions of the will; or in case of intestacy, against an adoptive son, or wife or daughter-in-law who was in the hand of the deceased; and this was conceded by the *Lex Papia* on account of the woman having three children, otherwise the daughter would not have this right.

(47) But where a freedwoman who had four children died testate, a daughter of the patron was entitled to an equal share with each child; this rule was not, as some authorities hold, established on account of the children, but the words of the *Lex Papia* state that she is entitled to an equal portion, even if the freedwoman should die intestate. If, however, a freedwoman dies after having made a will, the same right is granted the daughter of the patron as would be granted contrary to the provisions of the will of a freedman; that is, that the male children of patrons shall be entitled to possession of half the estate in opposition to the provisions of the will; although this part of the law has been written with very little care.

(48) From these observations it is apparent that the foreign heirs of patrons are far removed from the rights to which a patron is entitled, either with reference to the property of intestate children, or with reference to prætorian possession in opposition to the provisions of the will.

(49) Formerly, before the enactment of the *Lex Papia*, patronesses had only that right to the estates of their freedmen which was conferred upon patrons by the Law of the Twelve Tables; for they could not demand possession of half the estate of an ungrateful freedman contrary to the provisions of the will, or on the ground of intestacy, against an adopted son, a wife, or a daughter-in-law, which right was granted by the Prætor in the case of a patron and his children.

(50) The *Lex Papia* granted almost the same rights to a freeborn patroness, who had two children, and to a freedwoman who had three, which male patrons enjoy under the Edict of the Prætor. And the same rights were granted to a freeborn patroness if she had three children, as were conferred upon a male patron by the same law, but it did not bestow the same advantage upon a patroness who was a freedwoman.

(51) The *Lex Papia*, however, does not confer any new advantage upon a patroness on account of her children, so far as the estates of freedwomen are concerned, even if they should die intestate. Therefore, if neither the patroness herself, nor the freedwoman, has suffered a loss of civil rights, the estate will belong to her by the Law of the Twelve Tables, and the children of the freedwoman will be excluded, and this rule applies even if the patroness should have no children, for, as we stated above, women can never have a proper heir. But, on the other hand, if either of them has suffered a loss of civil rights, the children of the freedwoman will exclude the patroness, for the reason that her title is legally destroyed on account of the forfeiture of civil rights, so that the children of the freedwoman obtain the preference by the right of relationship.

(52) Moreover, when a freedwoman dies after having made a will, a patroness, who has no right through children, cannot claim possession contrary to the provisions of the will of the freedman; but one who is entitled through her children, has the same right conferred on her by the *Lex Papia* as a patron has under the Edict in opposition to the provisions of the will of his freedman.

(53) The same law bestows upon the son of a patroness almost the same rights as upon a patron; but in this instance a single son or daughter is sufficient to authorize the privilege.

(54) All that relates to this subject appears to have been sufficiently discussed up to this point; and a more minute explanation will be found in my Commentaries devoted to this subject.

(55) Let us in the next place examine the estates of Latin freedmen.

(56) In order that this branch of the law may become more clear, we should remember what we have stated elsewhere, namely, that those who are now styled *Latini Juniani* were formerly slaves under quiritarian right, but by the aid of the Prætor had been placed in a position of apparent freedom, so that their property belonged to their patron by the right of *peculium*. Afterwards, however, by the *Lex Junia*, all of those whom the Prætor had protected while in nominal freedom became actually free, and were styled *Latini Juniani; Latini*, because the law intended them to be free just as those Roman citizens were who, having left the City of Rome for Latin colonies, became Latin colonists; *Juniani*, because they were free under the *Lex Junia*, even though they did become Roman citizens. Hence the author of the *Lex Junia* understood that the result would be that by this fiction, the property of deceased *Latini* would no longer belong to their patrons, for the reason that, as they did not die slaves, their estates could not belong to their patrons by the right of *peculium*; nor could the property of a Latin freedman belong to his patron by the right of manumission, and he considered it necessary, in order to prevent the benefit granted to freedmen from becoming an injury to their patrons, to provide that their property should belong to those who manumitted them, just as if this law had not been enacted; and, therefore, the property of Latins by this law belongs as it were by the right of *peculium* to those who manumit them.

(57) Hence it happens that the title to the property of Latins under the *Lex Junia*, and that to the estates of freedmen who are Roman citizens, differ greatly.

(58) For the estate of a freedman who is a Roman citizen will, by no means, belong to the heirs of his patron; but it will belong absolutely to the son of the patron, and to his grandsons by a son, and to his great-grandsons by a grandson; even though they may have been disinherited by their father. Moreover, the estates of Latins will pass to the foreign heirs of a patron in the same way as the *peculium* of slaves, and will not belong to the children of the person who manumitted them, if they are disinherited.

(59) Likewise, the estate of a freedman who is a Roman citizen belongs in equal parts to two or more patrons; although they may have had unequal shares in said slave, if they were his owners; but the estate of a Latin belongs to his patrons, according to the shares which each one owned in him when he was his master.

(60) Also, with reference to the estate of a freedman who is a Roman citizen, one patron would exclude the son of another, and the son of one patron will exclude the grandson of another; but the estates of Latins belong jointly to a patron and the heir of another patron, in proportion to the share which would have belonged to the person who manumitted the slave.

(61) Likewise, if one patron leaves three children, and another one, the estate of a freedman, who is a Roman citizen, is divided *per capita*, that is to say, the three brothers will take three shares, and the other heir the fourth share. The estate of a Latin, however, belongs to his successors in the same proportion as it would have belonged to the person who himself manumitted the slave.

(62) Again, if one of the patrons rejects his share to the estate of a freedman who is a Roman citizen, or dies before he formally accepts it, the entire estate will belong to the other; but the property of a Latin will belong to the people, so far as the share of the patron who refuses to accept it is concerned.

(63) Subsequently, during the Consulate of Lupus and Largus, the Senate decreed that the estate of Latins should belong, in the first place, to the party who manumitted them; and next to the children of the latter, who were not disinherited by name, according to their proximity; and then, by the ancient law, to the heirs of those who manumitted them.

(64) Certain authorities hold that, under this Decree of the Senate, the same rule applies to the estates of Latins as to those of freedmen, who are Roman citizens; and this was the opinion of Pegasus. This doctrine, however, is evidently incorrect, for the estate of a freedman who is a Roman citizen never belongs to the foreign heirs of his patron; while the estate of a Latin citizen under this very Decree of the Senate, where the party who manumitted him left no children, will belong to his foreign heirs. Likewise, with reference to the estate of a freedman who is a Roman citizen, disinheritance does not in any way injure the children of the party who manumitted them; while in the case of the property of Latins, it is set forth in the said Decree of the Senate that where disinheritance is specifically made, they will be injured. Hence, the only actual effect of this Decree of the Senate is, that the children of the party who manumitted the slave, and who are not disinherited by name, are preferred to foreign heirs.

(65) Therefore, an emancipated son of the patron who has been passed over, although he may not demand prætorian possession of his father's estate, in opposition to the provisions of the will, is still preferred to foreign heirs, so far as the estates of Latins are concerned.

(66) Moreover, a daughter and other proper heirs, although they may have been disinherited with others under the Civil Law, and entirely excluded from sharing in the estate of their father; still, in the case of the estates of Latins, unless they have been specifically disinherited by their father, they will be preferred to foreign heirs.

(67) Again, the estates of Latins will, nevertheless, belong to children who have refused to accept the estate of their father, for they also can not, by any means, be said to have been disinherited, any more than those who have been passed over in silence in a will.

(68) From all these examples, it is perfectly clear that if he who makes a Latin . . . .[1]

(69) It also seems to be settled that if a patron has appointed his children his sole heirs to unequal shares of his estate, the property of a Latin belongs to them in the same relative proportions, for the reason that where there is no foreign heir, the Decree of the Senate becomes inoperative.

(70) If a patron should appoint a foreign heir along with his children, Cælius Sabinus says that the entire estate will belong to the children of the deceased in equal shares; because when a foreign heir appears, the *Lex Junia* does not apply, but the Decree of the Senate does. Javolenus, however, holds that the children of the patron will, under the Decree of the Senate, only be entitled to equal shares in that portion of the property to which foreign heirs would have been entitled under the *Lex Junia*, before the enactment of the Decree of the Senate; and that the remaining shares will belong to them in proportion to their interest in the estate of their father.

(71) Again, the question arises whether this Decree of the Senate refers to those children of a patron who are born of a daughter or granddaughter; that is to say, whether my grandson by my daughter will have a better right to the estate of my Latin than a foreign heir. The question also arises, whether this Decree of the Senate applies to Latins who belong to a mother; that is, whether, in the distribution of the estate of a Latin who belongs to a mother, the son of a patroness shall be preferred to the foreign heir of the mother. It was held by Cassius that, in both instances, there was ground for the application of the Decree of the Senate, but most authorities reject his opinion, for the reason that the Senate did not have in mind the children of female patrons who belong to another family, and this is evident from the fact that it excludes such as have been expressly disinherited; for it seems to have had in view those who are usually disinherited by their parent if they are not appointed heirs. For it is not necessary for a mother to disinherit her son or daughter,

---

[1] Original manuscript illegible.

nor a maternal grandfather his grandson or granddaughter, if he or she did not appoint them heirs; whether we consult the Civil Law or the Edict of the Prætor, by which the possession of an estate is granted to children who are passed over contrary to the provisions of the will.

(72) Sometimes, however, a freedman who is a Roman citizen dies as a Latin; for example, where a Latin has obtained the right of Roman citizenship from the Emperor, with the reservation of the rights of his patron. For the Divine Trajan decided in a case of this kind that if a Latin obtained the right of Roman citizenship from the Emperor without the knowledge or consent of his patron, the said freedman resembles other Roman citizens, and can beget lawful children; but he will die a Latin, and his children cannot become his heirs, and also that he can only make a will in such a way as to appoint his patron his heir, and substitute another for him if he should refuse to accept the estate.

(73) And for the reason that the effect of this Constitution seems to be that men of this kind never die as Roman citizens, even though they may subsequently have acquired the right of Roman citizenship under the *Lex Ælia, Sentia* or the Decree of the Senate. The Divine Hadrian, induced by the injustice of this law, caused a Decree of the Senate to be enacted providing that freedmen who had obtained the right of Roman citizenship from the Emperor without the knowledge, or against the will, of their patrons, and afterwards availed themselves of the right by which, under the *Lex Ælia, Sentia* or the Decree of the Senate, they would have obtained Roman citizenship if they had remained Latins, should be considered to occupy the same position as if they had acquired Roman citizenship under the provisions of the *Lex Ælia Sentia*, or the Decree of the Senate.

(74) Moreover, the estates of those whom the *Lex Ælia Sentia* places in the class of *dediticii*, belong to their patrons, sometimes as if they were freedmen and Roman citizens, and sometimes as if they were Latins.

(75) For the estates of those who, had it not been for some offence which they perpetrated after having been manumitted, would have become Roman citizens, are granted by this same law to their patrons, just as the estates of those who have become Roman citizens, for they have not the power to make a will; and this opinion was not unreasonably held by the greater number of authorities, for it seems incredible that the legislator intended to grant the right to make a will to men belonging to the lowest rank of freedmen.

(76) The estates of those who, if they had not committed some offence, would, after their manumission, have become Latins, are granted to their patrons, just as if they had died Latins. It has not escaped my observation, however, that the legislator did not express his intention in this manner in a way which is sufficiently clear.

(77) Let us now consider the succession to which we are entitled by the purchaser of property.

(78) The property of debtors may be sold either during their lifetime, or after their death. For example, it is sold during their lifetime when they conceal themselves for the purpose of defrauding their creditors, and are not defended while absent; and the same rule applies to those who surrender their property under the *Lex Julia*, or when judgment has been rendered against them after the time has elapsed which has been fixed for the payment of a debt, partly by the Law of the Twelve Tables, and partly by the Edict of the Prætor. The property of a debtor is sold after his death, for example, when it is certain that he has left no heirs, or persons entitled to prætorian possession, or any other legal successor.

(79) If the property of an insolvent debtor is sold during his lifetime, the Prætor orders it to be taken into possession and advertised for thirty consecutive days; but for fifteen days if he is dead. He afterwards orders the creditors to assemble, and select one of their number as their representative, that is, one by whom the estate may be sold. Therefore, where the property of a living debtor is sold, the Prætor orders the sale to take place within ten days, or if he is dead, within five days. If the debtor be living, he orders thirty days to

be added, and if he is dead he orders twenty. The reason why he orders a longer time to elapse before the sale of the property of a living debtor, is for the purpose of showing more care for the interests of the living by preventing too easy a sale of his estate.

(80) Moreover, the ownership of property under prætorian possession, or of the property of a debtor which is sold, is not absolute, but only provisional. Ownership under quiritarian right is only acquired by usucaption. Sometimes, however, it happens that ownership by usucaption can not be acquired by purchasers of the property of a debtor, for example, when an alien is the purchaser. . . .[1]

(81) Again, debts due to, or by the party from whom property is obtained, are not owed to, or by the prætorian possessor, or the purchaser of the property of the debtor; but can be collected by means of equitable actions, which we will explain in a subsequent Commentary.

(82) There are successions of other kinds which were not established by the Law of the Twelve Tables or by the Edict of the Prætor, but have been adopted by common consent.

(83) For when the head of a household gives himself in adoption, or a woman places herself in the hand of another, all their property, incorporeal and corporeal, as well as all debts due to them, are acquired by the adoptive father, or the purchaser, with the exception of those that are extinguished by the forfeiture of civil rights; as, for instance, usufructs, the obligation of the services of freedmen which is contracted by oath, and claims in legal actions where issue has been joined.

(84) On the other hand, any debt owed by the party who gave himself in adoption, or who came into the hand of another, does not pass to the purchaser or to the adoptive father, unless the indebtedness was hereditary; for then, because the adoptive father or the purchaser becomes the heir, they are directly liable; but he who gave himself in adoption, and the woman who came into the hand of another, cease to be heirs. But if the persons referred to are indebted in their own names, although neither the adoptive father nor the purchaser becomes liable, nor does he who gave himself in adoption, nor the woman who came into the hand of another remain bound, for the reason that they are released from liability by their loss of civil rights; still an equitable action is granted against both, on the ground that their forfeiture of civil rights has been rescinded, and if no defence is made to this action, the Prætor will permit all the property to be sold by the creditors which would have belonged to them, if they had not been subjected to the authority of another.

(85) Likewise, if an heir, before he declares his acceptance of the estate of an intestate, or acts as heir to the same, surrenders the estate in court, he to whom it was surrendered becomes the heir absolutely, just as if he himself had been legally called to the succession. If, however, the heir should surrender the estate after having accepted it, he will still remain the heir, and for this reason he will be liable to the creditors, and he must transfer the corporeal property belonging to the estate just as if he had surrendered the separate articles in court; but the debts are extinguished, and in this way the debtors to the estate profit by the transaction.

(86) The same rule of law applies where a testamentary heir accepts the estate, and then surrenders it in court; but if he surrenders the estate before entering on it, his act will be of no force or effect.

(87) The question arises whether a proper and necessary heir, by surrendering an estate in court, performs an act which is valid. Our preceptors hold that such an act is void; authorities of the other school, however, think that the same effect is produced as that caused by other heirs after the estate had been entered on; for it makes no difference whether a party becomes an heir either by declaring his acceptance, or as acting in

---

[1] Original manuscript illegible.

the capacity of heir, or whether he is compelled by law to accept the estate.

(88) Let us now pass to other obligations, the principal division of which is into two classes, for every obligation either arises from a contract, or from an offence.

(89) And first, let us examine those which arise from contracts, of which there are four different kinds; for an obligation is contracted either by delivery of property, verbally, by writing, or by consent.

(90) An obligation by the delivery of property is contracted, for example, in the case of a loan for consumption. This generally takes place with reference to articles which are susceptible of being weighed, counted, or measured; such as money, wine, oil, grain, bronze, silver, and gold. This kind of property we transfer either by counting, measuring or weighing it with the understanding that it shall belong to him who receives it, and that, at some time or other, not the same article, but another of the same nature, shall be returned to us, and therefore an obligation of this kind is called *mutuum*, because what was given to you by me, from being mine becomes yours.

(91) He also who received something that was not due from a person who paid him through mistake, is liable under a contract of this description, for a personal action can be brought against him under the formula, "If it appears that he was required to give"; just as if he had received the property as a loan for consumption. Hence certain authorities hold that a ward or a woman to whom payment was made of something which was not due, through mistake, and without the authority of his or her guardian, is not liable to a personal action; any more than they are for a loan for consumption. This species of obligation does not, however, appear to arise from a contract, for a party who gives with the intention of paying a debt, rather desires to discharge an obligation than to incur one.

(92) An obligation is verbally contracted by question and answer, as for instance: "Do you solemnly agree to give it to me?" "I do solemnly agree." "Will you give it?" "I will give it." "Do you promise?" "I do promise." "Do you pledge your faith?" "I do pledge my faith." "Do you guarantee?" "I do guarantee." "Will you do this?" "I will do it."

(93) The verbal obligation contracted by the expressions, "Do you solemnly agree to give?" "I do solemnly agree to give," is peculiar to Roman citizens; the others belong to the Law of Nations, and therefore they are valid among all men, whether they are Roman citizens or aliens. And even if they are uttered in the Greek language they are still valid, so far as Roman citizens are concerned, if they understand Greek; and on the other hand, although they may be stated in Latin, they will, nevertheless, be binding on foreigners, provided they are familiar with the Latin language. The obligation contracted by the words, "Do you solemnly agree to give?" "I do solemnly agree to give," is so peculiar to Roman citizens, that it cannot properly be expressed in the Greek language, although it is said to have been derived from the Greek.

(94) Therefore, it is said that there is one instance in which an alien may be bound by this phrase, that is to say, when our Emperor interrogates the ruler of a foreign people with reference to concluding peace, as follows: "Do you solemnly agree that peace shall exist?" or where the Emperor himself is interrogated in the same manner. This, however, is said to be too subtle a refinement, for if anything should be done to violate a treaty, an action is not brought under the stipulation, but the property is claimed by the law of war.

(95) It may be doubted if anyone . . . .[1]

(95a) . . . .[1] a debtor, by the order of his wife, provided her guardian consents, may make a statement of the

---

[1] Original manuscript illegible.

amount of dowry which he owes. Another, however, cannot be bound in this way, and therefore if any other person promises a dowry to the husband in behalf of his wife, he will be liable under the common law, provided the husband had previously stipulated.

(96) An obligation is likewise contracted by one of the parties speaking and promising the other without being interrogated; as where a freedman swears that he will give a present, or perform some labor or service for the benefit of his patron; and this is the sole instance in which an obligation is contracted by oath, for in no other are men rendered liable on account of having been sworn, as will be apparent if the Roman law is examined; although if we ascertain what the law is among aliens by searching the records of other states we might come to a different conclusion.

(97) If we stipulate that something shall be given to us which cannot be transferred, the stipulation is void; for example, if anyone stipulates for the transfer of a freeman whom he thinks to be a slave; or of a dead slave whom he believes to be living; or of a sacred or religious place which he supposes to be subject to human law.

(97a) Likewise, if anyone stipulates for something which cannot, in the nature of things, exist, as for instance, a hippocentaur, such a stipulation also is void.

(98) Moreover, if anyone stipulates under a condition which cannot take place, for example, if he should touch the sky with his finger, the stipulation is void. Our preceptors however, were of the opinion that a legacy bequeathed under an impossible condition should be paid, just as if it had been left unconditionally; but the authorities of the other school hold that a legacy is just as invalid as a stipulation, under such circumstances, and, indeed, no good reason can be given for establishing a distinction.

(99) Moreover, a stipulation is void if anyone ignorantly agrees that his own property shall be transferred to himself; as what already belongs to a person cannot be given to him. Finally, a stipulation is void where anyone stipulates as follows: "Do you solemnly agree to pay after my death?" or "Do you solemnly agree to give after your death?" The stipulation, however, is valid if anyone stipulates as follows, "Do you solemnly agree to give at the time of my death?" or "Do you solemnly agree to give when you die?" that is, the obligation is valid as it relates to the last moment of the life of the stipulator or promisor, for it has been considered contrary to legal principle to make the obligation attach to the person of the heir.

(100) Again, we cannot stipulate as follows, namely: "Do you solemnly agree to pay on the day before I die, or on the day before you die?" for the expression: "On the day before anyone dies," can only be ascertained after death has taken place; and, moreover, where death has occurred the stipulation becomes retrospective, and means the same as, "Do you solemnly agree to pay to my heir?" which is clearly void.

(101) What we have stated with reference to death must also be understood to apply to the loss of civil rights.

(102) A stipulation is also void when anyone does not answer the question which he was asked; for instance, if I stipulated for ten sesterces to be paid by you, and you promise five; or if I stipulate absolutely, and you promise conditionally.

(103) Moreover, a stipulation is void if we stipulate to pay a party to whose authority we are not subject. Hence the question arose to what extent the stipulation would be valid if a person should agree to pay one to whose authority he is not subject. Our preceptors are of the opinion that it would be valid for the entire amount, and that he who stipulated would be entitled to all of it, just as if he had not added the name of a stranger. The authorities of the other school, however, think that only half is due to him, and that the stipulation is void so far as the other half is concerned.

(103a) The case is different where, for instance, I stipulate as follows: "Do you solemnly agree to pay my slave or my son who is under my control?" for then it is settled that the entire amount is due, and that I can collect it from the promisor and the result is the same when I only stipulate for payment to my son who is under my control.

(104) Again, the stipulation is void where I stipulate with one who is under my control, and also if he should stipulate with me. Still, a slave belonging to the household, a daughter under paternal authority, and a woman in the hand of her husband, cannot only not bind themselves to the persons to whose authority they are subject, but they cannot bind themselves to anyone else.

(105) It is clear that a dumb person can neither stipulate nor promise; and the same rule applies to one who is deaf, because he who stipulates must hear the words of the promisor, and he who promises must hear those of the stipulator.

(106) An insane person cannot transact any business, because he does not understand what he is doing.

(107) A ward can transact all kinds of business, provided, however, that, as the authority of his guardian is necessary it be granted, just as if he himself was bound; for he can render another liable to himself even without the authority of his guardian.

(108) The same rule of law applies to women who are under guardianship.

(109) Still, what we have stated with reference to a ward is only true of one who has some intelligence; for an infant, and a child who is almost an infant, do not differ greatly from an insane person, because minors of this age have no judgment; but in the case of such minors a more indulgent interpretation of the law is made on account of the benefit resulting to them.

(110) Although, as we have already stated, a party not subject to our authority cannot stipulate for us, we can associate another with us in the stipulation which we make, who also stipulates for the same thing, and who is commonly called a joint stipulator.

(111) He, also, has a right of action as well as ourselves, and payment can be made to him as well as to us, but he can be compelled by the action of mandate to transfer to us anything which he may recover.

(112) Again a joint stipulator can also make use of other words than those which we employ. Hence, for example, if I stipulate, as follows: "Do you solemnly agree to pay?" the joint stipulator may say, "Do you pledge your faith for the same?" or "Do you guarantee the same?" or *vice versa*.

(113) Likewise, he may stipulate for less, but not for more, than the stipulator. Therefore, if I stipulate for ten sesterces, he can stipulate for five; but, on the other hand, he cannot stipulate for more. Moreover, if I stipulate absolutely, he can stipulate under a condition, but not *vice versa*. The term "more or less," is understood not only to refer to quantity, but also to time, for to make payment immediately is more, and to do so after a certain period is less.

(114) To this rule there are certain exceptions, for the heir of a joint stipulator has no right of action. Likewise, the act of a slave as joint stipulator is void, although in all other cases he acquires property for his master by a stipulation. The better opinion is, that, the same rule applies to a slave in domestic servitude, because he occupies the place of a slave. Moreover, a son who is under the control of his father can act as a joint stipulator, but he does not acquire anything for his father; although, under all other circumstances, by stipulating he makes acquisitions for his benefit. Nor will he be entitled to any right of action unless he has been released from paternal control without the forfeiture of civil rights; as, for instance, by the death of his father, or because he himself has been installed a priest of Jupiter. We

understand that the same rule applies to a daughter under the control of her father, and a woman in the hand of her husband.

(115) Others are usually liable for the party who promises, some of whom we call sponsors, others guarantors, and others still, sureties.

(116) A sponsor is interrogated as follows: "Do you solemnly agree to pay the same?" a guarantor as follows: "Do you guarantee the same?" and a surety as follows, "Do you pledge your faith for the same?" We shall see what names should be properly applied to those who are interrogated, as follows, namely: "Will you give the same?" "Do you promise the same?" "Will you do the same?"

(117) We often accept sponsors, guarantors, and sureties, when we desire to be provided with additional security; and we rarely make use of a joint stipulator, except when we stipulate that something shall be paid after our death. If we make such a stipulation ourselves, our act is void, and hence the joint stipulator is employed so that he may bring suit after our death; but if he should recover anything, he will be liable by an action of mandate to deliver it to our heir.

(118) The positions of a sponsor and a guarantor are similar, that of a surety is extremely unlike the others.

(119) For the former can enter into no obligations except verbal ones, although sometimes the party who promises is not bound, as for instance, where a ward or a woman without the authority of his or her guardian, promises to make a payment after his or her death. It is a question, however, if a slave or an alien should promise, whether his sponsor or guarantor will be liable. A surety can enter into every kind of obligation, that is to say, whether it is contracted either by words, or by writing, or by consent, and it makes no difference whether the obligation be a civil or natural one. To such an extent is this true, that he is also liable for a slave, whether it be a stranger who accepts him as security for the slave, or whether .it be the master himself who does so for a debt which is due to him.

(120) Moreover, the heir of a sponsor and a guarantor is not liable, unless we have reference to the heir of an alien guarantor, in whose State another rule than ours prevails; but the heir of a surety is also liable.

(121) Likewise, a sponsor and a guarantor are released by the *Lex Fufia* from liability at the expiration of two years; and no matter what may be the number of the sureties at the time when the debt can be collected the obligation is divided into as many parts as there were sureties at that time, and each one of them is only liable for his respective share. Sureties, however, are perpetually liable, and no matter what may be their number, each of them is bound for the entire amount of the debt; and therefore the creditor is at liberty to collect the whole debt from any one of them whom he may select. But, now, according to a letter of the Divine Hadrian, a creditor is compelled to collect the proportionate part of the debt from each of the sureties who is solvent at the time. Hence, this letter differs from the *Lex Fufia* in that if any one of the sponsors or guarantors should not be solvent, this does not increase the liability of the others; but if even only one of the sureties is solvent, the entire burden of all the others is imposed upon him. But, as the *Lex Fufia* only applies to Italy, the result is that in the other provinces both sponsors and guarantors, like "sureties, are perpetually liable; and each one of them is bound for the entire amount of the debt, unless they are, to a certain extent, relieved by the letter of the Divine Hadrian.

(122) Moreover the *Lex Apuleia*, introduces a certain partnership between sponsors and guarantors; for if any of them should pay more than his share he will have a right of action against the others to recover the surplus. This law was enacted before the *Lex Fufia*, and therefore the question arises whether, after the passage of the *Lex Fufia*, the benefit of the *Lex Apuleia* still remains. This is certainly the case outside of Italy, for the *Lex Fufia* is in force only in Italy, while the *Lex Apuleia* embraces also the other provinces; but whether the benefit of the *Lex Apuleia* still continues to exist in Italy, *is* a question. But the *Lex Apuleia*

does not apply to sureties, and therefore, if a creditor recovers his entire debt from one surety the latter alone must suffer the loss, that is to say, if the party for whom he became surety is not solvent. But, as appears from what has been already stated, he whom a creditor sues for the entire amount of the debt can, under the letter of the Divine Hadrian, petition for the action to be brought against him only for his proportionate share.

(123) Moreover, it is provided by the *Lex Cicereia*, that a creditor who accepts sponsors or guarantors, must previously publish and declare the amount of the claim for which he receives security, and the number of sponsors or guarantors that he will accept as sureties for the obligation; and unless he does so, the sponsors and guarantors are permitted within the term of thirty days to demand a preliminary trial, by which it may be ascertained whether the declaration required under this law had been made, and if it should be decided that it had not been made, they shall be released from liability. No mention of sureties was made in this law, but it is customary when we receive sureties to make this statement.

(124) Moreover, the benefit of the *Lex Cornelia* is common to all, and by its provisions the same person is forbidden to become a surety for the same debtor to the same creditor, during the same year, for a larger sum of money than twenty thousand sesterces; and although sponsors or guarantors may bind themselves for a larger amount, for example, for a hundred thousand sesterces, they will still only be liable for twenty thousand. Again, we say that money which is lent under this law includes not only that which was actually loaned, but all certain to be due at the time that the obligation was contracted; that is to say, whatever is unconditionally included in the obligation, and therefore the money which we stipulate to be paid on a certain day comes under this provision, for the reason that it is certain that it will be due, although it cannot be collected until after the time has elapsed. All kinds of property are comprehended in this law under the term "money," and therefore, if we stipulate for wine, grain, land, or a slave, this law must be observed.

(125) In some cases, however, the law permits security to be taken to an indefinite amount; as for instance, for the purpose of dowry, or for what may be due to you under a will. Security may also be taken by an order of court. It is also provided by the *Lex Julia*, which imposes a tax of one twentieth on estates, that the *Lex Cornelia* shall not apply to the securities referred to in this law.

(126) Under this rule, also, the condition of all sponsors, guarantors, and sureties is the same, in that they cannot be liable for more than their principal owes; on the other hand, however, they may be liable for less, as we have stated with reference to a joint stipulator; for as is in his case, their liability is also accessory to the obligation of the principal, and the liability of the accessory cannot be greater than that of the principal.

(127) A further similarity exists between them in that, if the sureties should pay anything for the principal debtor, they will have a right to the action of mandate against him to recover it. Sponsors also, under the *Lex Publilia* are entitled to still another remedy, as they have a right to bring an action for double the amount, which is called the action to recover money expended.

(128) An obligation contracted by writing is made, for instance, by the entry of claims on an account book. Entries of this description are of two kinds; either from a thing to a person, or from a person to a person.

(129) The record from a thing to a person is made, for example, where what you owe me on account of a purchase, a lease, or a partnership, is entered upon my book as having been paid to you.

(130) The record of a claim from a person to a person is made, for instance, when the amount that Titius owes me is charged to you on my book; that is to say as if Titius had substituted you for himself to me.

(131) The case of those claims which are designated as cash is different, as the obligation for them has reference to the thing itself, and not to a charge in writing; although they are not valid unless the money has

been actually paid; for the payment of money makes the obligation a legal one. For which reason we very properly say that the entry of a claim as cash does not constitute an obligation, but is merely evidence that the obligation has been contracted.

(132) Hence, it is not proper to say that aliens are also bound by claims as cash, because their liability does not depend upon the entry of the claim, but upon the payment of the money; and this kind of an obligation belongs to the Law of Nations.

(133) A reasonable doubt has arisen as to whether aliens are bound by claims which have been entered on an account book; for an obligation of this kind is, to a certain extent, one contracted under the Civil Law, which was the opinion of Nerva. It was, however, held by Sabinus and Cassius that if the entry was made as from a thing to a person, aliens would also be liable; but if it was entered as from a person to a person, this would not be the case.

(134) Moreover, an obligation by writing is considered to be created by written evidences of debt, or promises to pay; that is to say, where anyone states in writing that he owes a debt, or will make payment in such a way, of course, that a stipulation is not entered into on this account. This kind of obligation is peculiar to aliens.

(135) Obligations are created by consent, in purchase and sale, leasing and hiring, partnership and agency.

(136) Moreover, we say that obligations are contracted by consent in these different ways, because no form of words or writing is required, but it is sufficient for the parties to the transaction to have consented. Therefore, agreements of this kind can be entered into by persons who are absent, as for instance, by letter or by messenger; while, on the other hand, verbal obligations cannot be created between absent persons.

(137) Likewise, in contracts of this description the parties are reciprocally liable, because each is liable to the other to perform what is proper and just; while, on the other hand, in the case of verbal obligations one party stipulates and the other promises; and in the entry of claims one party creates an obligation by doing so, and the other becomes liable.

(138) An absent person can be charged in writing with the disbursement of money although a verbal obligation cannot be contracted with one who is absent.

(139) Purchase and sale are contracted as soon as the price is agreed upon, although the price may not have been paid,[1] or any earnest money given; for what is given by way of earnest money is only a proof of the conclusion of a contract of purchase and a sale.

---

[1] The Mohammedan law provides that the declaration and acceptance by vendor and purchaser is all that is requisite to conclude a sale, and render it binding. It is considered preferable to make the statement in the past tense, and that both the articles and the price should be at hand. The amount of the purchase-money must be certain, but where an exchange — which is to be held to be a sale — takes place, absolute certainty is not necessary. "Sell anything that is in exchange for a different kind, in whatever manner you please, and without regard to the quality." (The Hedaya XVI, 1.) The Ottoman Code defines a sale to be "the interchange of one thing with another." (The Medjille, Art. 105.)

Under the Mosaic Law, payment of the purchase-money caused the title to the object of the sale to at once vest in the purchaser. The rule of the Talmud changed this, however, and the property passed as soon as the vendor obtained possession, whether the price was, or was not paid. Actual transfer of possession was therefore indispensable. (Mishnah, Introduction to Chap. IV.) In England, the transfer of title to specific articles depends upon the agreement of the parties; where they are not specified, it does not pass until their identity has been determined. Where the sale is for cash, the purchaser has no right to the property till he tenders the entire amount. (Stephen, Commentaries on the Laws of England II, II, V, 3.) It is of the essence of the contract of sale in American law that the price must be certain, the article capable of identification, and that both parties must concur in the agreement. The sale must be complete for the right of ownership to pass without question. Delivery is not essential, as it was under the Roman system. (Parsons, The Law of Contracts, I, III, 4.) — ed.

(140) Moreover, the price must be certain; for, otherwise, if we agree that property shall be purchased for the amount at which Titius may estimate its value, Labeo denies that a transaction of this kind has any force or effect; and Cassius agrees with him. Ofilius holds that it is a purchase and sale, and Proculus adopts his opinion.

(141) Moreover, the price must consist of money, for it is seriously questioned whether it can consist of any other property, as for instance, a slave, a robe, or a tract of land. Our preceptors think that a price can consist of other property, and hence is derived the common opinion that purchase and sale are contracted by exchange of articles, and that this kind of purchase and sale is of the highest antiquity, and in proof of their contention, they adduce the statement of the Greek poet Homer, who somewhere says: "Here landed Achæan ships in search of wine. They purchased it with copper and with iron; With hides, with horned cattle, and with slaves." Authorities belonging to the other school dissent from this, and think that the exchange of articles is one thing, and purchase and sale another, as where property is exchanged it cannot be determined what is sold and what is given by way of price; and, on the other hand, it is absurd to consider that both articles are sold, and at the same time given by way of price. Cælius Sabinus says that if you have some property for sale, for example land, and I receive it, and give you a slave by way of price, the land should be considered to have been sold, and the slave given by way of price, as the land is what is received.

(142) Moreover, leasing and hiring are governed by similar rules, for, unless the amount paid is certain, the contract of leasing and hiring is not considered to have been concluded.

(143) Hence, if the price is left to the judgment of another, for instance, at the amount that Titius may deem proper, the question arises whether the contract of leasing and hiring has been made. Therefore, if I give clothing to a fuller to be cleaned and taken care of, or to a tailor to be repaired, and the price was not stated at the time, but I was to pay the amount afterwards agreed upon between us, the question arises whether a contract for leasing and hiring has been entered into.

(144) Likewise, if I lend an article to you to be used, and I receive, in turn, another article to be used by myself, the question arises whether a contract of leasing and hiring has been made.

(145) Purchase and sale and leasing and hiring are considered to be so nearly related to one another that in certain cases the question arises whether the contract is one of purchase and sale, or one of leasing and hiring. For instance, if land is perpetually leased — which happens in the case of real property belonging to municipalities — under the condition that, as long as the rent is paid, neither the lessee nor his heir shall be deprived of the land; the better opinion is that this is a contract of leasing and hiring.

(146) Again, if I deliver gladiators to you under the condition that twenty *denarii* shall be paid to me for the exertions of every one who issues safe and sound from the arena; and a thousand *denarii* for every one who is killed or disabled; the question arises whether a contract of purchase and sale, or one of leasing and hiring has been made. The better opinion is that, in the case of those who come forth safe and sound, a contract of leasing and hiring was concluded; but so far as those who have been killed or disabled are concerned the contract is one of purchase and sale, for it is apparent that the contract depends upon circumstances taking place as it were under a condition; a contract of sale or hiring having been entered into with reference to each gladiator, for there is no doubt now that property can be sold or leased conditionally.

(147) Likewise, where it is agreed upon between a goldsmith and myself that he shall make me a number of rings of a certain weight and style out of his own gold, and shall receive, for example, two hundred *denarii*; the question arises whether a contract of purchase and sale, or one of leasing and hiring is made. Cassius

says that the material is the object of purchase and sale, but that the labor depends upon a contract of leasing and hiring; still, the greater number of authorities are of the opinion that the contract is one of purchase and sale. But if I furnish him with my own gold, and the price of the work is agreed upon, it is settled that the contract is one of leasing and hiring.

(148) We are accustomed to form a partnership either of all the property of the partners, or with reference to one certain business, for example, the purchase and sale of slaves.

(149) An important discussion arose, however, as to whether a partnership could be formed in such a way that one partner would have a greater share in the profits and be liable for a smaller amount of the losses. Quintus Mucius held that this was contrary to the nature of a partnership, but Servius Sulpicius, whose opinion has prevailed, thought that a partnership could be formed in such a way that one of the partners should not be liable for any of the losses, and be entitled to a part of the profits, provided that his services were so valuable as to make it just for him to be admitted into the partnership under such an agreement. For it is settled that a partnership can be formed in such a way that one partner shall furnish all the money and that the other shall not furnish any, and the profits nevertheless be equally divided among them; for frequently the services of a person are worth as much as money.

(150) It is certain, however, that if no agreement concerning the division of profit and loss should be made among the parties, the benefit and the disadvantage shall be equally shared between them. If the share of each should be stated, so far as the profit is concerned, but omitted with reference to the loss, the loss must be shared in the same way as the profit.

(151) Moreover, a partnership continues to exist as long as the partners give their consent, and when any one of them renounces the partnership, it is dissolved. It is clear, however, if a person renounces a partnership in order that he alone may obtain some pecuniary advantage, for instance, if a partner of mine in the entire property should be left an heir by anyone, and should renounce the partnership in order that he alone may profit by the estate, he can be compelled to share this gain with his partners. If, however, he obtains any profit, without intending to do so, it shall belong to him alone, and I will only be entitled to whatever may be acquired by him after he renounces the partnership.

(152) A partnership is also dissolved by the death of a partner, for he who enters into one selects a certain person for his associate.

(153) It is also said that a partnership is dissolved by forfeiture of civil rights, for the reason that under the rule of the Civil Law loss of civil rights is considered as equivalent to death; but if the partners still consent to the continuance of the partnership a new one is considered to be formed.

(154) Likewise, a partnership is dissolved if the property of one of the partners is disposed of at either public or private sale. The kind of partnership, of which we are speaking, however, that is one which is formed by mere consent, belongs to the Law of Nations, and therefore continues to exist according to natural reason among all men.

(155) Agency is established whether we direct it to take place for our own benefit or for that of another; and hence whether I direct you to transact my business or that of another, the obligation of mandate is contracted, so that both of us will reciprocally be liable, for whatever you must do for me, or I must do for you, in good faith.

(156) If, however, I direct you to perform some act for your own benefit, the mandate will be to no purpose, for what you are about to do for your own advantage should depend on your own judgment, and not be done on account of my mandate. Therefore, if you have some idle money at home, and I advise you

to lend it at interest, and you lend it to a party from whom you cannot collect it, you will not be entitled to an action of mandate against me. Again, if I advise you to purchase some article, even though it will not be to your advantage to do so, I will still not be liable to you in an action of mandate. These rules have been so well established that the question arose whether a party is liable in an action of mandate who advised you to lend money to Titius. Servius denied that liability is incurred, and thought that an obligation could not arise in this instance, any more than in one where a person is generally advised to lend his money at interest. We, however, adopt the contrary opinion of Sabinus, for the reason, that you would not have lent money to Titius if you had not been advised to do so.

(157) It is evident that, where anyone directs an act to be done which is contrary to good morals, an obligation will not be contracted; for instance, if I direct you to commit a theft, or some injury against Titius.

(158) In like manner if I should be directed to perform some act after my death the mandate is void, for the reason that it has been generally decided that an obligation cannot begin to take place with an heir.

(159) Where a mandate was properly given and while the matter still remained unchanged was revoked, it is annulled.

(160) Again, if before a mandate was begun to be executed, the death of either of the parties should take place, that is the death of him who gave the mandate, or of him who received it, the mandate is annulled. However, for the sake of convenience, the rule has been adopted that if the party who gave me the mandate should be dead, and I, being ignorant of his death, should execute the mandate, an action of mandate can be brought against me; otherwise a just and natural want of information would occasion me loss. Similarly to this, it has been decided by the greater number of authorities that if my debtor should, through ignorance, pay my steward who has been manumitted, he will be released from liability; although, otherwise, he could not be released under the strict rule of law, because he paid another than the one whom he should have paid.

(161) If the person to whom I gave a proper mandate exceeds his authority, I will be entitled to an action of mandate against him for the amount of my interest in having the mandate executed, provided he was able to execute it; but he cannot bring an action against me. Hence, for example, if I should direct you to purchase a tract of land for me for a hundred thousand sesterces, and you purchase it for a hundred and fifty thousand, you cannot bring an action of mandate against me, even though you are willing to convey the land to me for the price for which I directed you to purchase it; and this opinion was held by Sabinus and Cassius. If, however, you should purchase it for a smaller sum, you will certainly be entitled to an action against me; for anyone who directs land to be bought for a hundred thousand sesterces is understood also to direct that it be bought for less if this can be done.

(162) In conclusion, it must be remembered that when I give any material to be manufactured gratuitously, in which case, if I had fixed a price for the work performed, a contract for leasing and hiring would be made, an action of mandate will lie; for instance, when I give clothing to a fuller to be cleaned or pressed, or to a tailor to be repaired.

(163) Having explained the different kinds of obligations which arise from contracts, we should observe that obligations can not only be acquired by us by what we do ourselves, but also through those persons who are subject to our authority, or are in our hand, or under our control by mancipation.

(164) Obligations are also acquired by us through freemen, and the slaves of others of whom we have possession in good faith; but only in two instances, that is, where they acquire anything by their own labor, or by means of our property.

(165) An obligation is also acquired by us in the two cases above mentioned through a slave in whom we have the usufruct.

(166) Anyone, however, who has the mere quiritarian right in a slave, although he may be his owner, is still understood to have less right to what he may acquire than an usufructuary, or a *bona fide* possessor, for it is established that, under no circumstances, can the slave acquire anything for himself; and to such an extent is this the rule, that even if the slave should expressly stipulate for something to be given to him, or should accept something in mancipation, in his name, some authorities hold that nothing is acquired for him.

(167) It is certain that a slave owned in common can acquire for his masters in proportion to their respective shares, except where by stipulating, or by accepting in mancipation expressly for one of them, he acquires for him alone. For example, if he should stipulate as follows: "Do you solemnly agree to pay to Titius, my master?" Or when he received by mancipation in the following manner: "I declare that this property belongs to my master Lucius Titius by quiritarian right, and let it be purchased for him with this piece of bronze and this bronze balance."

(167a) The question arises whether the addition of the name of one the masters, or the order of one of them, produces the same effect. Our preceptors hold that he alone will acquire who gave the order, just as if the slave had expressly stipulated, or had accepted in mancipation for the single master who was expressly mentioned. The authorities of the other school think that the acquisition will be made by all, as if no order had been given.

(168) An obligation is extinguished principally by the payment of what was due. Wherefore, the question arises that if anyone should pay something for another with the consent of his creditor, whether he would be released from liability by operation of law, and this opinion was held by our preceptors; or whether he remains bound by operation of law, but should defend himself by an exception on the ground of fraud against his creditor who brings the suit, which opinion was adopted by the authorities of the other school.

(169) An obligation is also extinguished by means of a release. A release is, as it were, a fictitious payment, for if I owe you something under a verbal obligation and you are willing to discharge me from liability, this can be done by permitting me to question you as follows: "Have you received what I promised you?" And you reply, "I have received it."

(170) In this manner, as we have already stated, only those obligations are discharged which have been contracted verbally, but no others; for it seems to be consistent that an obligation verbally contracted should be released by other words. Anything which is due for some other reason can be changed into a stipulation, and then be discharged by a release.

(171) But although we have stated that a release takes place by a fictitious payment, still a woman cannot make one without the authority of her guardian; while, on the other hand, payment can be made to her without her guardian's authority.

(172) Likewise, a portion of what is due may be legally paid; but it is doubtful whether it can be partially released when paid.

(173) There is another kind of imaginary payment which is effected by bronze and balance; but this is used only in certain cases; as, for instance, where something is due on the ground that there has been a transaction by bronze and balance, or for the reason that something is due on account of a judgment.

(174) This transaction takes place as follows: Not less than five witnesses and a balance-holder must be present, and then the party who is to be released must say, "For the reason that I have been condemned to pay you so many thousand sesterces, I pay and discharge this amount by means of this piece of bronze and

this bronze balance; and this is the first and last pound of bronze that I pay you in accordance with public law." Then he strikes the balance with the pound of bronze, and gives it to the party by whom he is released as if by payment.

(175) In the same way a legatee releases an heir from liability for a legacy which was left him by condemnation, except that, as the party against whom judgment was rendered mentions that he has been condemned; so the heir states that he has been charged by the terms of the will to pay the legacy. An heir, however, can only be released from liability in this way where the property constituting the legacy can be weighed or counted, and where the amount is certain. Some authorities hold that the same rule applies to articles which can be measured.

(176) Moreover, an obligation is extinguished by novation,[1] for instance, if I stipulate that what you owe me shall be paid by Titius; for *a* new obligation arises by the intervention of a new person, and the first obligation is annulled by being changed into the second one. To such an extent is this the case, that sometimes, although the subsequent stipulation may be void, still the first one is disposed of by novation; for example, if you owe me something and I stipulate that it shall be paid by Titius after his death, or by a woman, or a ward, without the authority of his or her guardian; in which case I lose my claim, for the first debtor is released from liability, and the subsequent obligation is void. The same rule of law does not apply if I stipulate with a slave, for then the former debtor remains liable, just as if I had not afterwards stipulated with anyone else.

(177) When, however, I subsequently stipulate with the same person, novation only takes place where something new is contained in the subsequent stipulation, that is to say, if some condition, date, or sponsor should be either added or omitted.

(178) What we have stated with reference to a sponsor has, however, not been absolutely settled; for it has been held by authorities of the other school that neither the addition or omission of a sponsor has the effect of causing novation.

(179) Moreover, what we stated with reference to the introduction of a condition effecting novation, must be understood to mean that a novation would take place if the condition should be fulfilled; but if it should fail, the former obligation will continue to be operative. But let us see, whether a party who brings an action in a case of this kind can be barred on the ground of fraud, or informal agreement; for it seems to have been agreed upon by the parties that suit could only be brought for the recovery of the property if the condition of the subsequent stipulation should be fulfilled. Nevertheless, Servius Sulpicius thought that a novation took place immediately, while the condition was in suspense, and if it should fail that there would be no cause of action on either ground, and in this way that the claim would be extinguished. In consequence of this, he gave it as his opinion that if anyone should stipulate with a slave for a debt which Lucius Titius owed to him, a novation would be created, and the claim would be lost; because an action could not be brought against the slave. In both these instances, however, we make use of another rule; and novation is not produced under these circumstances any more than if I should stipulate for what you owe me with an alien, who is not allowed to participate as a sponsor, by using the expression, "Do you solemnly agree?"

(180) An obligation is also extinguished by a joinder of issue, provided the action brought is authorized by law; for then the original obligation is dissolved, and the defendant begins to be held liable by the joinder of issue. But if judgment is rendered against him, the obligation produced by the joinder of issue is

---

[1] "Novatio est veteris obligationis in novam translatio et transfusio." — ed.

disposed of, and he becomes liable under the judgment. This is the reason why it was stated by the ancient authorities that a debtor is compelled to make payment before issue has been joined; for, after this has been done, he will be liable if judgment should be rendered against him, and if he is condemned, he will be compelled to satisfy the judgment.

(181) Hence, if I bring a legally authorized action for the collection of a debt, I cannot afterwards, under the strict rule of law, sue a second time, as the statement that the defendant is required to pay me something will be without effect; for the reason that by joinder of issue he ceases to be obliged to make payment. The case is different if in the first place I brought an action derived from the authority of a magistrate; for then the obligation will still continue to exist, and, therefore, by the strict rule of law, I can bring another action; but I can be barred by an exception grounded on a previous judgment, or on a former joinder of issue. We shall explain in a subsequent Commentary what actions are authorized by law, and what are derived from the authority of a magistrate.

(182) Let us now pass to obligations which arise from the commission of crime; for instance, where anyone perpetrates a theft or robbery, or damages property, or commits any injury; and the obligation growing out of all these matters is of one kind, while obligations arising from contracts are divided into four classes, as we already have explained.

(183) Servius Sulpicius and Masurius Sabinus state that there are four kinds of theft, manifest, non-manifest, the receiving of stolen property, and the delivery of stolen property to another. Labeo says that there are two, namely, manifest and non-manifest theft, for the receiving of stolen goods and their delivery to another rather give ground to actions connected with theft than are different kinds of theft, and this seems to be the more correct opinion, as will appear hereafter.

(184) Some authorities hold that manifest theft is "committed when the culprit is taken in the act; others, however, go further and say that it occurs when he is taken in the place where the theft was perpetrated, for instance, where olives are stolen from an olive orchard, or grapes from a vineyard, while the thief is in the olive orchard or the vineyard; or, if the theft was committed in a house, as long as the thief remains therein. Others go still further, and hold that manifest theft is committed until the thief has carried the stolen property to the place where he intends to leave it. Others go even further, and say that theft was committed as long as the thief holds the property. This last view has not been adopted, and the opinion of those who hold that if the thief is taken before he has conveyed the stolen property to the place where he intends to leave it, it is manifest theft, should not be accepted; for the reason that great uncertainty may arise whether the time for his detection should be limited to one day or to several. This doubt arises because thieves often intend to transport stolen property to other cities or into other provinces. Therefore, the first and second opinions have been generally approved, and the greater number of authorities accept the second one.

(185) From what we have already said it will be understood what non-manifest theft is, for what does not belong to this class belongs to the other.

(186) The receiving of stolen property takes place when it is sought for and found in the possession of anyone, in the presence of witnesses; for even though the party may not be the thief, a special action can be brought against him which is called a suit for the recovery of stolen property.

(187) Delivery of stolen goods is said to take place when the stolen property is offered to you by anyone in order that it may be found in your possession, and is given to you with the intention that it should be discovered on your premises rather than upon those of him who gave it to you. If the property should be found on your premises an action will lie in your favor against the party who gave it to you, even though he may not be the thief, which is called an action on account of the delivery of stolen property.

(188) An action for preventing the search for stolen goods may be brought against him who hinders anyone from searching for stolen property on his premises.

(189) The penalty for manifest theft was capital under the Law of the Twelve Tables, for a freeman, after having been scourged, was delivered up to the party against whom he committed the theft; and whether he became his slave by this proceeding, or was placed in the position of one against whom judgment had been rendered for a debt, was a matter of dispute among the ancient lawyers. The punishment of scourging was also inflicted upon a slave, but the harshness of the penalty was subsequently disapproved of, and in the case of a slave, as well as of that of a freeman, an action for fourfold damages was established by the Edict of the Prætor.

(190) The penalty for non-manifest theft was double damages by the Law of the Twelve Tables, and this the Prætor has preserved.

(191) The penalty for the concealment or delivery of stolen goods imposed by the Law of the Twelve Tables was triple damages, and this, in like manner, has been preserved by the Prætor.

(192) The action for preventing search, introduced by the Edict of the Prætor, requires the payment of fourfold damages. The ancient law, however, did not impose any penalty for this offence; but only prescribed that whoever desired to make search should do so naked, wearing a girdle, and carrying a dish; and if he found anything, it ordered that this should be considered manifest theft.

(193) The nature of the girdle was a matter of controversy, but the better opinion is that it was some kind of cloth by which the private parts were concealed. This entire rule is ridiculous, for anyone who would prevent a person from searching when clothed, would also do so if he were naked; and especially because, if anything were found under such circumstances he would be subjected to a more severe penalty. Then, whether he was ordered to have a dish in his hands for the reason that they being occupied, he might bring nothing secretly into the house; or whether if he found anything, he might place it in the dish; neither of these provisions would have any effect if the property sought for was of such a size or description that it could neither be brought into the house or be placed in the dish. There is no doubt whatever that the requirements of the law were satisfied, no matter what material the dish consisted of.

(194) For the reason that the law, in a case of this kind, declared such an offence to be manifest theft, there are some writers who hold that manifest theft may be either that defined by law, or that established by nature; that defined by law being what we are discussing, and that established by nature being what we have previously explained. The better opinion, however, is that manifest theft should be understood to be that which has been actually committed, for the law cannot cause a non-manifest thief to become a manifest one, any more than it can cause one who is not a thief at all, to become a thief, or anyone who is not an adulterer, or a homicide, to become an adulterer, or a homicide. The law, however, can cause anyone to be liable to a penalty, just as if he had committed theft, adultery, or homicide, even though he had not been guilty of any of these crimes.

(195) Again, theft is committed not only when a person removes the property of another with the intention of appropriating it, but, generally speaking, when anyone handles the property of another without the consent of the owner.

(196) Therefore, if anyone makes use of property deposited with him for safe keeping, he commits theft, and if having received an article for the purpose of using it, he employs it for some other purpose, he becomes liable for theft; for example, if anyone being about to invite friends to supper borrows silver plate and takes it away with him to a distance; or if anyone borrows a horse to carry him to a certain place, and takes it much further away, or, as the ancient lawyers stated by way of example, if he takes the horse into battle.

(197) It was decided, however, that those who use property for another purpose than that for which they received it, commit theft, provided they know that they do this contrary to the will of the owner, and that he, if he knew of it, would not allow it; but if they believe that he would permit them to do so, this should not be considered theft. And the distinction is perfectly proper, as theft is not committed without unlawful intent.

(198) If anyone thinks that he is handling an article contrary to the will of the owner, but the owner is in fact willing for him to do so this is said not to be theft; and hence the question arose and was discussed, whether if Titius should solicit my slave to steal certain property belonging to me, and deliver it to him; and the slave should notify me, and I, desiring to detect Titius in the crime, should permit my slave to take the property to him, whether Titius would be liable to me in the action of theft, or in the one for corrupting a slave, or whether he would be liable in neither. The answer is that he would be liable in neither action, for he would not be liable in the action of theft, for the reason that he did not handle the property contrary to my will; and he would not be liable in the action for corrupting the slave, for the reason that the slave was not rendered any worse.

(199) Sometimes, however, a theft of persons who are free is committed, for example where anyone of my children who is under my control, or a wife in my hand, or a judgment debtor, or a gladiator whom I have hired is secretly taken away.

(200) Anyone may even commit a theft of his own property, as for instance, where a debtor secretly removes an article which he has pledged to his creditor, or where I surreptitiously abstract my own property from a *bona fide* possessor of the same; and hence it has been decided that he who conceals the fact that a slave who is held by a *bona fide* possessor has returned to him, commits theft.

(201) Again, on the other hand, it is sometimes permitted to seize and acquire by usucaption property which belongs to another; and in such cases theft is not held to have been committed; as for instance, where property belonging to an estate of which the heir has not taken possession is seized, unless there is a necessary heir; for when there is a necessary heir, it has been decided that usucaption cannot take place in favor of a party acting as the heir. Likewise, in accordance with what we have stated in a former Commentary, a debtor who has transferred property to his creditor by mancipation or surrendered it in court on account of a trust, can take possession of the property, and acquire it by usucaption, without being guilty of theft.

(202) Sometimes a person is liable for theft who did not himself commit the offence; as is the case with one by whose aid and advice a theft has been perpetrated. To this class belongs a person who knocks money out of your hand in order that another may pick it up; or places himself in your way in order that another may seize it; or puts your sheep or oxen to flight in order that another may catch them, as in the example given by the ancient authorities, where a person put a herd of cattle to flight by means of a red cloth. If, however, this were done merely for the sake of amusement, and not for the purpose of committing a theft, we will examine whether an equitable action should be granted, as by the *Lex Aquilia*, which was enacted with reference to damages, even negligence may be punished.

(203) The action of theft will lie in favor of the party whose interest it is that the property shall be preserved, even though he may not be the owner; and hence it will not lie in favor of the owner, unless he is interested in the property not being destroyed.

(204) Therefore, it is settled that when an article which was pledged has been stolen, the creditor can bring the action of theft, and to such an extent is this true, that even if the owner himself, that is to say the debtor, steals the property, the action of theft can still be brought by the creditor.

(205) Moreover, if a fuller receives clothes to be cleaned or pressed, or a tailor receives them to be repaired, for a certain compensation, and loses them by theft, he, and not the owner, will be entitled to bring the action; because the owner is not interested in their not being lost; as he can recover the value of the clothing in the action of leasing against the fuller, or tailor, provided the said fuller or tailor has sufficient property to make good the loss; for if he should not be solvent, then, for the reason that the owner is unable to recover what belongs to him, he can himself bring the action of theft, because, in this case, it is to his interest that the property should be saved.

(206) What we have stated with reference to a fuller and a tailor, we can likewise apply to one to whom we lend an article for use, for, as the former, on account of the compensation they received, are liable for the safe keeping of the property, the latter in consideration of the benefit he derives from using the article, also becomes responsible for its safe keeping.

(207) But as he with whom property is deposited for safe keeping is only responsible where he has committed fraud, in like manner, if the property should be stolen from him, for the reason that he is not required to make restitution by the action of deposit he is not, on that account, interested in its being preserved; and hence he cannot bring the action of theft, but this action will lie in favor of the owner.

(208) In conclusion, it should be noted, that it is a question whether a child under the age of puberty becomes guilty of theft by removing property belonging to another. It is held by the greater number of authorities that, as a theft consists in the intention, a child under the age of puberty is not liable for this offence, unless he is very near puberty, and for this reason can understand that he is committing a crime.

(209) Anyone who seizes the property of another by violence, is also liable for theft; for who handles the property of another more against the consent of the owner than he who seizes it by violence? Therefore, it has been very properly said that he is an impudent thief. The Prætor, however, introduced a peculiar action to be brought in the case of a crime of this kind, which is called the action for robbery with violence; and it may be brought within a year for quadruple damages, and, after a year has elapsed, for simple damages. This action will lie even if the person took only one article, even of the smallest value, with violence.

(210) The action for unlawful damage was established by the *Lex Aquilia* in the first chapter of which it is provided that if anyone unlawfully kills a male or female slave, or any quadruped included in the cattle of another, he shall be required to pay to the owner of the same a sum equal to the highest value of the property during that year.

(211) To unlawfully kill is understood to mean where this happens with malicious intent or through the negligence of another; loss which results without the fault of the party who causes it not being punishable by any law, and therefore, he who occasions damage under any circumstances, without negligence or malicious intent will go unpunished.

(212) It is not only the body of the slave or of the animal which is appraised in the action brought under this law, but if by the death of the slave the owner sustained a greater loss than the value of the said slave amounted to; as for instance, if my slave was appointed heir by someone, and should be killed before he declared his acceptance of the estate by my order, not only his own value is taken into consideration, but also that of the estate which was lost. Likewise, if one of two twins, or one of a company of actors or musicians should be killed, an appraisement is not only made of the one who was killed, but also a computation of the depreciated value of those who remain. The same rule of law applies where one of a pair of mules, or one of a team of four chariot-horses is killed.

(213) Moreover, the person whose slave was killed has the choice either of prosecuting for a capital crime the person who killed him, or of bringing an action for damages against him under this law.

(214) The clause inserted in this law: "The greatest sum which the property was worth during the year," has the following effect. If the slave who was killed was crippled, or blind of an eye, but had been sound within a year, the estimate shall be made not of his value when he was killed, but of his greatest value during that year; the result of which is that sometimes the party will recover a larger amount than that of the loss which he sustained.

(215) By the provisions of the second chapter an action is granted for the amount of the claim against a joint stipulator who fraudulently released the payment of money due to the stipulator.

(216) It is clear that in this section of the law an action was introduced for the recovery of damages, although this provision was not necessary, as the action of mandate would have been sufficient for that purpose; except that under this law a suit for double damages can be brought against the defendant, if he makes a contest.

(217) In the third chapter, provision is made for all other kinds of damage. Therefore, if anyone wounds a slave, or a quadruped included under the head of cattle; or even one which is not so included, as for instance, a dog; or wounds or kills a wild beast, for example, a bear, or a lion; an action is authorized by this chapter. With reference to other animals also, as well as to all property which is destitute of life, damages can be recovered for injury by this section of the law. An action is also provided therein, where anything has been burned, dashed to pieces, or broken, although the single term "broken" is sufficient in all these cases, for it is understood to mean spoiled in any way. Therefore, where anything is burned, dashed to pieces, or broken, and also cut, crushed, spilled, or injured to any extent, or destroyed or deteriorated, it is comprehended in this term.

(218) In this chapter, however, the person who committed the damage is responsible, not only for the value of the property within the past year, but also for what it was worth within the thirty preceding days and the words "highest value" are not added. Therefore, certain authorities hold that it should be in the discretion of the judge to determine whether the estimate of the property ought to be made with reference to its greatest value, or to any inferior value which it may have had within the last thirty days; but it was the opinion of Sabinus that the law should be construed just as if the word "highest" had been inserted; and that the legislator was satisfied because he had used the expression in the first chapter of the law.

(219) Moreover, it was decided that an action will only lie under this law where the party caused the damage by means of his own body, and hence where damage has resulted in some other way, equitable actions should be granted; for instance, where anyone shuts up a slave or a head of cattle belonging to another, and kills him or it by starvation; or where a beast of burden is driven so hard that it perishes; and also where anyone persuades the slave of another to climb a tree, or descend into a well, and, in doing so, he falls, and is either killed or sustains some bodily injury. If, however, anyone pushes a slave off of a bridge or bank into a stream, and he is drowned, the party who pushed him may readily be understood to have caused the damage by means of his body.

(220) Injury is committed, for example, not only where anyone strikes another with his fist, or with a stick or a whip, but where he reviles him in a loud voice, or where well knowing, that nothing is due to himself, he seizes and advertises for sale the property of another as his debtor; or where he writes prose or poetry defaming another; or persistently follows the mother of a family or a boy wearing the *prætexta*; and finally in many other ways.

(221) We consider that injury may be suffered not only by ourselves, but also in the persons of our children who are subject to our authority, as well as by our wives, although they may not be in our hand. Hence if you commit an outrage against my daughter, who is married to Titius, an action for injury can (not) only be

brought against you in her name, but also in that of mine, as well as in that of Titius.

(222) It is understood that injury cannot be committed against a slave individually, but his master may be injured through him; not, however, in the same ways in which we are considered to suffer injury through our children or wives, but where some peculiarly atrocious act is committed, which clearly appears to have been perpetrated to insult the owner, for example, if anyone scourges a slave belonging to another; and a rule has been established to meet this case. If, however, anyone reviles a slave, or strikes him with his fist, no rule has been prescribed in this instance, and permission to bring an action would not readily be given.

(223) The penalties for injuries provided by the Law of the Twelve Tables were as follows: "For a broken limb, retaliation; for a bone broken, or crushed, three hundred asses, if the party was a freeman, but if he was a slave a hundred and fifty; and for all other injuries, twenty-five asses." These pecuniary penalties seemed to be sufficient compensation in those times of great indigence.

(224) At present, however, we make use of another rule; for we are permitted by the Prætor to estimate the damages ourselves, and the judge may either condemn the defendant for the amount of which we have estimated it, or for a smaller sum, as he may think proper. The Prætor usually fixes the amount of damages to be paid for an atrocious injury, and when he has once decided in what sum the defendant must give security to appear, he establishes this sum as the limit, and although the judge can render a decree for a smaller amount, still, as a rule, on account of his respect for the authority of the Prætor, he does not venture to do so.

(225) Again, an injury is rendered atrocious either by the act, as when anyone is wounded, beaten with rods, or severely whipped; or by the place, as for instance, where the injury is committed either in the theatre, or in the forum; or on account of the person, for example, where a magistrate is insulted, or an injury is inflicted upon a senator by a person of inferior rank.

FOURTH COMMENTARY

(1) It remains for us to speak of actions. And if we inquire how many kinds of actions there are, the better opinion seems to be that there are but two, real and personal; for those who say that there are four, and include such as arise from solemn agreements, do not perceive that some kinds of actions are subdivided into others.

(2) A personal action is one which we bring against anyone who is liable to us under a contract, or on account of a crime; that is, that (what) we claim is that he is bound to give something, to do something, or to perform some service.

(3) A real action is one in which we either claim some corporeal property to be ours, or that we are entitled to some particular right in the property, for instance, the right of use and enjoyment; or the right to walk or drive through the land of another; or to conduct water from his land; or to raise the height of a building, or to have the view unobstructed; or when a negative action is brought by the adverse party.

(4) Therefore, these actions being distinct, it is certain that we cannot make use of the following form to recover our property from another, namely: "If it appears that he should be required to transfer it." For what is ours cannot be transferred to us, as it is understood that what is given to us is given for the purpose that it may become ours, and property which already belongs to us cannot become ours any more than it now is. Through hatred of thieves, and for the purpose of making them liable to a greater number of actions, the

rule has been adopted that, in addition to the penalty of double and quadruple the value of the property obtained, thieves are also liable to the form: "If it appears that the defendant should be required to transfer the property"; even though the action by which we seek to recover what belongs to us may also be brought against him.

(5) Moreover, real actions are styled suits for the recovery of property, but personal actions, by which we assert that something must be given, or some act be performed, are called *condictiones*.

(6) Again, we sometimes bring suit merely to recover property; sometimes only to recover the penalty; and sometimes to recover both.

(7) For example, we sue merely to recover property in actions brought under a contract.

(8) We bring suit only to recover a penalty, for example, in the actions of theft and of injury; and, according to the opinion of certain authorities, in an action for goods taken by violence; for we are entitled to recover the property by either a real or a personal action.

(9) Moreover, we bring suit to recover both the property and a penalty; for instance, in those cases in which we bring our action for double damages against a party who defends the case; and this happens in an action to recover a judgment debt; or expenses paid for a principal; or damages for injury under the *Lex Aquilia;* or to recover legacies; or a certain sum which has been bequeathed by condemnation.

(10) Moreover, there are some actions which refer to the ancient form of judicial procedure upon which they are based; and others become operative by their own force and power. In order that this may be clear, we must first treat of those which are based upon ancient judicial procedure.

(11) These actions which the ancients employed were so designated, either for the reason that they were provided by the law — although at that time the edicts of the Prætor, by means of which many new actions were introduced, had not come into use — or, because they followed the words of the law, and therefore, like the law itself, were observed without any alteration. Hence, it was decided that, a person who brought an action against another for cutting his vines, and in the pleadings called them "vines," should lose his case, as he ought to have called them "trees," because the Law of the Twelve Tables, under which the action for cutting vines was brought, speaks in general terms of the cutting of trees.

(12) Actions were brought in five ways under the ancient form of judicial procedure, and were called *Sacramentum, Judicis Postulatio, Condictio, Manus Injectio, Pignoris Capio.*[1]

---

[1] The *legis actiones* were the earliest forms of judicial procedure known to the Roman law for the collection of claims and the enforcement of obligations. As will be observed, they are of a very primitive character, and it is surprising, when taking into consideration the wonderful progress of the Roman people in intelligence and knowledge, that these antiquated and cumbersome methods survived for so long a period. They were based upon the Twelve Tables; upon customs which, by continuous usage, had acquired full legal authority; upon the decision of the various popular tribunals; and upon statutes which were passed from time to time either for the purpose of explaining or confirming obscure or disputed points of ancient jurisprudence, that is, what was ordinarily designated the Civil Law. The extreme nicety with which the established forms were required to be observed, and which, if neglected in the slightest particular, caused the litigant to irretrievably lose his case, forcibly recalls the technical accuracy demanded by the old system of Common Law pleading that, for generations, exercised to the utmost the legal ingenuity and skill of the English practitioner. The equitable jurisdiction of the Prætor was expressly devised to remedy the abuses and relieve the distress to which rigid adherence to the rules of the *legis actiones* constantly gave rise. This innovation was deplored by the eminent juriconsults of Rome, who regarded any change introduced into the existing judicial procedure as unnecessary, dangerous, and revolutionary; an example which was subsequently followed to the letter by the lawyers of England upon the establishment of the Court of Chancery, of which the Prætorian Tribunal was the prototype.

The *Sacramentum*, so called from the wager or forfeit, which involved the deposit by the parties in the hands of the Pontiffs, for the benefit of the *sacra publica*, and by way of security, of a quantity of bronze or copper equal in value to double that of the property in controversy, half of which was lost by the one who was defeated, was originally the only method of civil procedure among the Romans.

(13) The action *Sacramentum* was a general one, for where no provision was made by the law in any other way for bringing suit with reference to certain property, it was done by means of an oath. This proceeding was attended with danger to the party swearing falsely; just as, at present, is the case in the action for the recovery of money lent, on account of the solemn agreement by which the defendant assumes a risk if he rashly denies the claim, and because of the counter engagement by which the plaintiff becomes liable if he did not recover the debt. Hence, the party who was defeated was obliged to pay the amount of money deposited by way of penalty, which was placed in the Public Treasury; and, for this reason, sureties were given to the Prætor; instead of, as at present, the amount deposited as penalty being for the benefit of the party who gained the case.

(14) The amount deposited by way of penalty in this proceeding was either five hundred, or fifty asses; five hundred were deposited when the property in question was worth a thousand or more asses, and fifty when it was worth less than a thousand; for this was provided by the Law of the Twelve Tables. When, however, the controversy was with reference to the freedom of a slave, although he may have been extremely valuable, still the amount deposited by way of penalty was only fifty asses. This was also provided by the Twelve Tables in favor of freedom, in order that the protector of the slave might not be unduly oppressed . . . .[1]

(15) Moreover, when all these actions were brought to enforce an obligation, the parties, having furnished sureties, agreed to again appear for the appointment of a judge; and having returned after thirty days, the judge was appointed in accordance with the *Lex Pinaria*; while before this law was enacted he was appointed immediately. We understand from what has been already stated, that if the property in dispute was worth less than a thousand asses, the amount deposited was usually only fifty, and not five hundred. Then, after the judge had been appointed, the parties gave notice to one another to appear before him on the third day following. Finally, when they came into court, and before the case was argued, it was customary to state it briefly, and in a concise manner; which was called the presentation of the case, which was, as it were, a mere summary of the same.

(16) When a real action was instituted, the movable property, and that which could move itself and be brought into court, was demanded as follows. The party making the claim, held a staff, and then grasping the object in dispute, as for instance, a slave, said: "I declare this slave to belong to me, on account of his condition, in accordance with quiritarian right. See! in accordance with what I have stated, I have placed my staff upon him"; and, at the same time, he laid the staff upon the slave. His opponent then said and did the same thing, and when both of them had asserted their claims, the Prætor said: "Both of you release your

---

Little of the *Judicis Postulatio* is known to us but the name, which has reference to an application to the magistrate to appoint a judge or arbiter to hear the case, after joinder of issue; and therefore, that it made provision for arbitration.

The *Condictio* was strictly a personal action for the recovery of a certain sum of money which had either been loaned, or paid by mistake. It was introduced as a convenient substitute for the preceding and more complex forms. The plaintiff, by appearing before the Prætor, could force the defendant to agree (*condicere*) to have a judge appointed within thirty days.

The *Manus Injectio* enabled a surety who had paid the debt, to seize and imprison the principal until the latter had fully reimbursed him, if six months had elapsed after payment.

The *Pignoris Capio*, as stated in the text, lay for the enforcement of obligations to soldiers for subsistence and pay, as well as to enable magistrates to compel parties against whom judgments had been rendered to comply with them. In effect, it was almost identical with levying a distress under the English law. The last two of the *legis actiones*, rather belong to the category of legal processes or forms of execution, than to lawsuits, in the strict sense of the term.

We are indebted to Gaius for the most complete account of these curious old methods of judicial procedure and which, while far from satisfactory, is still more detailed than those of other Roman writers on jurisprudence, who, for the most part, only vaguely refer to the subject. The *legis actiones* were nominally abolished B. C. 167. — ed.

[1] Original manuscript illegible.

hold upon the slave"; and they did so. The one who first asserted his claim, then interrogated the other as follows: "I ask whether you will state on what ground you make this claim?" and he replied, "I asserted my right to him by placing my staff upon him." The first claimant than said, "As you have wrongfully claimed him I call upon you to deposit five hundred asses by way of forfeit," and his opponent then said, "I call upon you to do the same"; (that is if the property was worth more than a thousand asses five hundred were deposited but if it is worth less only fifty was the amount of the forfeiture). After this the same proceedings took place as in a personal action, and then the Prætor made a temporary disposition of the property in favor of one of the parties, that is to say, he gave him possession of it for the time, and ordered him to furnish sureties to his adversary for the expenses of the suit as well as the mesne profits of the property which was the object of the action. The Prætor, moreover, took sureties for the forfeits, from both parties, for the benefit of the Public Treasury. The staff was employed instead of a spear, as an emblem of lawful ownership, for whatever was taken from an enemy a man considered to be absolutely his own; wherefore in cases tried before the *Centumviri*, a spear was placed in front of the tribunal.

(17) If the property was of such a nature that it could not be brought or led into court without inconvenience, as for instance, if it consisted of a column, or a drove of cattle of any kind, a certain portion was brought in, and then the claim was made for that portion just as if all of it was present. Therefore, if the property in dispute consisted of a flock of sheep or goats, a single sheep or goat was brought into court, or even a single tuft of wool was produced; or if it consisted of a ship, or a column, a small part was broken off; and, in like manner, if a tract of land or a building, or an estate was the subject of controversy, a small part was brought in, and a claim was made for it in the same manner as if all the property was there; as, for instance, a clod was taken from the land, or a tile was taken from the building; and if the dispute was with reference to an estate, in like manner the property itself, or some part of it was produced in court . . . .[1]

(17a) . . . .[1] For they observed the same time and the same manner in appointing a judge, and agreed upon a day when they would be ready to receive the judge, for to "agree upon" meant originally "to notify".

(18) Therefore, this action was very properly styled a notification, for the plaintiff was accustomed to notify his adversary to appear before the court on the thirtieth day to receive a judge. At present, however, we do not properly call a suit of this kind by which we institute proceedings to have property conveyed to us a personal action, for now no notice is given for this purpose.

(19) This form of judicial procedure was established by the *Lex Silia* and the *Lex Calpurnia*; by the *Lex Silia*, to receive a certain sum of money, and by the *Lex Calpurnia*, to recover any other property which was certain.

(20) It has frequently been asked why this action was required when we could either by *Sacramentum* or *Judicis Postulatio*, obtain the transfer of property to which we are entitled.

(21) The proceeding of *Manus Injectio* was employed in certain cases, as for instance, by the Law of the Twelve Tables, when judgment had been obtained against a debtor. This was as follows: the party who brought the suit said, "As judgment has been rendered against you, or you have been condemned to pay me ten thousand sesterces, and you have not paid them, for this reason I lay my hands upon you, as being indebted to me under the judgment for ten thousand sesterces"; and at the same time he seized him by some part of the body, and the debtor was not permitted to resist, or to protect himself by law, but he appointed a defender, who conducted the case for him, or, if he did not do so, he was taken to his house by the plaintiff and placed in chains.

---

[1] Original manuscript illegible.

(22) Subsequently, certain laws in some other cases, permitted the arrest of debtors against whom judgment had been rendered; as the *Lex Publilia* against a party for whom his sponsor had paid the debt, if, within the next six months from the time when it was paid, he had not indemnified him; likewise, the *Lex Fufia de Sponsu* against one who had collected from his sponsor more than his proportionate share; and finally, many other laws granted proceedings of this kind in numerous instances.

(23) Other enactments provided that, on certain grounds, proceedings could be instituted by the imposition of hands; but this was the simple act, and not authorized in the case of debtors against whom judgment had been rendered; for instance, the *Lex Fufia Testamentaria* permitted this to be done against a party who, as a legatee or the recipient of a donation *mortis causa*, had received more than a thousand asses, when he was not excepted under this law, and was entitled to receive more; also the *Lex Marcia* against money-lenders, so that if they collected interest, they could be compelled by this proceeding to refund it.

(24) By these laws and others similar to them, the defendant was permitted to resist arrest, and take legal measures to defend himself, for the plaintiff in this form of judicial procedure was not entitled to add the words, "On account of a judgment rendered"; but after having stated his cause of action, said: "For this reason I lay hands upon you"; just as he in whose favor proceedings were instituted on account of a judgment, after having stated his cause of action, said: "I arrest you on account of the judgment which has been rendered against you." It has not escaped my notice that in proceedings under the *Lex Fufia Testamentaria* the words, "On account of the judgment rendered against you," were inserted, although they do not appear in the law itself; which seems to have been done without any reason.

(25) Afterwards, however, by the *Lex Vallia* all other defendants, except judgment debtors and principals whose debts had been paid by their sureties, were permitted to resist arrest, and avail themselves of the law for their defence, when this proceeding was instituted against them. Therefore, the party against whom judgment was rendered, and one whose debt had been paid by his surety were, even after this law, required to appoint a defender; and if they did not do so, were taken to the house of their creditor; and this rule was observed as long as the ancient forms of procedure were employed. Hence, in our times, anyone against whom proceedings have been brought in an action on judgment or to recover the amount of the debt paid by a surety is compelled to furnish security to satisfy the claim.

(26) *Pignoris Capio* was employed in some instances through custom, and in others by virtue of law.

(27) It was introduced through custom into military affairs; for a soldier was entitled to employ this proceeding against the paymaster for his pay, if he did not give it, which compensation was designated *æs militare*, and he could also distrain for money for the purpose of purchasing a horse, which was called *æs equestre*, as well as for money with which to purchase barley for his horse which was called *æs hordiarium*.

(28) The detention of property in this manner was also legally authorized, for instance, by the Law of the Twelve Tables against a party who bought a victim for sacrifice and did not pay for it; and likewise against one who did not pay the hire of a beast of burden which he had leased for the purpose of raising money to meet the expenses of a festival, that is to say, of a sacrifice. In like manner, the right to distrain was granted by the law of Censors to the farmers of the revenue of the Roman people, against persons who owed taxes under any law.

(29) In all these instances the property was seized by the employment of certain words; and, on this account, it was held by most authorities that this proceeding was also a form of statute process. Others, however, were of the contrary opinion; first, because it took place out of court, that is to say, not in presence of the Prætor, and usually also during the absence of the adverse party; while, on the other hand,

other actions could not be made use of by any one except in the presence of both the Prætor, and the adverse party, and besides property could not be distrained on an unlawful day, that is to say, on one when it was not permitted to act under the law.

(30) All these forms of judicial procedure, however, gradually became unpopular on account of the extreme subtlety of the ancient legal authorities, so that the result was that anyone who committed the slightest error lost his case. Hence, by the *Lex Æbutia* and the two *Leges Julia*, proceedings under this law were abolished, and another form was substituted for them; so that at present in litigation we make use of written instructions, that is to say, formulas, for that purpose.

(31) In only two instances was permission granted to act under the ancient procedure, that is to say, those of threatened injury, and those before the Centumviral Tribunal. When application is made to the *Centumviri*, proceedings are first instituted by the deposit of forfeits before the Urban or the Foreign Prætor; but in the case of threatened injury, no one wishes to employ the ancient procedure, but prefers to bind his adversary by a stipulation provided for in the Edict; by which means his rights are more conveniently and thoroughly protected. By the seizure of property as security for debt . . . .[1] it is apparent.

(32) On the other hand, in the formula provided for the farmer of the revenue a fiction is inserted, ordering that the debtor be condemned to pay the same amount of money which he would have been compelled to pay in order to release his property, if it had been seized as security for the debt.

(33) No formula, however, is based on a fiction in a personal action for recovery; for whether we bring suit for a sum of money, or for any certain article of property as being due, we assert that the very thing itself should be transferred to us, and we do not add any fiction for the purpose of establishing the claim. Therefore, we understand these formulas to be those by which we allege that a definite sum of money, or certain specified property, should be transferred to us, and that the claim is valid by its own force and power. Actions of loan for use, trust, business transacted, as well as innumerable others are of the same nature.

(34) We make use of other fictions in certain formulas, for instance, when a party who claims possession of the property of an estate brings an action as a fictitious heir; for as he succeeds to the deceased by the prætorian, and not by the Civil Law, he is not entitled to a direct action, and cannot allege that what belongs to the deceased is his; nor can he demand that what was due to the latter should be paid to him; and therefore, under the fiction that he is the heir, he asserts his claim as follows: "Let So-and-So be judge. If Aulus Agerius" (that is to say, the plaintiff, himself) "should be the heir of Lucius Titius, and it is found that the land in question ought to belong to him by quiritarian right;" or if, in the case of a debt, a similar fiction having been employed by the party, as heir, there is added: "If it should appear that Numerius Negidius should pay to Aulus Agerius ten thousand sesterces."

(35) Likewise, the purchaser of the property of a bankrupt estate may proceed under the fiction that he is the heir, and sometimes he can do so in a different way; for in his statement of the claim he may mention the person whose property he purchased and himself in the condemnation; that is to say, that his adversary may be condemned to pay him on this account what belonged to the former or was due to him. This species of proceeding is called Rutilian, because it was devised by the Prætor Publius Rutilius, who is said to have also introduced the sale of bankrupt estates. The kind of action mentioned above, by which the purchaser of the property of an insolvent estate pretends to be the heir, is called Servian.

(36) Likewise, there is a pretended usucaption in the action which is styled Publician. This action is granted

---

[1] Original manuscript illegible.

to a party who claims property which has been delivered to him for some legal reason, and of which he lost possession before obtaining a title to it by usucaption; for because he cannot claim it as his under quiritarian right, the fiction is employed that he has acquired it by usucaption and hence, as it were, to have become its owner, by quiritarian right; for instance, as follows: "Let So-and-So be judge. If the slave whom Aulus Agerius purchased and who was delivered to him remained in his possession for a year, the said slave would then have lawfully belonged to the said Aulus Agerius by quiritarian right, etc."

(37) Likewise, Roman citizenship is feigned in the case of an alien, if he either sues or is sued in an action established by our laws; provided it is just that the said action may be extended to aliens. For example, if an alien sues or is sued for theft, or for aiding and abetting theft, the following formula should be employed, "Let So-and-So be judge. If it appears that a gold cup was stolen from Lucius Titius by Dio the son of Hermæus, or with his aid and advice for which he would have been compelled to make restitution for theft if he had been a Roman citizen, then let the said Dio, the son of Hermæus be convicted, etc." Again, if an alien brings the action of theft, or if, under the *Lex Aquilia* he sues or is sued for damage to property, he can avail himself of the fiction of Roman citizenship, and judgment can be rendered either for or against him.

(38) Moreover, sometimes we may feign that our adversary has not suffered a loss of civil rights; for if a man or a woman has become liable to us under a contract, and he or she has afterwards undergone forfeiture of civil rights — as, for instance, the woman by coemption, and the man by arrogation — he or she ceases to be indebted to us under the Civil Law, and we cannot directly claim that either is bound to transfer anything to us. In order, however, that the party may not have power to annul our rights, an equitable action is granted against him or her by a fictitious rescission of the loss of civil rights; that is to say, one in which it is feigned that the party had not suffered a disability of this kind.

(39) The divisions of the Formula are the following, the *Demonstratio*, the *Intentio*, the *Adjudicatio*, and the *Condemnatio*.

(40) The *Demonstratio* is that part of the Formula which designates the ground on which the case is brought, that is to say, the following part of the same: "For the reason that Aulus Agerius sold a slave to Numerius Negidius"; or "For the reason that Aulus Agerius left a slave in the keeping of Numerius Negidius".

(41) The *Intentio* is that part of the Formula in which the plaintiff states his claim; for instance, as follows: "If it appears that Numerius Negidius should pay ten thousand sesterces to Aulus Agerius"; or, "Whatever it appears that Numerius Negidius should pay to, or do for, Aulus Agerius"; likewise, "If it appears that the slave in dispute is the property of Aulus Agerius, by quiritarian right".

(42) *Adjudicatio* is that part of the Formula by which the judge is permitted to assign the property in question to one of the litigants; as for instance, where an action for the partition of an estate is brought between co-heirs; one for the division of common property between partners; one for the establishment of boundaries between neighbors. In cases of this kind, the following form is employed, namely: "Judge, award to Titius the amount to which he is entitled."

(43) *Condemnatio* is that part of the Formula by which authority is granted to the judge to condemn or discharge the defendant; for instance, as follows: "Judge, condemn Numerius Negidius to pay ten thousand sesterces to Aulus Agerius, and if the claim should not be proved, discharge him." Likewise, as follows: "Judge, condemn Numerius Negidius to pay to Aulus Agerius not more than ten thousand sesterces, and if the claim should not be proved, let him be discharged," or, as follows: "Judge, let Numerius Negidius be condemned to pay to Aulus Agerius"; etc., without adding the clause, "Not more than ten thousand sesterces".

(44) All these divisions are not found together but in every formula; where some of them appear, others do not, and in fact, sometimes the *Intentio* exists alone, as in prejudicial formulas, in which the question is whether a man is a freedman, or what the amount of a dowry may be, and numerous others. The *Demonstratio*. the *Adjudicatio*, and the *Condemnatio* are never found alone; for the *Demonstratio* without the *Intentio* and the *Condemnatio*, is of no effect; and, in like manner, the *Condemnatio* or the *Adjudicatio* has no force without the *Intentio*, and for this reason they are never found alone.

(45) We say that the formulas in which a question of right is involved, are founded in law; as for instance, when we assert that any property belongs to us by quiritarian right, or that the adverse party is obliged to pay us something, or make good a loss to us as a thief, for these formulas and others are those in which the claim is based on the Civil Law.

(46) We say that other formulas are based upon questions of fact, that is, where a claim of this kind is not made with reference to them; but, where a fact is stated in the beginning of a formula, words are added by which authority is given to the judge to condemn or discharge the defendant. This kind of a formula is employed by a patron against his freedman, when the latter brings him into court contrary to the Edict of the Prætor; for then it is in the following terms: "Let So-and-So be judges. If it is established that such-and-such a patron was brought into court by such-and-such a freedman, contrary to the edict of such-and-such a Prætor — judges, condemn the said freedman to pay to the said patron the sum of ten thousand sesterces. If the case should not be proved, discharge him." The other formulas mentioned in the Edict with reference to the summoning of parties into court, refer to matters of fact; as for instance, against a person who, having been summoned into court, neither appeared nor appointed anyone to defend him; and also against one who rescued by force a party who was summoned to appear; and, in conclusion, innumerable other formulas of this description are set forth in the Register of the Prætor.

(47) In some instances, however, the Prætor permits formulas having reference to either law or fact to be employed; for example, in actions of deposit, and loan for use. The following formula is one of law. "Let So-and-So be judge. Whereas Aulus Agerius deposited a silver table with Numerius Negidius, for which this action is brought, whatever Numerius Negidius is obliged to pay to, or do for, Aulus Agerius, in good faith, on this account, do you, judge, condemn Numerius Negidius to pay to, or do for Aulus Agerius, unless he makes restitution; and, if the case should not be proved, let him be discharged." The following formula: "Let Soand-So be judge. If it appears that Aulus Agerius deposited a silver table with Numerius Negidius, and, through the fraud of the said Numerius Negidius, the said table has not been restored to the said Aulus Agerius, do you, judge, condemn Numerius Negidius to pay to Aulus Agerius a sum of money equal to the value of the property, and if the case is not proved let him be discharged"; is one of fact. Similar formulas are employed in an action of loan for use.

(48) The condemnation clause of all formulas has reference to the pecuniary value of the property. Therefore if we claim any corporeal property, for instance, land, a slave, a garment, or gold or silver, the judge condemns the party against whom the suit was brought not to deliver the very thing itself, as was formerly the practice, but its estimated value in money.

(49) The judgment clause of the formula either mentions a certain, or an uncertain sum of money.

(50) The mention of a certain sum of money, for example, appears in the formula by which we demand the payment of a designated amount; for then the last part of the formula is as follows: "Judge, condemn Numerius Negidius to pay ten thousand sesterces to Aulus Agerius; and if the case is not proved, discharge him."

(51) A judgment for an uncertain sum of money has a two-fold signification. In the first instance, it is

preceded by some restriction called a limiting clause, as, for instance, where we bring an action for an uncertain amount; for then in the last part of the formula the following words are employed: "Judge, condemn Numerius Negidius to pay not more than ten thousand sesterces to Aulus Agerius; and if the case should not be proved discharge him." If, however, the amount is uncertain, and there is no limit; for instance, where we bring suit for property belonging to us, which is in the possession of another, that is to say, if we institute proceedings for the production of property in court, the following words are used: "Judge, condemn Numerius Negidius to pay to Aulus Agerius a sum of money equal to the value of the property; and if the case is not proved let him be discharged."

(52) What then is the rule? If the judge decides against the defendant, he must require him to pay a certain sum of money even though no specified amount may have been mentioned in the judgment. The judge should also be careful that, when a certain sum is stated in the judgment, not to require the defendant to pay a larger or a smaller amount, otherwise he makes the case his own. Again, if a limiting clause was inserted, he must take care not to condemn the defendant in a larger amount than is mentioned in said clause, otherwise, he will, in like manner, make the case his own; he is, however, permitted to render a judgment against him for a smaller sum; and even if there should be no limiting clause, he can condemn him in any amount that he may wish.

(52a) For the reason that the party who accepts the formula should state the amount which he claims, the judge is not required to render a decree for a larger sum; but the plaintiff cannot make use of the same formula a second time, and he should state in the condemnation the certain sum of money which he claims, in order that he may not recover less than he desires.

(53) If anyone claims more than he is entitled to he will lose his case, that is to say, he will lose his property, and he cannot obtain complete restitution through the Prætor; except in certain instances in which the Prætor does not permit all plaintiffs to suffer loss on account of their own errors; for he always comes to the relief of minors under the age of twenty-five years, as in other cases.

(53a) A plaintiff may demand more than he is entitled to in four ways; in the amount of property, in time, in place, and in the statement of his cause of action. He does so in the amount of property, if he demands twenty thousand sesterces, instead of ten thousand which are due to him; or, if he demands as his own, either the whole, or the greater part of the property, when he is only a joint owner. He demands more in point of time, if he asks for payment before the debt is due. He demands more in place, for instance, where payment is promised in a certain place, and he demands that it be made somewhere else, which was not mentioned in the contract; for example, if I stipulate with you as follows: "Do you solemnly agree to pay me ten thousand sesterces at Ephesus?" and afterwards bring suit at Rome under the formula, "If it appears by the stipulation that you are obliged to pay me ten thousand sesterces," I am understood to claim more than I am entitled to, for the reason that in this way I subject the promisor to more inconvenience than he would suffer if he paid at Ephesus. I can still absolutely demand payment at Ephesus, for this is not an additional place.

(53b) He demands too much in his statement of his cause of action, if he deprives the debtor of a choice which he had by the terms of the contract, for example, if anyone stipulates as follows: "Do you solemnly agree to either pay ten thousand sesterces, or deliver the slave Stichus?" as then he can demand either the one or the other. For although he may demand what is of lesser value, he still is considered to claim too much, because his adversary may sometimes more conveniently deliver what is not demanded. Likewise, if anyone stipulates for a genus, and afterwards claims a species; for instance, if he stipulates for purple, in general terms, and afterwards expressly demands Tyrian purple, even though he may demand that of the least value the same rule will apply, for the reason which we have just mentioned.

The same rule also applies where anyone stipulates for a slave in general terms, and afterwards demands a particular slave, for example, Stichus; although he may be almost worthless. Therefore, the phraseology of the formula designating the claim must exactly coincide with what was set forth in the stipulation.

(54) It is perfectly evident that too large an amount cannot be claimed by an uncertain formula, because as a definite amount is not demanded, but it is merely stated that the adversary shall give, or do only what he is required, no one can claim more. The same principle applies where a real action is granted to recover an uncertain share of property; as for example, when a plaintiff demands that there shall be transferred to him the share of the land in question to which he is entitled, which kind of action is granted in very few instances.

(55) It is also evident that if anyone claims one thing instead of another, he will run no risk, as he can bring another suit, because he is not considered to have previously done anything which was legal; for instance, where a party who had a right to claim the slave Stichus, demands Eros; or where anyone states that he is entitled to property under a will, when in fact he is entitled to it under the terms of a stipulation; or where an agent or attorney claims that property should be transferred to him, instead of to his principal.

(56) To claim more than one is entitled to, as we have stated above, involves risk; but anyone is permitted to claim less. He is not permitted, however, to bring suit to recover the remainder in the jurisdiction of the same Prætor, for anyone who does so, is barred by the exception styled the exception against division of actions.

(57) If more is claimed in the condemnation than is proper, the plaintiff runs no risk; but as the defendant has made use of a formula which was unjust, he may obtain complete restitution, in order that the amount of the judgment may be reduced. If, however, less be set out in the condemnation than the plaintiff has a right to, he only obtains the amount which he sued for, as the entire claim was brought into court, and he will be limited by the amount stated in the condemnation which the judge cannot exceed. In a case of this kind the Prætor does not grant complete restitution, for he more readily comes to the relief of defendants than plaintiffs. We, however, except minors under the age of twenty-five years, for the Prætor always comes to the relief of such persons, where loss of property has been sustained by them.

(58) Where more or less than is due is set forth in the *Demonstratio*, no case is brought into court, and hence the matter remains unaltered; and this is what is meant when it is said that a right is not extinguished by a false statement of the cause of action.

(59) Still, there are some authorities, who hold that less than is due may be properly included in the *Demonstratio*; so that a party who has purchased both Stichus and Eros, is considered to have properly stated his cause of action as follows: "Whereas I purchased the slave Eros from you"; and, if he desires to do so, he may bring an action for the recovery of Stichus by means of another formula; because it is true that anyone who purchased both slaves also purchased each of them; and this was especially the opinion of Labeo. If, however, he who purchased one of them, should bring an action to recover both, he makes a full statement of his cause of action. The same rule is applicable to other actions, for instance, to those of Loan for Use, and Deposit.

(60) We have found it stated in certain writers that, in the action of Deposit — and indeed in all others in which, the condemned party is branded with infamy — anyone who demands more than he is entitled to in the statement of his cause of action, will lose his case; for instance, where he who had deposited one article, alleges in his statement that he had deposited two; or where he who was struck on the cheek with the fist, states in an action for injury sustained that he was also struck in some other part of the body. Let us carefully examine whether we should hold this opinion to be correct. It is true that there are two formulas

employed in the Action of Deposit, one based upon the law and the other upon fact, as we mentioned above. The one based on the law, in the first place, designates the cause of action in the manner in which this is usually done, and then sets out the claim as being based upon the law in the following terms: "Whatever the defendant should, on this account, give or perform." But in the formula based upon fact, the cause of action is set forth in the beginning without any previous statement, as follows, "If it appears that So-and-So deposited such-and-such property with So-and-So"; we should entertain no doubt that if anyone in a formula based on fact alleges that he has deposited more articles than was actually the case he will lose his suit, because he is considered to have included in his claim more than he was entitled to. . . .[1]

(61) Set-offs frequently take place in such a way that each party receives less than he would otherwise be entitled to. For, as in *bona fide* actions, the judge is considered to have full power to estimate how much should justly and properly be paid to the plaintiff; on the other hand, he also has authority to determine how much the plaintiff should pay in the same case, and to render judgment against the defendant for the remainder.

(62) *Bona fide* actions are such as the following: purchase and sale; leasing and hiring; the transaction of the business of others without authority; deposit; trust; partnership; guardianship; dotal property.

(63) The judge also has a right not to consider any set-off, at all, as he is not expressly directed to do so by the terms of the formula; but, for the reason that this seems to be proper in a *bona fide* action, it is therefore held to be part of his duty.

(64) The case of an action brought by a banker is different, for he is compelled to take account of a set-off, and to mention it in his statement; and to such an extent is this true, that he must make allowance for it in the first place, and only demand that the remainder shall be paid to him. For example, if he owes ten thousand sesterces to Titius, and Titius owes him twenty thousand, he should state his claim as follows: "If it appears that Titius owes him ten thousand sesterces more than he owes Titius."

(65) Again, the purchaser of the estate of a bankrupt is directed to make a deduction when he brings his action, so that his adversary will only have judgment rendered against him for the balance which remains after having deducted what the purchaser of the estate owes the defendant on account of the insolvent debtor.

(66) Between the set-off which is made against the claim of the banker, and the deduction to be taken from the claim of the purchaser of a bankrupt estate, there is this difference, namely: that property of the same kind and nature is only included in the set-off; as for instance, money is set-off against money; wheat against wheat; wine against wine; and it is even held by some authorities that wine cannot be set off against wine, or wheat against wheat, unless it is of the same nature and quality. In making the deduction, however, property is included which is not of the same kind. Hence, if the purchaser of the estate of a bankrupt brings an action for money due the latter, and he himself owes a certain quantity of grain or wine, after it has been deducted, suit shall be brought only for the remainder, whatever it may be.

(67) Deduction is also made of what will be due hereafter at a certain time, but set-off only takes place where the debt is already due.

(68) Moreover, the amount of the set-off is inserted in the statement of the claim, the result of which is that if the banker demands in the set-off a single sesterce more than he is entitled to, he will lose his case, and therefore his property as well. The deduction, however, is inserted in the judgment, in which place the

---

[1] Original manuscript illegible.

claimant does not run any risk, for demanding too much; especially when the purchaser of a bankrupt estate brings a suit in which, although he makes a claim for a certain amount of money, he, nevertheless, sets out an uncertain amount in the condemnation.

(69) For the reason that we have previously mentioned the action brought against the *peculium* of sons under parental control and slaves, it is necessary for us to more clearly explain this, as well as the other actions, which are ordinarily brought against parents and masters, on account of their sons and slaves.

(70) In the first place, if a transaction was entered into with a son or a slave, by order of his father or his master, the Prætor will grant an action for the entire amount against the father or the master; and this is proper, because anyone who enters into a transaction of this kind takes into consideration their responsibility rather than that of the son, or the slave.

(71) For the same reason the Prætor grants two other actions, the *Actio Exercitoria*, and the *Actio Institoria*. The first will lie where the father or the master places his son or his slave in charge of a ship, and any business on this account is transacted by the party in charge. For whenever a debt has been contracted with the consent of the father or master, it appears to be perfectly just that an action for the entire amount should be granted against him. And even though a person appoints as the master of a ship either a slave belonging to another, or a freeman, the prætorian action will, nevertheless, be granted against him. This action is called "*Exercitoria*," for the reason that the party who obtains the daily returns from the ship is called "*Exercitor*." The Institorial Formula is employed when anyone places his son or slave, or the slave of another or a freeman, in charge of his shop, or of any kind of business whatsoever; and where the party placed in charge of the same contracts any debt which has reference to the said business. It is called "*Institoria*," for the reason that the party placed in charge of a shop is called "*Institor*"; and this formula is made use of for the collection of the entire amount which is due.

(72) In addition to these, the *Actio Tributoria* has been established against a father or a master, when his son or slave transacts some business with his *peculium*, with the knowledge of his father or his master. For if any contract having reference to said property should be made with either of them, the Prætor directs that whatever was invested in the said business, or any profits derived from the same, shall be distributed between the father or master, if anything is due to them, and among any other creditors, in proportion to their respective claims; and for the reason that he permits the distribution to be made to the father, or the master, if any creditor should complain of having received less than he was entitled to, he enables him to bring this action which is called "*Tributoria*."

(73) Moreover, the action *De Peculio* was introduced where any advantage accrued to the father, or the master; and although the business may have been transacted without the consent of either of them, still, whatever was expended for the benefit of their property should be paid in full; or if it was not expended for that purpose, payment should be made to the amount of the value of the *peculium*. It is supposed to have been expended for the benefit of the master's property if the slave should have disbursed anything necessarily for the advantage of his master; for instance, if he should pay borrowed money to his creditors; or should prop up buildings which are about to fall; or should purchase grain for his household; or should buy a tract of land, or any other property which it was necessary to acquire. Therefore, for example, if out of ten sesterces which your slave borrowed from Titius, he should pay five to your creditor, and should expend the remaining five in any way whatsoever, you ought to have judgment rendered against you for five, and for the other five to the amount of the *peculium*. From this it is apparent that if all of the ten sesterces were employed for the benefit of your property, Titius can recover the entire ten; for, although there is but one action having reference to the *peculium* to recover what was used for the benefit of the property of the father, or the master, still, he has the right to two judgments; and, therefore, the judge before

whom the action is brought, should investigate in the first place, whether the expenditure was made for the benefit of the property of the father, or master; and should not pass to the estimation of amount of the *peculium*, unless either nothing was understood to have been expended for the benefit of the property of the father, or master, or that not all of it was so employed; as, when the estimate is made of the amount of the *peculium*, that should previously be deducted which is due to the father or the master, by the son, or the slave who is under his control; and the remainder shall only be considered as *peculium*. Sometimes, however, the amount due by the son, or the slave, as aforesaid, is not deducted from the *peculium*; for instance, if he who owes it himself forms a part of the said *peculium*.

(74) But there is no doubt that either the *Actio Exercitoria*, or the *Actio Institoria* will lie in favor of anyone who has entered into a contract with a son or a slave, by the order of his father or master; and that he can bring the action of *peculium*, or that based on the employment of property for the benefit of another. No one, however, when he could undoubtedly obtain the whole amount of the debt by means of either of the above mentioned actions, would be so foolish as to take the trouble to prove that the party with whom he contracted had a *peculium*, and that his claim could be satisfied out of it; or that the money which he demanded had been employed for the benefit of the father, or master.

(74a) Again, he who is entitled to bring the *Actio Tributoria*, can also bring the *Actio de Peculio*, as well as the one for the recovery of money employed for the benefit of another: and it will generally be more advantageous for him to make use of this action than of the *Actio Tributoria*, for in the latter only the account of the *peculium* is considered which the son, or the slave made use of in the business in which he was engaged, and the profits of the same; in the *Actio de Peculio*, however, the entire *peculium* is involved; and anyone may transact business with a third or a fourth of it, or even with a smaller portion, and have the greater part of his *peculium* otherwise invested. This is even more true, and he should certainly have recourse to this action if it can be proved that what the party who contracted with the son or the slave gave was used for the benefit of the father or the master; for, as we stated above, the same formula is employed both in the action having reference to the *peculium*, and in the one to recover property used for the benefit of another.

(75) Noxal actions are granted on account of offences committed by sons under paternal control, or by slaves; as, for instance, where they commit theft or injury; so that the father or master is permitted either to pay the damages assessed, or to surrender the culprit by way of reparation; for it would be unjust for the misconduct of a son or a slave to cause any loss to his parent, or his master, except by the forfeiture of the body of the son or the slave.

(76) Moreover, noxal actions were established either by law or by the Edict of the Prætor; by law, for instance, in the action of theft under the provision of the Twelve Tables; the action for wrongful damage by the *Lex Aquilia*; the action for injury, and that for property taken with violence by the Edict of the Prætor.

(77) All noxal actions follow the person of the culprit. Hence, if your son, or your slave commits a wrongful act while he is under your control, an action will lie against you; if he comes under the power of another, an action can be brought against the latter; if he becomes his own master, a direct action can be brought against him, and his surrender by way of reparation is extinguished. On the other hand, a direct action may become a noxal one; for if the head of a household commits a wrongful act and he gives himself in arrogation to you, or becomes your slave; what we stated in the First Commentary might happen in certain cases takes place; that is to say, a noxal action can be brought against you, when, formerly, a direct action would lie against the offender himself.

(78) If, however, a son commits a wrongful act against his father, or a slave against his master, no right of action will arise; for no obligation can, under any circumstances, be created between me and one who is

under my control. Hence, although he may pass under the control of another, or becomes his own master, an action will lie neither against himself, nor against the party under whose control he now is. Therefore, the question arises where the son or the slave of another commits a wrongful act against me, and subsequently is subjected to my authority; whether, on this account the action is extinguished, or remains in suspense. Our preceptors hold that it is extinguished, because conditions have become such that it cannot be brought; and, therefore, if the party should be freed from my control, I cannot bring suit. The authorities of the other school are of the opinion that as long as he is in my power, the action remains in suspense, for the reason that I cannot sue myself; but that when he is no longer subject to my authority the action is revived.

(79) Moreover, when a son under paternal control is transferred by mancipation, on account of some wrongful act which he has committed, the authorities of the other school think that he should be sold three times, because it is provided by the Law of the Twelve Tables that a son cannot be released from the authority of his father unless he has been three times sold. Sabinus, Cassius, and the other authorities of our school, however, hold that one sale is sufficient, and that the three mentioned by the Law of the Twelve Tables only refer to voluntary sales.

(80) So much with reference to those persons who are under the control of their fathers and masters whether the controversy relates to their contracts, or their crimes. But with reference to such persons as are in hand, or are liable to mancipation, the law is said to be that when an action founded on contract is brought against them, unless they are defended against the entire amount by the party to whose authority they are subject, any property which would be theirs, if they had not been under control, shall be sold. When, however, their forfeiture of civil rights having been rescinded, an action based on the judicial power of the magistrate is brought against them and is not defended, the woman herself can be sued, while she is in the hand of her husband, because, in this instance the authority of the guardian is not necessary. . . .[1]

(81) What course then should be pursued? Although we stated that it was not permitted to surrender dead persons by way of reparation for the commission of a wrongful act; still, if anyone should surrender the body of such a person who had died, he will (be) legally released from liability.

(82) In the next place we should note that we can either sue in our own names, or in that of another, as for instance, our agent, attorney, guardian, or curator, while formerly, when the *legis actionis* were employed, a man could not bring an action in the name of another, except in certain cases.

(83) Moreover, the attorney in an action is appointed by prescribed forms of words in the presence of the adverse party. The plaintiff appoints an attorney as follows: "Whereas, I am bringing an action against you (for example) to recover a certain tract of land; I appoint Lucius Titius my attorney against you in this matter." The adverse party makes his appointment as follows: "Whereas, you have brought an action against me to recover a tract of land, I appoint Publius Mævius my attorney against you in this matter." The plaintiff may make use of the following words: "Whereas, I desire to bring an action against you, I appoint Lucius Titius my attorney in this matter." The defendant says: "Whereas, you desire to bring an action against me, I appoint Publius Mævius my attorney in this matter." It makes no difference whether the attorney appointed is present, or absent; but if an absent person is appointed, he will only become the attorney if he accepts and undertakes the duties of the office.

(84) An agent, however, is substituted in the case without the use of any special forms of words, merely by mandate alone, and his appointment can be made during the absence, and without the knowledge of the

---

[1] Original manuscript illegible.

adverse party. Moreover, there are some authorities who hold that one can become an agent, without having been directed to do so, provided he attends to the business in good faith, and gives security that his principal will ratify his acts; although he to whom the mandate was given is generally required to furnish security, because the mandate is frequently concealed in the beginning of the proceedings and is afterwards disclosed in court.

(85) We have stated in the First Commentary in what manner guardians and curators are appointed.

(86) He who brings an action in the name of another makes the claim in the name of his principal, and mentions his own name in the condemnation. If, for instance, Lucius Titius brings suit for Publius Mævius, the formula is in the following words: "If it appears that Numerius Negidius should pay to Publius Mævius ten thousand sesterces, Judge, condemn Numerius Negidius to pay ten thousand sesterces to Lucius Titius, and if his indebtedness should not be established discharge him from liability." Again, in a real action, the claim is made that the property belongs to Publius Mævius by quiritarian right, and the representative is mentioned in the condemnation.

(87) When anyone intervenes in behalf of the party against whom the action is brought, and the claim is made that "the principal should make payment," the condemnation is stated in the name of the representative of the party sued. In the case of a real action, however, the name of the party defendant is not mentioned in the claim, either when he appears in person, or by a representative; for the claim merely states that the property in question belongs to the plaintiff.

(88) Let us now consider under what circumstances either the defendant or the plaintiff may be compelled to give security.

(89) Hence, for example, if I bring a real action against you, you should furnish me security, for it appears to be but just as you are permitted to retain possession of the property, and it is doubtful whether it belongs to you, or not, that you should give security that if you are defeated, and do not restore the property itself, or refuse to pay its value, I may have the power to proceed against you, or your sponsors.

(90) There is all the more reason that you should furnish me security, if you are acting as the representative of another in the case.

(91) Moreover, a real action is of a twofold nature; for it is either brought by a formula stating the claim, or by one based on a solemn engagement; and, if it is made in the manner first mentioned, the stipulation called "security for the payment of a judgment" will apply; but if it is based on a solemn engagement, that form of stipulation styled "security for the property in dispute and the profits derived from the same," is the one made use of.

(92) The formula which states the claim contains the allegation of the plaintiff that the property belongs to him.

(93) In the proceeding based upon a solemn engagement, we proceed as follows, and we make this demand upon the adverse party: "If the slave in dispute is mine by quiritarian right, do you promise to pay me twenty-five sesterces?" And then we state the formula by which we claim that the sum mentioned in the promise should be paid to us; but we can only gain our case by means of this formula if we prove that the property is ours.

(94) The sum mentioned in the promise is not exacted, for it is not penal, but merely prejudicial, and is used only for the purpose of deciding the right to the property; therefore even the party against whom the action is brought does not make another stipulation with the plaintiff. Moreover, this kind of a stipulation instead of security for the property in dispute and for the profits of the same, was so called because it took the place

of personal sureties who formerly, when proceedings were instituted under the *legis actiones*, were given by the party in possession to the plaintiff, for the restoration of the property itself and the mesne profits of the same.

(95) When, however, the suit is brought before the *Centumviri*, we do not demand the sum mentioned in the solemn engagement, by the formula, but under the ancient form of procedure; for then we challenge the defendant by the deposit, and the promise of a hundred and twenty-five sesterces is made by virtue of the Lex . . . .[1]

(96) If a party brings a real action in his own name, he does not furnish security.

(97) And even if an action is brought by an agent, no security is required from him, or his principal, for he has been substituted for his principal by a prescribed and, as it were, solemn form of words; and he is very properly considered to occupy the place of his principal.

(98) If, however, an agent brings the action, he is ordered to give security that his principal will ratify his acts; for there is danger that, otherwise, the principal might bring a second action with reference to the same property, which danger does not exist where the suit was brought by an agent; for the reason that anyone who sues by an agent has no greater right of action than if he brought the suit himself.

(99) The terms of the Edict compel guardians and curators to furnish security in the same way as agents; sometimes, however, they are not required to do so.

(100) So much with reference to real actions. In the case of personal actions, when inquiry is made now and when security should be furnished by the plaintiff, we repeat what we have already said with reference to real actions.

(101) But with respect to the party against whom the action is brought, where anyone intervenes in his behalf, he must, by all means, furnish security, for the reason that no one is understood to be a proper defender of another's affairs without security. If the action is brought against an attorney, his principal is required to furnish security, but if brought against an agent, the latter must furnish it himself. The same rule applies to guardians and curators.

(102) If, however, a party undertakes his own defence in a personal action he usually gives security to pay the judgment, in certain cases which are indicated by the Prætor. In these cases there are two reasons why security is exacted; for this is either done on account of the nature of the action, or because the character of the defendant is suspicious. It is required on account of the nature of the action, for instance, where it is one to compel the payment of a judgment, or to collect money expended for a principal; or where the morals of a wife are involved. It is required on account of the suspicious character of the defendant, where he has squandered his property; or his creditors have obtained possession of it, or advertised it for sale; or when proceedings have been instituted against an heir whom the Prætor considers liable to suspicion.

(103) Actions are either founded upon law, or are derived from the authority of a magistrate.

(104) Actions founded upon law are those which are brought in the City of Rome, or within the first milestone from that city, between Roman citizens before a single judge. Those brought under the *Lex Julia Judiciaria* expire after the lapse of a year and six months, unless they have been previously decided; and this is the reason why it is commonly stated that under the *Lex Julia* a case dies after a year and six months have elapsed.

---

[1] Original manuscript illegible.

(105) Actions derived from the authority of a magistrate are those brought before several judges, or before a single judge, if either the latter or one of the litigants is an alien. These actions belong to the same class as those which are brought beyond the first mile-stone from the City of Rome; whether the parties litigant are Roman citizens or aliens. Cases of this kind are said to be derived from the authority of the magistrate, for the reason that the proceedings are only valid as long as he who directed them to be instituted retains his office.

(106) Where an action is brought under the authority of a magistrate, whether it is real or personal, or whether it was based upon a formula of fact, or a statement of law, it is not by operation of law a bar to subsequent proceedings having reference to the same matter, and therefore it is necessary to plead an exception on the ground that a decision has already been rendered, or that issue has been joined in the case.

(107) If, however, a personal action based on a legal statement has been brought by the formula relating to claims under the Civil Law, an action cannot subsequently be maintained with reference to the same matter by operation of law, and for this reason an exception will be superfluous. If, however, a real action, or an equitable personal action based upon fact, should be brought, proceedings may nevertheless subsequently be instituted, by operation of law; and on this account an exception on the ground that the question has already been decided, or that issue has been joined, will be necessary.

(108) The rule was formerly different when the ancient method to procedure was employed, for when proceedings concerning a matter had once been instituted, no legal action could be taken with reference to it, nor was the employment of exceptions in those times customary, as it is now.

(109) Moreover, an action may be founded upon law, and yet not be legal; and, on the other hand, it may not be founded upon law, but still be legal. For example, proceedings based upon the *Lex Aquilia, Publilia*, or *Furia*, when instituted in the provinces, are derived from the authority of the magistrate, and the rule is the same if we bring an action before several judges, or before a single judge if one of the parties is an alien; and, on the other hand, if an action in which all the parties are Roman citizens is brought at Rome before a single judge, for the same cause for which a right of action is granted to us by the Prætor, it will be legal.

(110) In this place we should note that those actions which are based upon a statute or a decree of the Senate are usually granted by the Prætor in perpetuity; but that those which are dependent upon the jurisdiction of the Prætor himself are only granted within a year from the time when the cause of action arose.

(111) Sometimes, however, he also grants such actions in perpetuity, as, for instance, those in which the Civil Law is imitated; such as the actions which he grants to the prætorian possessors of estates, and to other persons who occupy the place of an heir. The action of manifest theft, although it is derived from the jurisdiction of the Prætor himself, is granted without limitation of time, and this is reasonable, as a pecuniary penalty has been established instead of a capital one.

(112) All actions which lie against anyone, either by operation of law, or because they are granted by the Prætor, do not also lie against his heir, nor are usually granted by the Prætor; for this rule is so positive that penal actions arising from criminal offences do not lie, and are not usually granted against an heir; as, for instance, the action of theft, of the robbery of property by violence, or of injury, or of unlawful damage. Actions of this kind will, however, lie in favor of heirs, and will not be refused them by the Prætor, with the exception of the action for injury, and any other of the same description if it can be found.

(113) Sometimes, however, even an action based upon a contract will not lie for or against an heir; since the heir of a joint stipulator has no right of action, and the heir of a sponsor or guarantor is not liable.

(114) It remains for us to consider whether, if the party against whom the action was brought before judgment had been rendered but after issue had been joined, should satisfy the plaintiff, what course the judge should pursue; whether he has authority to discharge him from liability, or whether he should rather decide against him for the reason that at the time of the joinder of issue he was in such a position that he should have been condemned. Our preceptors think that he should be discharged, and that it makes no difference what kind of a judgment is rendered; and this is the reason why it is commonly said that it was the opinion of Sabinus and Cassius that a discharge from liability could be granted in all actions. The authorities of the other school agree in this point with reference to *bona fide* actions; because in cases of this kind no restraint is placed upon the judge; and their opinion is the same with reference to real actions, for the reason that there is an express provision of this kind stated in the terms of the formula, so that if the defendant should restore the property he shall be discharged from liability. This, of course, applies where the action was brought under the formula making the claim, in which the party is sued in such a way that the property in dispute is demanded, and the words above referred to are repeated in the beginning of the condemnation; for sometimes . . .[1] personal actions of this kind are brought in which it is not permitted . . . .[1]

(115) In the next place let us examine exceptions.[2]

(116) Exceptions have been introduced for the purpose of defending those against whom actions have been brought; for it often happens that a party is liable by the Civil Law, when it would be unjust for a judgment to be rendered against him. For example, if I stipulate for a sum of money from you on account of my having advanced it to you, when I never did so; as it is certain that I can bring an action against you for the money and you would be obliged to pay it as you are liable under the stipulation, but because it would be unjust for judgment to be rendered against you on this account, it is settled that you can defend yourself by the exception on the ground of fraud. Likewise, if I make an informal agreement with you not to bring suit for a debt which you owe me; I can nevertheless, bring an action against you for the amount, and you will be obliged to pay me because the obligation is not extinguished by a mere agreement, but if I should sue you, it is established that you can bar me by an exception on the ground of an agreement entered into.

(117) Again, exceptions can be pleaded in actions which are not personal; for example, if you compel me through fear, or induce me through fraud, to sell any property to you, and then you sue me for the said property, an exception will be granted me by which you will be barred, if I can prove that you have been guilty of intimidation or fraud. Likewise, if knowing that a case involving the title to a tract of land was pending in court, and you buy the land from a party who is not in possession, and claim it from one who is in possession, an exception can be pleaded against you by which you will be absolutely barred.

(118) The Prætor mentions other exceptions in his Edict, and he grants still others after having taken cognizance of the case. All of them are either based upon law or what is equivalent to it, or they are derived from the jurisdiction of the Prætor.

(119) Moreover, all exceptions are drawn up in language which is the opposite of what the party against whom the action is brought alleges. For if the defendant states that the plaintiff is guilty of fraud, for the reason that he brings suit for money which he never advanced, the exception is stated in the following words: "If in this matter no fraud was, or is committed by Aulus Agerius." Likewise, if he states that the

---

[1] Original copy illegible.

[2] The *exceptio*, or exception, was the answer of the defendant, and while by means of it he could traverse the plaintiff's allegations, this was not usually done; but the practice was to set forth circumstances, which, if they did not directly contravene the statements of the plaintiff — and they even sometimes admitted them — rendered these of no effect, by alleging bad faith, fraud, or flagrant injustice. Hence the *exceptio* almost exactly coincided with the English plea of confession and avoidance. — ed.

action was brought in opposition to an agreement not to demand the money, it is set forth as follows: "If it was not agreed between Aulus Agerius and Numerius Negidius that the said money should not be demanded"; and similar terms are ordinarily employed in other cases. Hence, because every exception is an objection made by the defendant but is inserted in the formula in such a way as to render the condemnation conditional, that is, the judge must not condemn the defendant unless no fraud was committed by the plaintiff with reference to the matter in question, the judge shall not render a decree against him if no informal agreement[1] was entered into not to bring suit to recover the money.

(120) Exceptions are said to be either peremptory or dilatory.

(121) Peremptory exceptions are those which are always valid, and cannot be avoided; for instance, the exception on the ground of intimidation or fraud, or of a violation of the law; or of a decree of the Senate; or because the case has already been decided; or that issue has been joined; or that an informal agreement was entered into "that suit should not, under any circumstances, be brought to recover the money.

(122) Dilatory exceptions are such as are only valid for a time; for instance, the exception based on an informal agreement that suit shall not be brought within five years, and after that time has expired the exception cannot be pleaded. The exception of a divided claim, or that of a residual claim, is similar to this; for if anyone brings an action for a part of a debt, and should then bring another for the remainder in the same prætorship, he will be barred by the exception which is called that of a divided claim. In like manner, if one who has several claims against the same person brings suit on some of them, and defers doing so with reference to the remainder in order that they may be brought before other judges, and he then brings an action within the same prætorship, to recover those which he postponed, he will be barred by the exception styled that of a residual claim.

(123) It should be observed, however, that the party against whom a dilatory exception may be pleaded ought to defer his action, otherwise, if he proceeds and the exception be pleaded against him, he will lose his claim; as if issue had been joined, and his case has been lost by this exception, he has no longer any power to sue after the time during which, if matters had remained unchanged, he could have avoided the effect of the exception.

(124) Exceptions are understood to be dilatory not only with reference to time, but also with regard to persons; and to this class belong those which are connected with the position of attorney; for instance, where a party who, under the terms of the Edict, has no right to appoint an attorney acts through one; or, if he has a right to appoint an attorney, but appoints one who is not legally qualified to undertake the duties of the *office*. If the exception to an attorney is pleaded, and the party himself is such a person that he cannot appoint an attorney, he himself can bring the action; if, however, the attorney is not permitted to assume the duties of the office, his principal has the power to bring the suit, either by another attorney, or in his own proper person, and he can, in either one of these ways, avoid the exception; but if he should pay no attention to this disability, and conduct the case by the attorney he will lose it.

(125) If the defendant, through mistake, should not avail himself of a peremptory exception, he can obtain complete restitution, by adding the exception to the pleadings; but if he should not make use of a dilatory exception, it is a question whether he will be entitled to complete restitution.

(126) It sometimes happens that an exception which, at first sight, appears to be just, will cause injury to

---

[1] *Pactum conventum.* An agreement of this kind was not absolutely binding unless authorized by the Prætor who, however, rarely refused his sanction. When this was obtained, no difference existed between this kind of obligation and the *contractus*, or formal convention, so far as their legal requirements were concerned. — ed.

the plaintiff, and when this is the case an addition is required to the pleadings for the purpose of affording protection to the plaintiff, which addition is called a *Replicatio*, because by means of it the force of the exception is weakened and destroyed. If, for example, I made an informal agreement with you not to sue you for money which you owe me, and afterwards we entered into a contrary agreement, that is to say, that I might be permitted to sue you, and then if I do sue you, you plead the exception against me that judgment should only be rendered against you where no agreement had been made that I should not bring suit for the money, this exception on the ground of an informal agreement prejudices my claim, as the first agreement still retains its force, even though we made a contrary one subsequently; but because it is unjust for me to be barred by an exception, a replication based on the subsequent agreement is granted me as follows: "If no agreement was entered into afterwards that I might be permitted to bring an action to recover the money."

(126a) Likewise, if a banker brings suit for the price of property sold at auction, the exception may be pleaded against him that judgment is only to be rendered against the purchaser where the property which he bought had been delivered; and this is apparently a just exception. If, however, the condition was imposed at the auction that the property should not be delivered to the purchaser until he had paid the price of the same, the broker can make use of the following replication: "Or if it was previously stated at the sale that the property would not be delivered to the purchaser before he paid the purchase money."

(127) Sometimes, however, it happens that a replication which, at first sight, appears to be equitable, unjustly inflicts an injury on the defendant; and when this takes place, an addition to the pleadings is required for the purpose of protecting the defendant, which is styled *Duplicatio*.

(128) Again, if this, though it appears at first sight to be just, for some reason or other injures the plaintiff, another addition to the pleadings is required by which the plaintiff may be protected, and this is called a *Triplicatio*.

(129) Sometimes the multiplicity of affairs requires the use of additional exceptions to those which we have already mentioned.[1]

(130) Let us now consider Prescriptions,[2] which have been adopted for the benefit of the plaintiff.

(131) For it is frequently the case that, under the same obligation a party is required to do something for us at present, and something more at a future time. For instance, where we have stipulated for the payment of a certain sum of money every year, or every month, and, at the end of the year or month, a sum of money is required to be paid to us for this time; and with reference to years to come, although an obligation is understood to have been contracted, the time of payment has not yet arrived. Therefore, if we desire to bring an action to recover what is now due, and to proceed to joinder of issue and leave the future discharge of the obligation unimpaired, it is necessary, when we bring suit, to make use of the following prescription: "Let the proceedings have reference only to what is at present due." Otherwise, if we bring suit without making use of this prescription, under the formula by which we sue for an uncertain amount, the statement of the claim is expressed as follows: "Whatever it appears that Numerius Negidius should transfer to, or do for Aulus Agerius," brings the entire obligation, that is to say, also what is due in the future, into court; and no matter what may be due hereafter it cannot be collected, nor can an action subsequently be brought to

---

[1] These terms and the order of their employment are strongly suggestive of the ancient forms of Common Law pleading, the Reply, Rejoinder, Surrejoinder, Rebutter and Surrebutter. Under both the Roman and English systems, the pleadings could be indefinitely multiplied, until joinder of issue was attained, but it was not customary to extend them beyond the *Triplicatio*, or Surrejoinder. — ed.

[2] *Præscriptio*. This was equivalent to an exception, or a demurrer, which took the place of the *Demonstratio*, and was inserted in the beginning of the Formula. It was subsequently known as the *Actio Præscriptis Verbis*, and operated as a limitation of the right of action. To have legal effect, it was essential that it should be specially pleaded. — ed.

recover the remainder.

(131a) Likewise, where for example, we bring an action on purchase, in order that land may be conveyed to us by sale, we must state the prescription as follows: "Let the proceedings only have reference to the sale of the land"; and, afterwards, if we desire vacant possession be delivered to us, we will be entitled to an action under the stipulation, or to one under the contract of purchase to compel its delivery. If we neglect to make use of this prescription, the obligation of our entire right embraced in the uncertain claim: "Whatever on this account Numerius Negidius. should give to, or do for Aulus Agerius," is disposed of by the statement of the claim in the former suit; so that afterwards we will not be entitled to any action to compel the delivery of vacant possession, if we should desire to bring one.

(132) Prescriptions are so called for the reason that they precede the formulas, which fact is perfectly obvious.

(133) At the present time, however, as we mentioned above, all prescriptions proceed from the plaintiff, while formerly some of them were pleaded in behalf of the defendant, as for instance, the following prescription: "Let this point be determined, if it does not prejudice the estate"; which is now changed into a species of exception, and is used when the claimant of the estate prejudices the right to the same by bringing another kind of action, for example, if he brings suit for certain articles belonging to the estate; for it would be unjust to render the result of an action involving the entire estate dependent upon a decision having reference to only a portion of the same . . . .[1]

(134) If suit is brought under a stipulation entered into by a slave, and the *Intentio* states to whom the amount is to be paid, that is to say, that what the slave stipulated for should be paid to his master; the allegations in the prescription should be true in accordance with their natural meaning.

(135) Moreover, what we have said with reference to slaves we understand to be applicable to all other persons subject to our authority.

(136) Again, we should observe that when we bring an action against a party who promised something which was uncertain, the formula should be drawn up so as to include a prescription, instead of a statement of the cause of action, as follows: "Let So-and-So be judge. For the reason that Aulus Agerius stipulated for something uncertain from Numerius Negidius, payment of which is now due, whatever on this account Numerius Negidius should transfer to, or do for, Aulus Agerius, etc."

(137) When an action is brought against a sponsor or surety, it is the practice, in the case of the sponsor, to employ the following form of prescription: "Let the action be tried on the ground that Aulus Agerius stipulated for something of uncertain amount from Lucius Titius, for which Numerius Negidius is sponsor for the amount which is now due." In the case of a surety, the following form is employed: "Let the case be tried on the ground that Numerius Negidius became surety for Lucius Titius for an uncertain amount, which is now due"; and then the formula is added.[2]

---

[1] Original manuscript illegible.

[2] The Formulary System of the Romans contributed much of value and importance to both the principles and forms of the Common Law. The maxims of the great lawyers of that age are still quoted authoritatively in our courts. The ancient writs of English legal procedure were directly derived from the Formula. As equity jurisprudence traces its origin to the broad and indulgent interpretation permitted the Prætorian Tribunal, so the modern bill in equity bears many striking resemblances to the instruments by means of which parties litigant were enabled to maintain their rights and protect their persons before the most powerful and distinguished of the Roman magistrates.

The *formulæ* were almost infinite in number and variety, and the party to a suit who failed to elect the one applicable to his case paid the penalty of his ignorance or negligence with the loss of his right of action. The abuses which grew out of the inflexible adherence to

(138) It remains for us to examine interdicts.

(139) The Prætor, or the Proconsul, interposes his authority directly in certain cases for the purpose of putting an end to controversies. This he especially does when there is a dispute between the parties with reference to possession or quasi possession; and, in short, he either orders something to be done, or forbids it to be done. Moreover, the formulas and the clauses made use of in this proceeding are styled interdicts and decrees.

(140) They are called decrees when he commands something to be done, for instance when he directs that something be produced in court, or restored; they are called interdicts when he forbids something to be done; for instance when he directs that no violence be employed against the party who is in possession without any defect; or that nothing be done on consecrated ground. Hence, all interdicts have reference to restitution, production, or prohibition.

(141) Still, when he orders that something shall be done, or prohibits some act from being performed, the affair is not immediately concluded, but recourse is had to one or more judges, and the formulas having been issued, an inquiry is held as to whether anything has been done, or some act which he ordered has not been performed, in opposition to the Edict of the Prætor. In a proceeding of this kind sometimes a penalty is involved, and sometimes it is not; it is penal, for instance, where a formal promise is concerned, and it is not where an arbiter is demanded. It is the practice to proceed under prohibitory interdicts always by way of solemn promise, and, in the case of orders for restitution or production, this is either done by way of formal promise or by means of the formula styled "arbitrary".

(142) Hence, the original division of interdicts is into prohibitory, or for restriction, or for production.

(143) The next division is into those instituted for the purpose of obtaining, retaining, or recovering possession.

(144) An interdict issued to the prætorian possessor of an estate for the purpose of obtaining possession begins: "Whatever portion of the property"; and its force and effect is that the possession of property held by anyone, as heir, or possessor, or who has fraudulently relinquished possession, shall be restored to the party to whom possession is granted by the interdict. He is considered to possess the property as heir, not only when he is the actual heir, but also when he thinks that he is the heir. He holds the property as the mere possessor who has anything belonging to an estate, or the entire estate, without any title to the same, knowing that he is in possession of something that does not belong to him. The interdict for the purpose of obtaining possession is so called because it is only advantageous to him who now, for the first time, attempts to acquire possession of the property; therefore, if anyone having obtained possession should lose it, the interdict ceases to be of any benefit to him.

(145) Again, an interdict is granted to the purchaser of a bankrupt estate, which some authorities call a possessory interdict.

(146) In like manner, an interdict of the same kind is granted to one who purchases confiscated property at a public sale, which is called *Sectorium* for the reason that those who purchase such property at public sale, are designated *Sectores*.

(147) The interdict called *Salvianum* was also one devised for the purpose of obtaining possession; and the owner of land can make use of it against the property of the tenant which the latter has pledged to him as

---

certain rules and forms which, encouraging chicanery and oppression, were often productive of gross injustice, eventually caused the abolition of the system. — ed.

security for the future payment of rent.

(148) It is the practice for interdicts for the purpose of retaining possession to be granted when a controversy arises between two parties with reference to the ownership of property; and it must be previously ascertained which one of the litigants should have possession, and which one should have a right to demand it; and it is for this purpose that the interdicts *Uti Possidetis* and *Utrubi* has been established.

(149) The interdict *Uti Possidetis* is granted with reference to the possession of land or buildings; the interdict *Utrubi* with reference to the possession of movable property.

(150) If the interdict has reference to land or houses, the Prætor orders that party to have the preference who, at the time when the interdict was issued, obtained possession from his adversary, neither by force nor clandestinely, nor with his acquiescence. When, however, it has reference to movable property, he orders that party to have the preference who, for the greater part of that year, has held possession against his adversary neither by force, nor clandestinely, or with his acquiescence; and this is sufficiently apparent from the terms of the interdicts themselves.

(151) But, in the interdict *Utrubi*, not only is the possession of every one a benefit to him, but that of another party which may be properly treated as accessory to it; for instance, that of a deceased person whose heir he is, and that of anyone from whom he has purchased property, or acquired it by means of a donation or a dowry. Hence, if the lawful possession of another party is added to our own, and it exceeds the possession of our adversary, we will be successful in the proceeding under that interdict. The accession of time is not granted, and cannot be granted to one who has no possession of his own, for whatever does not exist can have nothing added to it. If, however, a party should have defective possession, that is to say, if it had been acquired from his adversary either by violence, or clandestinely, or by mere acquiescence, no accession is granted, for his own possession is of no advantage to him.

(152) Moreover, the year is reckoned backward, and hence, for example, if you had possession eight months before I did, and I had it during the seven following months, I will be entitled to the preference, because your possession for the first three months would be of no advantage to you under this interdict, as the possession was in another year.

(153) We consider a party to be in possession not only where we ourselves possess, but also where anyone is in possession in our name, although he may not be subject to our authority; as, for instance, a tenant or a lessee. We are also considered to have possession by means of those with whom we have deposited property, or lent it for use, or to whom we have granted gratuitous lodging, or the usufruct or use; and this is what is commonly called the power of retaining possession of property by anyone who possesses it in our name. Again, many authorities hold that possession can be retained merely by intention; that is to say, that though we ourselves may not be in possession, nor anyone else in our name, still, if there be no intention of relinquishing possession, and we leave the property, intending afterwards to return, we are deemed to have retained possession of it. We stated in the Second Commentary by what persons we could obtain possession, nor is there any doubt that we cannot obtain it by mere intention.

(154) The interdict for the purpose of recovering possession is usually granted where anyone has been ejected by violence, for the interdict which is issued begins as follows: "In the place from which you have been forcibly ejected"; and by means of it the party who ejected the other is compelled to restore possession of the property to him, provided the latter did not himself obtain possession either by violence, or clandestinely, or by permission from the former; hence, I can eject with impunity anyone who has obtained possession from me either by violence, or clandestinely, or by permission.

(155) Sometimes, however, even though I should forcibly eject the party who obtained possession from me

either by violence, or clandestinely, or by permission, I can be compelled to restore possession to him; for instance, if I should eject him by force of arms, for, on account of the atrocity of the crime, I am liable to have proceedings instituted against me by which I shall be absolutely obliged to reinstate him in possession. We understand by the expression, "force of arms," not only the use of shields, swords, and helmets, but also that of sticks and stone.

(156) The third division of interdicts is into simple and double.

(157) Simple interdicts are, for instance, those in which one party is plaintiff and the other defendant, and of this description are all those established for the restitution or the production of property; for he is the plaintiff who demands that the property be either produced or restored, and he is the defendant from whom it is demanded that he produce or restore it.

(158) Of prohibitory interdicts some are double, and others simple.

(159) Simple interdicts are, for instance, those by which the Prætor forbids a defendant to perform any illegal act on consecrated ground, or in a public stream, or on its bank; for the plaintiff is he who demands that the act shall not be committed, and the defendant is he who attempts to commit it.

(160) Double interdicts are such, for instance, as *Uti Possidetis* and *Utrubi*. They are called double because the position of both litigants in them is the same, and neither is exclusively understood to be defendant or plaintiff, but both of them sustain the parts of defendant and plaintiff. In fact the Prætor addresses both in the same language, for the form of these interdicts is as follows: "I forbid force to be employed to prevent you from having possession of the property which you now possess." The terms of the other are as follows: "I forbid violence to be employed to prevent the party from removing the slave in dispute, and who has been in his possession for the greater part of the year."

(161) The different kinds of interdicts having been explained, let us next consider their order and effects, and we shall begin with those which are simple.

(162) Therefore, if an interdict for the restitution or the production of property is issued; for instance, for the restitution of possession to one who has been forcibly ejected, or for the production of a freedman whose services his patron desires to claim, the proceedings are sometimes brought to a conclusion without the risk of incurring the penalty, and sometimes with that risk.

(163) For, if he against whom the case is brought should demand an arbiter, he receives the formula which is called "arbitrary," and if, by the award of the judge, he is required to restore or produce any property, he either produces or restores it without any penalty, and thus is discharged from liability; or if he does not restore or produce it, he is compelled to indemnify the plaintiff for the loss sustained through his disobedience. The plaintiff, however, can, without incurring a penalty, bring an action against one who is not required to produce or restore any property, unless an action for vexatious litigation is brought against him to recover the tenth part of the property in question; although it is said to have been held by Proculus that an action for vexatious litigation should be refused to him who demands arbitration, because he is considered to have, as it were, admitted that he ought to restore or produce the property. We, however, make use of another rule, and very properly; for anyone who demands an arbiter rather shows his intention to litigate in a more moderate manner, than for the reason that he admits the validity of the claim of his adversary.

(164) It should be observed that he who desires to demand an arbiter must do so before leaving court, that is before he departs from the tribunal of the Prætor, for if such a demand is made later it will not be granted.

(165) Hence, if he does not demand an arbiter, but leaves the tribunal without doing so, the affair is brought to a conclusion at the risk of the parties; for the plaintiff challenges his adversary to deposit the forfeit which shall be paid if, in disobedience to the Edict of the Prætor, he does not produce or restore the property; and the defendant restipulates in opposition to the demand for a forfeit by his opponent. The plaintiff then delivers to his adversary the formula of the forfeit to be deposited, and the latter in his turn delivers that of the restipulation. The plaintiff, however, adds to the formula of the promise of a forfeit another action for the restipulation or the production of the property in question, so that if he should be successful, and the property is not either reduced or restored to him . . . . [1]

(166) When a double interdict has been granted, the mesne profits are sold at auction and the highest bidder is placed in possession of the property, provided he furnishes his adversary security under the stipulation for the enjoyment of the profits; the force and effect of which is that if judgment should be rendered against him with reference to possession, he shall pay his adversary the sum provided for in the stipulation. This bidding between the parties is designated the bidding for the profits, because they contend with one another for the profits of the property during the preliminary proceedings. After this, each one of them challenges the other to deposit the forfeit to be paid by the promisor, if he has by violence interfered with the possession of his adversary, and hence has violated the Edict of the Prætor; and each of them mutually bind themselves, or the two stipulations being united so that one promise is made between them, and also one restipulation is entered into by one party against the other, which is the more convenient way of proceeding, and therefore the one most generally in use.

(166a) Then, after the necessary formulas of all the promises and restipulations have been filed by both parties, the judge before whom the case is tried must examine the point introduced by the Prætor in the interdict; that is to say, which of the parties was in possession of the land or the house at the time when the interdict was issued, and that he did not obtain possession of it by violence, or clandestinely, or with the permission of the adverse party. When the judge has investigated this, and has, perhaps, decided in my favor, he condemns my adversary to pay the penal sums called for by the promise and the restipulation which I made with him, and in consequence discharges me from liability for the promise and restipulation which were made with me. Further, if my adversary had possession of the property for the reason that he made the highest bid for the profits of the same, and he does not restore possession to me, he can have judgment rendered against him in the action styled Cascellian or Secutorian.

(167) Therefore, if he who is the highest bidder does not prove that he is entitled to possession, he is ordered to pay the sums mentioned in the promise and restipulation, as well as the amount he offered in his bid for the mesne profits at auction, by way of penalty, and to restore possession of the property; and, in addition to this, he must return the profits which, in the meantime he has collected; for the sum of money mentioned in the bid for the profits is not the price of the same, but is paid as a penalty because the party attempted to retain possession belonging to another, for this time, and also to enjoy the profits derived from the property.

(168) Moreover, if he who made a lower bid for the profits at the auction does not prove that he is entitled to possession, he should only be required to pay the amount of the promise and restipulation by way of penalty.

(169) We should observe, however, that the unsuccessful bidder, without availing himself of the stipulation for the enjoyment of the profits, has a right to bring an action on the sale at auction, just as by the Cascellian or Secutorian action he can sue for the recovery of possession. A special action has been

---

[1] Original manuscript illegible.

introduced for this purpose, which is called "fructuary," by means of which the plaintiff receives satisfaction for his judgment. This action is also called Secutorian, because it follows the advantage of the promise, but it is not also called Cascellian.

(170) But, for the reason that, after an interdict has been issued, some of the parties are unwilling to institute other proceedings under it, and on this account matters cannot be expedited, the Prætor made provision for a case of this kind, and introduced interdicts which we call "secondary"; because they are issued in the second place, under such circumstances. The force and effect of these is that he who does not institute further proceedings under the interdict, for example, one who does not forcibly eject the other party; or does not make a bid for the mesne profits of the property; or does not furnish security for the same; or does not participate in the promise, or defend the case; shall, if he is in possession of the property, restore it to his adversary; for if he is not in possession, he shall not use violence against the other party who is. Hence, although, otherwise, he might have been able to succeed under the interdict *Uti Possidetis*, if he could have complied with the other requirements imposed by it, and did not do so, he will still lose his case by means of a secondary interdict . . . .[1]

(171) For the purpose of avoiding vexatious litigation, the parties are sometimes deterred by pecuniary penalties, and sometimes by an oath which is imposed by the Prætor. In certain cases an action for double damages is brought against a defendant; for instance, in the collection of a judgment debt, or for money expended for a principal, or for unlawful damage to property, or where proceedings are instituted to collect legacies left by condemnation. In some instances, the deposit of a forfeit is permitted to be made, for example, in an action for a certain sum of money which has been lent, or to collect a debt formerly incurred. Where suit is brought to collect a loan, the amount is one-third of the sum in question; and in the case of the acknowledgment of a balance due, it is one-half.

(172) If no deposit was made as a forfeit, and the penalty of double damages was not imposed upon the party against whom the action was brought, and under it, from the beginning, no more than simple damages can be collected; the Prætor permits the plaintiff to require the defendant to swear that he has not made a denial for the purpose of annoyance. Hence, although the heirs and those who are considered to occupy the position of heirs, are not subject to a penalty, and women and wards are exempted from the penalty of a forfeit, the Prætor, nevertheless, orders them to be sworn.

(173) Moreover, in some cases from the beginning an action for more than simple damages will lie; as in an action of manifest theft a fourfold penalty, in non-manifest theft a double penalty, and when stolen property has been delivered to another a threefold penalty can be collected; for in these and some other instances, the suit is for more than simple damages, whether the party denies, or admits the claim.

(174) Vexatious litigation by the plaintiff is also restrained sometimes by the action for this purpose, sometimes by the contrary action, sometimes by oath, and sometimes by a counter stipulation.

(175) The action of vexatious litigation is applicable as against all other actions, and is for the tenth part of the claim, but for the third part when brought against a joint stipulator.

(176) The party sued, however, has the right to choose whether he will bring the action of vexatious litigation, or exact an oath from his adversary that he has not brought suit for the purpose of causing annoyance.

(177) The counter action, however, is only applicable in certain cases; for instance, where suit is brought

---

[1] Original manuscript indistinct.

for injury, and where one is brought against a woman on the ground that having been placed in possession on account of her unborn child, she transferred it fraudulently to some other party; or where anyone brings an action alleging that he has been placed in possession by the Prætor and is refused admission by another. In the case of an action of injury it is granted for the tenth part of the amount in dispute; in the two others for the fifth.

(178) But, the most severe restraint is that produced by the counter action. For no one is condemned in the action of vexatious litigation to pay the tenth part of the amount in dispute, unless he knew that he had no right to bring suit, and did so only for the purpose of annoying his adversary and relies for success rather upon the error or injustice of the judge, than on account of the merits of his cause; for vexatious litigation, like the crime of theft, depends upon intention. In the contrary action, however, the plaintiff will, under all circumstances, be condemned if he should not prevail in the former action, although he had good reason to believe that he had a right to bring suit.

(179) Still, in all those cases in which the contrary action can be brought, the action for vexatious litigation will also lie; but it is only permitted to have recourse to one or the other of these proceedings. For which reason if an oath should be exacted that the action has not been brought for the purpose of annoyance, just as the action for vexatious litigation will not lie, so the contrary action should not be granted.

(180) The penalty of the counter engagement is usually required in certain cases, and, as in the contrary action the plaintiff is condemned under all circumstances if he should not gain his case, nor is it necessary for him to know that he had no good cause of action; so the penalty of the counter engagement must, under all circumstances, be paid by the plaintiff if he was unable to gain his case.

(181) Moreover, when anyone undergoes the penalty of the counter engagement neither the action for vexatious litigation can be brought against him, nor can the oath be administered, for it is clear that in cases of this kind the contrary action will not lie.

(182) In certain actions persons who are condemned become infamous, as in those of theft, robbery with violence, and injury, also in cases of partnership, trust, guardianship, mandate, and deposit. In actions of theft, robbery with violence, and injury, not only are the persons convicted branded with infamy, but also where a compromise is made, as is stated in the Edict of the *Prætor*; and this is proper, for it makes a great deal of difference whether anyone becomes a debtor on account of the commission of a crime, or under a contract. But while it is not expressly stated in any part of the Edict that a party is to become infamous, still he is said to be infamous who is forbidden to represent another in court, or to appoint, give, or have an agent or attorney, or to intervene as agent or attorney in a case.

(183) In conclusion, it should be noted that a person who desires to bring an action against another must summon him to appear in court, and if the party summoned does not appear, he will be liable to a penalty under the Edict of the Prætor. It is, however, not permitted to summon certain persons without the permission of the Prætor; for instance, parents, patrons, patronesses, and the children or parents of a patron or patroness; and anyone who violates this provision is liable to a penalty.

(184) However, when the adversary who has been summoned appears in court, and the business cannot be finished on the same day, the defendant must furnish security; that is to say he must promise to appear on some other designated day.

(185) Security in certain instances is simple, that is, given without sureties; and in others it is given with sureties; in still other instances, it is given by oath; and in some cases a reference is made to judges, that is to say, if the party does not appear, he may be immediately condemned to pay the amount of the security by the judges; and all these things are explained at length in the Edict of the *Prætor*.

(186) If proceedings have been instituted for the collection of a judgment, or for money expended for a principal, the amount of the security is equal to the value of the property in dispute. But in other cases the amount is that which the plaintiff swears that he has not brought suit for with the intention of causing annoyance; provided that the security is not more than half the sum in question, or more than a hundred thousand sesterces. Hence, if the property in dispute is valued at a hundred thousand sesterces, and the action is not for the collection of a judgment, or money expended for a principal, the amount of the security cannot be more than fifty thousand sesterces.

(187) Those persons whom we cannot summon to appear in court without the permission of the Prætor, we cannot compel to furnish security for their future appearance; unless the Prætor, after having been applied to, grants permission.

END OF THE INSTITUTES OF GAIUS

FRAGMENTS OF THE RULES OF DOMITIUS ULPIANUS

FRAGMENTS OF THE RULES OF DOMITIUS ULPIANUS

(1) A law is perfect, which forbids something to be done, and if it has been done rescinds it, such as the *Lex*. . . .[1] A law is imperfect, which forbids something to be done, and if it has been done does not rescind it, and imposes no penalty upon him who breaks the law; such as the *Lex Cincia*, which prohibits more than two thousand *asses* to be donated, except to certain relatives, and if more than that is given does not rescind the donation.

(2) A law is less than perfect, which forbids something to be done, and if it is done, does not rescind it, but imposes a penalty upon him who violates the law; such as the *Lex Furia* relating to wills, which forbids the acceptance of more than a thousand *asses* as a legacy, and inflicts a penalty of quadruple the amount upon him who accepts a larger sum.

(3) A law is either passed, that is, enacted; or abrogated, that is, a former law is repealed; or modified, that is, a part of the original law is annulled; or subrogated, that is, something is added to the first law; or opposed by another, that is to say some part of the first law is changed.

(4) Custom is the tacit consent of the people confirmed by long-established practice.

TITLE I. CONCERNING FREEDMEN.

(5) There are three classes of freedmen, Roman citizens, Junian Latins, and those included in the number of *dediticii*.

(6) Those freedmen are Roman citizens who have been legally manumitted, that is, either by the authority of an official, by the census, or by will, where no lawful impediment exists.

(7) Where they are manumitted under the authority of an official, the ceremony is performed before a magistrate of the Roman people, as for instance a consul, a proconsul, or a prætor.

(8) Those manumitted by the census are such as formerly, at the Lustral Census of Rome, by the order of their masters, offered themselves to be enrolled among Roman citizens.

(9) The Law of the Twelve Tables rendered those free who are manumitted by will, as it confirms testamentary grants of freedom in the following words: "It shall be legal for him to bequeath them as part of his property."

---

[1] Original manuscript illegible.

(10) Latins are those freedmen who have not been legally manumitted, as for instance, in the presence of friends, where no legal impediment exists, and whom the *Prætor* formerly only protected as having the mere form of freedom, for they remained slaves by operation of law; at present, however, they are free by operation of law under the terms of the *Lex Julia*, slaves manumitted in the presence of friends being by this law designated Junian Latins.

(11) Those are included in the number of *dediticii* who have been placed in chains by their masters as a punishment; or who have been branded; or who, having been tortured on account of some offence have been found to be guilty; or who have been delivered up to fight with the sword, or with wild beasts; or who have been thrust into some gladiatorial school, or thrown into prison, and afterwards manumitted in any way whatsoever. This is effective by the *Lex Ælia Sentia*.

(12) It is provided by the same law that a slave under thirty years of age, who has been manumitted before a magistrate, does not become a Roman citizen, unless cause is shown for it in the presence of the Council; hence, it is held that a slave manumitted without the permission of the Council remains a slave. The law also directs that a slave manumitted by will is in the same position as if he had been liberated with the consent of his master, and therefore he becomes a Latin.

(13) The same law prohibits a minor under the age of twenty years from manumitting a slave, unless he gives good reason for doing so before the Council.

(13a) At Rome the Council is composed of five senators and five Roman knights; in the provinces of twenty judges who are Roman citizens.

(14) A slave directed to be free, and appointed heir by the will of his master who is insolvent, becomes a Roman citizen and the heir; even though he may be under the age of thirty years, or in such a position that he should be classed among *dediticii*; provided, however, that there is no other heir under the will. If two or more slaves are ordered to be free and become heirs, the first one mentioned becomes free and the heir; and this also is prescribed by the *Lex Ælia Sentia*.

(15) The same law forbids the manumission of a slave for the purpose of defrauding a creditor or a patron.

(16) Anyone who holds a slave merely by bonitarian, but not by quiritarian right, makes him a Latin by manumitting him. A slave is only held by bonitarian right, where, for instance, one Roman citizen buys him from another and the slave is delivered to him, but is neither mancipated nor surrendered in court, nor possessed by the purchaser for the term of a year; for, unless one of these things takes place although the slave forms part of the property of the purchaser by bonitarian right, he still belongs to the vendor by quiritarian right.

(17) A woman who is under guardianship, or a male or female ward cannot manumit a slave without the authority of his or her guardian.

(18) One of two owners, by the manumission of a slave held in common, loses his share which accrues to his partner; and this is especially the case where he manumits him in such a way that if he had the entire ownership, he would have made the slave a Roman citizen; for if he should manumit him in the presence of friends it is held by most authorities that his act would be void.

(19) Where the usufruct of a slave is in one party and the ownership in another, and the slave is manumitted by the latter, he does not become free, but is a slave without an owner.

(20) Freedom cannot be granted by a will either after the death of the heir or before his appointment, except in the case of a military will.

(21) A grant of freedom made between two appointments of heirs where both enter on the estate, is not

valid; it, however, was valid, by ancient law where only the first heir appointed entered on the estate. But, after the enactment of the *Lex Papia Poppæa*, which leaves the share of the heir who does not accept without an owner; it was decided that the grant of freedom will still be valid, if the first heir appointed enjoys either the privilege of children, or the ancient right of accretion ; if, however, he does not do so it is settled that it is void, for the legatees who are fathers become the heirs of him who does not enter on the estate. There are some authorities, however, who hold that, even in this instance, the grant will be valid.

(22) A slave who is directed to be free by a will, becomes free just as soon as even one of the heirs enters on the estate.

(23) Lawful freedom can only be granted by a will to those slaves who, both at the time when the will was executed and at the death of the testator, belonged to him by quiritarian right.

(24) The *Lex Fufia Caninia* orders that out of three slaves not more than two shall be manumitted by will; and it permits half of those owned to be manumitted up to ten; from ten to thirty, a third, so that as many as five may be manumitted, as previously stated; from thirty to a hundred, the fourth, so that at least ten may be liberated as under the former number; from a hundred to five hundred, the fifth; and likewise, twenty-five may be freed under the preceding number. Finally, it directs that not more than a hundred shall become free under the will of any person whomsoever.

(25) The same law provides that grants of freedom to slaves shall be bestowed upon them by name.

TITLE II. CONCERNING A SLAVE, OR SLAVES, WHO ARE TO BE FREE UNDER A CONDITION.

(1) A slave who is ordered to be conditionally free under the terms of a will is called a *Statuliber*.

(2) He remains a slave of the heir as long as the condition is pending; when it is fulfilled he at once becomes free.

(3) Whether a slave of this kind is alienated by an heir, or anyone has the use and enjoyment of him, he carries the condition of his freedom with him.

(4) Where a slave is ordered to be free under the following condition : "If he should pay ten thousand sesterces to my heir"; even though he may have been alienated by the heir, by refunding the money to the purchaser he will obtain his freedom; and this is ordered by the Law of the Twelve Tables.

(5) If by any act of the heir the slave is prevented from complying with the condition, he becomes free, just as if the condition had been fulfilled.

(6) Where a slave is ordered to pay a certain sum of money to a stranger and become free, and he is ready to pay it, and the party to whom he was ordered to make payment either refuses to accept the money, or dies before receiving it, the slave becomes free, just as if he had paid the money.

(7) Freedom can be directly conferred as follows: "Be free"; "Let him be free"; "I order him to be free"; and by the terms of a trust, for instance: "I request," "I charge the good faith of my heir that he manumit the slave Stichus."

(8) A slave who is directly ordered to be free becomes the freedman of the testator; one to whom freedom has been granted by a trust becomes the freedman, not of the testator, but of the person who manumitted him.

(9) A party to whose good faith the transfer of property can be entrusted can also be entrusted to grant freedom to a slave.

(10) Freedom can be granted by a trust, not only to the testator's own slave but also to one belonging to the heir or legatee, or to any stranger whomsoever.

(11) When freedom is conferred by a trust upon the slave of another, and his owner will not sell him for a fair price, the grant of freedom is extinguished, since no computation of the value of freedom can be made.

(12) As freedom can be granted, so it can also be taken away by a will, or by a codicil confirmed by a will; provided, however, it is taken away in the same manner in which it was granted.

TITLE III. CONCERNING LATINS.

(1) Latins acquire the right of Roman citizenship in the following ways: by the favor of the Emperor, by children, by repetition, by service in the night-watch, by ship-building, by the construction of houses, by milling; and, in addition to this, a freeborn woman who has brought forth children three times, is entitled to this right under the Decree of the Senate.

(2) A Latin acquires Roman citizenship through the favor of the Emperor if he obtains it from the latter by petition.

(3) A Latin who was under the age of thirty years at the time of his manumission obtains the right of Roman citizenship by means of children, for it is provided by the *Lex Junia* that if he has married either a Roman citizen, or a Latin woman, and should state in the presence of witnesses that he did so for the purpose of having children; after the birth of a son or a daughter who has completed its first year, he may prove his case before the Prætor or Governor of the province, and he, as well as his son and daughter, and his wife, will become Roman citizens, provided she herself is a Latin; for if his wife is a Roman citizen, the child also becomes one by the Decree of the Senate enacted at the instance of the Divine Hadrian.

(4) A person becomes a Roman citizen by repetition who, having been made a Latin after he has passed his thirtieth year, is a second time legally manumitted by the person to whom he belonged as a slave by quiritarian right; such a person, however, under the Decree of the Senate is permitted to obtain the right of Roman citizenship by having children.

(5) A Latin acquires the right of Roman citizenship by the *Lex Visellia* if he serves for six years in the night-watch of Rome; and it is also granted to him by another Decree of the Senate if he has served for three years in the night-watch.

(6) A Latin acquires Roman citizenship by an Edict of the Divine Claudius, if he has built a ship having a capacity of not less than ten thousand measures of grain, and has used it during six years for the transport of grain to Rome.

TITLE IV. CONCERNING THOSE WHO ARE THEIR OWN MASTERS.

(1) Those who are the heads of their families are their own masters, that is to say, the father and the mother of the family.

(2) Children born to a mother who is known, and a father who is unknown, are called illegitimate.

TITLE V. CONCERNING THOSE WHO ARE UNDER CONTROL.

(1) Children born in lawful marriage are under the control of their parents.

(2) Matrimony is lawful when legal marriage takes place between those contracting it, if the male has

arrived at puberty, and the female is nubile, and when both consent, if they are their own masters; or their parents give their consent, if they are under their control.

(3) Marriage is the legal capacity for marrying a wife.

(4) Roman citizens can contract legal marriage with women who are Roman citizens; they can only do so, however, with Latins and aliens when the right has been especially granted them.

(5) Legal marriage cannot be contracted with slaves.

(6) Legal marriage cannot exist between blood relatives in the ascending or descending line. Formerly, marriage could not be contracted between blood relatives in the collateral line, as far as the fourth degree; now, however, a man can marry a wife related to him even in the third degree, but only the daughter of his brother; for he cannot marry the daughter of his sister, or his paternal or maternal aunt, although they are in the same degree. We cannot marry her who has been our stepmother, step-daughter, daughter-in-law, or mother-in-law.

(7) If anyone takes as a wife a woman whom he has no legal right to marry, he contracts an incestuous marriage; and hence his children are not subjected to his authority, but are illegitimate, as if conceived in promiscuous intercourse.

(8) When legal marriage takes place, the children always follow the father, but if it does not take place, they follow the condition of the mother; except where the child is born of an alien father, and a mother who is a Roman citizen, as the *Lex Mincia* directs that where a child is born of parents one of whom is an alien, it shall follow the condition of the inferior parent.

(9) A child born of a father who is a Roman citizen and a Latin mother, is a Latin; one born of a freeman and a female slave, is a slave; since the child follows the mother as in cases where there is no legal marriage.

(10) In the case of children who are the issue of a legally contracted marriage, the time of conception is considered; in the case of those who were not legitimately conceived, the time of their birth is considered; for instance, if a female slave conceives and brings forth a child after having been manumitted, the child will be free; for while she did not lawfully conceive, as she was free at the time the child was born the latter will also be free.

TITLE VI. CONCERNING DOWRIES.

(1) A dowry is either given, expressly stated, or promised.

(2) A woman who is about to be married can state her dowry, and her debtor can do so, at her direction; a male ascendant of the woman related to her through the male sex, such as her father or paternal grandfather, can likewise do so. Any person can give or promise a dowry.

(3) A dowry is either said to be profectitious, that is, one which the father of the woman gives; or adventitious, that is, one given by anyone else.

(4) When a woman dies during marriage, her dowry given by her father reverts to him, a fifth of the same for each child she leaves being retained by the husband, no matter what the number may be. If her father is not living the dowry remains in the hands of the husband.

(5) An adventitious dowry always remains in the hands of the husband unless the party who gave it expressly stipulated that it should be returned to him, and a dowry of this kind is specifically designated receptitious.

(6) When a divorce takes place, if the woman is her own mistress, she herself has the right to sue for recovery of the dowry. If, however, she is under the control of her father, he having been joined with [his] daughter, can bring the action for the recovery of the dowry; nor does it make any difference whether it is adventitious or profectitious.

(7) If the woman dies after the divorce, no right of action will be granted to her heir, unless her husband has been in default in restoring her dowry.

(8) If the property constituting the dowry is composed of articles which can be weighed, counted, or measured, it should be returned at the end of one, two, and three years; unless it was agreed that it should be returned at once. Other dowries are returned without delay.

(9) Portions of a dowry are retained either on account of children, on account of bad morals, on account of expenses, on account of donations, or on account of articles which have been abstracted.

(10) A portion is retained on account of children, when the divorce took place either through the fault of the wife, or her father; for then a sixth part of the dowry shall be retained in the name of each child, but no more than three-sixths altogether.

(11) These sixths can be retained, but cannot be recovered by a suit; for when a dowry has once been disposed of, it cannot again be brought in question except when another marriage takes place.

(12) A sixth of the dowry is also retained on the ground of a flagrant breach of morals; an eighth, where the offence is not so serious. Adultery alone comes under the head of a flagrant breach of morals, all other improper acts are classed as less serious.

(13) The adultery of a husband, if he is of age, is punished by requiring him to return the dowry at once, if it was to have been returned after a certain time; if his offence is less grave, it must be returned within six months. When, however, it is to be returned immediately, he is required to pay out of the profits an amount equal to the difference between immediate repayment, and payment in one, two, or three years.

(14) There are three kinds of expenses, which are designated either necessary, useful, or for the purpose of pleasure.

(15) Expenses are necessary, when, if they are not incurred, the property composing the dowry will become deteriorated; for instance, when anyone repairs a house which is falling into ruin.

(16) Expenses are useful when, if they are not incurred, the property constituting the dowry will not become diminished in value, but, if they are incurred, it will yield a better revenue; for instance, if vineyards and olive orchards should be planted.

(17) Expenses for the purpose of pleasure are such as, if not incurred, will not cause the property composing the dowry to become less valuable, and if incurred, will not cause it to yield a more profitable revenue, which takes place where pleasure gardens are laid out, and pictures and other articles of this description are purchased.

TITLE VII. CONCERNING THE LAW OF DONATIONS BETWEEN HUSBAND AND WIFE.

(1) A donation between husband and wife is not valid except in certain cases; that is to say, in apprehension of death, on account of divorce, or for the purpose of manumitting a slave. By the Imperial Constitutions, however, a woman is permitted to make a donation to her husband in order that he may be honored by the

FRAGMENTS OF THE RULES OF ULPIANUS

Emperor with the Senatorial or Equestrian dignity, or some other distinction of this kind.

(2) If a husband in anticipation of divorce abstracts anything belonging to his wife, he will be liable to an action for the clandestine removal of property.

(3) Where a husband obligates himself for his wife, or spends any money upon her property, when a divorce takes place, it is customary for him to provide for this by means of a tribunicial stipulation.

(4) Those children are also under parental authority, on account of whom a case of error is established, when marriage has been contracted by mistake among persons of unequal condition; for whether a Roman citizen marries a wife through ignorance supposing her to be a Roman citizen, when in fact she was a Latin, an alien, or one belonging to the class of *dedititii*; or whether a woman who is a Roman citizen through mistake marries an alien, or one belonging to the class of *dedititii*, thinking him to be a Roman citizen, marries a man whom she supposed to be a Latin; under the *Lex Ælia Sentia*, when the cause of the error has been proved, Roman citizenship shall be conferred upon the children, as well as the parents, with the exception of those who are *dediticii*; and in this way the children are placed under the control of their parents.

TITLE VIII. CONCERNING ADOPTIONS.

(1) Not only natural children, but also adopted children, are under the authority of their parents.

(2) Adoption takes place either by the act of the people, or by that of the Prætor or the Governor of a province. Adoption which occurs through the act of the people is specifically designated "arrogation".

(3) Those who are their own masters are arrogated by the act of the people; children under paternal control are, however, given by their parents in adoption, with the sanction of the Prætor.

(4) Arrogation only takes place at Rome; adoption takes place in the provinces before the governors thereof.

(5) Males, as well as females, can be adopted by the authority of the Prætor or Governor of a province; and this applies to those who are under and above the age of puberty. Women, however, cannot be arrogated by the act of the Roman people, and formerly minors also could not be arrogated, but they can be now by a Constitution of the Divine Antoninus, when proper cause has been shown.

(6) Those who are incapable of procreation, as for instance, eunuchs, may adopt in either way. The same rule applies to unmarried persons.

(7) Again, anyone who has no son may adopt a child as a grandson.

(7a) Women cannot adopt in either way, as they do not have even their natural children subject to their authority.

(8) Where the head of a household gives himself to be arrogated, his children also as grandchildren, pass under the control of the arrogator.

TITLE IX. CONCERNING THOSE WHO ARE IN THE HANDS OF THEIR HUSBANDS.

(1) . . . .[1] It is settled that a wife is placed in the hand of her husband by the use of certain words, in the

---

[1] Original manuscript illegible.

presence of ten witnesses, and by the offering of a solemn sacrifice, in which also a cake made of spelt is employed.[1] ....[2]

TITLE X. IN WHAT WAY PERSONS UNDER THE CONTROL OR SUBJECT TO THE AUTHORITY OF OTHERS ARE RELEASED FROM THE EXERCISE OF THAT RIGHT.

(1) Children are released from paternal control by emancipation, that is, if after having been sold they are manumitted. A son who has been sold three times, and manumitted three times, becomes his own master; for the Law of the Twelve Tables orders this in the following words: "If a father should sell his son three times, the son shall be free from his father." Other descendants both male and female, except sons, become their own masters by a single sale and manumission.

(2) Sons and daughters become independent by the death of their father, but grandsons only become free by the death of their grandfather, if, after the death of the latter, they do not pass under the control of their father; for instance, when at the time of their grandfather's death, their father had either already died, or had been released from parental authority; for, if at the time of the death of their grandfather, their father was under his control, by the decease of the former they come under the power of their father.

(3) If either the father or the son is interdicted from water and fire the right of parental authority is extinguished; because a person interdicted from water and fire becomes an alien, and an alien cannot have a Roman citizen, nor can a Roman citizen have an alien under his control.

(4) If a father is captured by the enemy, although he becomes the enemy's slave, still, when he returns he will recover all his former rights by the law of *postliminium*. As long as he is in the hands of the enemy, however, his authority over his son remains in abeyance, and when he returns he will again have him under his control; but if he should die in captivity, his son will become his own master. Likewise, if a son is captured by the enemy, the authority of his father will in the meantime remain in abeyance, on account of the law of *postliminium*.

(5) Those who are installed priests of Jupiter, or selected as vestal virgins, cease to be subject to parental authority.

TITLE XI. CONCERNING GUARDIANSHIP.

(1) Guardians are appointed for males as well as for females, but only for males under puberty, on account of their infirmity of age; for females, however, both under and over puberty, on account of the weakness of their sex as well as their ignorance of business matters.

(2) Guardians are either legal, or are appointed under Decrees of the Senate, or derive their authority from custom.

(3) Legal guardians are such as are appointed by some law, and those are especially styled legal who are

---

[1] Marriage by *confarreatio* was the oldest form of the ceremony known to the Romans, and was that used by the higher class of the people. The cake referred to was made of a hard grained wheat (*Triticum Spalta*), and, prepared and baked by the Vestal Virgins, was offered as a sacrifice to Jupiter in the presence of the highest dignitaries of the Roman priesthood, and then carried in solemn procession before the bride when she was taken to the home of the husband. It has been conjectured with much probability, that this cake was divided among the wedding guests, and if this be true, it discloses the origin of a custom which has survived to the present day. — ed.

[2] Original manuscript illegible.

FRAGMENTS OF THE RULES OF ULPIANUS

mentioned by the Law of the Twelve Tables, either openly, as agnates, or indirectly as patrons.

(4) Agnates are relatives of the male sex having a common father, and descending by the male sex through the members of the same family; as for instance, brothers, paternal uncles, the sons of brothers, and the sons of paternal uncles.

(5) . . . .[1] Anyone who has manumitted a person who was free and sold to him either by a parent, or by a party to the sale, becomes his guardian in the same way as a patron, and is called a fiduciary guardian.

(6) Legal guardians may transfer the guardianship to another person in court.

(7) He to whom the guardianship is transferred is styled a cessionary guardian, and if he should die, forfeit his civil rights, or, in his turn, transfer the guardianship to another, it reverts to the legal guardian; and if the legal guardian should die, or lose his civil rights, the cessionary guardianship is also extinguished.

(8) So far as agnates are concerned, no cessionary guardianship at present takes place; as it was only permitted to transfer the guardianship of females in court, but not that of males. The *Lex Claudia*, moreover, abolished the legal guardianship of women, with the exception of that of patrons.

(9) Legal guardianship is lost by forfeiture of civil rights.

(10) There are three kinds of forfeiture of civil rights, the greatest, the intermediate, and the least.

(11) The greatest is that by which both citizenship and freedom are lost; for instance, where anyone is sold for not having returned his property to the censor; or where a woman has formed a union with the slave of another, in defiance of the warning of his master, and has become a slave under the Claudian Decree of the Senate.

(12) The intermediate forfeiture of civil rights is said to occur when citizenship is lost, but freedom is retained; which happens where a party is interdicted from water and fire.

(13) The least forfeiture of civil rights is that by which both citizenship and freedom are preserved, but only the condition of the person is altered, which takes place in adoption, and where one is placed in the hand of another.

(14) Testamentary guardians appointed by name are also confirmed by the Law of the Twelve Tables in the following words: "Let it be the law that a man can dispose of his money or the guardianship of his property." Such guardians are designated Dative.

(15) Guardians may be appointed by will for children who are under the control of their parents.

(16) Testamentary guardians who have the right to make, or take under, a will, may be appointed with the exception of a Julian-Latin, for although a Latin has testamentary capacity, nevertheless, he cannot be appointed a guardian, as the *Lex Junia* forbids it.

(17) A testamentary guardian does not lose his guardianship if he has suffered a forfeiture of civil rights, but if he should refuse it, he ceases to be guardian, for to refuse means to say that he is unwilling to act as guardian. A testamentary guardian, however, cannot transfer the guardianship in court; a legal guardian can do so, but cannot decline the guardianship.

(18) The *Lex Atilia* directs that guardians for women and minors who have none shall be appointed by the Prætor and a majority of the tribunes of the people, and these we call Atilian guardians. But, for the reason

---

[1] Original manuscript illegible.

that the *Lex Atilia* only applies to Rome, it is provided by the *Lex Julia et Titia* that guardians of such persons may, in like manner, be appointed by governors in the provinces.

(19) The *Lex Junia* orders that he to whom the party belonged under quiritary right before his or her manumission shall be appointed the guardian of a Latin woman, or a Latin minor under the age of puberty.

(20) By the *Lex Julia* relating to the regulation of marriage, a guardian is appointed by the Prætor of the City for a woman or a virgin who is obliged to marry under the terms of this same law, for the purpose of giving, specifically stating, or promising a dowry when she has a minor as her legal guardian; but the Senate subsequently decreed that in the provinces guardians should also be appointed by the governors for this purpose.

(21) The Senate also decreed that another guardian should be appointed for the purpose of constituting a dowry, instead of a guardian who was dumb or insane.

(22) A guardian is likewise appointed by the Decree of the Senate for a woman whose guardian is absent, unless the latter is her patron; for another guardian cannot be demanded instead of her absent patron, except for the purpose of enabling her to enter on an estate, or to contract marriage.

(23) The Senate further decreed that if the guardian of a male or female ward should render himself liable to suspicion, and be removed from the guardianship, or if he should be excused for some good reason, another guardian shall be appointed in his stead.

(24) In accordance with custom, a guardian is appointed for a woman or a minor who desires to bring a legal action against her own guardian, in order that she may do so by him as her representative; (for a guardian cannot become the principal party in a matter of his own) ; and he is called a prætorian guardian; as it is customary for him to be appointed by the Prætor of the City.

(25) The guardians of male and female wards transact their business and sanction their acts; the guardians of women only sanction their acts.

(26) Where there are several guardians all of them should authorize every transaction, with the exception of those who are appointed by will; for the authority of any one of these is sufficient.

(27) The authority of a guardian is necessary for women in transactions of this kind, that is, where they bring a legal action, or bind themselves, or transact any civil business, or where they permit a freedwoman of theirs to cohabit with the slave of another, or alienate mancipable property. In addition to this, the authority of a guardian is required by wards in the alienation of property which is not mancipable.

(28) Males are released from guardianship by puberty. The Cassians say that anyone has reached puberty who bears the evidence of that condition upon his body; that is to say, who is capable of procreation. The Proculians hold that he has arrived at puberty who has completed his fourteenth year; but Priscus is of the opinion that he only has arrived at puberty in whom both of these qualifications coincide, namely, the condition of his body, and the number of his years.

(28a) Women are released from guardianship by the right of having three children, but freedwomen who are under the guardianship of a patron are only released by having four.

TITLE XII. CONCERNING CURATORS.

(1) Curators are either legal, that is, those who are appointed under the Law of the Twelve Tables, or Prætorian, that is such as are appointed by the Prætor.

(2) The Law of the Twelve Tables also directs a spendthrift who has been forbidden to have control of his property, to be under the curatorship of his agnates.

(3) A curator may be appointed by the Prætor for freedmen who are spendthrifts, as well as for freeborn persons who, having been appointed heirs by the will of a parent, are squandering their property; for a curator could not legally be appointed for persons of this kind, as a man who is freeborn becomes the heir of his father by will, and not on the ground of intestacy. A freedman, however, can, under no circumstances, become the heir of his father, because he is not considered to have had a father, as servile cognation does not exist.

(4) Moreover, the Prætor appoints a curator for one who, having recently arrived at the age of puberty, is not capable of transacting his own business. . . .[1]

TITLE XIII. CONCERNING A MAN WHO IS UNMARRIED, ONE WHO HAS NO CHILDREN, AND A FATHER WHO HAS BUT A SINGLE CHILD.

(1) By the *Lex Julia* Senators, as well as their children, are forbidden to marry their freedwomen or any women when either they themselves, or their fathers or mothers were professional actors.

(2) The same persons, and others who are freeborn, are forbidden to marry women who were public prostitutes, or procuresses, or any women manumitted by a procurer or a procuress; or one (who) had been taken in adultery or convicted of a crime, or who had belonged to the theatrical profession; and to these the Maurician Decree of the Senate adds a woman who has been convicted by the Senate. . . .[1]

TITLE XIV. CONCERNING THE PENALTY OF THE LEX JULIA.

(1) The *Lex Julia* granted exemption from its penalties to women for a year after the death of their husbands, and for six months after a divorce had taken place; the *Lex Papia* granted them two years from the death of their husbands, and a year and six months after a divorce . . . .[1]

TITLE XV. CONCERNING TENTHS.

(1) Husband and wife may, under a will, take one tenth of the estate of either on account of marriage; but if either of them have surviving children by a previous marriage, he or she may, in addition to the tenth on account of marriage, take as many more tenths as there are children.

(2) Any son or daughter born to both of them, who dies after the day when he or she was named adds another tenth; and two of them dying after the day when they were named add two tenths.

(3) In addition to the tenth, either of the parties can take the usufruct of the third portion of the estate of the other, and when they have children, the ownership of the said portion, as well; and further, the woman, in addition to the tenth, can take her dowry if it is left to her.

TITLE XVI. CONCERNING THE CAPACITY OF HUSBAND AND WIFE TO RECEIVE IN FULL WHAT MAY BE LEFT BY THE OTHER.

(1) Sometimes husband and wife can take the entire amount which one leaves to the other; for instance, where both, or either of them are not yet of the age at which the law requires children, that is, where the

---

[1] Original manuscript illegible.

husband is under twenty-five, or the wife under twenty; and likewise, if both of them have passed the age in marriage prescribed by the *Lex Papia*, that is to say where the husband has reached sixty years, and the wife fifty; and also if they are related to one another as far as the sixth degree.

(1a) They are free to make wills in favor of one another if they have obtained the right of children from the Emperor; or if the husband is absent on business for the State for a year and afterwards returns ; or if they have a son or daughter; or have lost a son fourteen years of age, or a daughter of twelve; or if they have lost two children of three years of age, or three after they have been named; and if a child of any age, under puberty, should be lost within eighteen months, the right will be granted them to take in full all that is left. Again, if the wife should have a child by her deceased husband within ten months after his death, she can take in full whatever he may have left her out of his estate.

(2) Sometimes they take nothing from one another; that is when they have contracted marriage in violation of the *Lex Julia Papia que Poppea;* for example, where a freeborn man marries a woman of infamous character, or a senator a freedwoman.

(3) Any man who has failed to comply with either provision of the law within his sixtieth year, or a woman within her fiftieth (although, after this age, he or she may be released by the same law), are always liable to the penalties of the Persician Decree of the Senate.

(4) By the Claudian Decree of the Senate, however, if a man over sixty years of age marries a woman under fifty the result will be the same as if he had married her while under sixty. But, on the other hand, if a woman who is over fifty marries a man under sixty, the marriage is called unequal, and provision is made by the Calvitian Decree of the Senate, that it shall be of no avail for the purpose of receiving an estate, a legacy, or a dowry. Hence, if the woman dies, the dowry will be without an owner . . . .[1]

TITLE XVII. CONCERNING LAPSED LEGACIES.

(1) Anything which is left to a person by a will in such a way that he could take it under the Civil Law, and he, for some reason failed to do so, is called "caducous" (as if it had fallen from his hands) ; for instance, where a legacy is bequeathed to an unmarried man, or to a Junian Latin, and the unmarried man does not comply with the law within a hundred days, or the Latin does not obtain the right of Roman citizenship; or where an heir appointed to a portion of an estate, or a legatee dies, or becomes an alien before the opening of the will. . . .[1]

(2) At present, by a Constitution of the Emperor Antoninus, all lapsed legacies are confiscated to the Treasury; but by the ancient law they were preserved for the descendants and ascendants of the testator.

(3) Legacies lapse with the burdens attaching to them; hence grants of freedom, bequests, and trusts with which the party on whose account the estate became caducous was charged, still remain operative. Both legacies and trusts, however, become caducous along with their burdens . . . .[1]

TITLE XVIII. WHO ARE GOVERNED BY THE ANCIENT LAW IN THE CASE OF LAPSED LEGACIES.

(1) Moreover, the *Lex Papia* granted the ancient right to the descendants and ascendants of the testator as far as the third degree, so that if they were appointed heirs, what any one of them did not take under the will would belong to the others, either wholly or in part, according to circumstances . . . .[1]

---

[1] Original manuscript illegible.

TITLE XIX. CONCERNING OWNERS, AND THEIR ACQUISITION OF PROPERTY.

(1) All property is either mancipable, or not mancipable. Mancipable property is land situated in Italy, both rustic, such as a field, and urban, such as a house; likewise all rights attaching to rustic estates, as the right of way, to pass, or drive; the right to conduct water, and also slaves, and quadrupeds broken to yoke or saddle, as for instance, oxen, mules, horses, and asses. All other property is not mancipable, for elephants and camels, although they are trained to haul loads and carry burdens, do not come under this category, as they are classed among wild beasts.

(2) The ownership of individual articles of property is acquired by us by mancipation, by delivery, by surrender in court, by usucaption, by adjudication, and by law.

(3) Mancipation is a kind of alienation peculiar to property of this kind, which is made by the use of certain words in the presence of a balance-holder and five witnesses.

(4) Mancipation takes place between Roman citizens, Latin colonists, Junian Latins, and those aliens to whom commercial privileges have been granted.

(5) Commerce is the right of reciprocal purchase and sale.

(6) Movable property cannot be mancipated, unless the parties are present, and not more than can be taken in the hand should be disposed of; several tracts of immovable property can, however, be mancipated at one time, even though they be situated in different places.

(7) Delivery is a species of alienation peculiar to property which cannot be mancipated. We acquire the ownership of property of this kind by mere delivery, provided it is transferred to us by a legal title.

(8) By usucaption we obtain the ownership of property which is either susceptible, or not susceptible of mancipation. Moreover, usucaption is the acquisition of ownership by uninterrupted possession for one or two years; for one year in the case of movable property, for two in the case of property which is immovable.

(9) Surrender in court is a kind of alienation common to property which can be mancipated as well as to that which cannot. It is effected by the agency of three persons, the one who surrenders, the one who claims, and the one who awards it.

(10) The owner surrenders the property in court, the party to whom it is surrendered claims it, the Prætor awards it.

(11) Incorporeal property, as, for instance, an usufruct, an inheritance, and the legal guardianship of a freedwoman, can also be surrendered in court.

(12) An estate is surrendered in court either before or after it has been entered on.

(13) Before it is entered on, it can be surrendered in court by the heir-at-law; after it has been entered on, it can be surrendered either by the heir-at-law, or by the testamentary heir.

(14) If an estate is surrendered in court before it is entered on, the party to whom it is surrendered becomes the heir, just as if he himself was the heir-at-law.

(15) If it is surrendered in court after it has been entered on, he who surrendered it remains the heir, and for this reason continues to be liable to the creditors of the deceased; but the debts are extinguished, that is, the debtors of the deceased are discharged from liability; the corporeal property, however, passes to the party to whom the estate was surrendered, just as if the articles had been transferred to him, one at a time.

(16) We obtain ownership through adjudication, by means of the proceeding in partition which is instituted among co-heirs; by that for the division of common property which applies to partners; and by that for the establishment of boundaries, which is employed by neighbors. For if a judge should adjudicate any property to one of several heirs, partners, or neighbors, it will immediately be acquired by the latter, whether it is susceptible of mancipation or not.

(17) Property is acquired by us by law, for example, where it has lapsed or been forfeited under the *Lex Papia Poppeæ*, and also where it has been bequeathed under the Law of the Twelve Tables; whether it is susceptible of mancipation or not.

(18) Moreover, property is acquired by us by means of those persons whom we hold subject to our authority, in our hand, or in servitude; hence, if they have received anything, for instance, by sale, or any property has been delivered to them, or if they have stipulated for something, it belongs to us.

(19) Again, if they have been appointed heirs, or a legacy has been bequeathed to them, and they enter on the estate by our order, they acquire it for us, and the legacy belongs to us.

(20) If a slave forms part of the property of one person by bonitarian right, and belongs to another by quiritarian right, in every instance he acquires for the party entitled to bonitarian right.

(21) Anyone whom we possess in good faith, whether he be free or the slave of another, only acquires for us in two instances, that is where he obtains anything by means of our property, or by his own labor; with the exception of these cases, if he is free, he acquires for himself, or if he is the slave of another, he acquires for his master. The same rule applies to a slave in whom we have only the usufruct . . . .[1]

TITLE XX. CONCERNING WILLS.

(1) A testament is the legal statement of our will, solemnly made in order that it may become operative after our death.

(2) There were formerly three kinds of wills, one made in the presence of the *Comitia*, one made when about to enter into battle, and one made by means of a piece of bronze and a balance. The two first having been abolished, at present the only one in use is that made by means of a piece of bronze and a balance, that is to say, by a fictitious sale. In the execution of this kind of a will a balance holder and a purchaser of an estate are present, as well as not less than five witnesses who have testamentary capacity.

(3) No one who is under the control of the testator or of the purchaser of the estate can act either as a witness or balance-holder; as the sale of the estate takes place between the testator and the purchaser, and for this reason members of their households cannot act as witnesses.

(4) If a son is the purchaser his father cannot be a witness.

(5) Of two brothers who are under the control of the same father, one cannot act as purchaser and the other as a witness; as what one of them receives by the sale he acquires for his father, and a son of the latter should not be a witness to this transaction.

(6) A father, however, and a son who is under his control, as well as two brothers who are under the control of the same father, can both be witnesses; or one can be a witness, and the other the balance-holder, when a third party is the purchaser of the estate; as no harm results where several witnesses are taken from the same household in a transaction with a stranger.

---

[1] Original manuscript illegible.

FRAGMENTS OF THE RULES OF ULPIANUS

(7) A person who is deaf, dumb, or insane, a minor, or a woman cannot act either as purchaser or balance-holder.

(8) A Junian Latin may act either as purchaser, witness, or balance-holder, as he has no right to make a will.

(9) In a will made by means of a piece of bronze and a balance, two things take place, the sale of the estate, and the declaration with reference to the will. The declaration with reference to the will is made in the following manner; the testator holding the will in his hands says: "Whatever is written in these waxen tablets I give, bequeath, and declare to be my will, and therefore do you, Roman citizens, give your testimony." This verbal statement is also called an attestation.

(10) A son under paternal control cannot execute a will as he has nothing of his own of which to make testamentary disposition. The Divine Augustus, however, granted as a military privilege, that a son under paternal control who was a soldier, could make a will disposing of the *peculium* which he had acquired while in camp.

(11) Anyone who is uncertain as to his condition, for instance, when he is ignorant that he is his own master because his father died while absent on a journey, cannot make a will.

(12) A person under the age of puberty, although he may not be subject to parental authority, cannot make a will; as he has not yet full mental capacity.

(13) One who is dumb, deaf, or insane, as well as a spendthrift interdicted by law from the control of his property, cannot make a will; a dumb person for the reason that he cannot speak the words of the declaration; one who is deaf, because he cannot hear the words uttered by the purchaser of the estate; an insane person, as he has not sufficient intelligence to permit him to make the declaration with reference to the property; the spendthrift, because he is forbidden to engage in commercial transactions, and hence cannot sell his estate.

(14) Likewise, a Junian Latin and one included among the *dediticii* cannot make a will. A Junian Latin is incapable as he is expressly forbidden by the Junian Law, nor can one of the *dedititii*, because he is unable to make a testamentary declaration as a Roman citizen, for the reason that he is an alien; and he is prevented from doing so, as an alien, since he is a citizen of no certain country, and cannot dispose of his property by will in accordance with its laws.

(15) Women who are over twelve years of age can make a will with the authority of their guardians, as long as they remain under guardianship.

(16) A public slave of the Roman people has the right to make a will disposing of half of his *peculium*.

TITLE XXI. HOW AN HEIR SHOULD BE APPOINTED.

(1) An heir can be properly appointed by the following words: "Let Titius be my heir", "I order Titius to be my heir"; but an appointment made as follows: "I appoint Titius my heir"; "I make Titius my heir"; is disapproved by the greater number of authorities. . . .[1]

TITLE XXII. WHO CAN BE APPOINTED HEIRS.

(1) Those can be appointed heirs who have a right to make a will with the testator.

(2) A person included in the number of *dedititii* cannot be appointed an heir because he is an alien, and has

---

[1] Original manuscript illegible.

not testamentary capacity.

(3) A Junian Latin can make a will, if at the time of the death of the testator he is, or before the term prescribed for the acceptance of the estate has elapsed, he becomes, a Roman citizen; but if he remains a Latin, he is prohibited by the Junian Law from taking the estate. The same rule applies to unmarried persons on account of the *Lex Julia*.

(4) A person who is uncertain cannot be appointed an heir, for instance, as follows: "Let whoever first comes to my funeral be my heir"; as the intention of the testator should be certain.

(5) Nor can municipalities, or the members of the same be appointed heirs, as the body is uncertain, and all of them cannot decide, or act as heirs in order to become such; still, by a Decree of the Senate they are permitted to be appointed heirs by their freedmen. An estate left in trust, however, may be transferred to the members of a municipality, for this is provided for by a Decree of the Senate.

(6) We cannot appoint any of the gods our heirs, except those whom we are permitted to appoint by a Decree of the Senate, or by the Imperial Constitutions; for instance, the Tarpeian Jove, the Didymaean Apollo of Miletus, Mars in Gaul, the Trojan Minerva, Hercules of Gades, Diana of Ephesus, the Sipylenian Mother of the gods worshipped at Smyrna, and the Heavenly Goddess Selene of Carthage.

(7) We can appoint slaves our heirs, our own with the grant of freedom, those of others without the grant of freedom, and slaves owned in common whether with or without the grant of freedom.

(8) We can not appoint a slave our heir, even with the grant of freedom, who belongs to us merely by bonitarian right, because he only obtains Latinity, which is no benefit to him in receiving an estate.

(9) We can only appoint slaves who belong to others our heirs when we have the right to make a will with their masters.[1]

(10) A slave owned in common by us and another party can properly be appointed an heir with the grant of his freedom, only so far as our share in him is concerned, and if appointed without the grant of freedom, only so far as the share of the partner is concerned.

(11) If a slave entirely owned by the testator is appointed his heir with the grant of his freedom and remains in the same condition, he becomes free, and the heir under the will, that is a necessary heir.

(12) But if he has been either manumitted or alienated by the testator himself during his lifetime, he can enter on the estate at his own discretion, or by the order of his purchaser. If, however, he was appointed without the grant of freedom his appointment is absolutely void.

(13) When a slave belonging to another is appointed an heir and remains in the same condition, he should enter on the estate by order of master, but if he has been manumitted or alienated by his master during the lifetime of the testator, he can either enter on the estate at his discretion, or do so by order of his purchaser.

(14) Proper heirs should either be appointed or disinherited. Proper heirs are children, natural as well as

---

[1] *Testamenti factio* signified not only testamentary capacity, but also competency to take under a will. The most important requisite of a will was that the designated heir should be legally capable of testamentary disposition along with the testator. This was not indispensable, however, as a slave who did not possess it might be appointed heir with the gift of freedom, when an estate was known, or supposed to be, insolvent, in order to prevent the reputation of the deceased from becoming infamous, which it otherwise would be, if, at the time of his death, he was unable to discharge his pecuniary obligations. It was also necessary that the property bequeathed should be susceptible of ownership or occupancy by the legatee, as, if this were not the case, it would be void. "*Quod si testamenti facti tempore decessisset testator, inutile foret, id legatem quandocunque decesserit non valere.*" (Digest, XXXIV, VII, 1.) — ed.

adopted, whom we have under our control, as well as our wives whom we have in our hand, and our daughter-in-law who is in the hand of a son subject to our authority.

(15) Posthumous children also, that is to say those who are yet unborn, where they are such that if they were already born they would be under our control, are included in the number of proper heirs.

(16) When a son, who is one of our proper heirs, is neither appointed heir nor disinherited by name, this prevents the will from being valid.

(17) If, however, other descendants, for example, a daughter, a grandson, or a granddaughter, are passed over, the will is valid, but they are entitled to share the estate with the appointed heirs; the proper heirs having a right to equal shares, and strangers having a right to half of the estate.

(18) Posthumous children, of either sex, if not mentioned in the will destroy its validity by their birth.

(19) If unborn children would be our proper heirs after their birth, we can appoint them heirs; if they are born after our death, we can make the appointment under the Civil Law; if born during our lifetime, we can do so by the *Lex Junia*.

(20) When a son who is under paternal control is not appointed heir, he should be disinherited by name, and the remaining proper heirs of either sex should be either disinherited by name, or among the others.

(21) A posthumous son should be disinherited by name. A posthumous daughter or any other descendant, should be disinherited either by name, or among the others; provided in the latter instance something is bequeathed to those who are disinherited.

(22) Grandsons, great-grandsons, and other male posthumous descendants should be either disinherited by name, or among the others, with the addition of a legacy; but the safer plan is to disinherit them by name, and this is generally practised.

(23) Although by the Civil Law, it is not necessary either to appoint or disinherit emancipated children, still, the Prætor orders that if they are not appointed heirs, they shall be disinherited; all the males by name, the females by name or among the others; otherwise, he promises them possession of the estate in opposition to the provisions of the will.

(24) Under the Civil Law no difference exists between necessary heirs, that is slaves who are appointed heirs with the grant of freedom, and proper and necessary heirs, that is, children who are under paternal control; for both of them become heirs even against their wishes. By the Prætorian Law, however, proper and necessary heirs are permitted to reject the estate of a parent, but authority to do this is not granted to heirs who are only necessary.

(24a) The Prætor places in the class of proper heirs children who have been sold by the party under whose authority they were, as well as those who have been remancipated, when they have been appointed heirs by their parents with the grant of freedom; and therefore power is given to them also to reject the estate.

(25) A foreign heir, if he was appointed with the right to declare his acceptance, becomes the heir by doing so; if, however, he was appointed without it, he will become the heir by acting as such.

(26) He acts as heir who makes use of the property of an estate as if he were the owner, for example, where he puts it up at auction, or provides the slaves of the estate with food.

(2?) The right of declaration is the privilege granted to an appointed heir to deliberate for a certain time as to whether it is expedient for him to enter on the estate, or not, as, for instance: "Titius, be my heir, and decide within the next hundred days after you have learned of your appointment, and can do so; and if you do not decide, you shall be disinherited."

(28) "To declare" is to state the words of the decision as follows: "As Mævius has appointed me his heir, I hereby enter on, and decide to accept, his estate."

(29) Where an heir who was appointed without the right to deliberate decides that he is unwilling to be the heir, he is immediately excluded from the estate, and cannot afterwards enter on it.

(30) When an heir is appointed with the right of deliberation, as by making his declaration he becomes the heir, so he cannot be excluded, unless he fails to state his decision within the time prescribed by law; and hence, even if he decides not to be the heir, and any of the time granted for the declaration remains, he can, by changing his mind, still become the heir, if he announces his acceptance of the estate.

(31) A declaration of acceptance is called either common, or continuous: common, in which the following words are added, namely, "In which you know and can do so"; continuous, in which they are not added.

(32) Only those days are computed against one who is entitled to the common declaration of acceptance during which he knew that he had been appointed heir and could have declared his acceptance; but those days are computed against him who has the continuous right to declare his acceptance in which he was ignorant that he was appointed heir, or if he knew it, was unable to make his declaration.

(33) Heirs are said to be either appointed or substituted. Appointed heirs are those mentioned in the first place in a will; substitutes are those mentioned as heirs in the second, or a subsequent place, for example: "Titius, be my heir, and make your declaration in the next hundred days after you have learned of your appointment, and can do so; and if you do not make your declaration in this way, be disinherited. Then Mævius, be my heir, and decide within the next hundred days, etc." In like manner other substitutes may afterwards be appointed.

(34) If an heir is appointed under an imperfect declaration clause, that is one in which the following words are not inserted: "If you do not make your declaration, be disinherited," but the following words are employed: "If you do not make your declaration, then Mævius be my heir"; the heir appointed by making this declaration excludes his substitute; but by not doing so, and by acting as heir, he admits his substitute to share in the estate; the Divine Marcus, however, afterwards decided that by acting as heir he will be entitled to the entire estate. But if he neither makes his declaration nor acts as heir, he will be excluded, and his substitute will become heir to the entire estate.

TITLE XXIII. HOW WILLS ARE BROKEN.

(1) A will legally executed becomes void in two ways, by being broken, or by becoming of no effect.

(2) A will is broken by change, that is, if another will is afterwards legally executed; also by birth, that is, if a proper heir should be born who was neither appointed heir nor disinherited, as is required.

(3) A proper heir either appears by birth, by adoption, by coming into the hand, by succeeding to the place of another proper heir, as for instance, a grandson, where the son either dies or is emancipated; or by manumission, that is, if a son, after having been manumitted by a first or second mancipation, again passes under the control of his father.

(4) A will becomes of no effect, if the testator should lose his civil rights, or, if having been executed according to law, no heir should appear.

(5) If the person who made the will is captured by the enemy, it still remains valid; if he returns it is valid by the law of *postliminium*; if he dies in the hands of the enemy, it is valid by the *Lex Cornelia* which confirms his succession, just as if he had died in his own country.

(6) If a will is sealed with the seals of seven witnesses, even though it may be broken, or become of no effect under the Civil Law, the Prætor grants possession of the property of the estate to the appointed heirs in accordance with the provisions of the will, if the testator, at the time of his death, was a Roman citizen, and his own master; and this possession of the estate becomes operative, that is to say, takes effect, if there is no other heir-at-law.

(7) Parents can substitute heirs for their children who are under the age of puberty and subject to their authority, whether they are born or not, in two ways; that is, either in that by which an heir is substituted for strangers, where there are no children who are heirs; or by their own right, that is, if they became heirs after the death of their parents, but died before reaching the age of puberty, for then the substitute shall become the heir.

(8) Parents are even permitted to make substitutions for their disinherited children.

(9) No one, however, can appoint an heir as a substitute for a child under the age of puberty, unless he either appointed the same child or someone else his heir.

(10) The wills of soldiers are valid, no matter how or when they are made; that is, even if they are executed without the observance of the legal formalities; for by the Imperial Constitutions they are permitted to make a testamentary disposition of their property in any way they desire, and in any way they can.[1] A will

---

[1] The military testament of the Roman legionary was the prototype of these adopted by most nations in subsequent times, by which important privileges were conceded to soldiers and sailors with reference to the testamentary disposal of their estates. The great latitude allowed those engaged in the defence of their country, is derived from a custom having the force of law, which was generally observed long before the compilation of the Twelve Tables. It was publicly sanctioned by Cæsar, and was confirmed by the edicts and ordinances of many succeeding emperors. In its original form it was designated *testamentum in procinctu factum*, through its being executed on the eve of an engagement by a soldier armed and "girded" for battle.

The *testamentum militare* was usually nuncupative; but it might be written in any manner and upon any substance when exigency demanded, and even be inscribed upon a part of his armor or equipment by the finger of the testator dipped in his own blood, or traced in the dust of the field with the point of a weapon. The privilege was not restricted to actual combatants, but was enjoyed by all persons in attendance upon, or attached to the army, including the wives and female companions of soldiers. In granting it, the general illiteracy of the favored class and their ignorance of legal formalities were also taken into consideration, as well as the honorable character of the profession to which they belonged. So extensive was this right that, in its exercise, even the most important laws were habitually disregarded. Only two witnesses were required to render a military will valid, where otherwise seven were indispensable; and foreigners or women, not competent under other circumstances, could act in this capacity; the testator could ignore the reservation of the Falcidian fourth for the benefit of the heir; the fact that he was deaf and dumb was not considered a disqualification; he could die partly testate and partly intestate; he could disinherit his children without naming them; he could make any number of wills, all of which would be valid if they did not contradict one another; he could appoint as his heirs aliens and other persons incapable of taking under a regular testament; and he was allowed to institute a direct heir by a codicil. The will of a soldier was probably only valid for a year after his honorable discharge from military service; dishonorable dismissal rendered it, *ipso facto*, void.

In England, by the Statute of Frauds, which so generally restricted the execution of nuncupative wills as almost absolutely to invalidate them, the following exception is made in favor of soldiers and sailors. "Soldiers in actual Military Service, and Mariners at Sea, may dispose of their Personal Estates, as before the making of this Act." (Stat. 29, Car. II. Cap. 3.) This privilege has been confirmed by subsequent legislation.

The ordinary legal formalities demanded in the execution of wills are largely dispensed with in the case of persons in the military or naval service of other European nations. (*Cod. Civ. de France*, Arts. 981, 988; *Cod. Civ. Annoté de Belgique*, Arts. 981, 988; *Cod. Civ. de Espana*, Arts. 716, 722; *Cod. Civ. Portuguez*, Arts. 1945, 1949; *Allgemeines Bürgerliches Gesetzbuch*. (Austria) Art. 601. The Japanese law on the subject is adapted from the French. (Civ. Code of Japan, Art. 1078.) Similar provisions with reference to the testation of soldiers and sailors are to be found in the statutes of several States of the Union. — ed.

made by a soldier contrary to the rules of law is only valid if he dies in the service, or within a year after his discharge.

TITLE XXIV. CONCERNING LEGACIES.

(1) A legacy is what is bequeathed by a will as a law, that is, imperatively. For anything left as a request is designated a trust.

(2) We bequeath legacies in four ways, by claim, by condemnation, by permission, and by preference.

(3) By claim we bequeath in the following terms: "I do give and bequeath"; "Let him take"; "Let him have for himself".

(4) By condemnation, we bequeath as follows: "Let my heir be required to give this"; "Let my heir give"; "Let my heir do"; "I order my heir to give."

(5) By permission, we bequeath as follows: "Let my heir be required to permit Lucius Titius to take such-and-such property, and have it for himself."

(6) By preference, we bequeath as follows: "Let Lucius Titius take such-and-such property as a preferred legacy."

(7) Property which belonged to the testator by quiritarian right both at the time of his death and when he executed his will, can be bequeathed by claim, with the exception of articles which can be weighed, counted, or measured; for, with reference to these, it is sufficient if they belonged to him by quiritarian right only at the time of his death.

(8) Every kind of property can be bequeathed by condemnation, even that which does not belong to the testator, provided it is of such a nature that it can be given.

(9) A man who is free, or property which belongs to the people or is either sacred or religious, cannot be bequeathed by condemnation; for the reason that it cannot be given.

(10) Property which belongs to the testator or his heir can be bequeathed by permission.

(11) The same property which can be bequeathed by claim can also be bequeathed as a preferred legacy.

(11a) If property which did not belong to the testator by quiritarian right at both times, is bequeathed by claim, although the legacy is not valid under the Civil Law, it is still confirmed by the Neronian Decree of the Senate; which provided that a legacy bequeathed in insufficient terms is considered just as if the bequest had been expressed in the best form possible, and the best form of a legacy is that which is left by condemnation.

(12) If the same property is bequeathed by claim to two persons either conjointly, as for instance: "I give and bequeath the slave Stichus to Titius and Seius"; or separately, as for instance: "I give and bequeath the slave Stichus to Titius, and I give and bequeath the same slave to Seius"; the shares in the slave are created by concurrence. If, however, one of the parties did not accept, his share accrued to the others under the Civil Law, but since the passage of the *Lex Papia Poppæa* the share of the one who did not accept lapses.

(13) When the same thing is bequeathed to two persons by condemnation, if this is done conjointly a share is due to each, and by the Civil Law, the share of the party who did not accept remained in the estate, but now it lapses; and if it was separately bequeathed all of it is due to each of the legatees.

(14) Where the option of a legacy is left by claim the legatee is given his choice as follows: "Select a slave," "Choose a slave," and the same rule applies if the right of selection is tacitly bequeathed in the following manner: "I give and bequeath a slave to Titius." If, however, the bequest was made by

condemnation, the following terms are employed: "Let my heir be condemned to give a slave to Titius"; and the heir has the option to give any slave he wishes.

(15) A legacy cannot be bequeathed before the appointment of an heir, as the force and effect of a will begin with the designation of the heir.

(16) A legacy cannot be bequeathed after the death of the heir, lest it may be considered that the heir was charged with it, which is not permitted by the rule of the Civil Law. A legacy may, however, be bequeathed at the moment of the death of the heir, as for instance: "When my heir dies."

(17) A legacy cannot be bequeathed as a penalty. A bequest is made as a penalty when it is left for the purpose of compelling the heir either to do, or to refrain from doing, something which has no reference to the legatee, as, for example, in the following manner: "If you should give your daughter in marriage to Titius, pay ten thousand sesterces to Seius."

(18) A legacy cannot be bequeathed to an uncertain person, for instance: "Let my heir pay so many thousand sesterces to anyone who gives his daughter in marriage to my son." A bequest, however, may be made to an uncertain person who is designated in a certain manner: "Let my heir give such-and-such an article to the one of my present relatives who comes first to my funeral."

(19) A legacy is not rendered void either by an incorrect description, or by a false statement of the reason for which it was made. An incorrect description is as follows: "I give and bequeath to Titius the land which I purchased from him"; when in reality the land was not purchased from Titius. A false reason for making the bequest, is as follows: "I give and bequeath the tract of land to Titius for the reason that he transacted my business for me"; when in fact Titius never transacted his business.

(20) A legatee cannot be charged with the payment of a legacy.

(21) He only can be charged with a legacy who was appointed the heir in the will, and therefore, if a son under paternal control, or a slave is appointed heir, neither his father nor his master can be charged with a legacy.

(22) An heir cannot be charged with a legacy payable to himself.

(23) A legacy may be bequeathed conditionally to a person who is under paternal control, in the hand, or subject to the authority of the appointed heir, in such a way that it shall be required that he be no longer in the power of the heir at the time when the legacy vests.

(24) A legacy cannot be bequeathed conditionally to anyone under whose control, in whose hand, or subject to whose authority, the appointed heir happens to be. This, however, can be done without a condition, provided the heir was appointed by the testator.

(25) Just as separate articles of property can be bequeathed, so also an aggregate amount of the estate of a testator can be left as a legacy, for example, as follows: "Let my heir share or divide my estate with Titius"; in which case it is held that half of the estate has been bequeathed to Titius, and any other portion, as a third, or a fourth, can be left.

(26) By the Civil Law the usufruct of property which can be used and enjoyed without diminishing its substance can be bequeathed; and this applies to the usufruct of one thing as well as of several.

(27) It is provided by a decree of the Senate that if the usufruct of property which consists of its consumption, as for instance, of wine, oil, or wheat, is bequeathed, it should be delivered to the legatee, if security is furnished by him to restore an equal amount of property of the same kind when the usufruct shall have ceased to belong to him.

(28) A legacy may be left to any city belonging to the Empire of the Roman people. This rule was first introduced by the Divine Nerva, and was afterwards, at the instance of the Emperor Hadrian, more specifically established by the Senate.

(29) A legacy which has been bequeathed can also be revoked by the same will, or by a codicil confirmed by the will; provided it is revoked in the same manner in which it was given.

(30) Legacies do not pass to the heir of the legatee unless they have already vested before the legatee died.

(31) Legacies left absolutely, or to be paid at a certain time vested by the ancient law at the death of the testator; but, by the *Lex Papia Poppæa*, they vest when the will is opened. Those, however, which are left under a condition vest when the condition is fulfilled.

(32) The *Lex Falcidia* directs that not more than three fourths of an estate shall be bequeathed, and that a fourth of the same shall, by all means, remain in the hands of the heir.

(33) Legacies by condemnation which have been improperly paid cannot be recovered.

TITLE XXV. CONCERNING TRUSTS.

(1) A trust which is not left in the terms prescribed as legal but as a request, according to the strict construction of the Civil Law is inoperative, but is granted solely in consideration of the wishes of the party bequeathing it.

(2) The words in common use which create a trust are the following: "I commit to your good faith to give"; "I entreat you to give"; "I desire to be given"; and others of the same description.

(3) It has been decided that, in practice, a trust can even be left by a nod.

(4) Persons can leave a trust who can make a will, even if they may not have done so, for anyone who is about to die intestate can leave a trust.

(5) Any property can be left by a trust which can also be bequeathed by condemnation.

(6) A trust can be left to those persons to whom a legacy can be bequeathed.

(7) Junian Latins can take under a trust, although they cannot take a legacy.

(8) A trust can be created both before the appointment of an heir, and after his death, or even by a codicil which was not confirmed by a will; although a legacy cannot be bequeathed in this manner.

(9) A trust written in the Greek language is also valid, although a legacy written in that language is void.

(10) When a son who is under paternal control or a slave is appointed an heir, or a legacy is bequeathed to him, the father, or master can be charged with the trust, although he cannot be charged with the legacy.

(11) An heir appointed by a will can be asked in a codicil to transfer the entire estate, or a portion of the same to another party, even if the codicil has not been confirmed by the will; although an heir cannot be directly appointed by a codicil, even if it has been confirmed by a will.

(12) Actions to compel the execution of trusts are not brought according to the Formula, as is the case with legacies; but the Consul, or the Prætor who is styled *Fideicommissarius*, has jurisdiction of them at Rome, and the governors in the provinces.

(13) Trusts cannot be created by way of penalty, or for the benefit of uncertain persons.

FRAGMENTS OF THE RULES OF ULPIANUS

(14) He who is asked to transfer an estate to another, where the Falcidian Law does not apply, because, for instance, he is not asked to transfer more than three fourths of the estate, does so under the Trebellian Decree of the Senate, in such a way that rights of action having reference to the estate are granted for and against the party to whom it is transferred.

If, however, the Falcidian Law becomes operative for the reason that the trustee is requested to transfer more than three fourths, or even the entire estate, he does so under the Pegasian Decree of the Senate; so that, after the deduction of the fourth part, actions can still be brought both for, and against him who was appointed heir, and he who received the estate is considered to occupy the position of legatee.

(15) When an estate is transferred under the Pegasian Decree of the Senate, both the advantages and disadvantages are shared between the heir and him to whom the remaining part of it has been transferred, stipulations being interposed, as in the case of those known as "of," and "for a share." Stipulations of this kind are properly so called which are usually entered into between the heir and the legatee of a part of the estate; that is, he with whom the heir shares the estate for the purpose of dividing the profit and loss.

(16) If the heir alleges that the estate will cause him loss, he will be forced by the Prætor to enter upon and transfer it so that actions may be granted both for and against the party who receives it; just as if it had been transferred under the Trebellian Decree of the Senate. It is expressly provided by the Pegasian Decree of the Senate that this course shall be pursued.

(17) If anyone should fraudulently and secretly promise to transfer property under a trust to one who has not the right to receive it, the Senate decreed that he cannot deduct his fourth, or if he has children, that he can not claim under the will any bequests which may have lapsed.

(18) Freedom can be granted by a trust.

TITLE XXVI. CONCERNING HEIRS-AT-LAW.

(1) The estates of freeborn persons dying intestate belong, in the first place, to their proper heirs, that is children who are under their control and others who occupy the position of children; and if there are no proper heirs, they belong to their nearest blood relatives, that is to brothers and sisters by the same father; and if there are none of these to the remaining nearest agnates, that is, relatives of the male sex descended through males of the same family. For it is provided by the Law of the Twelve Tables that "If a man dies intestate and leaves no proper heir, his nearest agnates shall have his estate."

(1a) If the deceased should not leave an agnate, the same Law of the Twelve Tables calls persons of the same family to the succession in the following words: "If there should be no agnate, persons of the same family shall have the estate." At present, however, this practice no longer prevails.

(2) If only one son survives the deceased together with one or more grandchild by another son who died previously, the estate belongs to all of them, and it is not divided *per capita*, but *per stirpes*, that is the only son shall be entitled to half of the estate, and the grandchildren, no matter how many there are, to the other half; for it is just that grandchildren should succeed to the place of their father, and have the share to which he would have been entitled if he had lived.

(3) As long as any hope is entertained that a proper heir may inherit, there is no place for the agnates; as, for instance, where the wife of the deceased is pregnant, or his son is in the hands of the enemy.

(4) The estates of agnates are divided *per capita*; for example, where there is one son of one brother and two or more children of another brother, and no matter how many of them there may be on both sides, the

estate is divided into a corresponding number of shares, so that each may receive one.

(5) Where there are several agnates in the same degree, and some of them refuse to accept the estate, or die before entering on the same, their shares will accrue to those who do enter on it; but if none of the heirs enter on the estate, it will not pass by law to those of the next degree as succession does not apply to estates which are transferred by law.

(6) An estate does not pass by law to females beyond the degree of sisters, and therefore a sister becomes the heir-at-law of her brother or sister. A maternal aunt, however, or the daughter of a brother, or their successors, do not become heirs-at-law.

(7) By the Law of the Twelve Tables, the estate of a mother who died intestate did not belong to her children even if she did not come into the hand of her husband, because women have no proper heirs; but subsequently, on account of an address of the Emperors Antoninus and Commodus delivered in the Senate, it was enacted that her estate shall belong to her children, to the exclusion of blood relatives and other agnates.

By the Law of the Twelve Tables, the estate of a son dying intestate does not belong to his mother, but if she enjoys the privilege derived from having had children, and, being a free woman, has three, or a freedwoman, has four, she becomes his heir under the Tertullian Decree of the Senate; provided, however, that there is no proper heir to her son, and that no one of the proper heirs is called to the possession of the estate by the Prætor, and that the son has no father to whom the estate or the possession of the property actually belongs by law, nor any full brother; if, however, a full sister survives, the estate shall belong to her and her mother.

TITLE XXVII. CONCERNING THE ESTATES AND PROPERTY OF FREEDMEN.

(1) The estate of a freedman dying intestate belongs, in the first place, to his proper heir; then to the party to whom the freedman belongs, for instance, his patron, his patroness, or the children of his patron.

(2) Where there is a patron and the son of another patron, the estate belongs entirely to the patron.

(3) The son of a patron also excludes the grandsons of another patron.

(4) The estate of the deceased belongs to the children of the patron, and is divided *per capita* and not *per stirpes*.

(5) The claim of an heir-at-law to an estate which is transmitted in accordance with the Law of the Twelve Tables, is extinguished by the forfeiture of civil rights. . . .[1]

TITLE XXVIII. CONCERNING THE GRANTING OF POSSESSION.

(1) The possession of an estate is granted either in opposition to the provisions of the will, or in accordance with them, or on the ground of intestacy.

(2) Possession in opposition to the provisions of a will is granted to emancipated children who have been passed over in the will, although, under the law, the estate does not belong to them.

(3) The possession of an estate in opposition to the provisions of the will is granted to both natural and adopted children, but only to natural children who have been emancipated and have not become the members of an adoptive family; and it is granted to adopted children only where they have remained under the control of their adoptive father.

---

[1] Original manuscript illegible.

(4) The possession of an estate is granted under the Edict to emancipated children if they are ready to give security to their brothers who have remained under the control of their father, that when the latter dies they will bring the estate into the common mass for division.

(5) Possession of an estate in accordance with the provisions of a will is granted to the heirs therein specified; provided there is no one entitled to take possession contrary to the provisions of the will, or if all of them refuse to demand it.

(6) Even if the will should not be valid under the Civil Law, for instance, because the sale of the estate or the declaration of the heir is lacking, still, if the will is impressed with the seals of not less than seven witnesses who are Roman citizens, possession of the estate will be granted.

(7) The possession of an estate on the ground of intestacy is granted through seven degrees; in the first degree to children, in the second, to heirs-at-law; in the third to the nearest cognates; in the fourth to the family of the patron; in the fifth to the patron, the patroness, and their children, or their ascendants; in the sixth to the husband or wife; in the seventh to the cognates of the manumitted who are entitled under the *Lex Furia* to receive more than a thousand asses. If there is no one entitled to the possession of the estate, or if anyone fails to exercise his right, the estate will pass to the people under the *Lex Julia* having reference to inheritances without ownership.

(8) The possession of an estate is granted not only to children who are under the control of their father at the time of his death, but also to such as have been emancipated, as well as to adopted children; provided they have not also been given in adoption.

(9) The nearest cognates not only acquire possession through persons of the female sex, but also agnates who have forfeited their civil rights, for, although they may have lost the legal right of agnation in this way, still, they continue to be relatives by nature.

(10) The possession of an estate is granted to ascendants and descendants within a year from the time when they were entitled to demand it, and to others within a hundred days.

(11) When all persons belonging to one degree have neglected to demand possession of an estate within the time prescribed by law, those in the next degree are admitted, just as if there had been none to precede them; and this is continued through the seven degrees.

(12) Those to whom possession of an estate is granted by the Edict having reference to successions, are not actually heirs, but through the privilege conferred by the Prætor are placed in the position of heirs. Therefore, whether they sue or are sued, fictitious actions in which they are feigned to be heirs should be brought.

(13) The possession of an estate is granted either effectively or inoperatively; effectively, when he who receives it can actually retain the property; inoperatively, when another can evict the estate under the Civil Law. For instance, if a proper heir is passed over in a will, although possession of the estate may, in accordance with the testamentary provisions, be given to the heirs therein mentioned it will still be inoperative, as the proper heir can legally evict the estate.

TITLE XXIX. CONCERNING THE ESTATES OF FREEDMEN.

(1) The Law of the Twelve Tables bestows the estate of a freedman who is a Roman citizen, upon his patron if the freedman dies intestate without leaving a proper heir; and therefore, whether he dies after having made a will, although he may have no proper heir, or whether he dies intestate, and his proper heir is not a natural one, for example, his wife who is in his hand, or an adopted son, the law gives nothing to

the patron. But, by the Edict of the Prætor, if the freedman dies testate and leaves his patron nothing, or less than half of his estate, possession of half of it is granted to the patron in opposition to the provisions of the will, unless the freedman left one of his natural children as his successor; or, if he dies intestate, and leaves a wife who was in his hand, or an adopted son, the possession of half of the estate is also granted to his patron to the exclusion of his proper heirs.

(2) No right to the estate of a freedwoman is granted by the Edict to her patron. Therefore, if she dies testate, the patron will only be entitled to the same right which was granted to him by the will under his authority as guardian; or if the freedwoman dies intestate, her estate will always belong to him, even if she leaves children, for, as they are not the proper heirs of their mother, they do not exclude the patron.

(3) The *Lex Papia Poppæa* subsequently released freedwomen from guardianship on account of their having four children; and as it gave them the privilege of making a will without the authority of their patron, it provided that the patron should be entitled to a share of the estate of a freedwoman, in proportion to the number of her surviving children.

(4) The male children of a patron have the same rights in the estates of their freedmen as the patron himself has.

(5) Moreover, by the Law of the Twelve Tables, the female descendants of a patron have the same rights as his male descendants; they are, however, not entitled to possession of the estate in opposition to the provisions of the will, or on the ground of intestacy, against proper heirs who are not natural ones. But, if they enjoy the privilege derived from having three children, they also acquire these rights under the *Lex Papia Poppæa*.

(6) Patronesses formerly had only that right to the estates of their freedmen which was established by the Law of the Twelve Tables; afterwards, however, the *Lex Papia Poppæa* bestowed upon a freeborn patroness, who had two children, and a freedwoman who had three, the same right that a patron possessed under the Edict.

(7) The same law also granted to a free-born patroness who had three children, the same right which it conferred upon a patron. . . .[1]

END OF THE RULES OF ULPIAN

---

[1] Original manuscript illegible.

THE OPINIONS OF JULIUS PAULUS ADDRESSED TO HIS SON

THE OPINIONS OF JULIUS PAULUS ADDRESSED TO HIS SON

BOOK I

TITLE I. CONCERNING AGREEMENTS AND CONTRACTS.

(1) We can enter into agreements with reference to matters which are lawful, and from them alone the obligation of a contract arises.

(2) In *bona fide* contracts one agreement is dissolved by another, and although it may give ground for an exception, it is, nevertheless, barred by a replication.

(3) The Aquilian stipulation is usually added to an informal agreement, but it is preferable to also add a penalty to it, for the reason that, if the agreement should be rescinded in any way, the penalty can be recovered under the stipulation.

(4) We cannot make a contract which is contrary to the laws or to good morals.

(5) We can make agreements and settlements with reference to matters in litigation.

(5a) An agreement entered into after a case has been decided should not be observed, unless it is introduced for the purpose of making a donation.

TITLE II. CONCERNING ATTORNEYS AND AGENTS.

(1) All infamous persons who are forbidden to bring actions at law cannot become attorneys, even with the consent of their adversaries.[1]

(2) Women are not forbidden to undertake the duties of attorneys where their own property is concerned.

(3) He can become an attorney or agent in his own behalf who sues for all parties.

(4) The action to enforce a judgment is not only granted for and against a principal, but also for and against an heir.

---

[1] Under the ancient Hindu law, persons accused of murder and other serious crimes were forbidden to employ attorneys, and were required to conduct their own cases in person. Women, minors, and idiots were, however, excepted from this rule. (Gentoo Code, III, 2.) — ed.

TITLE III. CONCERNING AGENTS.

(1) The appointment of an agent can be made either during his presence, or his absence; and it can be conferred either by mere words, or by a letter, or by a messenger, or in the presence of a governor or a magistrate.[1]

(2) An agent is appointed either for the purpose of conducting a suit, or to transact any business, wholly or in part, or for the general administration of affairs.

TITLE IV. CONCERNING THE TRANSACTION OF BUSINESS.

(1) He who transacts the business of another voluntarily should act in good faith, and observe strict diligence in the affairs of the party in whose behalf he has intervened.

(2) If a guardian continues in the administration after the termination of the guardianship, he will be liable to the ward or his curator in the action of business transacted.

(3) If anyone attends to pecuniary transactions, he is required to pay interest for the entire period, and to assume the risk for the sums which he has lent, if the party should not be solvent at the time that issue was joined. And this rule shall also be observed in *bona fide* actions.

(4) A mother who intervenes in the affairs of her children will be liable to them and their guardians, in an action for business transacted.

(5) If a son under paternal control, or a slave, transacts the business of anyone, an action will be granted against the father of the son, or the master of the slave, to the extent of the *peculium* of either.

(6) If the father or the owner charges the son or the slave with the transaction of the business of another, he will be liable for the entire amount.

(7) If the father of an emancipated son administers the property which he has given him without any restriction, he will be liable to his son in the action for business transacted.

(8) Anyone who, not being a guardian or curator, administers the property of a ward or a minor in that capacity, will be liable as guardian or curator in the action for business transacted.

---

[1] In the appointment of an agent or attorney, the law of the Jews demanded that the consent of the former, either expressed, or implied by some act indicating acceptance, be obtained, in order to give it validity. (Mishnah III. Chap. 1.)

According to Mohammedan law, mere information of his appointment conferred upon an agent the right to act, and if he did so at once, his act was valid. Much more ceremony was necessary to establish proof of his dismissal, of which he had to be formally notified by one person of high character, or by two whose reputation was unknown to him.

Like the Roman *procurator*, one person could be appointed by another to conduct his case in court; the consent of the adversary was, however, indispensable, unless the constituent was ill, or distant at least three days journey, at the time. This acquiescence was not required in the case of a woman, who had a right to appoint an attorney to represent her in court under all circumstances. The constituent must be competent, and the attorney or agent possessed of sufficient intelligence to enable him to discharge his duties properly. The appointment of an infant or a slave, with the consent of his guardian or master, was legal, provided the infant had the mental capacity to understand what he was doing. They could bind their constituent, but no liability attached to them. (Hedaya III, XXIII, 2.)

It was the ancient English rule that the principal, when he appointed his attorney, must be present in court. The presence of the adverse party was not necessary. "*Verum oportet eum esse præsent in curia qui alium ita loco suo ponit.*" "*Nec oportet adversarium ob id præsentem esse.*" (Glanvil, *Tractatus de Leg. et Consuet. Angliæ.* XI, 1.) — ed.

THE OPINIONS OF JULIUS PAULUS ADDRESSED TO HIS SON

TITLE V. CONCERNING CALUMNIATORS.

(1) He is guilty of calumny who knowingly and intentionally administers the property of another in a fraudulent manner.

(2) All calumniators are punished both in private and in public actions judicially, in accordance with the nature of the offence which they have committed.

TITLE VI.a. CONCERNING FUGITIVE SLAVES.

(1) A slave purchased from a dealer in fugitive slaves cannot be manumitted within ten years against the consent of his former master.

(2) It is not permitted either to purchase or sell a fugitive slave while in flight, contrary to the Decree of the Senate, and the penalty imposed upon each of the culprits is five hundred thousand sesterces.

(3) Guards at the boundaries, and soldiers stationed in garrisons are authorized by law to retain fugitive slaves in custody.

(4) Municipal magistrates can properly send fugitive slaves who have been arrested to the seat of the governor of the province or the proconsul.

(5) Fugitive slaves can be demanded, and included among the property of the Public Treasury.

(6) Fugitive slaves who are not claimed by their owners are sold by the prefect of the night watch.

(7) The purchaser can recover from the Treasury the price of a fugitive slave who has been claimed within three years from the time of sale.

TITLE VI.b. CONCERNING THE ACCUSATION OF DEFENDANTS.

(1) The accusation of a crime cannot be renewed where the culprit has been released by the party who accused him.

(2) If the son of the accuser desires to prosecute the defendant after he has been released for the crime of which he was accused by his father, he will not be permitted to do so.

(3) One party is not prevented from bringing an accusation for a crime, from the prosecution of which another desisted, or withdrew after having been defeated.

TITLE VII. CONCERNING COMPLETE RESTITUTION.

(1) Complete restitution is a proceeding for the restoration of the property or the case to its former condition.

(2) The Prætor grants complete restitution in the following instances, namely: where an act is said to have been performed through intimidation or fraud; where there has been a change of civil status; where a lawful error has been committed; and in case of necessary absence, or incapacity of age.

(3) Complete restitution cannot be permitted more than once, for the reason that it should be granted after proper cause has been shown.

(4) When complete restitution is granted on account of intimidation, either a real or a personal action will lie. A real action will lie in order that the actual property in dispute may be recovered; a personal action can be brought for a quadruple penalty within a year, or for a simple penalty after the expiration of that time.

(5) If anyone should either sell or promise any property in order to liberate himself from the violence of robbers, enemies, or the mob. this has no reference to intimidation, for he pays the price for being released from fear.

(6) Where a slave who has been emancipated through intimidation acquires or stipulates for anything, he acquires it for the person who suffered the violence.

(7) Superior force is an attack which cannot be resisted.

(8) Anyone who shuts another up in a house in order to compel him to sell or promise his property, is considered to have extorted the sale or the promise.[1]

(9) Anyone who has overcome another with a weapon, in order to compel him to deliver or sell him something, is considered to have employed violence. Anyone who throws another into prison for the purpose of extorting something from him, causes an act which has been performed on this account to be of no effect.

TITLE VIII. CONCERNING FRAUD.

(1) Fraud takes place when one thing is done, and another is pretended.

(2) Where one person employs fraud, and another intimidation, for the purpose of having property transferred to a third party, both will be liable in an action for fraud and intimidation.

TITLE IX. CONCERNING MINORS UNDER THE AGE OF TWENTY-FIVE YEARS.

(1) If a minor under the age of twenty-five years commits an offence which calls for public punishment, he cannot, on this account, obtain complete restitution.

(2) Anyone who directs a minor to transact his business, cannot personally obtain complete restitution, but if the minor voluntarily interfered in his business he should be restored to prevent the other party from suffering loss.

(3) If a person who is of age ratifies any transaction performed by a minor either by his act or by his silence, he will in vain demand complete restitution for this reason.

(4) If one minor is the heir of another, he can obtain complete restitution in transactions in which he became surety, guarantor, promissor, or mandator.

(6) Where anyone, knowingly and designedly, bound himself for a minor, and did so after deliberation, relief shall be granted to the minor, but none shall be granted to the other party.

(7) A minor who obtains complete restitution as against a purchaser, can recover the land sold if he returns the purchase money; for it has been established that the crops shall remain in the possession of the purchaser as a set-off for interest

(8) A minor can obtain complete restitution against the sale of his pledges and hypothecations, but not against those which were hypothecated by his father, if the case was such that it was necessary for them to be sold by the creditor.

---

[1] It is difficult to account for the antagonistic principles set forth in this and the Fifth Section. Both should certainly be included under the head of duress, and the former directly encourages the worst form of extortion. — ed.

TITLE X. CONCERNING ONE WHO LOSES HIS CASE BY CLAIMING MORE THAN HE IS ENTITLED TO.

(1) We lose our case by claiming more than we are entitled to either with reference to place, amount, time, or quality; with reference to place, by demanding another; with reference to amount, by claiming a larger sum; with reference to time, by bringing the action before the debt is due; with reference to quality, by demanding a different kind of property than is due, even though it be of inferior value.

TITLE XI. CONCERNING THE GIVING OF SECURITY.

(1) Whenever an estate is claimed, security is required by law, and if it is not given, the estate is transferred to the claimant who does give it. If the claimant is unwilling to furnish security, the estate remains in the hand of the possessor; for under similar circumstances the position of the possessor is preferable.

(2) An usufructuary should also give security with reference to the enjoyment of the usufruct, that is that he will make use of it as the head of a household himself ought to do.

TITLE XII. CONCERNING ALL CRIMINAL CASES.

(1) Persons who make use of a forged transfer are punished with exile by the *Lex Cornelia de Falsis*.

(2) Anyone who corrupts a female slave belonging to some one else is compelled to give another in her stead.

(3) Anyone who ignorantly makes a false allegation is not liable to the penalty of perjury.

(4) Neither a slave nor a freedman can be interrogated in behalf of his master or patron.

(5) Pregnant women cannot be tortured, or condemned to death, until after they have been delivered.

(6) Anyone who, by false allegations, has obtained a rescript from the Emperor is forbidden to use it.

(7) Anyone who makes a confession with reference to himself cannot be tortured against another, lest he who despaired of his own life may render that of another uncertain.

TITLE XIII. CONCERNING JUDGMENT.

(1) When anyone furnishes security to produce another in court and the party for whom he becomes surety dies, he will be released from liability under the bond.

(2) A son under paternal control can manumit a slave by the order of his father, but not by that of his mother.

(3) Anyone who erases, removes, or changes a public record, or interferes with anything else intended to give notice, shall be judicially punished.[1]

(4) If property which was sold is neither transferred nor delivered, the vendor can be compelled to transfer or deliver it.

(5) He depreciates the value of a slave who persuades him to take to flight or to commit theft, or who corrupts his morals or his body.

---

[1] That is to say the penalty shall be left to the discretion of the magistrate, without assignment of the case to *judices* to ascertain the facts. — ed.

(6) Anyone who debauches the female slave of another, who is an immature virgin, is liable to the penalty fixed by the *Lex Aquilia*.

TITLE XIII.a. WHERE AN ESTATE, OR ANY OTHER PROPERTY IS CLAIMED.

(1) In the claim for an estate all the property which the deceased left at the time of his death is included, or whatever was acquired by means of it after his death and before the estate was entered on.

(2) The possessor of an estate is compelled to surrender the price of any property which he fraudulently alienated, together with the interest on the same.

(3) The estimated value of the property belonging to an estate which has been alienated, depends upon the judgment of the claimant.

(4) The claim for an estate which was not contested by the deceased is not transmitted to his heir.

(5) . . . .[1]

(6) . . . .[1]

(7) . . . .[1]

(8) The possessor of an estate who neglected to gather or take possession of the crops, is required to pay double their value.

(9) In making restitution, the profits of property to be paid to the claimant are those which every diligent and honest head of a household would have been able to obtain.

TITLE XIV. CONCERNING THE PUBLIC HIGHWAY.

(1) Anyone who plows up a public highway is alone compelled to repair it.

TITLE XV. WHERE A QUADRUPED COMMITS DAMAGE.

(1) Where a quadruped causes any loss or commits any damage, or consumes anything; an action is granted against its owner to compel him to either pay the estimated amount of the damage, or surrender the quadruped; which was also provided by the *Lex Pesulania* concerning dogs.

(2) The Prætor forbids a wild beast to be tied up in any place where people pass, and, therefore, if any injury should be caused either by the animal itself, or on account of it, by one person to another, an extraordinary action will be granted against the owner or custodian for an amount of damages in proportion to the injury committed. This is especially the rule where a man loses his life, or is wounded on this account.

(3) No action, however, shall be granted against either the owner or keeper of an animal in favor of him who having irritated a wild beast, or any other quadruped, provoked it to attack and injure him.

TITLE XVI. CONCERNING THE ESTABLISHMENT OF BOUNDARIES.

(1) Anyone who forcibly destroys or removes landmarks shall be judicially punished.

---

[1] Original manuscript illegible.

TITLE XVII. CONCERNING SERVITUDES.

(1) Anyone who possesses a right of way, passage, or driving, or the right to conduct water, and does not make use of it for the term of two years is considered to have lost it; for rights which have been lost by non-user cannot be acquired by usucaption.

(2) The servitudes of drawing or conducting water, if not made use of for two years, is extinguished, and if unlawfully seized, can be recovered within two years.

TITLE XVIII. THE PARTITION OF ESTATES.

(1) An arbiter for the partition of an estate cannot be appointed more than once; and, therefore, an arbiter having been demanded shall adjudge the property which was not included in the first award by the division of what is now owned in common.

(2) In making the division, the judge should take cognizance of the entire property belonging to the estate, so that he may decide with reference to all of it at the same time.

(3) In rendering a decision in a case of partition, it is established that whatever each one receives from the entire estate must either be surrendered by him, or its value paid, in order that it may be divided among the co-heirs.

(4) In the partition of an estate the judge must be appointed, not with reference to certain property forming part of the estate, but with reference to all of it, and not to apportion the property among a few co-heirs, but among all of them; otherwise his appointment is void.

(5) All property belonging to the partners is divided among them separately in an action in partition brought for that purpose.

TITLE XIX. IN WHAT WAY ACTIONS MAY BE DOUBLED BY THE DENIAL OF THE DEFENDANT.

(1) Certain actions when contested by the defendant are doubled; as, for instance, those of judgment, of money expended for a principal, of a legacy left by condemnation, and of unlawful damage under the *Lex Aquilia*; as well as the one brought to determine the dimensions of a field when the purchaser has been deceived by the vendor.

(2) Cases of this kind which are doubled by the denial of the defendant cannot be settled by agreement.

TITLE XX. CONCERNING SURETIES AND SPONSORS.

(1) The obligation is divided between sureties under the Edict of the Prætor, if they are solvent; although each one is individually liable for the entire amount of the debt.

TITLE XXI. CONCERNING SEPULCHRES AND MOURNING.

(1) A body, after it has been permanently buried and solemn sacrifices have been made, can be transferred by night to another place on account of the overflow of a river, or the fear of impending ruin.

(2) It is not lawful for a corpse to be brought into a city, lest the sacred places of the latter may be polluted; and anyone who violates this law shall be arbitrarily punished.

(3) A body cannot be committed to burial within the walls of a city, or be burned therein.

(4) Anyone who strips a body permanently buried, or which has been deposited temporarily in some place, and exposes it to the rays of the sun, commits a crime, and therefore, if he is of superior station he is usually sentenced to deportation to an island, and if he is of inferior rank, he is condemned to the mines.

(5) Anyone who violates a tomb, or removes anything from it, shall either be sentenced to the mines, or deported to an island, according to his rank.

(6) Anyone who breaks or opens a sepulchre belonging to another, and places therein the body of a member of his own family, or that of a stranger, is considered to have violated the sepulchre.

(7) When land is sold, consecrated ground does not pass to the purchaser, nor does he acquire the right to inter bodies therein.

(8) Anyone who erases an inscription on a monument, or overturns a statue, or takes anything away which belongs to it, or removes a stone or a column therefrom, is considered to have violated the sepulchre.

(9) A body cannot be placed in the same sarcophagus or vault where another has already been deposited; and he who does so can be prosecuted as guilty of violation of a sepulchre.

(10) He who buries the body of a stranger and spends any of his own money for funeral expenses, can recover it from the heir, the father, or the master of the deceased.

(11) A husband can recover out of the dowry of his wife whatever he has expended upon her funeral.

(12) The right of residence near, or over a monument, does not exist, for a crime is committed even by the proximity of human habitation; and anyone who violates this law shall be punished either by being condemned to the public works, or by exile, according to his rank.

(13) Parents and children over ten years of age should be mourned for the term of a year; minors up to the age of three years, should be mourned for one month for each year of their age at the time of their death; a husband should be mourned for ten months, and cognates, under the sixth degree, for eight months. Whoever violates this law is included in the class of persons who are infamous.

(14) Anyone who is mourning should abstain from marriage, as well as from the use of ornaments, and purple and white garments.

(15) Anything which is expended for the funeral occupies the first place among the debts of the estate.

BOOK II

TITLE I. CONCERNING PROPERTY LOANED, AND OATHS.

(1) In pecuniary cases, if either of the litigants tenders the oath, he should be heard; for this is provided in order to shorten litigation, and is in accordance with the rules of equity.

(2) The plaintiff has the first right to tender the oath, but the defendant, on the other hand, can require him to swear that he did not bring the action for the purpose of causing annoyance.

(3) If when the defendant consents to take the oath, the plaintiff releases him from the necessity of doing so, and this is clearly apparent, the action shall not be granted him.

(4) He cannot tender the oath to the heir of the party with whom he made the contract, as the latter may be ignorant that the contract was made.

(5) If the debtor is shown to have admitted the existence of the debt, in any way whatsoever, an action shall not be granted to the creditor in the case to collect the claim, but the debtor shall be required to make payment.

THE OPINIONS OF JULIUS PAULUS ADDRESSED TO HIS SON

TITLE II. CONCERNING PREEXISTING PECUNIARY DEBTS.

(1) If you agree to pay what Lucius Titius owes me, you will be liable in an action for money already loaned.

TITLE III. CONCERNING CONTRACTS.

(1) A stipulation is a form of words to which a party, after having been properly interrogated answers, as for instance: "Do you solemnly promise?" "I do solemnly promise." "Will you pay ?" "I will pay." "Do you bind yourself?" "I do bind myself." "Do you pledge your faith?" "I do pledge my faith." Statements of this kind can be made absolutely as well as conditionally.

TITLE IV. CONCERNING LOANS FOR USE AND DEPOSIT, AND ALSO PLEDGES AND TRUSTS.

(1) Whenever anything is lent for use, and expense is incurred either on account of disease, or for any other reason, it can be recovered from the owner.

(2) If the property lent should be lost either through fire, the ruin of a house, shipwreck, or any other accident of this kind, the party to whom the property was lent will not be liable on this account, unless when he could have saved it he gave his own the preference.

(3) Where a slave, or a horse lent to another is killed by robbers, or in war, an action of loan is granted, as care and diligence must be exercised with reference to property lent.

(4) If I pay you the value of the property, so that if it is sold you may refund me the purchase money, and it is lost; if I requested you to sell it, it will be at my risk, but if you asked me for permission to do so, the risk will be yours.

TITLE V. CONCERNING PLEDGES.

(1) If a creditor merely desires to sell a pledge which has been deposited with him, he should notify the debtor three times, in order that he may release the pledge, and avoid its being sold.[1]

---

[1] This notification was necessary when an agreement had been entered into between the debtor and creditor that the property pledged should not be sold. It was substantially a demand for payment, and the creditor could not sell the property to which it had reference until two years had elapsed from the time when the last notice had been given. If he failed to comply with these rules he could be prosecuted for theft.

The general principles governing pledges at Civil Law were, in some respects, different from those recognized by Anglo-Saxon jurisprudence. Under the Roman system, any kind of corporeal property, including real-estate, could be pledged. Pledge implied possession by the creditor as security for a debt; where hypothecation took place, it was understood that while a lien existed in favor of the creditor, the debtor was entitled to retain possession of the article either by special agreement, operation of law, or testamentary provision. Generally speaking, the legal presumption was that the creditor could always sell the pledge if the debt was not paid when due.

The debtor was, however, still considered, to a certain extent, the owner; he could sell the property, tender the amount of the debt, recover the pledge, and deliver it to the purchaser. If he secured possession of it without the knowledge or consent of the creditor he could not be convicted of theft; and he might again acquire complete ownership by usucaption.

The creditor was liable for slight negligence, *culpa levis*, and could not use the profits of the property, or apply them in payment of interest in the absence of a special agreement, designated *pactum antichresis*, authorizing him to do so. In case a slave was pledged, any profit derived from his earnings was required to be credited on the debt. The creditor, on account of his quasi ownership, could not himself purchase the pledge, and if it was sold for more than the amount of his claim was obliged to immediately pay over the surplus to the debtor.

Property might be pledged to many creditors, one after the other, their liens being marshalled in the order of their priority. This principle, however, did not apply where a later creditor advanced funds to repair, or preserve the pledge from depreciation in value or

(2) When the debtor has the use of money lent without interest, the creditor can retain for himself the profits of the property pledged, at the legal rate of interest; but the issue or offspring of the property pledged cannot be retained by the law of pledge, unless this was agreed upon by the contracting parties.

(3) Set-off of a debt of the same kind but of a different amount is permitted; for instance, if I owe you money and you owe me money, grain, or anything else of this kind, although under a different contract, you should either avail yourself of the set-off, or produce the article; and if you demand the entire amount and claim more than you are entitled to, you cannot collect anything.

TITLE VI. CONCERNING SHIPMASTERS.

(1) If a son under paternal control has charge of a ship with his father's consent, he will bind his father for the entire amount of the cargo which he received in good condition.

TITLE VII. ON THE LEX RHODIA.

(1) It is provided by the *Lex Rhodia* that if merchandise is thrown overboard for the purpose of lightening a ship, the loss is made good by the assessment of all which is made for the benefit of all.

(2) If after a ship has been lightened by throwing the merchandise overboard, it should be lost, and the merchandise of others should be recovered by divers, it has been settled that he who threw his property overboard for the purpose of saving the ship will be entitled to an account of the same.

(3) Where either the ship, or a mast is lost in a storm the passengers are not liable to contribution, unless the vessel was saved through the passengers themselves cutting down the mast to insure their own preservation.

(4) Where, for the purpose of lightening a ship, merchandise is thrown into a boat and lost, it is established that the loss shall be made good by the assessment of the property which remained safe in the ship. If, however, the ship should be lost, no account should be taken of the boat which was saved, or of the merchandise it may have contained.

(5) Contribution by assessment should be made where property has been thrown into the sea, and the ship has been saved.[1]

---

loss, as he was entitled to preference on this account. It was not necessary to obtain an order of court to sell the article pledged, this power being ordinarily regulated by an agreement between the parties interested.

Encumbrance by implied hypothecation, had, at Civil Law, under certain conditions, a much broader application than under our legal system. A landlord had a lien for the rent upon the furniture or other personal effects brought into his house by a tenant; a rule still in force in many European countries, and in Louisiana. If anyone was indebted to the Public Treasury, his entire possessions were considered as tacitly hypothecated to secure payment. This was also the case where money was loaned to repair property, the creditor having a lien for the amount advanced.

In the countries whose legislation is founded on the law of Rome, hypothecation, from which our mortgage is derived, is considered under a separate head from pledge, and as distinct from it. In France it has reference solely to real-estate. (*Cod. Civ.*, Art. 2114.) The Spanish, Portuguese, and Italian Codes include incorporeal rights attaching to immovables, such as usufruct and emphyteusis. (*Cod. Civ. de España*, Art. 1874; *Cod. Civ. Portuguêz*, Art. 890; *Cod. Civ. d'Italia*, Art. 1967.) The Japanese law uses the word pledge as applicable to both real and personal property. (Civ. Cod. of Japan, Chap. IX, Secs. 2, 3.) In the Louisiana Code, the term mortgage is substituted for hypothecation, and applies only to immovables. In former times, slaves could also be mortgaged like real estate, a doctrine probably derived from the law of Feudalism, which declared villains regardant, or the lowest order of serfs, to be attached to the glebe and inalienable without it. — ed.

[1] The meager extracts set forth in this Title practically comprise all that survives of the maritime code of one of the most famous nations of antiquity, whose naval exploits are referred to by Homer as well known in his day, and whose wealth and power caused it to be feared and respected for a period of almost twelve hundred years. Its origin has, on plausible grounds, been attributed to the

TITLE VIII. CONCERNING AGENTS.

(1) As we derive advantages from the appointment of an agent so we should also suffer the inconvenience resulting therefrom; and therefore anyone who appoints a male or female slave, or a son or a daughter under paternal control, to transact his business, or to buy or sell merchandise, can be sued for the entire amount of any indebtedness contracted in his or her name.

(2) If a slave is placed in charge of money to be lent, or a tract of land to be cultivated, and on which crops are to be planted and sold, the owner of the land or the money will be bound for the entire amount involved in the contract made by the agent; and it makes no difference whether he is a slave or a freeman.

(3) Where a contract is made with the employees of those who have charge of factories or shops, an action is granted for the entire amount of the indebtedness against the masters or agents of said shops.

TITLE IX. CONCERNING PROPERTY EMPLOYED FOR THE BENEFIT OF ANOTHER.

(1) Where a slave, or a son under paternal control uses borrowed money for the benefit of the property of his owner or father, for instance, for the purpose of cultivating land, or for supporting a house, or for clothing slaves, or for the purchase of goods, or the payment of creditors, or to do anything of this description, he renders his father or his master liable for the entire amount expended for the benefit of his property; provided, however, that the money was furnished for this purpose.

TITLE X. CONCERNING THE MACEDONIAN DECREE OF THE SENATE.

(1) Anyone who lends money to a son under paternal control against the provisions of the Decree of the Senate, cannot, after the death of the father, bring an action to recover what he lent during the father's lifetime.

Phoenicians, who colonized so much territory belonging to the Mediterranean, and from that enterprising people, the commercial pioneers of the ancient world, no doubt came many of the rules of the sea which were accepted *en masse* by Augustus, in so far as they did not contravene the existing laws of the Empire.

It will be noticed that these provisions relate almost wholly to contribution, or what is now known as "general average". Two things were requisite to render this principle applicable, some portions of the vessel or the cargo must have been voluntarily thrown overboard in order to save the remainder, or the passengers; and this object must have been accomplished. Hence contribution could not be exacted if force was employed, or the vessel, despite the sacrifice made, was lost.

Everything was liable to contribution but provisions and articles of this description; even the personal effects of the passengers such as clothing, ornaments, and jewels were not exempt. The liability was estimated by using the ordinary market value of the property as a standard, and then making a comparison of what was saved with what was lost. Each person could only be assessed *pro rata* for his own share, except where one or more of the parties was insolvent, when his burden was assumed by the others. The rule also applied to the ransom of the ship from pirates. Nothing could be collected for the loss of life except in the case of a slave, as a freeman was not subject to appraisement; "*corporum liberorum æstimationem nullam fieri potest*".

In addition to contribution, the maritime law of Rhodes prescribed rules for the guidance of the officers and crews of vessels, and their passengers; penalties for misconduct of those in authority and their responsibility in case of negligence; and the forms of bills of lading, charter-parties, loans on bottomry and other contracts growing out of the prosecution of commercial transactions.

This equitable principle formulated by the greatest sailors and traders of antiquity; inherited by the Rhodians, a people scarcely inferior to them in maritime skill and enterprise; and transmitted to posterity by Roman authority and example survives in localities where one would least expect to encounter it. The *Lex Rhodia de jactu*, which the Romans borrowed from the Phoenicians, is now in great observance among the tribes of the Sahara as the customary mode of distributing the losses incurred by caravans crossing the desert between the company owning the camels, or what in railway language would be called the plant, and the passengers or owners of goods. The Khodja or scribe acts as a supercargo, and is said to be quite conversant with the distinction between general and special average. Whether the indigenous races of North Africa derived this custom from the Carthaginians and other Phoenician colonists directly, or whether it came to them indirectly through the Romans, is a point which it would probably be impossible to determine, and on which they themselves certainly could throw no light. (Lorimer, The Institutes of the Law of Nations, Vol. I, Page 30.) — ed.

TITLE XI. ON THE VELLEIAN DECREE OF THE SENATE.

(1) Women are forbidden to interfere in every kind of business matters and obligations, in behalf of males, as well as of females.

(2) A woman who, in her own behalf, promises indemnity to the guardians of her children, is not entitled to the benefit of the Decree of the Senate.

(1) . . . .[1]

(2) . . . .[1]

(3) . . . .[1]

(4) . . . .[1]

TITLE XII. CONCERNING DEPOSIT.

(5) If I deposit a sealed bag or a package of silver, and the party with whom it was deposited should handle it without my consent, an action of deposit, as well as one of theft, will lie in my favor against him.

(6) . . . .[1]

(7) In an action of deposit brought on account of delay, any profits which may accrue are included, and interest on the money deposited shall be paid.

(8) . . . .[1]

(9) . . . .[1]

(10) . . . .[1]

(11) . . . .[1]

(12) There is no ground for set-off in a case of deposit but the property itself must be returned.

TITLE XIII. CONCERNING THE LEX COMMISSORIA.[2]

(1) Where hypothecated property is sold by a creditor, the debtor has an action against him to recover the surplus.

(2) Any hypothecated property which a creditor acquires through a slave diminishes the principal of the debt.

(3) A debtor cannot sell hypothecated property to a creditor, but if he wishes to sell it to others, he can do so, in order that he may tender the purchase money to the creditor, and deliver the redeemed property to the purchaser.

(4) If the creditor purchases the property pledged from the debtor, without his consent, through the

---

[1] Original manuscript illegible.

[2] The *Lex Commissoria* was a provisional agreement by which the article pledged became the property of the creditor if the debt was not promptly paid at maturity. It also had reference to a contract of sale whereby the parties agreed that if the conditions were not complied with within a specified time it should be considered void; the purchase money be refunded; the profits, if any, be returned to the vendor; and everything connected with the transaction be placed, as far as practicable, in the same state in which it was before the agreement was entered into. This proceeding was abolished, as iniquitous, by Constantine, in 326. — ed.

intervention of a third party, the sale will be void; and therefore it can be set aside, as, the liability of the pledge or hypothecation cannot be released in this way.

(5) If an agreement is made between the creditor and the debtor that the property pledged shall not be sold, and the debtor should become insolvent, the creditor can formally notify him and sell the property, for an hypothecary action cannot arise from such an agreement.

(6) If the creditor should bequeath the hypothecated property either to one of his heirs, or to a stranger, an action for recovery will lie against all his heirs.

(7) If the creditor should improve the hypothecated property, he can hold the debtor liable in an action to recover the amount that he has expended upon it.

(8) The most recent creditor, if the money is tendered him, should satisfy the former creditor, to avoid having possession unjustly transferred to himself; the prior creditor, however, is not prevented from satisfying the second, although he himself has a better right to the property pledged.

(9) If a slave borrows money during the time of his servitude he cannot be sued on the obligation after he has been manumitted.

TITLE XIV. CONCERNING INTEREST.

(1) If a mere agreement for the payment of interest is interposed, it is of no effect; for no cause of action arises among Roman citizens from a mere agreement.

(2) Interest above one per cent a month is applied on the principal, and when the principal is paid it can be recovered.

(3) Money lent on bottomry can bear any amount of interest as long as the vessel sails, on account of the risk assumed by the creditor.

(4) Interest in excess of twelve per cent per annum can be recovered as paid by mistake.

(5) If anyone removes the pledges of a debtor without authority of court he is guilty of the crime of violence.

(6) A guardian cannot be sued for interest if he lends the money of his ward without taking sufficient security; and the trial of a case of this kind must be conducted before the governor of the province.

TITLE XV. CONCERNING MANDATES.

(1) A mandate for the transaction of business can be refused on account of sudden illness, or a necessary journey, or enmity, or for the reason that there is no property, before anything has been done.

(2) If I purchase anything for you with my money under your direction, even if you afterwards should be unwilling to take the property, an action of mandate will lie against you in my favor, and I can not only recover what has been expended but also the interest on the same.

(3) If a person ordered to sell property for a certain price sells it for less, the entire sum can be recovered by an action of mandate, for it has been held that the sale cannot be set aside.

TITLE XVI. ON PARTNERSHIP.

(1) Profits as well as losses are divided among partners, unless the loss has resulted either through the negligence or fraud of a partner.

TITLE XVII. CONCERNING PURCHASE AND SALE.

(1) If a person sells property of which he is not the owner, he will be liable on account of having received the purchase money, otherwise he cannot be held.

(2) If the property should be simply evicted, the vendor becomes still more liable to the purchaser if he provided against eviction by a stipulation.[1]

(3) If property which has been purchased is evicted after transfer and delivery have taken place, the vendor will be liable for double damages.

(4) Where land is sold, and the vendor makes a false allegation as to the quantity, he can be sued for double the amount which he falsely stated, and it is the duty of the judge to make the estimate of the same.

(5) The return of a defective slave, when the blemish has been concealed, can be required within six months.

(6) If, in order to sell a slave for more money, the vendor makes false statements with reference to his accomplishments, or his *peculium*, and an action on purchase is brought against him, the vendor will be compelled to pay to the purchaser the amount of the overvaluation, unless the purchaser is ready to return the slave.

(7) The crops, the labor of slaves, the increase of flocks, and the offspring of female slaves belong to the purchaser from the day of sale.

(8) You sold me a tract of land belonging to another person, and it afterwards became mine for a valuable consideration; if part of the purchase money was paid an action on purchase will lie in my favor against you to recover it.

(9) Unless the purchaser pays the price immediately after the delivery of the property he is required to pay interest on the same.

(10) A person who is dumb can both purchase and sell; an insane person, however, can do neither.

(11) Where a slave who has been purchased in good faith takes to flight on account of a former vicious habit, the party who sold him and was aware of the fraud, can not only be required to pay the value of the slave, but also that of any property which he may have taken with him in his flight.

(12) . . . .[2]

(13) When proof of his former habit of flight is lacking the statements of the slave should be believed, for he is considered to be interrogated with reference to himself, and not either for or against his master.

(14) In a contract executed in good faith, the obligation of written instruments is demanded without reason,

---

[1] Eviction was dispossession by legal procedure based upon concealed faults or a bad title. It was applicable to every species of property and every degree of ownership. An implied warranty in favor of the purchaser was considered to exist at the time of the sale; and sometimes a bond was given with a penalty for double the value of the article or land sold.

The vendor was obliged, under all circumstances, to indemnify the purchaser for the loss sustained. Proof in court of the existence of a lien of any description, or of a servitude which had not been disclosed, would be sufficient to cause eviction. When this was established, a demand could be made for the return of the object of the sale. Joint owners were liable *pro rata*, in proportion to their respective interests. A reservation of the right of eviction by the vendor, if assented to by the purchaser, barred the latter from instituting proceedings, even though he may have been aware at the time that the title to the property in question was defective. — ed.

[2] Original manuscript illegible.

provided the truth with reference to the good faith of the contract can be established.

(15) Land is considered to belong to him in whose name it was purchased and not to him by whom the money was paid, provided the land was delivered to the purchaser.

(16) Where the principal debtor is selected as being liable, his security or heir is released. The same rule does not apply to mandators.

TITLE XVIII. CONCERNING LEASING AND HIRING.

(1) A freeman who has control of his own condition can make it either better or worse, and hence can lease his services by day or by night.

(2) Where land is deteriorated through want of cultivation and failure to keep buildings in repair, the damage resulting from negligence must be made good by the lessee to the owner, according to the decision of the judge.

TITLE XIX. CONCERNING MARRIAGE.

(1) Betrothal can take place between persons over or under the age of puberty.

(2) Marriage cannot legally be contracted by persons who are subject to the control of their father, without their consent; such contracts, however, are not dissolved, for the consideration of the public welfare is preferred to the convenience of private individuals.

(3) . . . .[1]

(4) . . . .[1]

(5) . . . .[1]

(6) Marriage cannot be contracted, but cohabitation can exist between slaves and persons who are free.

(7) An insane person of either sex cannot contract marriage, but where marriage has been contracted it is not annulled by insanity.

(8) An absent man can marry a wife; an absent woman, however, cannot marry.

(9) It has been decided that a freedman who aspires to marry his patroness, or the daughter of the wife of his patron, shall be sentenced to the mines, or to labor on the public works, according to the dignity of the person in question.

TITLE XX. CONCERNING CONCUBINES.

(1) A man cannot keep a concubine at the same time that he has a wife.....[1] Hence a concubine differs from a wife only in the fact that she is entertained for pleasure.

TITLE XXI. CONCERNING WOMEN WHO FORM UNIONS WITH THE SLAVES OF OTHERS, AND ON THE CLAUDIAN DECREE OF THE SENATE.

(1) If a freeborn woman, who is also a Roman citizen or a Latin, forms a union with the slave belonging to another, and continues to cohabit with him against the consent and protest of the owner of the slave she becomes a female slave.

---

[1] Original manuscript illegible.

(2) If a freeborn woman forms a union with a slave who is a ward, she becomes a female slave by the denunciation of the guardian.

(3) Although a woman cannot permit her freed woman to cohabit with the slave of another without the permission of her guardian; still, by denouncing her who has formed such an union with her slave, she will acquire the woman as her slave.

(4) An attorney, a son under paternal control, and a slave, by the order of his father, master, or principal, makes a woman a female slave under such circumstances by denouncing her.

(5) If a free woman forms a union with a slave constituting part of the *peculium* of a son under paternal control, he will acquire the woman as his slave by operation of law, without any inquiry as to his father's consent.

(6) A freedwoman who, with the knowledge of her patron, forms a union with a slave of another, becomes the female slave of the person who denounces her.

(7) If a freedwoman, without the knowledge of her patron, forms a union with the slave of another, she becomes the female slave of the patron, under the condition that, at some time or other, he will confer Roman citizenship upon her.

(8) If a freeborn woman forms a union with a slave included in the *castrense peculium* of a son under paternal control, she becomes his female slave if he denounces her.

(9) If a daughter under paternal control, without the consent or knowledge of her father, forms a union with a slave belonging to another she will retain her position, even after being denounced; for the reason that the condition of a parent cannot become worse through any act of his children.

(10) If a daughter under paternal control, by order of her father, and against the will of his master, forms a union with the slave of another she becomes a female slave; because parents can render the condition of their children worse.

(11) A freedwoman who forms a union with the slave of her patron will remain in the same condition after having been denounced, because she is considered to have been unwilling to abandon the house of her patron.

(12) Any woman who erroneously thinks that she is a female slave, and on this account forms a union with the slave of another, and, after having ascertained that she is free, continues in the same relation with him, becomes a female slave.

(13) If a patroness forms a union with the slave of her freedman, it has been decided that she does not become a female slave by his denunciation.

(14) A freeborn woman, who knowingly forms a union with a slave belonging to a municipality, becomes a female slave without denunciation, but the rule is not the same if she was ignorant of his condition; and, moreover, she is considered to have been ignorant if, having ascertained the facts, she broke off relations with the slave or thought that he was a freedman.

(15) A free woman who forms a union with a slave that has several masters becomes the slave of the first one who denounces her, unless this is done by all of them at once.

(16) If a mother forms a union with the slave of her son, the Claudian Decree of the Senate does not abolish the filial reverence which should be entertained for a mother; even though she should blush on account of

her disgrace, as in the case of her who cohabits with the slave of her freedman.

(17) Although it is provided by the Decree of the Senate that a woman becomes a female slave after having been notified by three denunciations, still, this cannot be determined by the owner without the authority of a decree issued by the Prætor or the Governor, for he only should deprive a person of freedom who can confer it.

(18) If a daughter under paternal control continues to cohabit with a slave after the death of her father, she becomes a female slave in accordance with the terms of the Claudian Decree of the Senate.

TITLE XXI.a. CONCERNING DOWRIES.

(1) A dowry either precedes or follows marriage, and hence it can be given either before or after the ceremony, but where it is given before marriage it anticipates its occurrence.

(2) It is provided by the *Lex Julia* concerning adultery that a husband cannot alienate any land given by way of dowry, without the consent of his wife.

TITLE XXII. CONCERNING AGREEMENTS ENTERED INTO BETWEEN HUSBAND AND WIFE.

(1) The crops of dotal land are gathered for the benefit of the husband during the existence of the marriage, and also proportionately during the year in which a divorce takes place.

(2) A stipulation should be attached to all agreements, so that an action on the stipulation can be brought.

TITLE XXIII. CONCERNING DONATIONS BETWEEN HUSBAND AND WIFE.

(1) A *donatio causa mortis* is one made under apprehension of impending death; as, for instance, on account of illness, a journey, a sea voyage, or war.

(2) A donation for the sake of manumission is permitted between husband and wife through favor to freedom, or, in fact, for the reason that no one is pecuniarily benefited by it; and therefore they are not prohibited from making reciprocal donations for the purpose of manumitting slaves.

(3) A donation cannot be made between husband and wife through the intermediation of a third party.

(4) A fictitious sale with the intention of making a donation cannot be contracted between husband and wife.

(5) Where the party who made a donation at the time of marriage survives the other to whom it was made, the property donated remains in the hands of the donor.

(6) No matter at what time a donation in anticipation of death was made between husband and wife, it vests as soon as death takes place.

TITLE XXIV. CONCERNING THE BIRTH OF CHILDREN.

(1) If a female slave conceives, and has a child after she has been manumitted, the child will be free.

(2) If a free woman conceives and has a child after having become a slave, the child will be free; for this is demanded by the favor conceded to freedom.

(3) If a female slave conceives, and in the meantime is manumitted, but, having subsequently again become a slave, has a child, it will be free; for the intermediate time can benefit, but not injure freedom.

(4) A child born to a woman who should have been manumitted under the terms of a trust, is born free, if it comes into the world after the grant of freedom is in default.

(5) If, after a divorce has taken place, a woman finds herself to be pregnant, she should within three hundred days notify either her husband, or his father to send witnesses for the purpose of making an examination of her condition; and if this is not done, they shall, by all means, be compelled to recognize the child of the woman.

(6) If the woman should not announce that she is pregnant, and should not permit the witnesses sent to make an examination of her, neither the father nor the grandfather will be compelled to support the child; but the neglect of the mother will not offer any impediment to the child being considered the proper heir of his father.

(7) Where a woman denies that she is pregnant by her husband, the latter is permitted to make an examination of her, and appoint persons to watch her.[1]

(8) The physical examination of the woman is made by five midwives, and the decision of the majority shall be held to be true.

(9) It has been decided that a midwife who introduces the child of another in order that it may be substituted, shall be punished with death.

TITLE XXV. IN WHAT WAY CHILDREN BECOME THEIR OWN MASTERS.

(1) A father captured by the enemy ceases to have his children under his authority, but, having returned, he will recover control of them as well as of all his property, by the law of *postliminium*, just as if he had never been taken captive by the enemy.

(2) Separate mancipations can be made in the presence of the same or different witnesses, and either on the same day, or at different times.

(3) Emancipation can take place even upon a holiday.

(4) Emancipation and manumission can take place before municipal magistrates having legal jurisdiction.

(5) A son under paternal control is not compelled to be emancipated against his will.

---

[1] This is no doubt the origin of the ancient English writ *De ventre inspiciendo*, issued on the application of the heir presumptive to ascertain whether or not the widow of a deceased ancestor was feigning pregnancy for the ultimate purpose of producing a supposititious heir to the estate. Bracton describes the examination as follows: "*Vbi se fecerit pregnantem, cum no sit, ad querelam veri heredis, per præceptum domini regis, faciet vic. venire talem muliarem coram eo, et coram custodibus placitorum coronæ, vel etiam coram aliquo quem dominus rex iustic, constituent et faciet eam videri a discretis mulieribus, et tractari per vbera, et per ventrem, ad inquirendam veritatem, et si suspitio habeatur alicujus falsitatis, qualiter debeat custodiri.*" (Bracton, *De Leg. et Consuet. Ang.* II, 69.) Britton says that if the woman was decided to be pregnant, or if any doubt existed on that point, she was shut up in a castle or some other secure place under guard, and excluded from the society of all persons liable to suspicion, until she was delivered, or her condition definitely ascertained. By virtue of this writ, she could thus be taken from her family and secluded for an indefinite period. (Britton, *De Legibus Anglicanis*, Cap. 66, *De Gardes*, 444.)

Extraordinary precautions against fraud are prescribed by the *Partidas*. The woman alleged to be pregnant was compelled to notify her deceased husband's relatives of the fact twice every month from the time of his death up to the date of her confinement, or until it was absolutely certain that she was not *enceinte*. They had a right to select a jury of five reputable women to examine her, and if she was found to be pregnant, to ask the judge of the district to appoint a woman to guard her. A second examination could be made thirty days before her anticipated delivery. She was never left alone for a moment, night or day; no pregnant woman, nor any child, was permitted to approach her; and when the birth took place, two midwives and sixteen other women were legally allowed to be present. Three lights were required to be kept burning in the house for several nights previously, in order to prevent the introduction of a supposititious heir. — ed.

THE OPINIONS OF JULIUS PAULUS ADDRESSED TO HIS SON

TITLE XXVI. CONCERNING ADULTERY.

(1) In the second chapter of the *Lex Julia* concerning adultery, either an adoptive or a natural father is permitted to kill an adulterer caught in the act with his daughter in his own house or in that of his son-in-law, no matter what his rank may be.

(2) If a son under paternal control, who is the father, should surprise his daughter in the act of adultery, while it is inferred from the terms of the law that he cannot kill her, still, he ought to be permitted to do so.

(3) Again, it is provided in the fifth chapter of the *Lex Julia* that it is permitted to detain witnesses for twenty hours, in order to convict an adulterer taken in the act.

(4) A husband cannot kill any one taken in adultery except persons who are infamous, and those who sell their bodies for gain, as well as slaves, and the freedmen of his wife, and those of his parents and children; his wife, however, is excepted, and he is forbidden to kill her.

(5) It has been decided that a husband who kills his wife when caught with an adulterer, should be punished more leniently, for the reason that he committed the act through impatience caused by just suffering.[1]

(6) After having killed the adulterer, the husband should at once dismiss his wife, and publicly declare within the next three days with what adulterer, and in what place he found his wife.

(7) An angry husband who surprises his wife in adultery can only kill the adulterer, when he finds him in his own house.

(8) It has been decided that a husband who does not at once dismiss his wife whom he has taken in adultery, can be prosecuted as a pander.

(9) ....[1]

(10) It should be noted that two adulterers can be accused at the same time with the wife, but more than that number cannot be.

(11) It has been decided that adultery cannot be committed with women who have charge of any business or shop.

(12) Anyone who debauches a male who is free, against his consent, shall be punished with death.

(13) ....[1]

(14) It has been held that women convicted of adultery shall be punished with the loss of half of their

---

[1] It seems more than probable that from this source has been derived the principle of what is known in the United States as "the unwritten law". As will be noted, its application was more restricted among the Romans, who required the homicide to be committed in the house of the aggrieved party in order to render it justifiable. Greece, as we learn from Plutarch's Life of Solon, was the first nation that recognized it; in that country indemnity was absolute, and no limitation of place was prescribed, the only essential being that the parties should be taken in *flagrante delicto*. Mohammedan law does not accept this doctrine, for, as the preservation of female chastity is, by Moslem custom, entrusted to eunuchs, the husband is to blame if he did not take sufficient precautions to secure it. In Scotland, in former times, no distinction was made between homicide under these circumstances and murder, but it was customary to recommend the culprit to mercy. (Mackenzie, The Laws and Customes of Scotland in Matters Criminal, XI, 14.) The killing of a married woman and her lover by the husband of the former, when they are surprised in the act of adultery, is excusable homicide under both the French and Belgian Codes. (*Code Pénal de France*, Art. 324. *Code de Lois Pénales Beiges*, Art. 413.) Under the English law the provocation suffered renders the offence manslaughter. (Stephen, A Digest of the Criminal Law, Art. 224d.) The rule is the same in the United States. (Wharton, A Treatise of Criminal Law, Vol. 1, Sec. 425.) — ed.

[1] Original manuscript illegible.

dowry and the third of their estates, and by relegation to an island. The adulterer, however, shall be deprived of half his property, and shall also be punished by relegation to an island; provided the parties are exiled to different islands.

(15) It has been decided that the penalty for incest, which in case of a man is deportation to an island, shall not be inflicted upon the woman; that is to say when she has not been convicted under the *Lex Julia* concerning adultery.

(16) Fornication committed with female slaves, unless they are deteriorated in value or an attempt is made against their mistress through them, is not considered an injury.

(17) If a delay is demanded in a case of adultery it cannot be obtained.

TITLE XXVII. CONCERNING THE EXCUSES OF GUARDIANS.

(1) Deadly enmity entertained by anyone against the father of a ward excuses a person from guardianship, to prevent wards from being committed to the care of an enemy of their father.

(2) A party cannot, without his consent, be called to take charge of him whose guardianship he administered.

TITLE XXVIII. CONCERNING THE APPOINTMENT OF PERSONS OF SUPERIOR POWER.

(1) He is not considered to have properly appointed a person of superior power who does not state the reason for the appointment.

(2) The party appointed should not only be superior in rank but also in point of property.

TITLE XXIX. WHO CANNOT APPOINT PERSONS OF SUPERIOR AUTHORITY.

(1) Where a freedman whom a father has appointed a guardian is said to be insolvent, he cannot be excused, but a curator may be associated with him.

TITLE XXX. ON THE RESCRIPT OF THE DIVINE SEVERUS.

(1) When a guardian or curator has been detected in the commission of fraud, he shall be fined double the sum of money out of which he attempted to defraud the minor.

TITLE XXXI. CONCERNING THEFTS.

(1) A thief is one who handles the property of another with evil intent.

(2) There are four kinds of theft, namely: manifest, non-manifest, the receiving of stolen goods, and the delivery of stolen property to another. A manifest thief is one who is caught in the act, and who is taken with the property within the boundaries of the place from whence he removed it, or before he arrived at the place where he intended to take it on that day. A non-manifest thief is one who is not caught in the act, or with the property in his possession; but, still cannot deny that he has committed the theft.

(3) A person in whose possession the proceeds of the theft are found is liable in the action for receiving stolen goods. He is liable in an action for having offered stolen property who delivered it to another to avoid having it found in his possession.

(4) He can bring an action of theft whose interest it is that the property should not be lost.

THE OPINIONS OF JULIUS PAULUS ADDRESSED TO HIS SON

(5) He can bring an action to recover stolen goods who detected the presence of the property, that is to say, found it. He with whom the property was found can bring the action for offering stolen goods.

(6) The actions for all four kinds of theft lie in favor of an heir but are not granted against an heir.

(7) A slave who is guilty of theft or has committed damage can, if his master is not prepared to make good the loss according to his means, be surrendered by way of reparation.

(8) Where a slave commits a theft, and is subsequently manumitted or alienated, an action can be brought against him after his manumission, or against his purchaser, if he is sold; for the damage follows the person.

(9) If a son under paternal control commits a theft and is afterwards emancipated, an action of theft is granted against him, because in all cases the damage follows the person.

(10) Not only he who actually perpetrated the theft, but he also by whose aid or advice the offence was committed, is liable in the action of theft.

(11) Property belonging to an estate cannot be stolen before it comes into the possession of the heir.

(12) It has been decided that anyone who carries away and conceals a harlot for the purpose of debauchery is liable in the action of theft.

(13) The action of manifest theft includes the penalty of quadruple the value of the property in addition to the recovery of the same, by a species of claim and personal suit.

(14) The penalty for receiving stolen goods, and for offering the same imposed upon him who offered it, is triple the value in addition to the recovery of the property itself.

(15) A person convicted of any kind of theft becomes infamous.

(16) The action of theft lies against the proprietor of an inn or stable kept for hire, for any property which is lost therein.

(17) If property which has been sold is stolen before being delivered, both the purchaser and the vendor can bring the action of theft, as both of them are interested in delivering the property, or in having it delivered.

(18) If any property is lost in a ship or boat the action of theft will be granted against the master of the vessel.

(19) A debtor commits a theft if he removes property given in pledge to his creditor, and if he himself, should lose it, he can in like manner be prosecuted in his own name.

(20) A father, or a master can bring the action of theft for property which a son under paternal control, or a slave, has surreptitiously removed; for it is important that proceedings should be instituted against him who can be sued for the *peculium*.

(21) If I should afterwards surreptitiously remove property which I lent to you for use, you will have no right to bring the action of theft against me, for we cannot steal something which is our own.

(22) Anyone who is about to search for stolen property should previously say what he is looking for, and should state the name and the nature of the articles.

(23) If anyone commits unlawful injury while searching for stolen property, he will be liable in an action under the *Lex Aquilia*.

(24) A reward promised for information leading to the apprehension of a thief is legally due.

(25) If growing grain, or trees of any kind are cut down for the purpose of being stolen, the culprit can be sued for double the value of the property.

(26) If anyone steals a slave held in common, the action of theft is also granted to the joint owner.

(27) Anyone who takes property supposed to be abandoned, does not commit theft; even though it has not been left by the owner with the intention of abandoning it.

(28) If a slave commits a theft in company with his master, the action of theft is granted against his master in addition to a personal action for the recovery of the property.

(29) A fuller, or a tailor, who receives clothing for the purpose of cleaning or repairing it, and makes use of it, is considered to have committed theft by merely handling it, because he is not understood to have received it for that purpose.

(30) Where crops have been stolen from land, the tenant or the owner can bring the action of theft, for the reason that it is to the interest of both of them to pursue the property.

(31) Anyone who steals a female slave, who is not a harlot, for the purpose of debauchery, is liable in the action of theft; and if he conceals her he can be punished under the *Lex Favia*.

(32) Anyone who steals any documents or written evidence of an obligation is liable in the action of theft for the sum mentioned therein; nor does it make any difference whether they have been cancelled or not, because it can be proved by means of them that a debt has been discharged.

(33) Anyone who advises a slave to take to flight is not liable in the action of theft, but is in the one for corrupting a slave.

(34) If stolen property is returned to the possession of the owner, the right of action for theft is extinguished.[1]

(35) Anyone who breaks into, or opens a place which is closed, but removes nothing, cannot be sued in the action of theft, but the action of injury can be brought against him.

(36) Anyone who steals his own property is not liable in the action of theft, provided that in doing so he does not injure another.

---

[1] The disposition of stolen goods does not, in England, when it takes place publicly, in the ordinary course of trade, and in good faith, cause any loss to the parties directly concerned. "The common law did ordaine (to encourage men thereunto) that all sales and contracts of any thing vendible in faires or markets overt should not be good onely between the parties, but should bind those that right had thereunto." (Coke, Institutes, II, Page 713.)

"Where goods are sold in market overt according to the usage of the market, the buyer acquires a title to the goods provided he buys them in good faith and without notice of any defect or want of title on the part of the seller." (Sales of Goods Act, 1893.) This rule has been appropriated, almost without alteration, from the laws of Menu. "He who has received a chattel, by purchase in open market, before a number of men, justly acquires the absolute property, by having paid the price of it, if he can produce the vendor:

"But, if the vendor be not producible, and the vendee prove the public sale, the latter must be dismissed by the king without punishment; and the former owner, who lost the chattel, may take it back on paying the vendee half its value." (Sir Wm. Jones Works, Vol. III, Page 304.)

This doctrine is not applicable in the United States. "A sale *ex vi termini*, imports nothing more than that the *bona fide* purchaser succeeds to the rights of the vendor. It has been frequently held in this country, that the English law of the market overt had not been adopted; and consequently, as a general rule the title of the true owner cannot be lost without his own free act and consent." (Kent, Commentaries on American Law, Vol. II, Page 390.) — ed.

(37) A fugitive slave still remains in the possession of his owner, but his owner is not liable to the action of theft on his account, because he is not under his control.

TITLE XXXII. CONCERNING THE SERVICES OF FREEDMEN.

(1) A freedman is compelled to support his patron, if he is in want, by means of gifts, presents, and services, to the extent of his means.

BOOK III

TITLE I. CONCERNING THE CARBONIAN EDICT.

(1) When a controversy is raised by a brother of the age of puberty as to whether the trial of a case should be deferred until the heir in question arrives at puberty, a difference of opinion exists, but it is generally held that it should not be deferred.

TITLE II. CONCERNING THE ESTATES OF FREEDMEN.

(1) A patron has a better right to the estate of a freedman than the son of another patron; likewise, the son of a patron is to be preferred to the grandson of another patron.

(2) The freedman of two patrons appointed other heirs, one of whom died during the lifetime of the freedman, and the survivor very properly demanded possession of the estate contrary to the provisions of the will.

(3) The estate of a freedman is divided *per capita* and not *per stirpes*; and therefore, if there are two children of one patron, and four of another, each of them will be entitled to equal shares of the estate. The patron, or the children of the patron who have been appointed heirs to half the estate of a freedman, can be compelled to pay the debts of the deceased, in proportion to their shares of his estate.

TITLE III. CONCERNING THE FABIAN FORMULA.

(1) Property which has been alienated in any way by a freedman for the purpose of defrauding his patron, can be recovered under the Fabian formula, by the patron himself, as well as by his children.

TITLE IV.a. CONCERNING WILLS.

(1) Males can make a will after having completed their fourteenth year, females after having completed their twelfth; but not where they have the right of children under the authority of a guardian.

(2) Eunuchs can make a will at the time when most males arrive at the age of puberty, that is to say, when they have reached their eighteenth year.

(3) A son under paternal control who is a soldier, or who has served in the army, can make a will disposing of his *castrense peculium*, not only at common law, but through the privilege which he enjoys. *Castrense peculium* is property acquired in camp, or which is given to a soldier while on his way to the army.

(4) A blind man can make a will, because he can request witnesses to be present, and hear them give their testimony.

(5) An insane person can make a will during a lucid interval of his insanity.

(6) A woman can be forbidden to dispose of her property if she is living a depraved life.

(7) A person can be prohibited by the Prætor from receiving an estate on account of his or her morals, in the following terms: "To prevent you from squandering the estate of your father, (or grandfather), by your profligacy, and bringing your children to want, I exclude you from the house and from all commercial intercourse."

(8) A person captured by the enemy cannot make a will, as he occupies the position of a slave. A will, however, which was made before captivity is valid, if the party returns under the law of *postliminium*; or, if he dies in captivity, he will be entitled to the benefit of the *Lex Cornelia*, by which lawful guardianship and inheritances are confirmed.

(9) A person who has been relegated to an island, or sentenced for a time to labor on the public works, can make a will, and take under a will, for the reason that he retains his citizenship.

(10) Where more than seven persons are called to witness a will no harm is done; for any superfluous act is a benefit to the right of testation, and cannot injure it.

(11) A person who has lost his senses on account of bodily illness cannot make a will during the time that this condition exists.

(12) A spendthrift who leads a proper life after having reformed can make a will and act as a witness to testamentary execution.

(13) If any of those who are called to witness a will do not know or understand Latin, but still are aware for what purpose they are present, and act as witnesses, this will not vitiate the will.[1]

---

[1] The right of testamentary disposition is of comparatively modern origin, the Greeks being the first nation to recognize it under the legal system established by Solon. "He is likewise much commended for his law concerning wills; for before him none could be made, but all the wealth and estate of the deceased belonged to his family." (Plutarch, Life of Solon.) Wills are not mentioned in the Code of Hammurabi, the Avesta, the Pentateuch, or the Gentoo Code; the first and the last of which compilations devote much space to the rules of inheritance. The declaration of Abraham that Eliezer was his heir, (Genesis XV, 3) can hardly be considered either as a nuncupative will, or *a donatio mortis causa*. The Germans of the time of Tacitus knew nothing of wills. (*De Germ.* XX.)

By the Visigothic Code a minor of ten years of age, if supposed to be *in extremis*, could make a testamentary disposal of his property; otherwise he was required to be fourteen years old. (*Forum Judicum*, II, VI, 10.) The collection of Alfonso X follows the rule of the text. (*Las Siete Partidas*, VI, I, 13.) Under Moslem law, no person is competent to make a will until the attainment of majority, incapacity being removed by arrival at the age of puberty, which period, when proof of precocious development is not adduced, is fixed at eighteen years for males, and seventeen for females. It may, however, be as early as twelve and nine years, respectively. A great divergence of opinion on this point exists among jurists. Some concede this right to a child over ten years of age; "if he is capable of discernment"; others deny it to a youth who has not arrived at puberty; others again, hold that only adults are capable. (*Syed Ameer Ali*, Mohammedan Law, Vol. II, Chap. XVI, Pages 470-471.) (The Hedaya, IV, LIII, 1.) (Hughes, Dict, of Islam, Page 476.) In France and Belgium, the age of capacity for testation is sixteen years, (Cod. *Civ.*, Art. 904. *Code Civil Annoté*, Art. 903) ; in Spain and Portugal, it is fourteen years, (*Cod. Civ.*, Art. 763. *Cod. Civ.*, Art. 1764) ; in Italy, eighteen years, (*Cod. Civ.*, Art. 763); in Sweden twenty-one years — but a minor over fifteen can bequeath property acquired by his or her own industry, (*Sveriges Rikes Lag. Ärvdabalk* XVI. *Kap.* 3); in Holland and Austria, eighteen years — minors under that age can, in Austria, under certain conditions, execute a nuncupative will; (*Burgerlijk Wetboek*, Art. 944; *Allgemeines Bürgerliches Gesetzbuch*, Art. 569) ; in Japan, fifteen years, (Civil Code of Japan, Art. 1601). The age of puberty is adopted by Scottish law. "Minors after puberty can test without their curators." (Erskine, Principles of the Law of Scotland, III, IX, 5.) At Common Law a male infant of fifteen and a female of twelve, could bequeath personal property, as by the Civil Law. Under tenures in Socage, Coke lays down the rule as being eighteen years. "If after his marriage he accomplish his age of eighteen years, at what time he may make his testament, and constitute executors for his goods and chattels." (Coke, Institutes, I, 89b.) In this country no established rule exists, the age being regulated by statute, but, generally speaking, a minor has not testamentary capacity. The age in most instances is the same as in England, twenty-one years; in many States it is eighteen; in Georgia, where it is the lowest, it is fourteen years. — ed.

THE OPINIONS OF JULIUS PAULUS ADDRESSED TO HIS SON

TITLE IV.b. CONCERNING THE APPOINTMENT OF HEIRS.

(1) There are two kinds of conditions, those which are possible and those which are impossible. A possible condition is one which in the nature of things can take place, an impossible condition is one which cannot take place; the occurrence of one of which may be expected, but the fulfillment of the other is suggested as impossible.

(2) Conditions which are contrary to the laws and decrees of the emperors, or are opposed to good morals, are of no force or effect, for instance, the following: "If you should not marry a wife; if you should not have children; if you should not commit homicide; if you should appear in the costume of a barbarian, or a spectre;" and others of the same description.

(3) When it is not apparent what heir was appointed, the appointment is not valid; which occurs when the testator had several friends of the same name.

(4) Heirs are said to be either appointed or substituted; those that are appointed are placed in the first degree, those that are substituted are placed in the second, or third degree.

(5) A testator can substitute an heir either absolutely or conditionally; and this applies to his own heirs as well as strangers, and to children over and under puberty.

(6) A testator can divide his estate into as many shares as he wishes; and where the entire estate is disposed of, heirs who are appointed without any share will be entitled to equal portions of the first half of the estate.

(7) If a slave belonging to another is appointed an heir with his freedom, this does not annul the appointment; but the grant of freedom is considered to be superfluous as the slave belongs to another person.

(8) Where a son and a stranger are appointed heirs to an estate, and a daughter has been passed over, she can only claim as her share the amount left to the stranger; but where the two sons have been appointed heirs, she will take a third from them, and half from the stranger.

(9) When an appointment of posthumous heirs is made as follows: "Let my children born after my death be my heirs"; any children born during his lifetime will break the will.

(10) A posthumous grandchild who can succeed to the place of his father, and who should either be appointed heir by his grandfather, or disinherited by name, does not break the will by his birth.

(11) Anyone who has once decided to accept an estate and meddles with the property belonging to it, cannot repudiate it, even though it may cause him loss.

TITLE V. ON THE SILANIAN DECREE OF THE SENATE.

(1) Under the terms of the Silanian Decree of the Senate, the estate of a person who is said to have been killed by his slaves cannot be entered on before torture has been applied; nor can the prætorian possession of it legally be demanded.

(2) One is said to have been killed not only where death took place through violence, or murder, as where a man's throat was cut, or he was hurled down from a precipice, but also where he is alleged to have been killed by poison; for the honor of the heir is involved in not allowing any kind of homicide of the testator to go unavenged.

(3) When the owner is killed, torture should be applied to those slaves who are under the same roof, or who were outside of the house with their master at the time he was murdered.

(4) When a person is said to have been killed, and it is established that he took his own life in some way, his slaves should not be tortured, unless they are able to prevent it, and did not do so.

(5) It is provided by the Neronian Decree of the Senate that where a wife has been killed, the slaves of the husband should be tortured; and, on the other hand, where the husband is alleged to have been killed, the same rule shall be applied to the slaves devoted to the personal service of the wife.

(6) Slaves living under the same roof where the master is said to have been killed, shall be tortured and punished, even though they have been manumitted by the will of the deceased; and those also shall be tortured who accompanied him, if he was killed on a journey.

(7) Slaves who were near at hand are punished if they could have heard the cries of their master and did not go to his assistance.

(8) It has been decided that slaves who abandoned their master and took to flight when he was surrounded by robbers while on a journey, shall be arrested, tortured, and put to death.

(9) Torture shall be inflicted upon slaves if the heir is alleged to have killed the testator; and it makes no difference whether he is a stranger, or one of his children.

(10) Heirs are deprived of an estate and it is confiscated by the Treasury, if, when the murder of the testator is suspected, they entered upon the estate after the opening of the will, or after he has been declared intestate, or they obtained prætorian possession of the same; and, in addition to this, the penalty of a hundred thousand sesterces is imposed upon them; nor does it make any difference by whom, or in what way, the head of the household is said to have been killed.

(l0a) In conclusion, it should be noted that torture must be applied to all those who, for any reason, are under suspicion.

(11) The following order is observed in subjecting those to torture whose master is said to have been murdered. In the first place it should be established that the master was killed, and then it should be made clear what slaves should be put to torture and in this way the guilty parties be detected.

(12) Although it may be certain who struck the fatal blow, the slaves should, nevertheless, be put to torture, in order that the instigator of the murder may be discovered.

(13) All those who have acted contrary to the intentions of the deceased shall be deprived of the estate as being unworthy, if nothing was provided in the will for the purpose of evading the law.

(14) The appointed heir can demand to be placed in possession of the estate unless the will is alleged to be forged, broken, or void.

(15) If a controversy arises between the appointed heir and the substitute, the better opinion is that the heir who was appointed in the first place should obtain possession of the property of the estate.

(16) The heir appointed in writing can legally demand to be immediately placed in possession. He cannot, however, obtain possession by law after a year has elapsed.

(17) The heir appointed in writing is not entitled to demand possession under a will which has not been produced and publicly read, as is required.

(18) The heir appointed in writing cannot with propriety demand to be placed in possession of any property which the testator did not possess at the time of his death, before the question has been decided in the ordinary course of law.

THE OPINIONS OF JULIUS PAULUS ADDRESSED TO HIS SON

TITLE VI. CONCERNING LEGACIES.

(1) A preferred legacy of money left to one of several heirs who were not at home, must be paid by the co-heirs by order of court in a suit for partition.

(2) A bequest cannot be made before the appointment of an heir; it can, however, be made between the appointments of heirs, without one or both being present; and sometimes half, and sometimes all will be due; half where the legacy is bequeathed to be claimed, all, where it is left by condemnation.

(3) . . . .[1]

(4) A legacy can be left to a slave owner in common either with the grant of his freedom or without it, and the entire legacy is acquired for the partner of the testator.

(5) A legacy cannot be bequeathed after the death of the heir, because the heir of an heir cannot be charged with the payment of a legacy.

(6) A legacy can be bequeathed to take effect at the time of the death of the heir, or when he dies, as follows: "I give and bequeath to Lucius Titius, when he dies my heir", or, "Let my heir be required to pay".

(7) Although the legatee may not yet have determined to claim the legacy, still, if he should die after the will has been opened, and before the estate has been entered on, he will transmit the legacy to his heir.

(8) If the property bequeathed by condemnation was hypothecated to a creditor, and the testator was not ignorant of the fact, the heir is expected to release the claim.

(9) If the slave should die, the loss must be sustained by the legatee, for the reason that the legacy lapsed through no fault of the heir.

(10) An heir can be charged to build a house for anyone, or to pay another's debt.

(11) Corporeal property, as well as that consisting merely of rights, can be bequeathed by way of permission; and therefore what was owed by a debtor may legally be bequeathed to him.

(12) A legatee cannot reject a part of the legacy bequeathed, and accept a part, as in the case of an heir.

(13) Unless the legacy consists of property which is certain, and is left to a certain person, it is of no force or effect.

(14) If anyone leaves a legacy, to himself and to Titius, the better opinion is that the entire legacy belongs to the joint legatees.

(15) Anyone who appoints himself guardian to the son of the testator, who is under the age of puberty, should as being suspicious, be removed from the guardianship which he is considered to have voluntarily attempted to obtain.

(16) If a testator subsequently pledges or hypothecates property which he has bequeathed, he will not, for this reason, be considered to have changed his mind.

(17) The usufruct of any kind of property can be bequeathed, and either vests by operation of law, or is transferred by the heir; hence, where left by condemnation it must be transferred by the heir, and where left to be claimed it vests by operation of law.

---

[1] Original manuscript illegible.

(18) The usufruct of a slave who is insane, ill, or an infant, may legally be bequeathed; for he may either recover his senses, or his health, or grow up.

(19) When the usufruct of a female slave is bequeathed, her offspring does not belong to the usufructuary.

(20) Where the usufruct of a flock is left, and it sustains no loss, the increase belongs to the usufructuary; that is to say, except in the case where some of the animals die, when the loss must be made up from their young.

(21) Where the usufruct of a piece of land is bequeathed, buildings cannot be constructed upon it.

(22) The accession of the alluvion of land does not belong to the usufructuary, for the reason that it is not the product of the soil, but any animals or birds taken in hunting will become the property of the usufructuary.

(23) An usufructuary can neither torture, scourge, nor, by any act of his, cause the deterioration of slaves.

(24) Where the profits of anything are bequeathed, and the use to be made of them is not stated, the better opinion is that the usufruct should be held to be included where profits cannot exist without use.

(25) If the use of a thing is left to one person, and the profits of it to another, the usufructuary will share in the use, which the person who has only the use cannot do, so far as the profits are concerned.

(26) Where the usufruct is bequeathed to two persons conjointly, by the expression: "I give and bequeath"; and one of them dies, the entire legacy will belong to the other.

(27) When the usufruct of anything is bequeathed, it is customary for the usufructuary to furnish security as to the way he will make use of it; and having furnished security, he is obliged to agree that he will use the property in the same way as the most careful head of the household would do.

(28) When an usufruct is lost it reverts to the ownership, and it is lost in five ways, namely: by the forfeiture of civil rights; by change in the property itself; by failure to make use of it; by its surrender in court; and by purchase of its ownership.

(29) It is lost by the forfeiture of civil rights, if the usufructuary is deported to an island, or if, for some reason, he is sentenced to the mines, or changes his condition either by arrogation or adoption.

(30) An usufruct is lost by failure to make use of it, where the usufructuary, being in possession, does not use the land for the term of two years, or movable property for the term of one year.

(31) The usufruct is lost by change in the property, where the usufruct of a house is bequeathed, and the house is destroyed by fire, or becomes ruined, although it may subsequently be rebuilt.

(32) An usufruct is lost by surrender in court, whenever the usufructuary, in a judicial proceeding, transfers it to the owner of the property.

(33) An usufruct is terminated either by death or by lapse of time; by death, when the usufructuary dies, by lapse of time, whenever the usufruct is bequeathed for a certain time, for instance, for two or three years.

(34) When a tract of land, or a slave is bequeathed, neither the appurtenances of the land nor the *peculium* of the slave belongs to the legatee.

(35) Those who perform farm labor are considered necessary for the securing of crops, as superintendents, stewards, and foresters; as well as oxen for plowing, plows, pruning hooks, and grain stored up for seed.

THE OPINIONS OF JULIUS PAULUS ADDRESSED TO HIS SON

(36) Various articles are included among the implements, as, for instance, baskets, sickles, and scythes for cutting grain and hay, and also olive-oil mills.

(37) Among the implements and appurtenances for preserving the crops are casks, vats, farm vehicles, provisions for men and animals, millers, asses, ovens, likewise female slaves who make garments for the laborers, leather and shoemakers are also included.

(38) The better opinion is that the wives of the laborers also form part of the appurtenances; and also flocks and their shepherds — if the former are kept on account of their manure — are also included.

(39) Those things, however, which are for the purpose of taking care of the property, rather than for the use of the head of the household, are not included in the category of appurtenances.

(40) The wives of those who are accustomed to pay wages are not included in the terms furnishings or appurtenances.

(41) Articles used for fishing and hunting are only included among the appurtenances of land when the income therefrom is for the most part derived from their employment.

(42) Gathered crops are only included where they were ordinarily consumed on the ground by the testator.

(43) Where land situated in the country or in a city is bequeathed with its appurtenances and the slaves thereon, all the seed and provisions will be due under the legacy.

(44) When land with all its appurtenances both rustic and urban and the slaves thereon is bequeathed, the furniture, the brazen and silver vessels, and the clothing which the head of the household was accustomed to keep there for the purpose of caring for, or cultivating the property, will be due under the legacy; as well as any slaves ordinarily employed by the head of the household, and any fowls or flocks which are kept on the land to be used in banquets, with the exception of those left there for safe keeping.

(45) Where land is left "to be maintained in the very best condition", nets to capture wild boars, and other implements used for hunting are included. These also are part of the appurtenances if the greater portion of the income of the land consists of the produce of the chase.

(46) Any crops attached to the soil at the time of the death of the testator belong to the legatee; those previously gathered belong to the heir.

(47) Where land is bequeathed with its slaves and flocks and all its rustic and urban appurtenances, the better opinion is that the *peculium* of the steward, if he dies before the testator and if it was on the same land, will also belong to the legatee.

(48) A steward, or tenant who was brought from the land of another and bequeathed with all the appurtenances does not belong to the legatee, unless the testator intended that he should be attached to the land in question.

(49) It has been decided that any additions derived from different purchases which the testator to the land bequeathed will belong to the legatee.

(50) When the land is bequeathed furnished, blacksmiths, carpenters, and pruners who live on the land for the purpose of working there are included in the bequest.

(51) Where land is bequeathed with its appurtenances, books, and libraries situated thereon, are included in the bequest.

(52) It has been decided that where a slave was on the land for the purpose of studying, and the land was bequeathed with its slaves, if he was transferred elsewhere he belongs to the legatee.

(53) Where land is bequeathed in such a way that possession may be obtained, both urban and rustic slaves, and gold and clothing which are on the land at the same time, belong to the legatee.

(54) Pastures subsequently purchased, which the testator added to the land bequeathed, if included in that appellation, belong to the legatee.

(55) Any property in the same house which the owner bequeathed furnished, and which he kept there to be constantly used, passes to the legatee.

(56) Any articles bequeathed with the house, and by which the building is better provided, or rendered safe from fire, are embraced in the legacy; hence tiles, mirrors, and curtains are included, likewise, coverlets, beds, mattresses, pillows, benches, chairs, tables, chests, tripods, toilet-boxes, wash-basins, candelabra, lamps, and similar objects, no matter of what material they may be composed.

(57) When a house is bequeathed, the bath attached to it, which is for common use, passes to the legatee, where it is not otherwise separated from it.

(58) Where a house is bequeathed furnished, with all the rights attached to the same, the urban slaves, together with the artisans, porters, and water-carriers employed in the service of the house, are comprised in the legacy.

(59) When all the contents of a house are bequeathed, written evidences of debt and bills of sales of slaves are not included in the legacy.

(60) When jewelry is bequeathed, gold and silver plate is not included, unless it can be shown clearly that the testator intended that it should be.

(61) When an inn is bequeathed with its appurtenances which are said to belong to the inn-keeper, all those things are included which are provided for the use of the proprietor; for instance, vessels in which wine is poured, and dishes and cups for eating and drinking, but those who serve food or drink by means of these utensils do not pass with the legacy.

(62) Where the instruments of a physician are bequeathed, eyewashes and plasters, all the apparatus for compounding medicines, as well as surgical instruments, are comprised in the legacy.

(63) When the studio of a painter is bequeathed, paints, brushes, branding irons, and vessels for mixing colors are included.

(64) Where the shop of a baker is bequeathed, sieves, asses, mills, and slaves who are employed in the bakery, as well as the machines with which flour is kneaded, are included in the legacy.

(65) When the establishment of a bather is bequeathed, the bather himself, benches, footstools, pipes, cauldrons, spigots, water-wheels, and also the beasts of burden by which wood is carried, are embraced in the legacy.

(66) When the equipment of a fisherman is bequeathed, nets, baskets, tridents, boats, hooks, and everything else of this kind intended for the use of fishermen is included.

(67) Where furniture is bequeathed, boxes and chests — except such as are solely intended for books or clothing — are included; as well as vessels of Phoenician, and other glass, or crystal, and of silver, both for eating and drinking purposes, together with cloths used for covering, are included in the legacy.

THE OPINIONS OF JULIUS PAULUS ADDRESSED TO HIS SON

(68) When a house and a field are bequeathed separately, one is included in the other.

(69) Where slaves are bequeathed by the formula: "I do give and bequeath", female slaves are also included; but where male slaves are bequeathed, females are not included. In the term female slaves, virgins, as well as the sons of slaves are included. Those, however, are excepted who are left in trust.

(70) When slaves who are secretaries are bequeathed, all who are engaged in that service in the city will be included, unless some of them have been permanently transferred to work in the country.

(71) It is doubtful whether hunters or bird-catchers should be included among those employed in service in a city, and the question therefore depends upon the intention. Still, if they are kept for the purpose of daily attendance upon the table they will be included.

(72) Muleteers and stewards are included in those employed in urban services, as well as purveyors and valets, butlers, chamberlains, cooks, cake-bakers, barbers, litter-bearers, and grooms.

(73) When flocks are bequeathed, all quadrupeds are included which feed together in herds.

(74) When beasts of burden are bequeathed, oxen are not included; and where horses are bequeathed, it has been decided that mares are included; where sheep are bequeathed, lambs are not included, unless they are a year old.

(75) Where a flock of sheep is bequeathed, rams are also included.

(76) Where fowls are bequeathed, geese, pheasants, chickens, and the places where they are kept are included, but whether the keepers of pheasants and of geese are included, depends upon the intention of the testator.

(77) When sweets are bequeathed, wine which has been boiled down either with or without spices; mead; sweet wine; dates; figs; and raisins are included. On this point, also, there is a question of the intention, because this term includes some kinds of apples.

(78) When vegetables are bequeathed, not only leguminous plants, but also barley and wheat are included.

(79) When cloth is bequeathed, it includes everything woven of wool and flax as well as of silk and cotton which is prepared for the purpose of wear or covering, as for girdles, or for placing under or upon one. Skins suitable for wear are also included.

(80) When clothing for males is bequeathed, this only applies to garments used by men for reasons of modesty, and any kind of covering is embraced in a bequest of this description.

(81) When female clothing is bequeathed, all garments intended for the use of women are included.

(82) When wool is bequeathed, it is included in the legacy whether it has been cut off, or washed, and whether it has been carded or dyed; purple, however, whether in the web or the woof, is not comprised in this category.

(83) When articles suitable for the use of women are bequeathed, everything intended to render them more neat and elegant is included; for instance, mirrors, toilet-boxes, vessels for water, ointments, and the vases in which they are contained, and also a stool for the bath, and other things of this kind.

(84) Where ornaments are bequeathed, all those things used for the adornment of women are included; as for instance rings, chains, nets, and other things with which women adorn their necks, heads, or hands.

(85) When silver is bequeathed, it only is due in the mass, for vessels which are designated by their own

names are not included in the legacy; for when wool is bequeathed, clothing is not due.

(86) When silver vessels are bequeathed, all those are included which are fashioned for any purpose, and therefore such as are used for eating or drinking, as well as the slaves who handle them at banquets are due; as for instance, small pitchers, bowls, dishes, pepper, cruets, spoons, ladles, goblets, and other utensils of this kind.

(87) When books are bequeathed, volumes of paper, parchment, and papyrus are included, and wooden tablets covered with wax, as well. By the term "books" not merely volumes of leaves of paper, but also any kind of writing which is enclosed in anything is understood.

(88) When gold is bequeathed, precious stones are also included, and pearls and emeralds pass with the legacy; the better opinion, however, is that this is a question of intention, for gold which is not manufactured is due, but where it is manufactured, it is comprised in the category with ornaments.

(89) Where silver plate is bequeathed, any inlaid decoration of gold is also embraced in the legacy.

(90) Where a silver drinking service is bequeathed, every kind of drinking vessel is included; as for instance, bowls, cups, goblets, pitchers, wine-jars, and spoons.

(91) When a carriage with its belongings is bequeathed, mules are also included in the legacy but the muleteer does not seem to be, according to the daily custom of speaking.

(92) When a codicil, or any other kind of a testament, is produced, from which a legacy has been erased, or cut away, its payment cannot legally be demanded.

TITLE VII. CONCERNING DONATIONS MORTIS CAUSA.

(1) A person makes a donation *mortis causa* who, on departing for war, or being about to undertake a sea voyage, does so upon the condition that if he should return the property shall be restored to him, and if he should die, it shall belong to him to whom he gave it.

(2) A donation *mortis causa* made on account of illness, on the recovery of health is also revoked by a change of mind; for it becomes effective only through death.

TITLE VIII. ON THE LEX FALCIDIA.

(1) When an estate has been exhausted by legacies, trusts, or donations *mortis causa*, the appointed heir can, by the aid of the *Lex Falcidia*, retain a fourth part of the same.

(2) Whenever a question arises with reference to the portion to be retained, on account of the risk of the heir demanding more than he is entitled to, after an appraisement of all the property has been made by the judge, the amount of the fourth to which the heir is entitled is determined; or a bond is executed from the legatee that if he receives any more than the fourth of the estate he will return it.

(3) Property donated to a son by a mother during her lifetime, is not subject to the reservation of the Falcidian fourth.

(4) Where default occurs in the payment of trusts or legacies, suit can be brought to recover the profits and interest; and default is held to be committed when the property left in trust or bequeathed is not delivered to the party claiming it.

THE OPINIONS OF JULIUS PAULUS ADDRESSED TO HIS SON

BOOK IV

TITLE I. CONCERNING TRUSTS.

(1) A wife to whom her husband left the dowry as a preferred legacy cannot be charged with a trust, for the reason that she does not obtain any pecuniary benefit from the will, but is considered merely to receive that to which she is entitled.

(2) A posthumous child, who has been appointed heir, can be charged with the execution of a trust.

(3) If the Emperor is appointed heir, he can be charged with the payment of a legacy and the execution of a trust.

(4) A person who is deaf or dumb, whether he receives a legacy, is appointed an heir, or succeeds on the ground of intestacy, can legally be charged with the execution of a trust.

(5) Anyone who leaves a trust can charge the party to whom he leaves it, as follows: "I request you, Gaius Seius, to be content with the said property"; or, "Or I desire that that property be delivered to you".

(6) We can create a trust in the following words: "I ask, I request, I desire, I direct, I pray, I wish, I enjoin." The expressions "I desire", and "I command" create a valid trust. The terms "I leave", and "I recommend", do not furnish ground for an action of trust.

(7) We can leave our own property, as well as that of others, subject to the terms of a trust; but our own must be delivered immediately, and that of others must either be purchased, or its value paid.

(8) If a testator leaves property belonging to someone else, as his own, in trust, he should not do so if he is aware that it belongs to another, as is the practice with legacies; for the trust will be of no force or effect.

(9) If the testator survives, and sells the property which he bequeathed the trust is extinguished.

(10) A trust included in a codicil which is not confirmed by a will is legally due.

(11) A trust left by a father to a son, no matter in what words it is expressed, is due according to law; for among persons who are related it is sufficient for the intention to be stated in any words whatsoever, as is the case with donations; and therefore a trust is considered to be legally bequeathed even on the day before the death of the deceased.

(12) If a trust be left, in any manner whatsoever, to take effect at the time of the emancipation of a son, or when he becomes his own master; he will be entitled to it when freed from paternal control.

(13) Where children are requested to transfer an estate if they should die without issue, and one of them dies without leaving children, the estate will pass to the survivor; nor can the parties, with reference to this make any agreement which is contrary to the will of the testator.

(14) An heir cannot execute a trust before entering on the estate, or a legatee before receiving his legacy.

(15) If the heir should sell the property left in trust and knowingly should purchase it, the beneficiary of the trust can still legally demand to be placed in possession.

(16) Whenever a trust is left to freedmen, it has been decided that it can only belong to such as have been manumitted, or who are among the legal number of those who have obtained their freedom under the terms of the same will.

(17) An heir can not only be charged with a trust involving the property of the estate, but also with one relating to his own property.

(18) All the rights attaching to a trust consist not in bringing an action to recover the property, but in making a demand for it.

TITLE II. CONCERNING THE TREBELLIAN DECREE OF THE SENATE.

(1) It was provided by the Trebellian Decree of the Senate that the heir should not be burdened with all the actions which might be brought against the estate; and therefore, whenever the estate is transferred under the terms of a trust, the actions relating to it are also transferred to the beneficiary, for the reason that both parties should not be liable to loss.

TITLE III. CONCERNING THE PEGASIAN DECREE OF THE SENATE.

(1) A stipulation is entered into between the heir and the beneficiary of a trust to whom an estate is transferred under the Pegasian Decree of the Senate, in such a way that a fourth part of the actions will lie in favor of the appointed heir, and the remainder in favor of the beneficiary of the trust in proportion to his share of the estate.

(2) If the heir is asked to transfer the entire estate and is unwilling to retain the fourth, the better opinion is that he should transfer it under the Trebellian Decree of the Senate; for then all actions are granted to the beneficiary of the trust.

(3) Again, the *Lex Falcidia* and the Pegasian Decree of the Senate as well, permit the fourth of the remainder of the estate to belong to the heir, after the debts and the gifts to the gods have been deducted.

(4) An heir who transfers the entire estate, and does not retain the fourth part of it under the Pegasian Decree of the Senate, as he should have done, cannot recover it; for he who prefers to discharge his entire duty to the deceased is not considered to have paid something which was not due.

TITLE IV. CONCERNING THE REJECTION OF AN ESTATE.

(1) An estate can not only be refused by words but also by acts, and by any indication of the intention whatsoever.

(2) An heir can be compelled by municipal magistrates, under the authority of the governor, to enter upon and transfer an estate, on the demand of the beneficiary of the trust.

(3) If the beneficiary alleges that the heir refuses to enter on the estate he can demand that a decree be rendered in his absence, and that he legally be placed in possession.

(4) An heir who is compelled to enter on an estate which is supposed to be insolvent, transfers all the property belonging to the same under the Trebellian Decree of the Senate.[1]

---

[1] Trusts, or bequests for the benefit of a third party, and known as *fideicommissa*, were invented to evade the rule of law by which a Roman citizen was prohibited from leaving property directly by will to foreigners and other persons legally incompetent to receive it. At first, no legal measures could be taken to enforce compliance with the wishes of the testator, the legacy absolutely vested in the trustee who was the testamentary heir, and was only in honor bound to carry out the provisions of the will, so far as the beneficiary of the trust was concerned. Violation of this moral obligation, however, occurred so often that the Emperor Augustus declared it to be legally binding, and provided for the enforcement of its performance. It is related of him that he himself scrupulously observed the directions of a testator with reference to the transfer to a beneficiary of property bequeathed for the benefit of the latter; thus affording a laudable example for the observance of his subjects. The consuls, and subsequently two prætors especially appointed for that purpose, were invested with jurisdiction over trusts. As difficulties arose in their execution, owing to the reluctance of the heir to assume responsibilities that in many cases were productive of no advantage, and which might result in serious loss, various decrees of the Senate were enacted to remove these drawbacks. By this means the heir, on the transfer of the estate, was released from all liability, which was assumed by the beneficiary; and he was entitled to a fourth of his share which, however, he forfeited if he refused

THE OPINIONS OF JULIUS PAULUS ADDRESSED TO HIS SON

TITLE V. CONCERNING THE COMPLAINT THAT A WILL IS INOFFICIOUS.

(1) A will is said to be inofficious, because the children having been improperly disinherited, it does not appear to have been drawn up in accordance with the duty of parental affection.

(2) When a son is born after a will has been made by his mother, and her intention does not seem to have been changed when it could have been done; the son can properly file a complaint for inofficiousness, as in the case of an heir who has been passed over.

(3) A will in which the Emperor is appointed heir can be declared inofficious; for it is but fitting that he who makes the laws should with equal dignity obey them.

(4) Anyone who can allege a will to be inofficious is not prevented from claiming the estate.

(5) A son who is appointed heir to an entire estate cannot declare the will to be inofficious, nor does it make any difference whether the estate is exhausted or not, for he still will be entitled to the fourth part of the same by the benefit of either the *Lex Falcidia* or the Pegasian Decree of the Senate.

(6) The fourth part of the estate, after the debts and funeral expenses have been deducted, should be given to the children, in order that they may be prevented from making a complaint of inofficiousness. It is settled that grants of freedom also diminish this part.

(7) If a son obtains less than a fourth part of the estate under the will of his father, he can legally demand that the remainder of his share be made good by his brothers, his co-heirs, without filing a complaint of inofficiousness.

(8) An agreement not to declare a will inofficious does not bar a future complaint with reference to the will, for it has been decided that the claims of children should be considered rather than any agreement.

(9) Where an heir is requested to transfer the estate, no injury is done to the beneficiary of the trust, even though the heir might be able to file a complaint of inofficiousness; for he only loses a fourth part of the estate which he could have had under the terms of the Decree of the Senate. .

(10) If the appointed heir has a substitute, and makes a complaint of inofficiousness but fails to gain his case, the property will not belong to the Treasury, but to the substitute.

---

to enter on the estate and legal measures were required to compel him to do so.

Trusts were either universal or special; the first involved the transfer of an entire inheritance, the second had reference to some designated article or a specified sum of money. An universal trust was, in its effect, merely a kind of substitution, entirely dependent upon the previous entry of the heir upon the estate. It was not necessary for the heir to even accept the execution of the trust in order to transmit it to his successors; and when certain property, which included his fourth, was bequeathed to him, he was held to occupy the position of an ordinary legatee. The beneficiary of a trust, as well as an heir, had the right to reject an estate or a legacy if he thought that it would prove burdensome, or disadvantageous.

Fideicommissa, which are treated under the head of Substitutions, are recognized by nearly all the Codes of Continental Europe. They were introduced into England under the name of "uses", during the reign of Edward III, for the purpose of evading the Statutes of Mortmain by enabling the clergy to enjoy the use and benefit of lands which could not be directly devised to them. The trustee was called the feoffee to uses, and the *fideicommissarius*, or beneficiary, the *cestuy que use*, and afterwards the *cestuy que trust*. The Statute 15, Richard II, 2, 5, effectively disposed of this ingenious expedient to avoid the requirements of the law. "If any be seized of any lands or other Possessions to the use of any Spiritual Person with purpose of Amortize them, and whereof such Spiritual Person takes the Profits, he shall before the Feast of St. Michael next, cause them to be Amortized by the Licence of the King and other Lords, or dispose of them to some use; otherwise they shall be Forfeit according to the Form of said Statute, as Lands purchased by People of Religion; And no such Purchase to the use of such Spiritual Person shall be hereafter made, upon like pain." (Wingate, An Exact Abridgment of all the Statutes from the beginning of Magna Charta, Title Mortmain, Page 433.) — ed.

TITLE VI. CONCERNING THE TAX OF THE TWENTIETH.

(1) A will is opened in the following manner: either all the witnesses who attached their seals to the will, or the majority of them are summoned, so that, having acknowledged their seals, and the cord having been broken, the will may be opened and read, and the opportunity to make a copy of the same may be afforded; and then, having been sealed with the public seal, it is placed among the public records, in order that if the copy should be destroyed, it may be known where the original can be found.

(2) Wills executed in provincial towns, colonies, fortified places, prefectures, villages, castles, and places of assembly should be opened and read in the presence of the witnesses or of respectable citizens in the forum or the church between the second and the tenth hour of the day. A copy having been made, the will is again sealed up in the presence of the magistrates in whose presence it was opened.

(2a) Anyone who opens or reads a will in any other manner, or in any other place than those required by law, is liable to a penalty of five thousand sesterces.

(3) The law directs a will to be opened immediately after the death of the testator; and although this rule has been changed by rescripts, still, under those at present in force a will should be opened within three to five days after the death of the testator, and where the parties are absent, within the same number of days after their return; for this is not a matter of such importance to the heirs, legatees, or recipients of grants of freedom, as it is that no delay should take place in the payment of the necessary tax.

TITLE VII. CONCERNING THE LEX CORNELIA.

(1) Anyone who writes, reads, substitutes, or seals a forged will, or knowingly and maliciously suppresses one which is genuine, or removes it, re-seals it, or destroys it, is liable to the penalty for forgery under the *Lex Cornelia*; that is to say, he shall be deported to an island.

(2) Not only he who substitutes, suppresses, or destroys a will, is punished by the penalty of the *Lex Cornelia*, but also he who knowingly and maliciously orders this to be done, or takes care that it shall be done.

(3) He suppresses a will who knowingly, intentionally and for the purpose of defrauding the heir, the legatees, the beneficiaries of a trust, or the slaves entitled to freedom under the will does not produce it.

(4) He is considered to suppress a will who having it in his possession and being able to produce it, takes care not to do so.

(5) If a codicil is concealed and not produced, it is considered to be suppressed.

(6) It is provided by the Perpetual Edict[1] that if a will is not produced proceedings can be instituted within

---

[1] The Prætor was invested with extraordinary power with reference to subjects included in his jurisdiction. His edict, inscribed upon the "album" or "tablet" — so called from its white color — posted conspicuously in the Forum, announced to all the formulas of practice, and the principles which were to form the bases of his decrees for the ensuing year. It is true that he usually adopted, with slight modification, those promulgated by his predecessors, but he was, by no means, obliged to do so. A new order of proceeding, other rules of judicial conduct, were ever at his disposal, on the assumption of his magisterial duties; provided, of course, that he could frame them, that they were not inequitable, and did not interfere with the rights of the litigants who appeared before him. This vast authority, which, to a certain extent, practically conferred upon the person in whom it was vested the privilege of legislation, was naturally liable to abuse; and led to the enactment of the *Edictum Perpetuum*, or "Continuous Edict", by whose provisions the Prætor was deprived of the arbitrary power to issue new edicts arising from the circumstances of any particular case, and was compelled to adhere to the rules which he himself had prescribed for his guidance during his term of office. This regulation, whose observance was originally optional with the Prætor, became compulsory with the passage of the *Lex Cornelia*, 67 B. C.; and effectively disposed of the *Edicta Repentina* or *Extraordinaria*, which has reference only to individual cases, and too frequently had been inspired by the caprice

THE OPINIONS OF JULIUS PAULUS ADDRESSED TO HIS SON

the year to compel its production through an interdict, by means of which the party who suppressed it can be forced to produce it. Where the instrument is written either on papyrus or parchment, it comes under the head of a will.

TITLE VIII. CONCERNING THE SUCCESSION OF PERSONS DYING INTESTATE.

(1) ....[1]

(2) ....[1]

(3) ....[1]

(4) ....[1]

(5) ....[1]

(6) ....[1]

(7) ....[1]

(8) ....[1]

(9) ....[1]

(10) ....[1]

(11) ....[1]

(12) ....[1]

(13) ....[1]

(14) The following difference exists between agnates and cognates, namely, cognates are included among agnates, but agnates are not included among cognates; and therefore a paternal uncle is both an agnate and a cognate, but a maternal uncle is a cognate but not an agnate.

(15) ....[1]

(16) ....[1]

(17) ....[1]

(18) Where one brother is dead, his surviving brother has a living son and there is a grandson of the deceased brother, the son of the former will be preferred to the grandson of the latter.

(19) ....[1]

---

or prejudice of the occupant of the Prætorian Tribunal.

In A. D. 131, during the reign of Hadrian, the Prætorian Edict, the interpretation and enforcement of which had previously been largely left to the discretion of the magistrate, acquired new legal authority through express Imperial sanction. Salvius Julianus, one of the most renowned jurists of the age, was ordered by the Emperor to revise the Edict as it then stood, with a view to having it enacted as a law. During the process of revision, many changes appear to have been made, some of them arbitrarily in accordance with the opinions of the compiler, others at the suggestion of the Emperor himself. The result of this was that, as strict construction and rigid application of the terms of the Edict now became obligatory on the Prætor, his equitable jurisdiction was greatly curtailed, often to the serious embarrassment and hardship of litigants, who sought relief in his Court from the severe and inflexible principles prescribed by the Civil Law. — ed.

[1] Original manuscript illegible.

(20) The son of a brother is preferred to the son of a sister, where the property of an intestate estate is concerned.

(21) By the ancient Civil Law, if legal heirs merely enter upon an estate within a hundred days the succession is transferred to the next of kin.

(22) Women beyond the degree of sisters are not admitted to the succession of intestate estates; and this is considered to have been established by the Voconian rule under the Civil Law. The Law of the Twelve Tables, however, admits agnates without this distinction of sex.

(22a) Although women beyond the degree of sisters are not admitted to the succession of intestate estates, they are, nevertheless, not prevented from demanding prætorian possession on the ground of relationship.

(23) The rule of succession does not apply to inheritance by law, and therefore, if a brother dies before entering on an estate, or rejects it, the son of his brother cannot be admitted, although if the succession were lost it would pass to the next of kin.

(24) Anyone who is captured by the enemy and returns under the law of *postliminium*, does not lose his right either as a proper heir or an heir-at-law. It has been decided that the same rule shall apply to those who have been deported to an island or sentenced to penal servitude, if, through the indulgence of the Emperor, they are completely restored to the enjoyment of all their rights.

(25) To act as the heir is to assume the management of some property belonging to an estate with the intention of afterwards claiming it; and hence he is considered to act as an heir who arranges for the cultivation of land belonging to an estate, and who makes use of slaves, animals, and other property forming part of the same.

(26) Where some of several heirs-at-law have neglected to accept an estate, or have been prevented from entering on it for some reason or other, those who did enter on it, or their heirs, will obtain by accrual the shares of any who failed to do so. The rule which applies to an appointed heir who fails to accept an estate, namely, that he can have a substitute, is not applicable in this instance, for a difference exists between a testamentary heir and an heir-at-law.

TITLE IX. ON THE TREBELLIAN DECREE OF THE SENATE.

(1) It is sufficient for mothers — and this includes not only those who are freeborn, but also freedwomen who are Roman citizens — in order to be entitled to the right of children, to have had children three or four times provided the latter were born alive and after full term.

(2) A woman who has three children at a birth is not entitled to this right, for she did not have children three times, but is considered to have had but one birth, unless she should have had them at intervals.

(3) If a woman brings forth a monster or a prodigy, this is of no avail, for creatures having forms contrary to that of the human race are not children.

(4) It has been decided that a mother can take advantage of a child whose membranes serve a double purpose, for the reason that it seems, to a certain extent, to be human.

(5) A child born after the seventh month is an advantage to its mother in this respect, for the rule of the Pythagorean number seems to admit that the child appears to be mature after the seventh or the tenth month.

(6) An abortion or a miscarriage is not considered to constitute a birth.

(7) In order that a freedwoman, who is a Latin, may obtain the right attaching to the birth of a number of children, it is sufficient if she has had four, as in the case of a woman who is free born.

(8) A Latin woman, who is freeborn, obtains the right of Roman citizenship if she has had children three times and is admitted as heir-at-law to her son, for she was not manumitted.

(9) A mother is entitled to the right attaching to the birth of a number of children who, either has, or has had three sons, even though she may not have them, nor has had them. She has them when they survive, she has had them after she has lost them; and she neither has, or has had them, when, through the kindness of the Emperor, she obtains the right attaching to their birth.

TITLE X. ON THE ORPHITIAN DECREE OF THE SENATE.

(1) Children born of promiscuous intercourse are not prevented from claiming the estate of their mother, if she died intestate; because, as their estates pass to their mother so the estate of their mother should vest in them.

(2) Through the operation of the Claudian Decree of the Senate, the estate of a mother who died intestate cannot pass to a daughter who is either a female slave, or a freedwoman; because neither slaves nor freedmen are understood to have mothers under the Civil Law.

(3) Children who are Roman citizens, but not Latins, are admitted as heirs-at-law to the estate of their mother who died intestate; they must, however, be Roman citizens at the time when the intestate estate passed to them, and could be entered on; just as when children become certain that their mother is dead, although they have not been notified, and it is clearly ascertained that she died intestate.

(4) A son cannot acquire the estate of his mother as heir-at-law without entering on the same.

TITLE XI. CONCERNING DEGREES.

(1) In the first degree of the ascending line are the father and the mother; in the first degree of the descending line, are the son and the daughter, and no other persons.

(2) In the second degree of the ascending line are the grandfather and the grandmother; in the second degree of the descending line are the grandson and the granddaughter; in the collateral line are the brother and the sister. These persons are doubled for the grandfather and grandmother on the father's as well as the mother's side, and the grandson and the granddaughter born of the son as well as of the daughter, and the brother and the sister on the father's as well as the mother's side, are included. Moreover, these persons are also doubled in the same order and in the same manner in the succeeding degrees, according to their positions in each degree.

(3) In the third ascending degree are the great-grandfather and the great-grandmother; in the third descending degree the great-grandson and the great-granddaughter; in the collateral degree the son and the daughter of the brother and the sister; the paternal uncle and the paternal aunt, that is to say, the brother and sister of the father, and the maternal uncle and the maternal aunt, that is to say, the brother and sister of the mother.

(4) In the fourth ascending degree are the great-great-grandfather and the great-great-grandmother; in the fourth descending degree the great-great-grandson and the great-great-granddaughter; in the collateral line the grandson and the granddaughter of the brother and the sister, the son and the daughter of the father's brother, that is, the son and daughter of the paternal uncle, the son and daughter of the father's sister, that is the son and daughter of the paternal aunt and the son and daughter of the maternal aunt; although this term of relationship is properly applied to children born of two sisters, to which is added the great paternal uncle

and the great paternal aunt, that is, the brother and sister of the paternal grandfather; and the great maternal uncle and the great maternal aunt, that is, the brother and the sister of both the paternal and the maternal grandmother, and of the maternal grandfather.

(5) In the fifth degree in the ascending line, are included the great-great-great-grandfather, and the great-great-great-grandmother; in the descending line, the great-great-great-grandson, and the great-great-great-granddaughter; in the collateral line the great-grandson and the great-granddaughter of the brother and sister, the paternal uncle of the brother, and the paternal uncle of the sister, the maternal uncle of the brother, and the maternal aunt of the sister, and their children; and then the cousins of both sexes, that is to say, the sons and daughters of the great paternal uncle and the great paternal aunt, and of the great maternal uncle and the great maternal aunt. Next in order of these come the great paternal uncle and the great paternal aunt, the brother and sister of the paternal greatgrandfather, and the great maternal uncle and the great maternal aunt, the brother and sister of the paternal and the maternal greatgrandfather, and the maternal great-grandparents.

(6) In the sixth degree in the ascending line are the great-great-great-great-grandfather and the great-great-great-great-grandmother; in the descending line are the great-great-great-great-grandson and the great-great-great-great-granddaughter, in the collateral line the great-great-great-grandson and the great-great-great-granddaughter of the brother and sister, the paternal uncle of the brother and sister, the maternal uncle and aunts, and the grandson and the granddaughter of cousins, the grandson and granddaughter of the paternal great uncle and the paternal great aunt and of the maternal great uncle and the maternal great aunt, that is, they are more properly called cousins, as the son and the daughter of a cousin are also styled cousins. Next in the collateral line come the son and the daughter of the paternal great-great-uncle, and the paternal great-great-aunt, and of the maternal great-great-uncle, and the maternal great-great-aunt, and the brother and sister of the paternal and maternal great-great-grandfather; and the brother and sister of the paternal and maternal great-great-grandmother, and the maternal great-great-grandparents.

(7) Those who are related in the seventh degree are not designated by peculiar names in either the direct ascending or descending lines; but in the collateral lines are the great-great-grandsons and the great-great-granddaughters of the brother and sister and the cousins or great-great-grandsons and great-great-granddaughters, and their sons and daughters.

(8) Only seven degrees of succession have been established, because in the nature of things neither names can be found nor life be prolonged, for those who succeed.

TITLE XII. CONCERNING MANUMISSIONS.

(1) Where one of his owners manumits a slave held in common he does not render him a Latin, nor still less a Roman citizen, and the share in the slave who, if he had belonged to but one person, would have obtained Roman citizenship, accrues to the other joint owner.

(2) A person who is dumb and deaf cannot liberate a slave under the wand of the Prætor; but he is not forbidden to manumit him in the presence of friends, or by means of a letter. Moreover, in order that the slave may obtain legal freedom, he can be excepted by his owners from the condition of the sale.

(3) A slave who has been subjected to torture in the presence of the governor and does not confess any crime, can receive lawful freedom.

(4) Where freedom is granted to a slave under the terms of a trust it is not annulled by the act of the heir, if he puts in chains the slave whom he was ordered to manumit.

(5) One of the joint-owners of a slave does not prejudice his future freedom by placing him in chains, for among similar opinions the more merciful is preferred to the more severe. It is certainly the part of human reason to favor the wretched, and to say that those are almost innocent whom we cannot declare to be absolutely bad.

(6) A creditor, or a debtor cannot, by placing a slave who has been pledged in chains, put him in the position of an enemy who has surrendered at discretion; for one of them cannot, without the other, cause deterioration of the property pledged.

(7) A slave who has been placed in chains by the order of an insane master or one who is a minor, is not to be classed in the number of persons who have surrendered at discretion, for the reason that neither an insane person nor a minor is capable of exercising good judgment.

(8) Not even if the master himself should place him in chains, will he prejudice his right to freedom; but if he should order this to be done, or should ratify the act of his attorney or agent who have placed him in chains, this will not affect the prospect of his future freedom; even if before he knew that he had been placed in chains, he should approve of his release.

(9) A curator cannot be appointed for a blind man, because he himself can appoint an attorney.

TITLE XIII. CONCERNING GRANTS OF FREEDOM UNDER A TRUST.

(1) Where an heir is appointed on the condition that he will emancipate his children, he is, by all means, required to emancipate them; for in this instance emancipation is considered to be conditional.

(2) Where the party who has been charged with a grant of freedom under the terms of a trust dies, his heirs should be required to bestow it.

(3) If a person at the time of his death grants freedom to his slaves, as follows, namely: "I wish So-and-So and So-and-So to be free, and I appoint them guardians of my children"; the grant of freedom under the trust will be prevented, because wards cannot manumit without the authority of their guardian, and a guardian cannot be appointed for those who already have one. In the meantime, however, wards are considered as being absent, and under the Decree of the Senate freedom can first be granted, and guardianship be established afterwards.

TITLE XIV. ON THE LEX FUFIA CANINIA.

(1) Slaves can be manumitted by will only by name, according to the *Lex Fufia*. They are understood to be properly manumitted by name when the following forms are employed: "Let Stichus be free"; or "I desire my steward", or "the child of my female slave to be free". By the Orphitian Decree of the Senate freedom can be granted just as if the slave had been mentioned by name, for the reference to his occupation and trade makes no change in his designation, unless there are several slaves who discharge the same duties; for then the name should be added in order that it may be clear which one the testator seems to have meant.

(2) Where grants of freedom mentioned in a codicil confirmed by a will agree with those granted by the will, they are considered the most recent because both are confirmed by it whether they precede or follow the will in point of time.

(3) Whenever a number of slaves is referred to on account of the *Lex Fufia Caninia*, fugitives also, whose possession is always supposed to be retained, should be included.

(4) It is provided by the *Lex Fufia Caninia* that a certain number of slaves can be manumitted by will; therefore, where two have been stolen, half of the remainder from three to ten, can be manumitted; from ten to thirty, the third; from thirty to a hundred, the fourth; from a hundred to five hundred, the fifth; but it is not lawful for more than a hundred to be manumitted from the greater number of slaves.

BOOK V

TITLE I. CONCERNING CASES INVOLVING FREEDOM.

(1) Where persons, on account of extreme necessity or through want of food, sell their children, they do not prejudice their rights of freedom, for a freeman can not be valued at any price. Nor can children be pledged or hypothecated by their parents; for which reason any creditor who knowingly permits this to be done shall be deported. The services of children can however be hired.

(2) Manumission, no matter in what way it may take place, does not prejudice true and original free birth.

(3) The division of free born persons made by public authority among slaves belonging to the Treasury, cannot prejudice the right of free birth.

(4) Anyone who, through intimidation and the effect of terror of any kind, falsely declares himself to be a slave before the tribunal of the governor, does not prejudice his condition, if he subsequently defends himself.

(5) Where anyone undertakes to defend a slave, and after proceedings have been instituted to declare him free abandons the case, it has been decided that it can be entirely transferred to another defender, and the first one be judicially punished for his act in betraying the cause of freedom; for where a case involving a man's condition has been undertaken, it cannot be relinquished except under urgent necessity.

TITLE II. CONCERNING USUCAPTION.

(1) We acquire possession by means of both the mind and the body, by our minds through our own exertions, by our bodies through our own exertions or those of others; we cannot, however, obtain possession by mere intention, but we can retain it in this manner, as happens in the case of winter and summer pastures.

(2) Nothing can be acquired for us by free persons who are under our control, but it has been decided that, for the sake of convenience, possession can be acquired for us by an agent. When the principal is absent, anything which is purchased is not acquired for him, unless he subsequently ratifies the act.

(3) Prescription of long time is established where the parties are present, by continuous occupation for the term of ten years; where the parties are absent, by continuous occupation for twenty years.

(4) Prescription for ten or twenty years also runs against public property, in favor of a person who had lawful possession in the beginning, and which was not in the meantime interrupted. The action of public property for damages is granted against those who have neglected to attend to matters of this kind.

(5) If, after a question as to the ownership of property has arisen, it in the meantime passes to a new owner by purchase, and he is not disturbed in its possession for twenty years, he cannot be deprived of it.

TITLE III. CONCERNING ACTS COMMITTED BY A CROWD.

(1) A claim for double damages, if the matter is a pecuniary one, can be brought against those who have either caused injury to anyone, or have been responsible for so doing, as members of a crowd or during the course of a sedition. If, however, any person has been injured by loss of life or limb on this account, extraordinary punishment may be inflicted.[1]

---

[1] *Cognitio extraordinaria*, or extraordinary procedure, consisted in the union of the duties of the judges of law and fact in a single

(2) Where any property obtained from a fire, the ruin of a building, shipwreck, or the plunder of a vessel, has been stolen or concealed, the party who concealed, stole, or took it by violence, can, within a year, be sued for fourfold damages, and, after the lapse of a year, for simple damages.

(3) Those who pillage, break into, or rob the residences or buildings of others, shall be punished with death if the act was committed by an assembled crowd armed with weapons. By the term "weapons" is understood everything by which the safety of a man can be endangered.

(4) Those who harbor the aggressors are punished with the same penalty as the robbers themselves, for the desires of the parties who are not active participants do not differ from that of those who steal, or conceal the property.

(5) Thieves and robbers of baths are generally sentenced to the mines or to labor on the public works; sometimes, however, the sentence of the judge is mitigated on account of the great number of the guilty parties.

(6) Incendiaries who intentionally set fire to property are punished with death. If, however, the fire was caused by the negligence of the occupants of a house, it has been decided that a loss of this kind must be made good by the owner of the property.

TITLE IV. CONCERNING INJURIES.

(1) We suffer injuries either in our bodies or outside of them; in our bodies, by blows and through debauchery; outside of our bodies by insults, and infamous libels, the effect of which is estimated by the position of both the party who suffers it and the party who inflicts it.

(2) An insane person, as well as an infant, are legally incapable of malicious intent and the power to insult, and therefore the action for injuries cannot be brought against them.

(3) If an injury is committed against our children who are under our control, or against our wives, it is to our interest to see that punishment is inflicted; therefore an action can be brought by us, provided the party who committed the act can be shown to have done so to our injury.

(4) A corporeal injury is inflicted when anyone is struck; it is different where adultery is committed, or an accusation is brought for the offence, which is punished judicially, as the forcible violation of modesty is punished capitally.

(5) Those who solicit married women, and those also who interfere with marriages, even if they are unable to consummate their crimes, are extraordinarily punished, on account of their intention to perpetrate acts of injurious debauchery.

(6) The action for injury is based either upon law or custom, or upon both. Punishment is provided by the Law of the Twelve Tables for libellous poems, broken limbs, and fractured bones.

---

official, usually a magistrate of the highest rank. Much was left to his discretion, and his rulings were often arbitrary and noted for their severity in criminal cases. This violation of the ancient principle which had prevailed in Roman judicature from the time of the Republic, was largely due to the disinclination of responsible citizens to serve as *judices* and *recuperatores*, judges of fact, who to a certain extent, exercised the functions of modern jurymen in the courts of the Empire. Although the practice was not unusual when circumstances appeared to demand it, it was first legally authorized by Diocletian in 294, who conferred absolute and sole jurisdiction on the governors of provinces in the hearing of causes brought before their tribunals. This privilege, manifestly susceptible of great abuse by unscrupulous individuals, was afterwards, by a series of enactments, conferred upon the other prominent members of the Roman magistracy. — ed.

(7) So far as custom is concerned, this takes place whenever the damage caused by an act is estimated by the judge according to its nature, and is punished by the infliction of a suitable penalty.

(8) The action for injury arising from both law and custom is established under the *Lex Cornelia*, whenever anyone is beaten, or his house is entered, not by those who are ordinarily called *derectarii*, and who are extraordinarily punished; so that the design of the thief who enters a house — as in the case of the intentional commission of fraud — is punished by the penalty of exile, or sentenced to the mines or to the public works.

(9) Anyone who is civilly convicted of having caused an injury is required to pay the damage and becomes infamous.

(10) An atrocious injury depends either upon the place, time, or person; upon the place, whenever it is committed in public; upon the time, when it is committed by day; upon the person, when it is committed against a senator, a Roman knight, a decurion, or any other person high in authority; and whether a plebeian, or a person of inferior rank commits the injury against a senator, a Roman knight, or a decurion, or whether a plebeian commits the injury against a magistrate, an ædile, or a judge, or against all of them.

(11) Anyone who brings the action for injury for the purpose of causing annoyance is extraordinarily punished; for it has been decided that all calumniators shall be punished by exile, by relegation to an island, or by the loss of their rank.

(12) Persons cannot bring an accusation of injury unless they are present, for the crime which is punished by the action of calumny cannot be prosecuted by others.

(13) An injury is committed against good morals, when anyone smears or bedaubs anyone with manure, filth, or mud; or defiles pipes, reservoirs, or anything else to the public injury. Persons of this kind are generally severely punished.

(14) Anyone who debauches a boy under the age of seventeen, or commits any other outrage on him, whether he is abducted by him or by a corrupt companion; or who solicits a woman or a girl, or does anything for the purpose of corrupting their chastity, or offers his house for that purpose, or gives them any reward in order to persuade them, and the crime is consummated, shall be punished with death; if it is not consummated, he shall be deported to an island, and his profligate accomplices shall suffer the extreme penalty.

(15) Anyone who composes a libellous song to the injury of another, or any poem by which the party may be recognized, shall be deported to an island by the authority of a Decree of the Senate; for it is in the interest of public order that the reputation of everyone should be protected from the infamy caused by vile poetry. He not only composes poetry of this kind who writes satires and epigrams, but also he who composes anything else of any other description. Nothing, however, is provided with reference to a speech composed for the purpose of lawfully prosecuting anyone, or for the arraignment of the opposite party in court, as the person of our adversary should in every way be attacked, but in doing so a certain moderation and judgment should be observed for a man's reputation may also be injured in this way.

(16) A *Psalterium*, as a song is commonly called which is composed and publicly sung for the purpose of disgracing another, causes the infliction of extraordinary punishment upon those who sing, as well as upon those who compose it; and the punishment is the more severe if the dignity of the person should be protected from injury of this kind.

(17) Persons who purchase infamous libels for the purpose of distributing them to insult others are punished extraordinarily, even to the extent of relegation to an island.

(18) A judge should not be abused by appellants, otherwise they are branded with infamy.

(19) Curses and abuse publicly uttered call for the punishment of injury, and when this is inflicted the condemned party becomes infamous.

(20) Not only he who uttered the curses and abuse, becomes infamous if convicted, but also he by whose aid and counsel the act is alleged to have been committed.

(21) Abuse is said to be against good morals when anyone uses obscene language, or exposes the lower part of his person in the presence of a woman; and an act of this kind in consideration of good morals and on account of public virtue, demands punishment of extraordinary severity.

(22) Where a slave has perpetrated an injury or insult, which is atrocious, he shall be condemned to the mines; if, however, it is not serious, after having been scourged, he shall be restored to his master under the penalty of being confined in chains for a time.

TITLE V. CONCERNING THE EFFECT OF DECISIONS AND THE TERMINATION OF ACTIONS AT LAW.

(1) Actions-at-law are decided by those who have the authority and power to do so, or by the authority of persons selected by the parties themselves, and likewise by municipal magistrates up to the amount for which they have the legal right to render judgment; and by those who have been appointed by the Emperor out of the regular order. Moreover, a judge appointed in a case involving a joint promise does not render a final decision, but if a penalty has been promised by the defendants, and the case is afterwards brought into court, the penalty can be collected under the stipulation.

(2) Debtors who have confessed their liability are considered as having judgment rendered against them, and therefore the time for payment is reckoned from the day of the confession.

(3) Anyone can acknowledge his liability in court, not only verbally but in writing, or in any other way whatsoever. He cannot be defeated, however, unless by written evidence, or by that of witnesses.

(4) The pledges of those who have acknowledged their indebtedness can be seized and sold.

(5) A defendant cannot revoke his confession a second time.

(6) A decision rendered in the absence of the other party does not obtain the force of *res judicata*.

(7) When a party is summoned by three letters or proclamations, or by one served for all, or by three public notices, and he does not appear before the court which notified him, or by whose letters or proclamation he was summoned, and a judgment is rendered against him as contumacious, it obtains the authority of a final decision for an appeal can by no means be taken from it.

(7a) An appeal cannot be taken from a judgment rendered against a person for contumacy, nor can it be brought up a second time.

(8) Formerly, a case which had been finally decided could not be brought into court after a long silence, nor could it be revoked on that account. A long term of silence, as in the case of long prescription, runs for ten years, where the parties are present; and is computed at twenty years, when they are absent.

(9) No person who is absent can be condemned in a capital case, nor can one who is absent either accuse or be accused by another.

(10) Where the judge has been deceived by the introduction of forged documents, the renewal of the case

can be legally demanded, provided the decision was pronounced before it was proved that the crime was committed.

(11) An error in calculation frequently takes place and therefore can be reconsidered at any time, if the right is not extinguished by a prolonged silence.

TITLE V.b. CONCERNING THE POSSESSION OF PROPERTY GRANTED BY THE AUTHORITY OF A JUDGE.

(1) Where creditors are placed in possession of the property of a minor for whom no defence is made, they are required to furnish him support until he reaches the age of puberty.

(2) The property of a person who has been captured by the enemy cannot be sold until he returns.

TITLE VI. CONCERNING INTERDICTS.

(1) Interdicts were introduced for the purpose of retaining possession, and by means of them we retain the possession which we already have. To this class belong the interdicts *Uti Possidetis*, which has reference to property attached to the soil, and *Utrubi*, which applies to movable property. In the case of the first, the position of that party is preferable who, at the time that the interdict was issued, had not obtained possession from his adversary, either by force, clandestinely, or by permission of the latter; and in the second, his position is preferable who has obtained possession neither by violence, nor clandestinely, nor by permission, and has retained it for the greater part of the past year.

(2) An interdict, like an action, will lie to prevent anyone from interfering with the public highway, the care of which devolves upon the officials having charge of highways. No one is exempt from repairing highways, still, if a person, while working, obstructs one so that those who pass to and fro are hindered, after the obstruction has been demolished he shall be condemned.

(3) Not only is an interdict available when the owner of property deprives anyone of possession, but also where his family does so; and only two slaves are sufficient to constitute a family.

(4) A person is forcibly ejected, not only where he is terrified through the oppression of a multitude of persons, or intimidated by clubs, darts, or other weapons, but also if he relinquishes possession through apprehension of violence, provided his adversary has entered on the property.

(5) Proceedings cannot be instituted under this interdict by a party who has been forcibly ejected from a ship; but an equitable action for the recovery of property, such as is granted as in the case of goods taken by violence will lie. The same rule also applies where anyone is deprived of a vehicle, or a horse, and if they are not removed, an action for injury is granted.

(6) He also is held to be forcibly ejected who is restrained by violence, and terrified upon the highway, so that he cannot approach his own land.

(7) Anyone who has obtained possession from his adversary either by violence, or clandestinely, or by his consent, can be ejected with impunity.

(8) Where possession of buildings has been obtained by violence, and any property belonging to the same is burned, or any slaves found there die; although this may have occurred without the malicious intent of the party guilty of the violence, still, he who desired to obtain property belonging to another will be condemned to pay the value of what was lost or destroyed.

(9) When water is taken from a stream forming the boundary between neighbors it should first be divided;

and force is forbidden to be exerted against anyone who conducts water from those parts of the stream from which it has been customary for each one of the parties to draw his supply. A pecuniary fine is imposed upon anyone who unlawfully makes use of water belonging to another. The regulation of this matter is part of the duty of the governor.

(10) When an interdict is issued, a certain right of action arises from the fact that anyone who has possession with the consent of another must restore the property; still, a civil action will lie to recover it, as if it had been loaned for use, or especially on the ground that no one should suffer injury on account of the favor which he has granted.

(11) Anyone is considered to have possession by the consent of another, not only where he has asked that it be granted to him by a letter, or in any other way, but also where he has possession through no indication of the consent of the owner, but merely through his sufferance.

(12) The heir of the party who held possession with the consent of another, and still retains it, is considered to hold possession clandestinely, according to the better opinion; for he does not appear to have made any request to that effect, therefore the owner has always the right to claim his property, and there is no ground for an interdict.

(13) Where a tree overhangs the house of another, or the field of a neighbor, so as to obstruct the light, the owner should be notified to trim it; and if, after having been notified to do so, he refuses, the overgrowth of branches may be cut by the neighbor, and this any owner of land whosoever is not prevented from doing.

(14) An interdict as well as an action authorized by the *Lex Favia*, will lie against a party who places a freeman in chains, conceals him, shuts him up, or gives any assistance to enable this to be done; and proceedings under an interdict may also be instituted to compel the party who detains him to produce him under the *Lex Favia*, so that he also may be liable to a pecuniary penalty.

(15) The Divine Pius forbade persons living harmoniously in marriage to be separated by a father. He also forbade a freedman to be separated from his patron, or a son or a daughter from their parents, unless a question arose as to where one of the parties could live more advantageously.

(16) Where all the property which anyone has at present, or may acquire in the future, is hypothecated, neither a concubine, nor a natural son, nor a foster-child, nor any articles which he may have for daily use are included; and therefore an interdict is not issued with reference to them.

TITLE VII. CONCERNING VERBAL OBLIGATIONS.

(1) Stipulations were introduced for the purpose of confirming obligations which are contracted merely by a form of words; and they are so called because by means of them the force of obligations is strengthened, for the ancients used the term *stipulum* to denote firm.

(2) Verbal obligations are contracted between present, but not between absent persons. If, however, it should be stated in an instrument in writing that anyone had made a promise, it is considered the same as if an answer had been made to a preceding interrogation.

(3) If a slave belonging to an usufructuary acquires anything by the property of the latter, or by his own labor, it will belong to the usufructuary; and, moreover, whatever he acquires from any other source, or from the property of the owner, he acquires for the owner.

(4) When, by the act of the promisor, property included in the stipulation is destroyed, an action can be brought under the stipulation just as if the said property was still in existence; and therefore the promisor is

punished by being compelled to pay its value, and especially is this the case where the stipulation was entered into with any fraud on his part.

TITLE VIII. CONCERNING NOVATIONS.

(1) Not only can we ourselves create novations with reference to what is due to us, but we can also do so through others by whom we can stipulate, for instance, through a son under paternal control, or a slave, by giving him orders, or by ratifying his act. It is settled that our attorney can also make a novation by our order.[1]

TITLE IX. CONCERNING STIPULATIONS.

(1) Where an heir was appointed under a condition, and is charged with the substitution of another, he can legally compel the party appointed by him to provide by stipulation that he will not diminish the property belonging to the estate by demanding prætorian possession; for, in this instance, he is compelled to pay double the amount of the profits from the day when the stipulation was entered into. The terms of this differ from those of the former one in which inquiry was made whether the property in question was worth more than a hundred sesterces, and therefore a longer time was established.

(2) The double profits are computed from the day when issue was joined by the party who instituted proceedings, and security was given for costs and damages. Both those who give and receive security and their heirs, attorneys, agents, and sponsors, are included in the same stipulation, as well as the other parties in whose name the promise is made.

(3) Whenever security is given in a stipulation for the payment of a judgment and an action is not brought under it, this does not prevent prosecution under the judgment.

(4) If emancipated children who have been passed over, desire to meddle with the estate of their father, and they remain with those who are still under paternal control, and desire to have the estate of their common father divided before demanding prætorian possession; they should give security for placing all the property in a mass. If they cannot furnish security, they should be immediately compelled to faithfully bring all the property in confusion,[2] with the exception of any *peculium castrense* which may exist.

---

[1] Novation, in Roman jurisprudence, meant something more than the mere extinction or renewal of an obligation, but, as the name implies, had reference to any alteration whatever which either did, or did not, increase the liability of the debtor. There were two kinds, the *novatio privativa*, which operated as a renewal, and disposed of the prior claim; and the *novatio cumulativa*, by means of which a second debt was created, leaving the already existing one in full force. When a new debtor, styled an *expromissor*, assumed the liability of the older one and the latter was, in consequence, released by the creditor, the proceeding was known as "delegation". Consent of the parties was absolutely essential to effect delegation; an *expromissor* could, however, agree to discharge the indebtedness without the knowledge or consent of the debtor.

Novation could not be created by presumption, and unless it was expressly stated that the former debt was cancelled by the new one, it was held to be cumulative, or supplementary, which, properly speaking, was not really a novation. In a transaction of this kind the *animus novandi* must be manifest, as its validity was entirely dependent upon the intention of the parties interested. — ed.

[2] *Confusio*, or merger of obligations, caused them to be extinguished by operation of law when the same person through force of circumstances, came to occupy the position of debtor as well as creditor, and hence the rights of both coincided. This might occur in the inheritance of an estate, where either became the heir of the other, or when the creditor succeeded to the surety, or *vice-versa*. Where the principal alone was affected, the surety was at once released; but if the confusion had reference to the person of the latter it is obvious that the obligation, as far as the liability of the principal was concerned, was not extinguished. — ed.

TITLE X. CONCERNING AUTHORITY FOR MAKING CONTRACTS.

(1) One neighbor should give security to another to provide against impending damage, and sponsors should be added with reference to the damage which might take place.

(2) For the sake of convenience, it should be observed with reference to a party wall, that he whose interest it is to build it ought to do so, but the other joint owner should be compelled to contribute his share of the expense.

TITLE XI. CONCERNING DONATIONS.

(1) Where articles, over and above the dowry, are presented by the mother, in honor of the marriage, to her son-in-law in the presence of her daughter, they are considered to have perfected the donation.

(2) The proof that possession has, or has not been delivered, does not consist so much in law, as in fact; and therefore if I actually have the property in my hands it will be sufficient evidence.

(3) If a father donates anything to his son under paternal control and does not change his mind before he dies, the donation will vest at the death of the father.

(4) Where a donation of the same thing is made to two persons, he has the preference to whom the article was delivered; nor does it make any difference who received it last, or first, or whether certain persons are excepted or not.

(5) A donor who is unwilling, is not compelled to promise with reference to the eviction of the property donated, nor is he rendered liable on this account if he did promise; because the possessor of property which benefits him is barred from bringing the action of eviction by the reason of the law itself.

(6) Any amount can be donated to a person who has rescued another from robbers, or the enemy, provided the donation is not called a reward for extraordinary exertion; because it has been decided that no limit can be placed upon the preservation of safety.

TITLE XII. CONCERNING THE RIGHT OF THE TREASURY AND THE PEOPLE.

(1) The property of one who kills himself on account of the commission of some atrocious crime, is confiscated to the Treasury. If, however, through weariness of life, or shame for indebtedness contracted, or inability to endure suffering caused by disease, he commits this offence, his property is not interfered with, but passes to his heirs by the ordinary rules of succession.

(2) He is deprived of an estate as being unworthy, who prevents anyone from making a will who is connected with, or related to him, and to whom he would succeed if he should die intestate; or intentionally interferes with his rights.

(3) Where a father or a master alleges that a will by which his son or slave is appointed an heir, or is entitled to a legacy, is false, and he does not prove his case, there is ground for confiscation by the Treasury.

(4) It is customary to come to the relief of a minor for the amount that he has lost where he alleges that a will is forged and he does not gain his case, and this is especially true where the action was brought by the advice of a guardian or a curator.

(5) A person is forbidden to hold any office connected with the Treasury in the province in which he was born, in order that he may not appear to favor or oppress his neighbor.

(6) Whenever officials take possession of the property of others, or publish it for sale, or place it under guard without authority of court, the Imperial Steward can be applied to, the wrong redressed, and those responsible for the act sent to the prætorian prefecture to be punished.

(7) A right of action can not be donated to the Treasury to the injury of private persons, nor, if donated, can it be accepted by it.

(8) It is odious to appoint the Emperor an heir for the purpose of litigation, for the power of causing annoyance should not be assumed by Imperial Majesty.

(9) No cause of action arises from a mere promise, and therefore the property of one who boasts that he is going to make the Emperor his heir cannot be confiscated by the Treasury.

(10) It is the privilege of the Treasury to hold the first place among all creditors.

(11) Anyone who is sued by the Treasury should not be summoned by the judge under a copy of any document, but under the original, so that the terms of the contract can be shown. It is settled, however, that an instrument intended to cause vexatious litigation cannot have the force of a just claim in court.

(12) The property of one who is alleged to have counterfeited money is confiscated to the Treasury. If, however, slaves are said to have done this without the knowledge of their master, they shall be put to death; but their master shall not be deprived of any property, for the reason that slaves cannot cause the condition of their master to become worse, unless he happened to know what they were doing.

TITLE XIII. CONCERNING INFORMERS.

(1) All persons are specially prohibited from accusing others, and bringing pecuniary cases to the notice of the Treasury; nor does it make any difference whether those who do this are males or females, slaves, freeborn persons, or freedmen; or whether they denounce their own relatives or strangers; for they, by all means, shall be punished.

(2) Slaves belonging to the Treasury who give information and notice to their owner are not considered to have denounced anyone. Persons who have been suborned are compelled to betray the culprit, in order to prevent a party who cannot denounce anyone himself from doing it through another. Suborners are punished in the same way as informers.

(3) Slaves who have been condemned, and confess the crimes of their masters before or after they have been sentenced, shall under no circumstances be heard; unless they accuse them of high treason.

TITLE XIV. CONCERNING THE INFLICTION OF TORTURE.

(1) Torture is employed in the detection of crime, but a beginning should not be made with its application; and, therefore, in the first place, evidence should be resorted to, and if the party is liable to suspicion, he shall be compelled by torture to reveal his accomplices and crimes.

(2) Where several culprits are implicated in the same offence, they should be examined in such a way as to begin with the one who appears to be more timid than the others, and of tender age.

TITLE XV. CONCERNING WITNESSES.

(1) It has been decided that witnesses who are suspected of partiality, and especially, such as the accuser produces from his own household, or whose low station in life renders them of bad repute, should not be interrogated; for in the case of witnesses, their social position, as well as their dignity, should be considered.

THE OPINIONS OF JULIUS PAULUS ADDRESSED TO HIS SON

(2) Witnesses cannot be examined with reference to anyone related to them by either marriage or blood.

(3) Neither parents, children, patrons, nor freedmen should be admitted to testify against one another, if they are unwilling to do so; for the near relationship of persons generally destroys the truth of evidence.

(4) Witnesses cannot be interrogated against documentary evidence unless its genuineness has previously been alleged to be doubtful.

(5) Witnesses who have testified falsely, or in different ways or have betrayed either party in the case, are either sent into exile, relegated to an island, or dismissed from the *curia*.

(6) Torture is not applied in pecuniary matters, unless when an investigation is made with reference to property belonging to an estate; other things, however, are established by oath, or by the evidence of witnesses.

TITLE XVI. CONCERNING THE TORTURE OF SLAVES.

(1) The rule of equity plainly shows that a slave can be interrogated with reference to his own acts, and against himself; for no obstacle should be placed in the way of him who lends or deposits anything by a slave without obtaining security.

(2) A judge having jurisdiction of guardianship, as well as the *Centumviri*, can apply torture to slaves belonging to an estate if they cannot otherwise obtain information concerning the property of the estate, or the honor of the family.

(3) A slave belonging to one master cannot be tortured against the person of another, unless this is done separately; and it is not permitted if his owner is unwilling, unless the informer, who has an interest in proving what he claims, is ready to pay the value of the slave to the amount estimated by his owner, or to make good any deterioration which he may be undergone by the slave.

(4) No attention shall be paid to a slave who voluntarily makes any confession with reference to his master, for where matters are in doubt, it is not proper that the safety of masters should depend upon the discretion of their slaves.

(5) Slaves cannot be interrogated against their masters by governors or public prosecutors, either in pecuniary or capital cases.

(6) A slave owned in common cannot be tortured in a case involving the life of either of his masters.

(7) Where anyone purchases a slave in order to prevent his being tortured to obtain evidence against him, the slave can be interrogated after the purchase money has been returned.

(8) A slave cannot be interrogated in a case involving the life of the master by whom he was sold, and in whose service he was for some time, through respect for his former master.

(9) When a slave has been manumitted in order to avoid his being put to the torture, this can still be done.

(10) No faith should be placed in the evidence obtained by the torture of a robber, whom someone has offered as having made a confession with reference to himself; unless this is shown to have been done for the purpose of concealing the guilty knowledge of the crime which he shared with the defendant.

(11) An accuser cannot bring an accusation by another, nor can one accused person be defended by another; unless a patron accuses his freedman of ingratitude, or a defence is made during the absence of the party accused.

(12) If a defendant is alleged to have been acquitted on account of money paid to the judge, and this should be proved against him, he shall be sentenced to the same penalty to which the defendant could have been sentenced.

(13) It should be determined by the nature of the crime which has been committed, whether a person who has been convicted may, or may not, be tortured.

(14) Accusers should be compelled to notify defendants of what crimes they are accused; for it is necessary that they should know for what offences they will be required to answer.

TITLE XVII. CONCERNING ACQUITTALS.

(1) An acquittal is the destruction, oblivion, or extinction of an accusation.

(2) After a public acquittal a defendant can again be prosecuted by his informer within thirty days, but after that time this cannot be done.

(3) Extreme punishments are crucifixion, burning alive, beheading; the penalties for less serious offences are condemnation to the mines, contests with gladiators, deportation; the mildest punishments are relegation, exile, labor on the public works, confinement in chains. Those who are sentenced to death must be executed within a year.

TITLE XVIII. CONCERNING CATTLE THIEVES.

(1) Cattle thieves are those who drive away one horse or two mares, or the same number of oxen, or ten sheep or goats, or five hogs. Anyone who drives away an animal within the aforesaid number shall be sued for double or quadruple its value, according to his rank, as a penalty for theft; or, after having been beaten with rods, he shall be sentenced to labor on the public works for a year; or, if he is a slave, he shall be restored to his master to be placed in chains.

(2) . . . .[1]

(3) If anyone drives away cattle, the ownership of which is in litigation, he shall be brought into court, and if convicted, shall be sentenced to pay double or quadruple their value as a thief.

(4) . . . .[1]

TITLE XIX. CONCERNING SACRILEGE.

(1) Persons who break into a temple at night for the purpose of robbery and plunder, shall be thrown to wild beasts; where, however, during the day they steal anything from a temple which can be easily carried off, if they are of high rank, they shall be deported, if of inferior station, they shall be sentenced to the mines.

TITLE XX. CONCERNING INCENDIARIES.

(1) Any persons who cause fires in a town for the purpose of plunder shall be punished with death.

(2) Those who set fire to a house or country residence through enmity, if they are of low rank, shall be sentenced to the mines or to labor on the public works; those of higher rank shall be relegated to an island.

(3) Where fires are accidental, or where, through the neglect of the person who starts them, they are carried by the wind, and spread to the fields of a neighbor, and growing grain, vines, olives, or fruit trees are destroyed, the estimated damage which has been caused must be made good.

---

[1] Original manuscript illegible.

(4) If a slave started the fire, and his master is responsible, the damage shall be made good through his surrender by way of reparation.

(5) Those who maliciously set fire to growing crops of grain, or vines, or olive trees, if of inferior station, shall be sentenced to the mines, if of superior rank, shall be relegated to an island.

(6) Those who cut down fruit trees at night are generally sentenced to labor on the public works for a term of years, or, if they are of superior rank, are either compelled to make good the damage, or are expelled from their *curia*, or relegated.

TITLE XXI. CONCERNING SOOTHSAYERS AND ASTROLOGERS.

(1) It has been decided that soothsayers who assume the characteristics of divinity, shall be expelled from the city to prevent public morals from being corrupted through human credulity entertaining faith in anything of this kind, for there is no doubt that the popular mind is disturbed by these things. Therefore, such persons, after having been beaten with rods, are driven from the city; and if they continue to practise their arts, they are either publicly placed in chains, or deported to an island, or relegated.

(2) Those who introduce new religious doctrines which are unknown to use or reason, and by which the minds of men are influenced, if they are of higher rank, shall be deported, if of inferior station, they shall be punished with death.

(3) Those who consult astrologers, male or female soothsayers, or diviners, with reference to the life of the Emperor or the safety of the State, shall be punished with death, together with the party who answered their questions.

(4) Every one should abstain not only from divination but also from the books teaching that science. If slaves consult a soothsayer with reference to the life of their master, they shall be subjected to extreme punishment, that is to say, to crucifixion; and if those who are consulted give any answer, they shall either be sentenced to the mines, or deported to an island.

TITLE XXII. CONCERNING SEDITIOUS PERSONS.

(1) The authors of sedition and tumult, or those who stir up the people, shall, according to their rank, either be crucified, thrown to wild beasts, or deported to an island.

(2) Those who dig up, or plow out landmarks, or overturn trees used for that purpose; if they are slaves, and commit the act voluntarily, shall be sentenced to the mines; persons of inferior rank shall be sentenced to labor on the public works; those of higher rank, after having been deprived of the third part of their property, shall be relegated to an island, or exiled.

(3) Roman citizens who permit either themselves or their slaves to be circumcised in accordance with the Jewish rite, after having had their property confiscated, shall be relegated to an island for life; and the physicians who performed the operation shall be put to death.[1]

---

[1] The rite of circumcision is of remote antiquity, and is a purely hygienic measure, whose observance was compelled by its intimate association with religion. It is supposed to have first been practised by the Phoenicians, from whom the Egyptians and other nations derived it. So important was it considered by the denizens of the Valley of the Nile that foreigners, even residing temporarily in Egypt, were forced to submit to its performance. Its practice is one of the cardinal precepts of Islamism, and was well known to the people of pagan Arabia. Abraham was ninety-nine years old when the Lord ordered him to be circumcised. (Genesis XVII, 24) ; and so strictly was the custom observed by his descendants that during mediæval times, when Jews occasionally apostatized to Christianity, their coreligionists circumcised them after death. The rite is wide spread and extends to the savage and semi-barbarous nations of Africa, Asia, America, and Australia. Its adoption as a sanitary precaution, confirmed by the experience of ages, is to-day recommended by all

(4) If Jews circumcise slaves whom they have purchased and who belong to another nation, they shall either be deported or capitally punished.

TITLE XXIII. ON THE LEX CORNELIA HAVING REFERENCE TO ASSASSINS AND POISONERS.

(1) The *Lex Cornelia* imposes the penalty of deportation upon anyone who kills a man, if he does so with a weapon for the purpose of stealing his property; or if he has in his possession, sells, or prepares poison for the purpose of killing another; or if he gives false testimony through which anyone might lose his life, or which might afford occasion for his death. It has been decided that persons of superior rank who commit crimes of this kind shall be capitally punished, and those of inferior rank shall be crucified, or thrown to wild beasts.

(2) ....[1]

(3) A man who kills another is sometimes acquitted, and one who does not kill is convicted of homicide; for the advice of everyone, and not his mere act should be punished. Therefore, a person who intends to kill another, but fails to perpetrate the crime on account of some fortuitous circumstance, is punished as a homicide, and he who accidentally, and negligently kills a man by throwing a weapon is acquitted.

(4) ....[1]

(5) ....[1]

(6) ....[1]

(7) ....[1]

(8) It has been decided that a person who kills a robber making an attack upon him, or any person whomsoever who attacks him for the purpose of committing the crime against nature, cannot be punished; for one of them defends his life, and the other his chastity from a public crime.

(9) ....[1]

(10) A judge who accepts money for a decision against the life or property of anyone, after having been deprived of his possessions, shall be deported to an island.

(11) The instigators of a murder are punished as homicides.

(12) If a person who is trimming a tree throws down a branch, and does not give warning so that it may be avoided, and a passer-by is killed by being struck with it, although the party responsible may not strictly come within the provisions of the law, he shall still be sentenced to the mines.

(13) Any one who castrates, or procures the castration of a man against his consent, either for the purpose of debauchery, or for reward, whether he is a slave or a freeman, shall be punished with death. Persons of higher rank shall be deported to an island, after their property has been confiscated.

(14) Persons who administer potions for the purpose of causing abortion, or love philtres, even if they do

---

well-informed and intelligent physicians. It was severely punished by the Canon Law, and has always been a favorite subject of ecclesiastical reprobation.

The extreme penalty was denounced by the Visigoths against Jews who either performed the ceremony of circumcision, or permitted it to be done. (For. Jud. XII, II, 7.) It was not specifically punishable at Common Law. — ed.

[1] Original manuscript illegible.

THE OPINIONS OF JULIUS PAULUS ADDRESSED TO HIS SON

not do so maliciously, still, because the act affords a bad example, shall if of inferior rank, be sentenced to the mines; if of superior rank, they shall be relegated to an island, after having been deprived of their property. Where, however, the man or the woman loses his or her life in consequence of their act they shall undergo the extreme penalty.

(15) Persons who celebrate, or cause to be celebrated impious or nocturnal rites, so as to enchant, bewitch, or bind anyone, shall be crucified, or thrown to wild beasts.

(16) Anyone who sacrifices a man, or attempts to obtain auspices by means of his blood, or pollutes a shrine or a temple, shall be thrown to wild beasts, or, if he is of superior rank, shall be punished with death.

(17) It has been decided that persons who are addicted to the art of magic, shall suffer extreme punishment; that is to say they shall be thrown to wild beasts, or crucified. Magicians themselves shall be burned alive.

(18) No one shall be permitted to have books on the art of magic in his possession, and when they are found with anyone, they shall be publicly burnt, and those who have them, after being deprived of their property, if they are of superior rank shall be deported to an island, and if they are of inferior station shall be put to death; for not only is the practice of this art prohibited, but also the knowledge of the same.

(19) If a man dies from the effects of a drug which is administered for the preservation of health, or as a remedy for disease, and the party who administered it is of superior rank, he shall be relegated to an island, and if he is of inferior station, he shall be punished capitally.

TITLE XXIV. ON THE LEX POMPEIA RELATING TO PARRICIDES.

(1) He who kills his father, his mother, his grandfather, his grandmother, his brother, his sister, his paternal or maternal uncle or aunt, his male or female cousin, a wife, a husband, a son-in-law, a mother-in-law, a stepfather, a step-son, a step-daughter, a patron or a patroness, is liable under the *Lex Pompeia* having reference to parricides. Anyone who kills his or her father or mother, grandfather or grandmother, brother or sister, patron or patroness, although they were formerly sewed up in a sack and thrown into the sea, are at present burned alive, or abandoned to wild beasts.

TITLE XXV. ON THE LEX CORNELIA HAVING REFERENCE TO WILLS.

(1) Anyone who knowingly and maliciously writes or reads publicly, substitutes, suppresses, removes, re-seals, or erases a will, or any other written instrument; and anyone who engraves a false seal, or makes one, or impresses it, or exhibits it; and anyone who counterfeits gold or silver money, or washes, melts, scrapes, spoils, or adulterates any coin bearing the impression of the face of the Emperor, or refuses to accept it, unless it is counterfeit, shall, if of superior rank, be deported to an island, and if of inferior station, be sentenced to the mines, or punished capitally. Slaves if manumitted after the crime has been perpetrated, shall be crucified.

(2) Anyone who receives or pays money for the purpose of giving false testimony, or to suppress that which is true; or who corrupts, or attempts to corrupt, a judge, in order to induce him either to render, or to not render a decision, shall, if of inferior station, be punished with death; and if of superior rank, shall be deported to an island, along with the judge, after the confiscation of their property.

(3) . . . .[1]

(4) A judge who renders a decision in opposition to an Imperial Constitution, or contrary to a public law which was read in his presence, shall be deported to an island.

---

[1] Original manuscript illegible.

(5) Anyone who knowingly and maliciously, and for the purpose of defrauding another, erases, changes, substitutes, or signs any register, decree, petition, public record, attestation, bond, note, or letter; or anyone who covers brass with gold or silver, or while melting silver or gold, substitutes brass or tin for it, shall be punished with the penalty for forgery.

(6) The Senate decreed that tablets containing either public or private contracts should be signed by the witnesses summoned, in such a way that having been perforated from the upper margin to the centre, they should be fastened with a triple cord; and that wax seals should be impressed upon the cord so that the writing contained therein might be preserved unimpaired. Where a tablet is produced which is sealed in any other way it has no force or effect.

(7) Anyone who opens, reads publicly, or reseals, the will of a person who is still living, is liable to the penalty imposed by the *Lex Cornelia*; and, in general, persons of inferior station who are guilty of this offence are condemned to the mines, and those of higher rank are deported to an island.

(8) When anyone proves that the contents of a legal instrument belonging to him has been betrayed to his adversary, either by his attorney or his agent, the said attorney or agent, if of inferior station, shall be condemned to the mines, and if of superior rank, shall be deprived of half his property, and relegated for life.

(9) If anyone should reveal the contents of, or deliver any written instrument deposited with him for safe keeping to the other party or adversary in the case during the absence of the owner, the culprit shall either be condemned to the mines, or relegated to an island, according to his condition.[1]

(10) Anyone who knowingly and maliciously makes use of forged instruments, decrees, letters, or rescripts, shall be punished with the penalty for forgery; that is to say, if he is of inferior station, he shall be condemned to the mines, and if he is of superior rank, he shall be deported to an island.

(11) Anyone who assumes a false name, race, or parentage, for the purpose of appropriating and possessing property belonging to another, shall be punished under the *Lex Cornelia* relating to forgery.

(12) Those who make use of the insignia of a higher rank than that to which they are entitled, or pretend to belong to the army for the purpose of terrifying or oppressing anyone; if they are of inferior station, shall be punished with death, and if they are of superior rank shall be deported to an island.

(13) Where anyone by means of false representations of his friendship or intimacy with a judge, sells his decisions, or pretends to do so anything in his name, he shall after conviction be either relegated or executed, according to the gravity of his offence.

TITLE XXVI. ON THE LEX JULIA RELATING TO PUBLIC AND PRIVATE VIOLENCE.

(1) Anyone invested with authority who puts to death or orders to be put to death, tortures, scourges, condemns, or directs a Roman citizen who first appealed to the people, and has now appealed to the Emperor to be publicly placed in chains, shall be condemned under the *Lex Julia* relating to public violence. The punishment of this crime is death, where the parties are of inferior station; deportation to an island, where they are of superior rank.

---

[1] The betrayal of secrets by one to whom they had been entrusted was punished by the *Partidas* with perpetual exile and the confiscation of property. (*Las Siete Partidas* VII, VII, I, 6.) The laws of the nations of Continental Europe on this question generally relate to privileged communications. (*Cód. Pénal de France*, Art. 378; *Cód. Pénal de España*, Arts. 512, 513; *Cod. Penale, d'Italia*, Art. 161; *Strafgesetzbuch für das Deutsche Reich*, Art. 300; *Wetboek van Strafrecht*, Art. 272.) — ed.

(2) Those are excepted from the operation of this law who exercise the art of actors, together with those who have been tried and have acknowledged their guilt, and persons who are ordered to be placed in prison because they did not obey the magistrate who stated the law; and individuals who commit acts against the public welfare; as well as military tribunals, and the commanders of fleets and of the wings of the army, so that military offences may be punished by them without any impediment arising from the *Lex Julia*.

(3) Anyone who, with the assistance of armed men, ejects or forcibly deprives another of the possession of a villa, or a field, or besieges or shuts him up therein, or, in order that this may be done, either employs, hires, or leads a body of men; or sets fire to property while in a crowd, an assembly, or a mob or during a sedition; or forbids the funeral rites or burial of anyone to take place; or interferes with, or disturbs funeral ceremonies; or receives, conceals, or harbors anyone interdicted from water and fire; or who, appearing armed in public and in company with armed men, besieges, surrounds, closes, or occupies, any temple, gate, or other public property; is liable under the *Lex Julia* relating to public and private violence. All persons convicted of this offence, if they are of superior rank, shall be deprived of the third part of their possessions and relegated to an island; if they are of inferior station, they shall be condemned to the mines.

(4) If a creditor, whose claim is in writing, should, without the order of the governor, forcibly seize as a pledge any property of his debtor which was not encumbered to him; he violates the *Lex Julia* relating to private violence. A creditor, however, without invoking the authority of court, is not prevented from claiming and seizing any property which was pledged or hypothecated, and deposited with him.

TITLE XXVII. ON THE LEX JULIA RELATING TO PECULATION.

(1) If anyone appropriates, steals, exchanges, or converts to his own use money belonging to the Public Treasury, he shall be condemned to pay fourfold the amount which he took.

TITLE XXVIII. ON THE LEX JULIA RELATING TO EXTORTION.

(1) Where judges are said to have been corrupted with money, they are generally either removed by the governor from their *curia*, or sent into exile, or relegated for a certain time.

TITLE XXIX. ON THE LEX JULIA RELATING TO TREASON.

(1) He by whose aid or advice arms have been taken up against the Emperor or the State, or an army is led into an ambuscade; or where anyone, without the order of the Emperor, carries on war, or enrolls, or prepares an army, or solicits soldiers to desert the Emperor, is liable under the *Lex Julia* relating to treason. Formerly, persons of this kind were interdicted from water and fire for life; but now those of inferior station are thrown to wild beasts, or burned alive, and those of superior rank are capitally punished. This crime is not only perpetrated by the act itself, but is aggravated by the utterance of impious words and maledictions.

(2) In the trial of anyone accused of treason inquiry should first be made with what resources, as a member of what faction, and through the instigation of what persons, he committed the offence; for a person accused of the crime should be punished, not under the pretext of flattering anyone, but on account of what he himself has done; hence, when he is examined his rank will not exempt him from torture.

TITLE XXX.a. ON THE LEX JULIA RELATING TO CORRUPT INTRIGUING FOR OFFICE.

(1) Where anyone desiring to obtain the office of magistrate or priest of the province, collects a mob to secure their votes, or assembles slaves, or calls together any other crowd of persons, he shall, if convicted, be deported to an island as a person guilty of having employed public violence.

TITLE XXX.b. ON THE LEX FAVIA.

(1) . . . .[1]

(2) . . . .[1]

TITLE XXXI. CONCERNING MILITARY PUNISHMENTS.

(1) If a soldier, through having received money, released a prisoner, he shall be punished with death; and inquiry should certainly be made of what offence the party released was accused.

(2) Anyone who by means of superior force releases a prisoner from the custody of a soldier shall be capitally punished.

TITLE XXXII. WHEN AN APPEAL CAN BE TAKEN.

(1) Whenever an oath is demanded, an appeal should be taken at the time when it is tendered, and not when it is made.

TITLE XXXIII. CONCERNING THE SECURITIES AND THE PENALTIES OF APPEALS.

(1) In order that no one may have full and free right to retract and revoke an opinion rendered, both a penalty and certain requirements with reference to time have been imposed upon appellants. To avoid improper appeals from being taken, the term of five days has been prescribed for the purpose of furnishing security for the payment of a penalty in an appeal. Therefore, a party who resides in the place where he appealed, should furnish security so that five continuous days may be reckoned from the day when the order was received; and if he should be at a distance from that place, five days are allowed for the journey, and are computed in addition to the one on which he received the order.

(2) In order that no one may be taken unawares by the words employed in furnishing security, it is very desirable that the penalty itself, or some other property in its stead should be deposited; for it is not necessary that the party should have a sponsor, or give a guarantor or a surety, or even be present, but if judgment is rendered against him, he will lose what he deposited.

(3) Whenever security is given for a penalty in an appeal, one or more sureties who are solvent may be furnished; for it is sufficient for even one who is solvent to be provided to insure the payment of the penalty.

(4) Where several parties appeal one bond is sufficient, and if only one person furnishes security he provides for all.

(5) Where an appeal is taken from several decisions separate bonds are required, and security should be furnished for each penalty.

(6) The amount of the penalty for which each party must furnish security should be expressly stated in the bond, so that each one may know who is bound by the stipulation; otherwise, security will not be considered to have been legally given.

(7) If a defender appeals, he should provide security for the third of the amount involved in the case.

---

[1] Original manuscript illegible.

(8) The better opinion is that, in all pecuniary cases, security must be furnished for the third of the sum in question.

TITLE XXXIV. CONCERNING PROCEEDINGS SENT UP ON APPEAL.

(1) Notice of proceedings sent up on appeal is served by the party who takes the appeal on him who should be notified; which notice is commonly called a summons, and acceptance of the same should be officially made within five days.

(2) A party who does not demand or receive notice of the case sent up on appeal, or make the proper return, is barred by prescription from proceeding further, and is compelled to pay the penalty of the appeal.

TITLE XXXV. CONCERNING THE RETURN OF CASES WHICH HAVE BEEN APPEALED.

(1) We can only ourselves, in person, prosecute an appeal taken for the purpose of establishing the condition of a party in a capital case; for no one who is absent can either be reduced to slavery, or condemned to death.

(2) It has been decided that appeals made for the purpose of delay, and those taken by avengers, and persons who have confessed, cannot be received.

(3) The party who appeals should not do so with abuse of the judge who decided the case; and therefore, when it is done in this way, it shall be punished in the discretion of the Emperor.

TITLE XXXVI. WHAT SHOULD BE OBSERVED AFTER AN APPEAL.

(1) It is settled that whenever a party in possession takes an appeal the mesne profits shall be deposited. If, however, the plaintiff appeals the profits shall not be deposited, nor can security for them legally be demanded.

(2) Where an appeal is taken with reference to urban estates or slaves their hire or wages, and the freight also (if the proceedings relate to a ship) are usually deposited.

TITLE XXXVII. CONCERNING THE MERITS OF APPEALS.

(1) It should by all means be established that, where an appeal is decided to be unjust, not the mere amount, but fourfold the expenses incurred by the adversary in defending the case, should be paid by the other party.

END OF THE OPINIONS OF PAULUS.

GENERAL INDEX

GENERAL INDEX

(Page references inside parentheses refer to Volume I of
S. P. Scott's 1932 publication of **The Civil Law**.)

-A-

ABSENT, person, when liable, 86 (169).
ACCOUNT BOOK, liability incurred by witness in, different claims recorded in, 85, 86 (168,169).
ACCUSATIONS, how made, 157 (261, 262).
ACQUITTAL, meaning of, 206 (323).
ACTIO DE PECULIO, why introduced, 109 (198).
ACTIO EXERCITORIA, when it lies, 108, 109 (198).
ACTIO INSTITORIA, nature of, 108, 109 (198).
ACTIO TRIBUTORIA, against whom brought, 108, 109 (198).
ACTION, to which heirs entitled under a trust, 68 (146); decree of Senate relating to, 68 (146); relating to Roman citizenship, 103 (191); in loss of civil rights, 103 (191).
ACTION AT LAW, decision of, 199 (314); cause of, 199 (314).
ADOPTED.CHILDREN, when emancipated, strangers, 55 (129).
ADOPTION, how obtained, 29 (96); deprives parent of authority, 32 (101); of independent son, 55 (129); confers parental authority, 133 (230); methods of, 133 (230); who capable of, 133 (231); how effected, 134 (234); rules concerning, 135 (234); who can adopt, 136,137 (235); kinds of, 137 (236); who not susceptible of, 137 (236); when applicable to ward, 138 (237); gives right of agnation, 138, 139 (237, 238); rank not diminished by, 140 (239); not available a second time, 140 (239); when illegal may be confirmed by emperor, 140 (239).
AGENCY, how established, 88 (172); voluntary, operation of, 156 (260); liability for, 156 (260).
AGNATES, who they are, 35,46 (104,118); who entitled to guardianship, 36 (105); curator of insane person can alienate property, 46 (118); not succeeded by next agnate in degree, 72 (151); civilly dead, not admitted to an estate, 73 (152); definition of, 134 (232); not cessionary guardians, 135 (233); acceptance by, 149,150 (251, 252); appointment of agents, 156 (260).
AGNATION, right of extinguished by loss of civil rights, 35 (104).
ALIEN, bound by claims, 86 (169); claim belongs to Law of Nations, 86 (169); as to claims on account book, 86 (169); under Civil Law, 86 (169); liability of, 86 (169); cannot acquire property by usucaption, 94 (163).
ALLUVION, law of, 47 (119).
APPEAL, how taken, 212 (331).
ARREST, by plaintiff, 3 (57).
ARROGATION, only at Rome, and who capable of, 133 (231).
ARSON, penalty for, 11, 206-207, 211 (70, 324, 329).
ASCENDANT, legal guardianship by, 36 (106).
ASSEMBLY of people forbidden, when, 14 (76).
ATTORNEY, who excluded as, 155 (259); woman can act as an, 155 (259).

-B-

BANKER, action by, must take set-off in, 107 (197).

217

BANKRUPT, purchase of estate of, 107 (197); set-off only allowed when debt due, 107 (197); amount of the indebtedness of inserted in statement of claim, 107 (197).

BASTARDS, who are, 130 (227); follow mother, 131 (228).

BENEFICIARY, of a trust can be charged with one in favor of another, 70 (148).

BEQUEST, what property object of, 61 (138); by permission, form of, 63 (140); by preferred legacy, how made, 63 (140); when right given to larger share of than heir entitled to, 64 (141); when made to stranger, void, 64 (141); limited to property of testator, 64 (141); when property held by quiritarian right to, 65 (142); of same property of two or more legatees, 65 (142); before heir appointed, void, 65 (143); difference between those left under a trust and those left directly, 70 (148).

BETROTHALS, when legal, 169 (276).

BONA FIDE ACTIONS, what they are, 107 (197).

BOOKS OF PARCHMENTS, ownership of, 48 (120); rule opposite with paintings, 48 (120).

BOOTY, acquired by natural law, 47 (119).

BOUNDARY, settlement of, 11 (72).

BRONZE AND BALANCE, sale by, 91 (175).

BUILDING MATERIALS, appropriation of, 10 (69).

-C-

CALUMNY, what it is, 157 (261).

CATTLE THIEVES, penalty of, 206 (323).

CHATTELS, not readily acquired by usucaption, 45 (116); production of in court, 100 (187); made of proceeding in action for, 100 (187); when a party brought into court because of, 100 (187).

CHILDREN, paternal control of, 24 (89); follow condition of mother, 27 (93); status of, female citizen who becomes a slave, 28 (95); natural and adoptive subject to paternal control, 29 (96); adoption of by popular vote, 29 (96); how freed from paternal authority, 31 (99); adoption of one who has been convicted of crime, interdicted from fire and water, 32 (100); released when priests, or vestal virgins, 32 (100); of colonists released, 32 (100); also those emancipated, 32 (100); sale of by father, 32 (100); when passed over, testament valid, 53 (127); who are Roman citizens and independent, 55 (129); called to the succession by Praetor, 73 (153); illegitimate, who are, 130 (227); follow mother, 131 (228); who are Latin, 131 (228); of slaves, 171 (279).

CIRCUMCISION, penalty for, 207-208 (325).

CIVIL LAW, what it consists of, 17 (81).

CIVIL RIGHTS, loss of, what it is, 35 (104); division of, 35-36 (104); forfeiture of, 135 (233).

CLAUDIAN DECREE OF THE SENATE, effect of, 27 (93).

COEMPTION, marriage by, 30 (97); method of, 30 (98); fiduciary, for what purpose, 30 (98); and mancipation, difference between, 31 (99); with stranger, effect of, 33 (102); persons sold by are slaves, 33 (102).

COGNATES, when not admitted, 73 (153).

CO-HEIRS, rights of, 9 (67).

CONCEALING stolen goods, penalty, 93 (178),

CONCUBINE, when forbidden, 169 (277).

CONFUSION, what it is, 202 (318).

CONTINUANCE, causes for, 4 (59).

CONTRACTS, different kinds of, 80-81 (162); obligations of, 155 (259); *bona fide*, 155 (259).

COUNCIL OF ROME, composition of, 20 (84).

COURT, appearance in, 3 (57).
CRETIO, meaning and derivation of, 58 (133).
CROP, penalty for destruction of, 11 (70).
CURATOR, when appointed, 40 (110); kinds of, 136 (235); for whom appointed, 137 (235).
CUSTOMS, what they are, 127 (223).

-D-

DAMAGE, liability for, 11 (69); by water, how settled, 11-12 (72); unlawful, action for, 95 (181); to property, action for, 96 (182); when it lies, 96 (182).
DEBTOR, sale of property of, when allowed, 79 (161); arrest of, 101 (188).
DECISION, before sunset, 4 (58).
DECREES, what they are, 118 (211).
DEDITITII, who they were, 19, 128 (84, 224); disabilities of, 21 (85).
DEFENDANT, when can resist arrest, 101 (189); summons of, 123 (218).
DELIBERATION, for acceptance of estate, time for, how computed, reason for, 59 (134).
DELIVERY, obligations for, 81 (162).
DEPOSIT, when used, theft, 93 (179); action on, two formulas of, 106, 107 (196); no set-off for, 166 (273)
DEPOSITARY, fraud by, 95 (181).
DETECTION, by dish and girdle, 6 (61).
DETENTION, of property, when legal, 101 (189).
DISINHERITANCE, necessary form of, 54 (128).
DIVORCE, reason must be given for, 11 (69).
DONATION, by husband and wife, 171 (279); *mortis causa,* 186 (297); when forfeited, 203 (319); when made to two persons, 203 (319).
DOWRY, how obtained, 131 (228).
DUPLICATIO, what it is, 116 (209).

-E-

EMANCIPATED DAUGHTER, rule concerning, 53-54 (127).
EMANCIPATION, effect of, 172 (280).
ERROR, in marriage with foreigner, consequences of, 25-27 (91-93).
ESTATE, not subject to sale, when, 41-42 (112); surrender of by testamentary heir, when void, 44 (114, 115); when rejected, 61 (132); must be formally accepted by heir, 63 (134); distribution of profit and loss *pro* rate, 68 (146); belongs to agnates when no proper heirs, 72 (151); of freedmen, division of per capita, 77 (158); of criminal freedmen granted to patrons, 79 (160); rejection of, 188 (300); how effected, 188 (300); when forbidden, 188 (300).
EUNUCHS, can adopt, 29 (96).
EXCEPTIONS, how drawn up, 114 (207); peremptory always valid, dilatory for a time, 114 (207).
EXPENSES, kinds of, 132 (229); definitions of, 132 (229, 230).

-F-

FALLEN FRUIT, right to, 11 (72).
FATHER, power of over son, 7 (64); absolute right of to dispose of estate, 9 (66); adopter can give adopted son in adoption, 29 (96); when considered to have reserved authority, 34 (102)
FEMALE, alone in hand of another, 30 (97); how disinherited, 54 (128).

FEMALE AGNATES, called in the third degree, 73 (153).
FEMALE CHILDREN of slave mother, property of master, 28 (94).
FICTIONS, in personal action, 102 (190); in certain formulas, 102 (190); in bankruptcy, 103 (191); in Publician Action, 103 (191); in Roman citizenship, 103 (191); in loss of civil rights, 103 (191).
FIDUCIARY GUARDIANSHIP, what it is, 36, 37 (105, 106).
FIDUCIARY OWNERSHIP, when contracted, 46 (118).
FORM of bequest of freedom, 70 (148).
FORMULA, division of, 104 (192); ground of action in, statement of case assigned by judge in authority granted to dismiss action, 104 (192); actions of law and fact in, 104 (192); duty of Praetor in use of, 105 (193); judgment for unliquidated damages in, 105 (193); rules for judge, 105 (194); must be certain, 106 (195).
FORMULARY SYSTEM, suit can be brought for legacies under, 71 (149).
FRAUD, liability for, 157 (262); expenses, how recovered, 163 (267).
FRAUDULENT CLAIM TO PROPERTY, penalty for making, 14 (77).
FREEDMAN, cannot pass over his patron in will, 75 (155); when obtain citizenship without consent of patrons, right of, 79 (160); classes of, 127 (223); various kinds of manumissions of, 127 (223); estates of, how divided, 150, 177 (252, 286); rights of patron to, 151,152 (254); services of, 177 (286).
FREEDWOMAN, guardianship of, 39, 40 (109); when has four children released from guardianship of patron, 39, 75 (109, 155).
FUNERAL, only one can take place, 13 (75).
FUNERAL CEREMONIES, not expensive, 13 (74).
FUNERAL PYRE, where erected, 14 (76).
FUNERAL WREATHS, 13 (75).

-G-

GENTILES, when called to the inheritance, 73 (152).
GRANDCHILDREN, succession of, 72 (151).
GRANDSON, not released with father, 31 (101).
GUARDIAN, penalty for fraud by, 11, 174 (71, 72, 283); for wife in hand, 33 (103); how appointed, 33, 134 (103, 232); liberty of choice, 35 (104); different privileges of, selection of, 35 (104); dative, 35, 135 (104, 233); nearest agnates appointed, 35 (104); demanded in place of absent patron, 37 (107); *ad litem,* when appointed, 37 (107); under *Lex Atilia,* 38 (107); when captured, substitute demanded, 38 (108); curators to furnish security for, 40 (110); exception to this, 40 (110); of woman when forced to give consent to will, 53 (127); when appointed must be certain person, 66 (144); with curator, must give security, 112 (203); legal, 134 (232); cessionary, 135 (233); by decree of Senate, 134 (234); excuses of, 174 (283).
GUARDIANSHIP, who are subject to, 33, 34 (102, 103); of freedmen, who entitled to, 36 (105); of Latins under puberty, 36 (105); cessionary, what is, 36 (106); how males and females released from, 137 (234, 235).

-H-

HANDLING, another's property, theft, 93 (179).
HEIR, of intestate, 9, 10 (67, 68); must be appointed in regular form, how this is done, 52 (126); how appointed to render will valid, 54 (128); kinds of, 57 (131); proper and necessary, who they are, why so called, may relinquish possession, rule applies to wife, 57 (132); foreign, who, 58 (133); power of

deliberation granted to, interference with property by, 58 (133); when appointed without time for deliberation, 58 (133); substitution of, 59 (134); slave when appointed must be freed, 61 (136); must enter on estate by order of master, 61 (137); under control when appointed, can be charged with legacy, 67 (145); when appointed trustee, 67 (145); stipulation of with beneficiary, 68 (146); liability of when estate accepted, 68 (147); when refuses to accept may be compelled to transfer it, 68 (147); may be asked by a codicil to transfer the estate, 70 (148); when disputes legacy, sued for simple damages, 71 (149); surrender of estate by, 79 (162); released by legatee, when, 91 (175); how appointed, 141 (241); who eligible, 141, 142 (241, 242); how slave may be appointed, 142 (242); acceptance by, 144 (244); condition of appointment of, 179 (288); when substituted, 179 (288, 289).

HOMICIDE, unlawful, definitions of, 95 (181); justifiable, 208 (326).

HUSBAND AND WIFE, capacity to take under will, 137 (236).

-I-

ILLEGAL CLAIM, penalty for, 14 (77).

IN HAND, ceremony of, 30 (97).

INFORMER, who can be, 204 (320, 321).

INHERITANCES, nature of, 51 (124).

INJURY, how suffered, 197 (312); who can commit, 197 (312); kinds of, 197 (312, 313); action for, 197 (312); penalty for, 198 (312); accusation for, 198 (313).

INSOLVENT DEBTOR, when property of is sold during his lifetime, 79 (161).

INTERDICTS, object of, 118 (211); kinds of, 118 (211); for possession, 118 (211); when confiscated property is purchased, 119 (212); Salvian decree, 119 (212); prohibitory, 120 (214); order and effect of, 120 (214); secondary, 122 (216); description of, 200 (315); proceedings under, 200 (316); effect of when issued, 201 (316); when they lie, 201 (316).

INTEREST, rate of, 167 (274).

-J-

JOINT LEGATEES, rights of, 63 (140).

JOINT OWNERS, right of in estate of former slave, 77 (158).

JOINT STIPULATOR, liability of, 96 (182).

JUDICIAL CORRUPTION, penalty for, 12 (73).

-L-

LAND, enclosure of, 11 (72); in provinces not subject to usucaption, 45 (116); possession of, when vacant, 45 (116); acquired by alluvion under natural law, 47 (119).

LAND MARKS, removal of crime, 160 (265).

LAPSED LEGACY, disposal of, 138 (237).

LATINI JUNIANI, who they were, 21 (85); rights of, 77 (157).

LATINITY, rights of, 29 (96).

LATINS, can take under the terms of a trust, 71 (149); not legally manumitted, 128 (224); how obtain citizenship, 130 (226, 227); how gained by repetition, 130 (227).

LATIUM, same laws operative in as at Rome, 12 (73).

LAW, division of, 19 (83); perfect and imperfect, 127 (223); definition of, 127 (223).

LEASING AND HIRING, rule of, 89 (171).

LEGACY, how many kinds of, 61 (137); forms of bequests of, 61 (137); of property of another, when valid, 61 (138); when left to two or more persons, 61 (138); when bequeathed as a claim, conditionally, 62 (138); how bequeathed by condemnation, 62 (139); of property not in existence, 62 (139); when of property not subject to mancipation, 62 (139); when no owner of, 62, 63 (139); when left to uncertain person, void, 66 (144); to a posthumous stranger, void, 66 (144); bequeathed conditionally, question as to validity of, 67 (145); left by a codicil, not valid unless confirmed by testator, 70 (148); bequeathed in Greek, not valid, 71 (149); preferred, how paid, 181 (291); heir appointed before payment, 181 (291); when property hypothecated, 181 (291); when consists of usufruct, 181, 182 (292, 293); articles included in, 183 (293, 294); of land and crops, 183, 184 (294, 295); other property bequeathed, 184-186 (295-297).

LEGATEE, when appointed heir to military will, 52 (125); cannot be charged with a legacy, 70 (148).

LEGITIMACY, after death of husband, 8 (65).

LEX AEBUTIA, effect of, 102 (190).

LEX ÆLIA SENTIA, provisions of, 23 (88).

LEX APULEIA, as to partnership, right of action of recovery, not applicable to sureties, 84 (167); effect of, 84 (167).

LEX ASINIA ANTISTIA, effect of, 32 (101).

LEX ATILIA, 135 (233).

LEX CALPURNIA, effect of, 101 (188).

LEX CICEREIA, publication of claim, amount, number of sureties, 85 (167, 168); preliminary trial, release from liability under, 85 (168); effect of, 85 (168).

LEX CLAUDIA, effect of, 35 (104); abolition of guardianship by, 36 (106).

LEX COMMISSORIA, provisions of, 166 (273).

LEX CORNELIA, on sureties, 85 (168); penalties under, 207, 208 (325).

LEX FALCIDIA, provisions of, 65, 148 (143, 249); retention by, 186 (297); what not subject to, 186 (297).

LEX FUFIA, limitation of bequests by, 65 (142); applicable to Italy, 84 (167); liability of sponsor and guarantor, unless for debt, 84 (167); when applicable, 84 (167).

LEX FUFIA CANINIA, restricts grant of freedom, 65 (143); effect of, 129, 195 (225, 309); forms of, 129 (225, 226).

LEX JULIA, 46 (118); prohibits unmarried persons from taking estates and legacies, 71 (150); on taxes, 85, 134 (168, 234); exemption from penalties, 136, 137 (235); effect of, 211 (329, 330).

LEX JULIA ET PAPIA, effect of, 33 (103).

LEX JUNIA, provisions of, 134 (234).

LEX MINICIA, provisions of, 26 (92).

LEX PAPIA, provisions of, 75 (155).

LEX PINARIA, effect of, 99 (186).

LEX POMPEIA, provisions of, 209 (327).

LEX PUBLILIA, for money expended, 85 (168); obligation by writing, 85 (168); as to purchase, lease, or partnership, 86 (169); validity after money paid, 86 (169); effect of, 101 (188).

LEX RHODIA, effect of, 164 (270); general average under, 164 (271).

LEX VALLIA, effect of, 101 (189).

LEX VISCELLIA, 130 (227).

LEX VOCONIA, effect of, 65 (142).

LIBERTY, judgment in favor of, 10 (68).

LOANS, kinds of, 162 (268).

LUCRATIVE POSSESSION, and usucaption, 46 (117).

-M-

MACEDONIAN DECREE OF SENATE, 165 (272).
MAGIC ARTS, penalty for, 11 (69).
MAGISTRATES, jurisdiction of, 18 (82).
MALES, at puberty, released from guardianship, 40 (110).
MANCIPATION, persons subject to, 30 (98); what it is, 30, 139 (98, 238); who and what are included, 30 (98); difference between land and other property, 31 (99); what subject to it, 139 (238).
MANDATE, effect of, 88, 89 (173); when against good morals, void, 89 (173); revocation of, 89 (173); when death occurs, annulled, 89 (173); action of, when lies, 89 (173); when may be refused, 167 (274).
MANIFEST THEFT, penalty, 93 (178).
MANUMISSION, requisites of, 20 (84); power of, restricted, 22 (87); causes for, 22 (87); of slaves, limitation of, 22, 23 (87, 88); by joint-owner, 129 (225); when usufruct and ownership exist, 129 (225); not granted after death of heir, 129 (225); when void, 129 (225); operative when heir accepts estate, 129 (225); must be definite, 129 (225); forms of, 130 (226); rules of, 194, 195 (307).
MANUS INJECTIO, form of, 101 (188).
MARRIAGE, of Senators with plebeians, prohibited, 14 (76); with slaves, forbidden, 24 (89); restriction of, 24 (90); with foreigners, consequences of, 25 (91); when legal, 130 (227); definition of, 130 (227); not legal with slaves or blood relatives, 131 (228); when incestuous, 131 (228); of free persons with slaves, illegal, 169 (277); who cannot contract, 169 (276).
MASTER, when responsible for theft by slave, 176 (284); who is his own, 130 (227).
MEN, conditions of, 19 (83).
MINOR, under puberty cannot manumit a slave, 128 (224).
MONSTERS, to be killed, 8 (65).
MOTHER, of three children, when released from guardianship, 39 (109).
MOURNING, term of, 162 (267).

-N-

NEAREST AGNATE, guardian, 9 (67).
NOCTURNAL ASSEMBLIES, penalty for, 12 (74).
NOVATION, force of, 91 (176); how affected by a condition, 91 (176); how created, 202 (317).
NOXAL ACTION, when granted, 109 (200); how established, 109 (200); follows person of culprit, 109 (200); does not lie against father or master, 109 (200); when right of action in suspense, 109 (200); effect of after mancipation, 109 (200).

-O-

OATH, force of, 12 (74); when tendered, and by whom, 162 (268); effect of, 162 (268).
OBLIGATIONS, only transferable by agreement, 44 (115); division of, 81 (162); verbally contracted by question and answer, 81 (162); formula of, 81 (162); contraction of, 82 (163, 164); how created, 82 (169); reciprocal liability of, 82 (169); by dependent, binding, 89, 90 (174); when acquired by slave, 90 (174); when extinguished, 90 (174, 175); by novation, 91 (175, 176); by joinder of issue, 94 (180); when released verbally, 86 (175); for commission of crime, 88 (177); verbal, how contracted, 201, 202 (317).
ORPHITIAN DECREE OF THE SENATE, 193 (305).
OWNER, of property by different titles, 44 (115); when no power to alienate property, 46 (118); when forbidden by *Lex Julia*, 46 (118).
OWNERSHIP, when nature of article changed, 48 (120).

-P-

PARTITION of estates, all property to be divided, 161 (266).
PARTNERS, liability of, 88 (172); agreement of, 88 (172).
PARTNERSHIP, dissolution of, 88 (172).
PATERNAL CONTROL, who under, 130 (227).
PATRON, penalty for defrauding client, 11 (72).
PATRON AND PARENTS, legal guardianship by, 39, 40 (109); daughter of, can demand half of estate of freedman, 76 (156); foreign heirs of do not enjoy right, 76 (156); rejection by, of share to freedman's estate, 77 (158); emancipated son of, when passed over, preferred to foreign heirs, 78 (159).
PATRONESS, right of, 76, 77 (156, 157).
PAYMENT, by bronze and balance, 91 (175); method of, 91 (175).
PEGASIAN DECREE OF THE SENATE, when applies, 68 (147); prohibits those who have no children from enjoying trusts, 71 (150).
PENALTY, for theft of deposit, 6 (62); for illegal interest, 6 (62); for non-payment of debt, 7 (63, 64); for arson, 11, 206, 207 (70, 324, 329); for serious personal injury, 11 (70, 71); for public abuse, 11 (70); for perjury, 11 (71); for homicide, 11 (71); for magic incantations, 11 (71); for homicide of an ascendant, 11 (71); for theft by slave with master's knowledge, 14 (77); amount deposited, 99 (186); and forfeits, 122 (217); when not enforced, 122 (217); in what actions allowed, 122 (217).
PEOPLE, vote of, when necessary, 14 (76); vote of, essential in important affairs, 14 (76).
PIGNORIS CAPIO, when employed, 101 (189); introduced in military affairs, 101 (189).
PLACES, when holy, 41 (111).
PLEDGE, sale by creditors, 163, 164 (269); when recovered by use, 46 (118); theft of, and action for, 94 (180).
POPULAR ASSEMBLIES, none to be held during obsequies, 14 (76).
POSSESSION, how inoperative when granted, 74 (154); when party is in, 114 (213); how retained, 114 (213); intention necessary, 114 (213); interdict to recover, 114 (213); by order of court, 200 (315).
POSTHUMOUS CHILDREN, can have guardians, 33 (103); must be appointed heirs or disinherited, 54 (128); rights of, 143 (243).
POSTHUMOUS STRANGER, cannot be appointed heir, 66 (144).
POSTLIMINIUM, law of, 32 (100).
POWER OF OTHERS, release from, 31 (99).
PRAETOR, interposition of, 118 (211).
PRAETORIAN POSSESSION, not excluded by *Lex Julia,* 57 (131).
PREGNANCY, proof of, 172 (280).
PRESCRIPTION, why so called, 117 (210); when operative, 196 (310, 311).
PRICE, must be certain, 87 (170); when left to another, 88 (171).
PRIVATE RELIGIOUS RITES, when used, 12 (74).
PRIVILEGES, to the injury of others illegal, 12 (73).
PROCEDURE, ancient form of used before *Centumviri,* 112 (203).
PROFITS, bidding for, 121 (215, 216).
PROPER HEIRS AND AGNATES, called by Praetor to possession *ab intestato,* 74 (154).
PROPERTY, in litigation cannot be rendered sacred, 14 (76); how transferred in court, 42 (113); when not acquired by usucaption, 45 (116); how acquired by delivery, 46 (118); acquisition of, through others, 49 (121); not acquired through freeman when independent, 50 (123); left by condemnation, rule of, 63 (140); heir not bound by such legacy, 63 (140); who is entitled to the same, 63 (140); left to another

under a trust, must be delivered or paid for, 68 (147); ownership of, praetorian possession, not absolute, 79 (161); division of, 139 (238); how acquired, 139 (238); surrender in court, 139 (238); how obtained, as by slave, 140 (239); used for another's benefit, 165 (272).
PROSECUTION, barred by compromise, 6 (62).
PUNISHMENTS, military, nature of, 212 (331).

-Q-

QUADRUPEDS, damage by, 11, 160 (69, 265).

-R-

REAL ACTION, of twofold nature, 111 (202); no security when in plaintiff's name, 112 (203).
RELEASE, of children from paternal control, how effected, 133 (231)
REPLICATIO, when filed, 122 (208)
RESPONSA PRUDENTUM, what they were, 19 (83).
RESTITUTION, nature of complete, 157 (262); when not available, 157 (263).
RIGHT OF ASSEMBLY, 11 (72).
ROAD, width of, 12 (73).

-S-

SACRED AND RELIGIOUS things, 41 (111).
SACRILEGE, definition, 206 (323).
SALE, by verbal agreement valid, 10 (68); dependent upon payment, 10 (68); how and when contracted, 86, 87 (169, 170); of other property, liability for, 168 (275); when title passes, 168 (275).
SECURITY, when for indefinite sum, 85 (168); when given by litigant, 111 (202); when not to be given, 112 (203); by defendant, when given, 112 (203); nature of action, when required, 112, 113 (204); how given, kinds of, 123 (218, 219); when demanded, 157 (263).
SEDITION, penalty for, 207, 208 (325).
SENATORS, cannot marry plebeians, 14 (76); when forbidden to marry, 136, 137 (235).
SEPULCHRE, violation of, 163 (267).
SERVITUDES, not subject to sale, 41, 42 (112).
SET-OFF, each party must receive less than is due, when pleaded, 106, 107 (196); when judge need not consider, 107 (197); difference in, 107 (197); only allowed when debt due, 107 (197); amount of inserted in statement of claim, 107 (197); of different debt, when allowed, 164 (270).
SETTLEMENT, by litigants, 4 (58).
SILANIAN DECREE OF THE SENATE, 179 (289).
SLAVES, restrictions of funerals of, 13 (75); for what reasons manumitted, 20 (84); when they become Latins, 21, 22 (86); power of masters over, 23 (88); harshness to, forbidden, 23 (88); female, issue of, and Roman citizen, status of, 28 (94); acquire for themselves everything obtained after patron's death, 61 (132); may be liberated under a trust, 70 (148); if belonging to another must be purchased and manumitted, 70 (148); when manumitted under a trust are freedmen of emancipator, 70 (148); under thirty years cannot be appointed heirs and declared free, 70 (148); or animal killed, appraised, 95 (181); suit, or prosecution for act, 96 (182); cause for manumission, necessary, 128 (224); statement of, free when manumitted by insolvent master, 128 (224); cannot be manumitted to defraud creditors, 128 (224); when made by a Latin, 128 (224); free on condition, 129, 130 (225, 226); of whom the freedmen, 130 (226); fugitive, rules

governing, 157 (261); female, debauchery of, 159 (264); are tortured, 179 (289, 290); defence of, 196 (310).

SOLDIERS' WILLS, favor to, 145, 146 (246).

SON, free when sold three times, 8 (65); under control, when appointed heir or disinherited, 53 (127); must be expressly disinherited, 53 (127); when passed over in silence, will broken, 55 (130).

SOOTHSAYERS, penalty of, 207 (324, 326).

SPONSOR, what he is, 84 (166); heir not liable, 84 (167).

SPONSORS AND GUARANTORS, who they are, 84 (166); form of interrogation of, 84 (166); when accepted, 84 (166); differences between, 84 (166, 167); heirs of, when liable, 84 (167); when released, 84 (167); release of, 84 (167).

STIPULATION, made for something impossible, void, 82 (164); instances of invalidation of, 82 (164); void when question not asked, 82 (164); not valid when made with one without authority, 83 (165); or with person who is deaf or dumb, or insane, 83 (165); when joint, how made, 83 (165); less, but not more may be agreed upon, 84 (166); act of slave making, void, 84 (166); when void, 82 (164, 165); joint, when legal, may be for less, not more, 84 (166); form of, 162 (268); effect of, security for, 202 (318).

STOLEN GOODS, recovery of, 93 (178); delivery of, 93 (178); search for, 93 (178).

SUBSTITUTION, rules of, 59, 60 (134, 135); must be publicly made, 60, 61 (135, 136); applicable to posthumous children, for strangers, 61 (136).

SUCCESSION, *per stirpes* and *per capita*, 73 (152); exclusion of sons and grandson's of different patrons from, 77 (158); to estates of Latins, 77 (158).

SUIT, for more than is due, in what way brought, 105 (194); less than debt may be claimed in, 106, 107 (196); when more is claimed case is lost, 107 (196); under stipulation by slave, 117 (210).

SURETY, perpetually liable, 84 (167); right of recovery of, 85 (168); unlike sponsor and guarantor, 84 (166).

-T-

TAX, of five percent, 190 (302).

TESTAMENTARY CAPACITY, how ascertained, 52 (126).

TESTAMENTARY GUARDIANS, for whom appointed, 33 (103).

TESTIFY, penalty for refusal to, 11 (71).

THEFT, by day, punishment of, 5 (60); kinds of, 88, 174 (177, 283); action for, 94 (180); by violence, 95 (181); rules governing, 93 (179); of persons, 93 (179); of own property, 94 (180); when committed by avarice, 94 (180); consists of intent, 95 (181); child under puberty, not liable, 95 (181); object of action for, 174 (283); when it lies, 174 (283); penalty, 176 (284); when debtor commits, 176 (284); committed by slave, 176 (284); of slave, 285 (285).

THIEF, legally killed in act, 4 (59); suit against, 6 (62).

THINGS, division of, 41 (111); public or private, 41 (111); corporeal and incorporeal, 41 (111); susceptible of mancipation, 42 (112); unsalable, pass by delivery, 42 (112).

TIME, allowed to pay judgment, 7 (63); for title by usucaption, 10 (68).

TITLE, to stolen property does not pass, 6 (62).

TOMB, not acquired by usucaption, 14 (76).

TOOTH, penalty for loss of, 11 (71).

TORTURE, when inflicted, 204 (321, 322); of slaves, 205, 206 (322).

TRANSACTION, with son or slave, who responsible for, 109 (198).

TREASON, trial and penalty for, 13, 211 (74, 330).
TREASURY, rights of, 203 (319); preference of, 204 (320).
TREBELLIAN DECREE OF THE SENATE, effect of, 68, 188, 193 (146, 299, 305).
TREES, penalty for cutting, 6 (62).
TRESPASS BY CATTLE, penalty for, 11 (70).
TRIAL, of case, 4 (59).
TRIPLICATIO, use of, 116 (209).
TRUST, form of words to create a, 67 (145); extinguished when estate rejected, 68 (146); any article may be left under a, 68 (147); applies to property of heir, legatee or anyone else, 68 (147); bequeathed in Greek, valid, 71 (149); property cannot be left under, by way of penalty, 71 (150); form of bequest of, 148 (249); what may be left by, 149 (250); when valid, 149 (250); cannot be created by way of penalty, 149 (250); freedom can be granted by a, 149 (251); who charged with, 187 (298); form of charge of, 187 (298); when void, 187 (298); when title to vests, 187 (298); how executed, 187 (299).
TRUSTEE, is still heir after transference of estate, 67 (145).

-U-

URBAN PRAETOR, when guardian demanded of, 38 (107).
USUCAPTION, of chattels complete in year, land in two years, 44 (115); sacred property not acquired by, 45 (116).
USUFRUCT, only transferable in court, 43 (113); creation of, in slaves, 43 (114).
USUFRUCTUARY, cannot acquire a slave by usucaption, 50 (123).
UTI POSSIDETIS, 119 (212).
UTRUBI, when available, 119 (212).

-V-

VELLEIAN DECREE OP SENATE, 165 (272).
VENDOR, false statement by, 168 (275).
VETERANS, privileges of, 24 (89).
VEXATIOUS LITIGATION, action of, 122 (217); when applicable, 122 (217); oath may be exacted instead of, 122 (217).
VOTE OF GREATER COMITIA, necessary, when, 12 (73).

-W-

WARD, female, transfer of guardianship of, 36 (106); no right of action against guardian, 39 (109); cannot alienate property, 48 (120); loan of money by, 49 (121); acquisition of property by delivery to, 49 (121); authority of guardian necessary, 83 (165).
WIFE, released from hand of husband by remancipation, 33 (102); while in hands of husband a proper heir, 71 (150).
WILD BEASTS, not subject to sale, 42 (112); how long owned, 47 (119).
WILL, different kinds of, 51, 140 (124, 239); by bronze and balance, 51 (124); witnesses to, 51 (124); who are disqualified as witnesses, 52 (124); military, 52 (125); who appointed heirs to military, 52 (125); male under fourteen cannot make, 52 (125); testamentary capacity, how ascertained, 52 (126); how validity is ascertained, 52 (126); heir appointed in regular form, how this is done, 52 (126); of woman, void without guardian's consent, 52 (126); attestation of seals of seven witnesses necessary, 53 (126); guardians of women forced to give consent to, 53 (127); son under control, when appointed heir or

disinherited, 53 (127); when children passed over, valid, 53 (127); rule of, concerning emancipated daughter, 54 (127); form of disinheritance necessary, 54 (128); when invalidated by manumitted son, 55 (129); revoked by one subsequently executed, 55 (130); void when testator loses civil rights, 56 (130); when illegal not absolutely void, 56 (130); invalidated by contrary intention, 56 (131); how executed, 140 (240); who can execute, 140, 141 (240, 241); disposal of *peculium* by, 140 (240); how broken, 144 (245); when void, 144 (245); who can make, 177 (286, 287); who disqualified to make, 178 (287); inofficious, 189 (300, 301); penalty for opening, 210 (328).

WINE, must not be poured on a corpse or funeral pyre, 13 (75).

WITNESS, when disqualified, 204 (321, 322).

WOMAN, who has lived with a husband for year, is legal wife, 10 (68); restraint of mourning by, 13 (75); how adopted, 29 (96); cannot adopt, 29 (96); in hand, not released from paternal control without coemption, 32 (101); generally in tutelage, 39 (109); loan of money by, 49 (121); legally paid without tutelary authority, 49 (121); estate of passes by right of agnation, 73 (152); when cannot manumit, 128 (224); in hand of husband, meaning of, 133 (231); freeborn, marriage with a slave, 169, 170 (277, 278).

WREATHS, of large size forbidden at funerals, 13 (75).

-Y-

YEAR, how reckoned, 119 (213).

OTHER TITLES OF INTEREST AVAILABLE EXCLUSIVELY THROUGH

R. A. SITES BOOKS

THE HOLY BIBLE
(In Five Volumes)
TRANSLATED BY JOHN WYCLIFFE

Unavailable since the late 1800's, this text-only edition of THE HOLY BIBLE is based upon the extremely rare first complete printing of the John Wycliffe Middle-English translation of THE HOLY BIBLE (Oxford: University Press, 1850). While Middle English spelling of words has been retained, alphabetic and runic symbols which are no longer in current usage have been replaced by their modern equivalents.

THE OLD TESTAMENT (PART ONE)
This Volume contains the Books of Genesis, Exodus, Leviticus, Numbers, Deuteronomy, Joshua, Judges and Ruth.

THE OLD TESTAMENT (PART TWO)
This Volume contains the Books of I, II, III and IV Kings, I and II Chronicles, I, II and III Ezra, Tobit, Judith, and Esther (with Apocryphal Additions).

THE OLD TESTAMENT (PART THREE)
This Volume contains the Books of Job, Psalms, Proverbs, Ecclesiastes, Song of Solomon, Wisdom, Syrach, and I & II Maccabees.

THE OLD TESTAMENT (PART FOUR)
This Volume contains all the Books of the Major and Minor Prophets and includes the Apocryphal Books of The Prayer of Jeremiah, Baruk, and the Apocryphal Chapters from Daniel – The Prayer of Azariah, The Song of the Three Young Men, Susanna and Bel and the Dragon.

THE NEW TESTAMENT
This Volume contains all the Books of the recognized Canon and includes the rare Apocryphal Letter of St. Paul to the Laodiceans.

A CONCISE DICTIONARY OF MIDDLE ENGLISH

A re-publication of the highly significant 1888 A CONCISE DICTIONARY OF MIDDLE ENGLISH by Mayhew and Skeat. This is not a facsimile edition. With over 300 pages of word entries, and including the original Middle English and Greek characters of the original publication, this is undoubtedly the best edition of this important reference work available.

THE SIBYLLINE ORACLES
TRANSLATED FROM THE GREEK INTO ENGLISH BLANK VERSE
By Milton S. Terry

THE SIBYLLINE ORACLES are a fascinating blend of mysticism, spirituality, philosophy and history emanating from the depths of antiquity. A gold mine for students of Classical mythology and early first millennium Jewish, Gnostic and Christian beliefs, they were widely referenced by the early Church Fathers, and despite their pagan content, almost attained Canonical status. Like a first draft of the Biblical Book of Revelation, the ORACLES have many of the same characteristics as the prophecies of Nostradamus. Cryptic and Apocalyptic, they present the reader with an enigma that has puzzled the world for 2500 years, an enigma still waiting to be solved. This edition includes three versions of the famous CHRISTIAN ACROSTIC, several Appendices and a lengthy Index.

THE HOPE OF THE GOSPEL
By George MacDonald

THE HOPE OF THE GOSPEL is a series of beautifully written sermons by one of the most prolific and celebrated Scottish writers and novelists of the Victorian era. As C. S. Lewis once said, "I know hardly any other writer who seems to be closer, or more continually close, to the Spirit of Christ Himself."

MORE TITLES OF INTEREST AVAILABLE EXCLUSIVELY THROUGH

R. A. SITES BOOKS

THE MIRACLES OF OUR LORD
By George MacDonald

THE MIRACLES OF OUR LORD is a series of beautifully written sermons by George MacDonald (1824 - 1905), an internationally renowned speaker who counted Mark Twain, Lewis Carroll, Ralph Waldo Emerson and John Greenleaf Whittier among his friends and admirers. In MacDonald's world, God's Love is no empty platitude. God becomes Flesh and dwells among us, tender and severe. He is Love nailed to the Cross....

THE BOOK OF WERE-WOLVES
By Sabine Baring-Gould
WITH 45 ILLUSTRATIONS AND PHOTOGRAPHS!

Sabine Baring-Gould (Celebrated composer of the famous Christian hymn, "Onward Christian Soldiers"), created a definitive foundation work of modern supernatural lore when he published THE BOOK OF WERE-WOLVES in 1862. Thirty years before Jack the Ripper, Baring-Gould concluded that were-wolves are what the modern era would later come to know as serial killers. And his conclusions have withstood the test of time. Baring-Gould presents the reader with a surprising and intriguing journey through a poorly understood and dark side of legend, history and human nature.

THE DIARY OF AN OLD SOUL
By George MacDonald

THE DIARY OF AN OLD SOUL is a series of beautifully written daily devotionals by one of the most prolific and celebrated Scottish writers and novelists of the Victorian era – George MacDonald (1824 - 1905). Day-by-day MacDonald reflects on the sweet and bitter, the happy and sad as he faces the challenges of living the true Christian life. This volume follows the original design of the 1880 edition. Each page of poetry is offset with an illustrated page for the recording of the reader's own thoughts throughout the year in the good company of George MacDonald. *ILLUSTRATED!*

THE MAN WHO WAS THURSDAY
By G. K. Chesterton

"A powerful picture of the loneliness and bewilderment which each of us encounters
in his single-handed struggle with the universe." -- C. S. Lewis

THE MAN WHO WAS THURSDAY cannot be classified. It is a detective story, a tale of international espionage, a story of master criminals pursued by courageous and brilliant policemen. It is full of mystery and the fog shrouded gas-lit streets of London at the beginning of the nineteenth century. It is about terrorism and anarchy – the throwing of bombs into innocent crowds. It is about political assassinations and the end of the world. It is about disguises and identity theft. It is a supernatural thriller of the first order.... Yet this still does not reveal the secret of THE MAN WHO WAS THURSDAY. From the celebrated author of the FATHER BROWN MYSTERIES and ORTHODOXY, G. K. Chesterton takes the reader on a journey as humorous and unexpected today as it was in 1908.

UNSPOKEN SERMONS - Series One, Two and Three
By George MacDonald

"A wonderful series of insightful, thought- and spirit-provoking sermons, written over a period of twenty-five years, UNSPOKEN SERMONS shows the breadth and depth of George MacDonald's developing vision of the Love of God as incarnated in the person of Jesus Christ. Never one to shy away from a difficulty, MacDonald explores some of the most challenging and perplexing passages in the Gospels, each time rising to newer heights in his elucidation of the mysteries of God's Love.

MORE TITLES OF INTEREST AVAILABLE EXCLUSIVELY THROUGH

R. A. SITES BOOKS

THE 1811 DICTIONARY OF THE VULGAR TONGUE
A Dictionary Of Buckish Slang, University Wit, and Pickpocket Eloquence.
By Captain Francis Grose, et. al.

THE 1811 DICTIONARY OF THE VULGAR TONGUE is a wonderful and hilarious compendium of street jargon, phrases of an indelicate nature, and other expressions of the riff-raff, university students, men of fashion, and other unsavory types popularly in use in and around London at the beginning of the Nineteenth Century. This is one of the most controversial dictionaries ever produced and not for the faint-hearted. Totally out of line with today's standards of propriety and political correctness, Captain Grose's Dictionary unapologetically takes aim at every human foible, quirk and oddity. Nothing is spared. If you love the English language, if you are curious about the true origins of much of the slang and street talk in use today, if you are not easily shocked, this is the Dictionary for you. This edition preserves the original spellings found in Grose's work and include his own interesting methods of censoring words even he found to be objectionable. This is **NOT** the King's English!

THE NEW CONSTITUTIONS OF THE EMPEROR LEO

By Late Antiquity Roman Law was seriously deteriorated and in a state of confusion. Centuries of non-systematic legal enactments by various Emperors, poorly kept records and numerous conflicting opinions presented by legal experts, especially during the even more tumultuous third to fourth centuries A. D., created a tangled web of laws and profound legal and political abuse. This is a vigorous translation by Henry Agylaeus of Emperor Leo's NEW CONSTITUTIONS, a direct precursor to the most comprehensive re-codification of law in the history of the world – the Emperor Justinian's CORPUS JURIS CIVILIS.

THE NEW FREEDOM
By Woodrow Wilson

THE NEW FREEDOM… "is not a discussion of measures or of programs. It is an attempt to express the new spirit of our politics and to set forth, in large terms which may stick in the imagination, what it is that must be done if we are to restore our politics to their full spiritual vigor again, and our national life, whether in trade, in industry, or in what concerns us only as families and individuals, to its purity, its self-respect, and its pristine strength and freedom. THE NEW FREEDOM is only the old revived and clothed in the unconquerable strength of modern America."   ~ Woodrow Wilson ~

THE NEW CONSTITUTIONS OF JUSTINIAN
(In Two Volumes)

By Late Antiquity Roman Law was seriously deteriorated and in a state of confusion. Justinian commissioned teams of legal scholars to completely examine and re-codify all the ancient laws of the Empire (over a thousand years of enactments and thousands of pages). The Commissions accomplished this task in what can best be described as record time, producing four profound works of law - The Code, The Digest, The Institutes and The New Constitutions - collectively known as the Corpus Juris Civilis. Samuel P. Scott's vigorous and highly readable translation of Justinian's New Constitutions, the final part of the most comprehensive re-codification of law in the history of the world, is now available for the first time in an affordable two volume paperback edition.

THE HAUNTED HOUSE
OR THE GREAT AMHERST MYSTERY OF 1879
AN ANTHOLOGY OF FORGOTTEN FRIGHTS

Macabre "true" stories and poetry from the Victorian past by such notable persons as George MacDonald, Abraham Lincoln, Theodore "Teddy" Roosevelt, Mark Twain, J. Sheridan Le Fanu, Daniel Defoe, Benjamin Disraeli, and others....

COMING 2014

R A SITES BOOKS
RARE AND IMPORTANT WORKS FOR THE CASUAL READER

Made in the USA
Lexington, KY
13 June 2015